Donald F. Power

© 1986 · Jocundry's Books · east Lansing, mi

THE ARBITRATION OF
INDUSTRIAL ENGINEERING DISPUTES

THE ARBITRATION OF
INDUSTRIAL ENGINEERING DISPUTES

by

Ronald L. Wiggins

Professor of Management
Colorado State University

The Bureau of National Affairs, Inc., Washington, D.C.

Printed in the United States of America
Library of Congress Catalog Card Number: 77-106490
Standard Book Number: 87179-106-4

31

To Ruth

ACKNOWLEDGMENTS

This study concerns a specialized segment of labor-management arbitration. The primary and principal sources of ideas are the analyses and conclusions of arbitrators as reflected in disputes referred to them, or their thoughts about and experiences with the arbitral process as summarized in thoughtful papers and articles.

Thus, a particular expression of gratitude for their decisions and commentaries is due the many arbitrators represented herein. Appreciation is also expressed to those arbitrators who have contributed to my practical knowledge of the subject—over a period of nearly 20 years of professional activity, including participation in a considerable number of grievance arbitrations.

A special word of thanks is due to five arbitrators. Not only is his thinking substantially represented in this report, but also Emeritus Professor Paul N. Lehoczky, Ohio State University, played an important part—both professionally and personally—in encouraging my early interest in arbitration. Dr. Lehoczky is widely recognized as the arbitrator most closely identified with industrial engineering cases.

Professor Harold W. Davey, Iowa State University, gave courteous and thoughtful consideration to some questions about his article in the *California Management Review;*[1] his comments contributed much to my thinking about arbitrator qualifications.

Professors Irving Bernstein, Joseph D. Carrabino, and Wayne L. McNaughton, all of U.C.L.A., were involved in my early research and analysis on this subject. To them, and especially to Professor McNaughton, go my sincere thanks for their encouragement.

---

[1] *The Arbitrator Views the Industrial Engineer,* VII CALIF. MGMT. REV. 1, 23 (1964).

The support and consideration of The Bureau of National Affairs, Inc., has been particularly significant in this effort. Not only is the organization publishing this book, but it has also granted permission to cite and/or quote from the cases selected from its *Labor Arbitration* series and a substantial number of the references.

Permission has been granted to cite and/or quote from the other publications which appear in the Bibliography. This courtesy is appreciated.

Finally, but importantly, appreciation is expressed to the members of my family for their many contributions to this study, not excluding forbearance. The involvement of my beloved wife, both directly and indirectly, is but symbolized by the dedication.

PREFACE

From the studies noted below, it is reasonable to infer that at least one in five grievance disputes culminating in arbitration involves industrial engineering principles and procedures. This proportion may well be low when it is considered that these same principles and procedures are often involved in grievance-arbitration problems primarily nontechnical in nature, for example, discharge and promotion problems.[1]

In a research study of the Impartial Chairmanship in the Full-Fashioned Hosiery Industry, over the years 1929 to 1945, the statistics indicated that 40 percent of the cases handled involved piece-rate questions and another 13.6 percent were concerned with other types of rate problems.[2] Mr. William E. Simkin, former Director of the Federal Mediation and Conciliation Service, reported that, for a five-year period under a permanent arbitratorship in which he had been involved, 23.5 percent of all decisions dealt with what he had identified as the three major types of technical disputes—*i.e.,* piecework and incentive, job evaluation, and workload.[3] In a report on the John Deere—UAW permanent arbitration experience, arbitrator Harold W. Davey's analysis indicated 20 percent incentive-pay grievances and 12.4 percent job-classification disputes.[4]

Of 1,003 arbitration cases included in a study of experiences under Bethlehem Steel agreements, 485, or nearly one half, pertained to wages or job classifications—the author noting that

---

[1] Simkin, *The Arbitration of Technical Disputes,* NEW YORK UNIVERSITY SIXTH ANNUAL CONFERENCE ON LABOR 181 (1953).

[2] T. KENNEDY, EFFECTIVE LABOR ARBITRATION (1948).

[3] Simkin, *supra* note 1.

[4] Davey, *The John Deere—UAW Permanent Arbitration System,* CRITICAL ISSUES IN LABOR ARBITRATION 161 (1957).

many involved incentive rates.[5] On the basis of unpublished statistics of the American Arbitration Association, it was stated that ". . . technical disputes related to incentives, job evaluation or individual job assignments have moved up into a close second in the last few years, averaging about 20 per cent." (First came discipline cases at 25 percent.) In this same article it was stated: "Nevertheless, the large volume of technical cases arbitrated every year shows the problem of wage rates, job evaluation, etc. to be a continuing and increasing labor relations difficulty."[6] Some qualitative corroboration is expressed in this opinion: "The number of wage incentive cases has risen consistently and markedly."[7]

Since the number of grievance arbitrations involving industrial engineering principles and procedures is substantial, continuing, and increasing, it is interesting that comparatively little has been written in the field. The one study [8] which seeks to consider industrial engineering problems generally is the predecessor to the present volume. Another study [9] deals with incentive and piece-rate plans and contains opinions solicited through interviews with personnel concerned with the arbitration process. Other publications also deal with particularized aspects of industrial engineering disputes,[10] or with such disputes in a particular context [11] or as a part of a general text on arbitration.[12]

The grievance problems involving or related to industrial engineering are both similar to and different from other issues which come to arbitration, as the arbitration cases in the area indicate. A detailed review and analysis of a large number of arbitration cases showed that disputes usually fell into the areas

---

[5] F. Murphy, *Job Classification Arbitrations under Bethlehem Steel Agreements*, 16 ARB. J. 8 (1961).

[6] J. Murphy, *Arbitration: Evaluation of its Role in Labor Relations*, NEW YORK UNIVERSITY TWELFTH ANNUAL CONFERENCE ON LABOR 281 (1959).

[7] Unterberger, *The Arbitration of Wage Incentive Cases*, 23 ARB. J. 236 (1968).

[8] Wiggins, *Arbitration of Industrial Engineering Cases*, 26 DISS. ABSTRS. 5105 (1966).

[9] McCullough, *Basic Patterns that Emerge from the Arbitration of Grievances Associated with Incentive Wage and Piece Rate Plans*, 28 DISS. ABSTRS. 4764-A (1968).

[10] M. STONE, MANAGERIAL FREEDOM AND JOB SECURITY (1964).

[11] HUTCHINSON, MANAGING A FAIR DAY'S WORK (1963); L. STESSIN, THE PRACTICE OF PERSONNEL AND INDUSTRIAL RELATIONS (1964).

[12] F. ELKOURI & E. ELKOURI, HOW ARBITRATION WORKS (2nd ed. 1960); C. UPDEGRAFF, ARBITRATION AND LABOR RELATIONS (3rd ed. 1970).

of Job Structuring and Work Performance (Measurement), as these terms are used herein.

Procedures Employed

Five hundred and two cases were selected from Volumes 1 through 51 of *Labor Arbitration,* published by The Bureau of National Affairs, Inc., for the analysis and exposition reflected herein. All but a small minority of the cases used were selected because they reflect Job Structuring or Work Performance (Measurement).

A few cases are included to round out one or more of the topics developed in the analysis. The more troublesome selections were those related, but peripheral, to industrial engineering as herein defined. Thus, arbitrations about discipline and discharge, assignments, and subcontracting—to indicate some exclusionary areas—sometimes involve the defined industrial engineering content, directly or basically. Assignments, in particular, often relate to job descriptions or classifications; so do questions of bargaining-unit work being done by others, or transferred out of the unit.

One category and one group of arbitrated disputes gave particular difficulty with respect to coverage. The category of subcontracting was omitted, not only because it has been given considerable attention in the literature but also because subcontracting deserves a detailed and intensive study by itself. Subcontracting cases appear herein only when one or more other industrial engineering ideas are exemplified.

The group referred to is the large and, apparently, growing number of steel-industry disputes, some of which appear in the *Labor Arbitration Reports* (LA). Such cases are collectively reported and form a valuable record of arbitration under a specific (basic) agreement. Utilization of such cases was limited to those which appear to offer industrial engineering applications, in keeping with the generality intended by the method used in selecting cases.

The rule was to include arbitrations in which industrial engineering content seemed to be involved substantially, and to exclude otherwise. The resulting selections include, no doubt, some cases which logically could be omitted and omit some which logically could be included. On balance, it is believed that industrial engineering disputes are fairly represented herein.

In the analysis of the 502 arbitration cases, cases were grouped to bring out common areas of industrial engineering content and closely related aspects of the cases themselves. A considerable number of non-industrial-engineering issues—such as seniority and discipline—were not included; they appear in the exposition only as necessary to understand the question (s) for arbitral decision.

The categories derived from such content analysis are presented in the following chapters, including the Introduction. It will be seen that the analysis resulted in classification of many of the cases into several categories. This is consistent with the basic purposes of the study. However, it does mean that there is no place in the book where the entire report of a particular arbitration can be read; the appropriate LA volume has the complete report.

The literature was reviewed in terms of some of these major areas, and appropriately noted where it would contribute to an understanding of the material. However, it was soon evident that little in the literature was directly related to the main themes of the study, although some attention was paid to desirable characteristics for arbitrators of industrial engineering cases, as will be noted later on. Also, there were some relevant areas which could, of themselves, become detailed studies if elaborated beyond the constraints of this book.

This last is illustrated by the subject area of custom and practice in arbitration cases. This is a rather substantial area herein—as might be expected—and the teachings of the cases studied are set forth in Chapter VI. However, if this subject area were generalized as to case and subject content and combined with the literature thereon, the result would be a substantial study in itself.

It was from the case studies, primarily, and from bibliographical sources, that generalized criteria applicable to the arbitration of industrial engineering disputes were evolved.

The observations on the educational preparation and professional experience of the arbitrators who decided the cases analyzed herein were developed through the *Labor Arbitration Reports*. Also, a review of the literature was made to reflect the opinions of persons involved in the arbitration process conccrning the professional preparation for those arbitrating industrial engineering cases.

From this background study of the arbitrators in the cases analyzed, the literature-opinion study, consideration of the developed criteria, and the fundamental nature of the profession of industrial engineering, it was possible to draw conclusions as to the extent to which competence in the profession should be a requisite for the arbitration of industrial engineering disputes.

TABLE OF CONTENTS

CHAPTER I. INTRODUCTION 1

1. Definition of Industrial Engineering 2
2. Arbitration 5
3. The Basic Problem 15

CHAPTER II. MANAGEMENT AND UNION "RIGHTS" 21

1. Bargaining-Unit Work Affected by Change 22
2. Bargaining-Unit Work Performed by Nonunion
   Personnel 28
3. Changes Within the Bargaining Unit 39
4. Problems of Sex 44
5. Classification Changes for Efficiency 48
6. Workload and Crew Size 54
7. Production Standards 60
8. Methods and Incentives 64
9 What About "Rights"? 70

CHAPTER III. A FAIR DAY'S WORK 75

1. Definition 75
2. Meaning and Measurement 77
3. Quantification 83
4. Employee Reactions 87
5. Understanding 90

CHAPTER IV. CLASSIFICATION AND EVALUATION ISSUES 91

1. Equal Pay for Equal Work 94
2. Varying Views About Job Changes 95
3. Evaluation Plans and Evaluation Concepts 103
4. Precepts and Principles 108
5. Procedures and Practices 115

CHAPTER V. STANDARDS AND INCENTIVE ISSUES 123

1. Earnings Opportunity 125
2. Earnings Guarantees 129
3. Plans and Their Utilization 134
4. Some Applications 140

5. Changeovers 144
6. Principles and Procedures 148

CHAPTER VI. PRACTICE 159

1. Definition, Function, and Interpretation 160
2. Classification and Assignment Practices 164
3. Interunit Practices 174
4. Workload and Methods Practices 177
5. Work Standards and Incentive Practices 181

CHAPTER VII.   METHODS AND PROCESSES 187

1. Equipment 190
2. Assembly 194
3. Metal Forming 197
4. Metal Working 201
5. General Manufacturing 206
6. Processes 210
7. Effect on Other Operations 213

CHAPTER VIII. THE IMPACT OF CHANGE ON JOBS 217

1. Establishing New Jobs or Classifications 218
2. Job Elimination 223
3. Combining or Splitting Jobs 227
4. Adding or Removing Duties 232
5. Claims of Classification Errors 236

CHAPTER IX. WORKLOAD AND CREW SIZE 241

1. The Nature of Workloads 241
2. Workload Problems 246
3. Problems of Crew Size 252
4. Working Conditions 259

CHAPTER X. STANDARDS PROBLEMS 265

1. Temporary Standards 267
2. Work-Cycle Problems 271
3. Machine Speeds and Feeds 276
4. Pace 281
5. Allowances 292

Chapter XI. Arbitrator Qualifications 301
  1. A Critique of Industrial Engineering Disputes 301
  2. The Arbitrators Who Decided the Cases 304
  3. The Need for Technical Qualifications 306
  4. When Is Technical Knowledge Required? 313

Chapter XII. Summary and Conclusions 315
  1. General Considerations 315
  2. Principal Bases for Arbitral Decisions 318
  3. Applications 320
  4. Uniqueness 323

Bibliography 325
Table of Cases 333
Topical Index 345

CHAPTER I

INTRODUCTION

There are three interrelated conceptual areas involved in the grievance arbitrations which are the substance of this book. Two of these—industrial engineering and arbitration—are reflected in the title. The third involves the imperatives of change, reflected in the common thrust of most of the arbitration reports considered. To put it another way, relatively few grievances in the industrial engineering area would be advanced to arbitration if there were stabilization—and, presumably, mutual understanding—of structure and performance.

The definition of industrial engineering utilized herein is designed for the particular problems reflected in the arbitration reports. However, industrial engineers will recognize the content as within the profession. The inclusion of the American Institute of Industrial Engineering definition not only permits comparison with the definition used, but also points up the most fundamental issue of all—the understanding of both the human and the manufacturing aspects of the stated integration. This point will have further elaboration.

Examination of the processes of arbitration is not an objective of the book. Contrary to the sincere doubts expressed by one observer,[1] it is believed that arbitration is appropriate for final resolution of industrial engineering grievances—quite aside from consideration of the judicial support for the process, or even judicial criticism. [2] The problem inherent in industrial engineering disputes is believed to be one of arbitrator qualifications, as will be developed. What is contained in the present

---

[1] Presgrave, *Grievance Arbitration and the Industrial Engineer*, XVIII J. OF INDUS. ENG'R 605 (1967).
[2] P. HAYS, LABOR ARBITRATION: A DISSENTING VIEW (1966).

chapter about arbitration is primarily the consideration of certain philosophical perspectives.

1. DEFINITION OF INDUSTRIAL ENGINEERING

Generally speaking, the industrial engineering content of the cases studied falls into two broad categories herein labelled Job Structuring and Work Performance (Measurement). These designations are synthetic and designed to sum up a number of problem areas which appear in the cases. For the purposes of this study, industrial engineering means these categories, as further exemplified.

Such areas as job descriptions, classification systems and procedures, job slotting, job-evaluation programs and procedures, and the various dynamics of job changes (eliminations, combinations, new jobs, and classification errors) are included within the term Job Structuring. Problems of crew size and workloads can fall within Job Structuring; they can also fall within the other category of Work Performance (Measurement). In fact, workload problems represent a bridge between the two main categories, in that workload always contains a performance component as well as an effort component which could be, for example, measured within a formal evaluation program. This is further exemplified (and sometimes confused) by the common phraseology used in referring to pace measurement as effort rating. Crew-size problems may or may not fall within both major categories.

The designation Work Performance (Measurement) refers to problems arising from performance requirements on jobs, either subjective or based upon industrial engineering precepts —i.e., measurement. There is, of course, "measurement" when a foreman applies his experience to estimate how long a particular job will take to complete and requires employees to perform within that "standard." However, "standard" in industrial engineering requires the objectivity of detailed job breakdown and accurate measurement, directly or indirectly. Areas summed up under this category heading include both kinds of performance requirements, time-study programs and procedures, various other means for measuring tasks—such as standard data; MTM (methods-time-motion measurement), Work Factor, and similar copyrighted, predetermined time systems; work-cycle problems; work scheduling and line balancing; machine feeds and speeds; the concept of "normal" pace; and allowances of various kinds.

It will be observed that many areas of industrial engineering activity—such as plant location, feasibility studies, cost estimating and controls, production planning and control, and quality control—are not included in the above definition. Grievance arbitrations sometimes touch on these, but usually only incidentally to problems encompassed within Job Structuring and Work Performance (Measurement). The same is approximately so for the important industrial engineering areas of process engineering and methods engineering. However, it will be seen that the areas of process engineering and methods engineering are of fundamental significance for understanding the arbitration of industrial engineering cases and for considering the qualifications of arbitrators who hear and decide such cases.

Both categories used in defining industrial engineering are intimately related to wages, directly or indirectly. Job Structuring is concerned with the "pricing" of jobs, usually when something happens to them, both absolutely and in relationships with each other within the negotiated wage structure. Work Performance (Measurement) is concerned with the work requirements necessary to earn the established rates as well as work requirements for additional earnings when some form of incentive exists. This association with wages is the reason so many grievances involving industrial engineering, as defined, reach arbitration, as well as why industrial engineering cases are so defined herein.

One of the early cases, in which the arbitrator was speaking about time study and job evaluation, illustrates the interrelationship of the two selected categories of industrial engineering (and also encapsulates some of the general functions of the profession) :

"In order to understand the problem, one must examine the objectives of time study. In the narrow sense, the only objective of time study is to analyze a job, standardize the cycle, time the accepted cycle (best method, all things considered), add allowances, set a standard. Once the standard is set, it may be used for wage incentive purposes, for estimating of machine loads, of production capacities, and of costs. When properly used, time study becomes a key cost control function.

"But in the broad labor relations sense, time study has a much more important function: in conjunction with job evaluation (which determines relative base rates) it actually evaluates each incentive job in like terms and makes the ideal of 'equal pay for equal work' possible. When properly carried out all jobs in the plant pay relatively equally well, and an expenditure of extra effort or skill applied to any job pays off equally well. . . ." [3]

Other Relationships

It is a mistake to consider industrial engineering grievance problems only in terms of a wages relationship, even though this relationship is exceedingly important. Labor—meaning both employees and unions—is frequently in dispute with management about "equity" [4] for employees, as that term may be used to identify the concepts developed in the reference. For example, a dispute about a workload requirement can involve fairness of the requirement, in relationship to a previous workload, a fellow employee's workload, the general requirement in the plant, or appropriateness generally. Interestingly enough, however, even such considerations of equity are often related, at least indirectly, to wages.

Industrial engineering may be interrelated with many other topics in collective bargaining, but in those cases is not usually the principal focus of the grievance problem. Illustrative are job bidding, promotions, transfers, demotions, and layoffs. Seniority problems, generally, are within this list, whereas work jurisdiction problems, while closely related to seniority, may be principally grounded on industrial engineering concepts (and within the limits of this study if the subject of a grievance).

Two arbitrators, in different cases but in similar language, have noted the distinction between seniority and work-jurisdiction problems. Selections from their opinions clarify this particular demarcation of the definition of industrial engineering:

"Seniority defines the rights and privileges to which an employee is entitled by virtue of his length of service in his current classification or department, whichever is the appropriate seniority unit. Jurisdiction, on the other hand, relates to the scope and content of the classification or job." [5]

"Seniority is a relationship between employees in the same seniority unit, rather than a relationship between jobs." [6]

---

[3] 6 LA 979.
[4] E. GINZBERG & I. BERG, DEMOCRATIC VALUES AND THE RIGHTS OF MANAGEMENT (1963).
[5] 30 LA 705.
[6] 35 LA 63.

The American Institute of Industrial Engineers defines the field as follows:

> "Industrial engineering is concerned with the design, improvement, and installation of integrated systems of men, materials, and equipment; drawing upon specialized knowledge and skill in the mathematical, physical and social sciences together with the principles and methods of engineering analysis and design, to specify, predict, and evaluate the results to be obtained from such systems." [7]

Implicit in this activity is a primary concern with the effective and efficient use of mechanical equipment in integration with men and materials. [8] Such use postulates a substantial knowledge of the principles by which mechanical equipment operates and materials function; it also postulates substantial knowlege of human behavior in work environs.

No further efforts at definition or exposition of the content of the industrial engineering field will be included herein, except as develops through the study. There is an extensive literature about both the field and specific subject areas.

2. ARBITRATION

As with the field of industrial engineering, there is no intent to analyze the process of arbitration—except for scope delineations, perspectives, and what evolves from the study. Here, too, there is a large and growing literature.

Suffice it to say that the principal feature of arbitration considered herein involves the mutual undertakings of managements and unions, in their collective bargaining agreements, to submit their disputes voluntarily to a jointly selected impartial arbitrator for final and binding resolution. As Labor Arbitration reflects, there are, sometimes, questions about the extent and applicability of the mutual undertakings, however expressed, leading to decisions about arbitrability.

This process is essentially the resolution of controversy, but it may also involve problem solving.[9] Unquestionably, the functions of therapy, politics, education, peace, and stability [10] are involved and appear, at least implicitly, in the arbitrations

---

[7] Emerson, *The New Outlook*, VII J. OF INDUS. ENG'R 139 (1956).
[8] INDUSTRIAL ENGINEERING HANDBOOK (H. Maynard ed., 2nd ed. 1963).
[9] Levitt, *When to Take a Grievance to Arbitration*, LABOR RELATIONS YEARBOOK—1967, at 59 (1968).
[10] *Id.*

considered. Other aspects of what is becoming the institution of labor-management arbitration are also present, implicitly or otherwise. However, the major thrust is disputes settlement.

Thus, this analysis is limited to arbitrations arising from disputes or grievances between management and labor about the proper resolution of problems within the framework of existing collective bargaining relationships. These are "rights" disputes [11] with the standards or criteria of reference extant—as opposed to "interests" disputes [12] where the purpose of arbitration is to establish the guidelines.

Arbitrator Capabilities

The qualifications and aptitudes of the individuals who act as arbitrators are germane to the arbitration process. The comments of two arbitrators will serve to exemplify.

"First, I submit that labor arbitration is in fact a distinct specialty and that the generality of arbitrators who are experienced do have a knowledge of industrial relations, an understanding of the problems of the interrelationship of levels of authority in multilayered organizations such as companies and unions, some knowledge of the problems of trade union administration, some feeling for the problems of production and of the roadblocks and obstacles to smooth in-plant administration, a considerable knowledge of the processes of industry, and a wide acquaintanceship with the techniques of wage incentives, job evaluation, and other features of wage administration that are basically simple, but until mastered, are gibberish to the uninformed. Furthermore, they need this knowledge to analyze intelligently and decide many, though by no means all, of the cases that come before them."[13]

In addition, an arbitrator should be able to: first, grasp the issue in a particular controversy; second, relate to a particular clause or clauses relied upon by the parties; third, relate these clauses to the basic purpose of the entire contract; fourth, relate the contract as a whole to the purpose of the collective bargaining process; fifth, act fairly, honestly, courageously, and intelligently; sixth, make up his mind; and seventh, use sound judgment.[14] Presumably, in view of the third requisite and the

---

[11] F. ELKOURI & E. ELKOURI, HOW ARBITRATION WORKS (2nd ed. 1960).
[12] *Id.*
[13] Wallen, *Arbitrators and Judges—Dispelling the Hays Haze,* IX CALIF. MGMT. REV. 17 (1967).
[14] Feinsinger, *Collective Bargaining and the Arbitrator,* COLLECTIVE BARGAINING AND THE ARBITRATOR'S ROLE 54 (1962).

fact that the contract would need to be available to the arbitrator to accomplish it, other pertinent clauses not relied upon by the parties, through inadvertance or otherwise, should also be related to the issue by the arbitrator.

Some of the philosophical differences among arbitrators are pertinent to the present subject. The study of a large number of grievance arbitrations indicates that such differences can and do have an impact on the decisions and awards quite often without explicit identification. In this connection, it is interesting to note a study based upon an hypothesis that "labor arbitrators are influenced by values or predelictions which not only condition their thinking but also provide them with ultimate standards for judgment." [15]

Arbitrator's Role

One of the philosophical differences concerns the particular role which the arbitrator is expected to play in the arbitration process. One school of thought holds that his function is essentially judicial in nature (quasi-judicial) and that he should restrict himself to a decision based upon the facts and evidence in interpretation of the terms of the contract then existing between the parties. This view is said to be historical, being grounded in the common law, and is identified—in terms of the recent history of American arbitration—with J. Noble Braden.[16]

The other view, originally identified with George W. Taylor,[17] holds that the arbitrator's role is primarily one of promoting harmony between the parties to the contract and that this is accomplished through mediation between the parties, where this will promote harmony, as well as through the judicial process.

Since the late 1940s, when the two referenced articles appeared, there has been considerable discussion of the two positions. Various theories evolved in support of these two positions are reviewed in considerable detail by one arbitrator.[18]

One perspective [19] on the harmony-promotion viewpoint de-

---

[15] Gross, *Value Judgments in the Decisions of Labor Arbitrators*, 21 Indus & Lab. Rel. Rev. 55 (1967).

[16] Braden, *The Function of the Arbitrator in Labor-Management Disputes*, 4 Arb. J. 35 (1949).

[17] Taylor, *Effectuating the Labor Contract Through Arbitration*, 26 Personnel 232 (1949).

[18] 42 LA 1025.

[19] Meyers, *The Task of the Labor Arbitrator*, 22 Personnel Ad. 24 (1959).

scribes the arbitrator as both judge and jury—like the judicial position—as well as an agent for the parties. Noted in this article is the constitutional/legislative analogy, which is contained in the often-quoted article by Dean Shulman.[20] The idea of the arbitrator acting as the mutual agent for management and labor has this emphasis in another article: "If the parties have not empowered their agent to make a 'contract of settlement' of their dispute, he is without *jurisdiction* to make one—and, to that extent, the dispute is not arbitrable." [21]

"Meditration" describes an interesting procedure for harmony promotion, culminating in formal arbitration if settlement of the dispute has not been accomplished.[22] It involves a permanent-umpire relationship.

Effects of the Trilogy

Unquestionably, the U.S. Supreme Court in the Steelworkers Trilogy [23] and later decisions,[24] along with stated policy of the National Labor Relations Board,[25] plays a part in these philosophical considerations. What the decisions themselves reflect, simply stated, is a policy favoring arbitration in labor-management disputes, including both arbitrable decisions on questions of arbitrability and a presumption of arbitrability, absent explicit exclusionary language. This policy is amenable to judicial surveillance, although all of the dimensions thereof are, probably, still to be spelled out through further adjudication. That is, the general rule that an arbitrator's award is enforceable in court, or cannot be successfully attacked in court, unless fraud or collusion can be established or unless the award

---

[20] Shulman, *Reason, Contract, and Law in Labor Relations*, MANAGEMENT RIGHTS AND THE ARBITRATION PROCESS 169 (1956).
[21] Justin, *Arbitrability and the Arbitrator's Jurisdiction*, MANAGEMENT RIGHTS AND THE ARBITRATION PROCESS 1 (1956).
[22] *Prescription for Curing 'Troubled' Grievance Procedures*, LABOR RELATIONS YEARBOOK—1966, at 184 (1967).
[23] United Steelworkers v. American Mfg. Co., 363 U.S. 564, 46 LRRM 2414 (1960); United Steelworkers v. Warrior & Gulf Nav. Co., 363 U.S. 574, 46 LRRM 2416 (1960); United Steelworkers v. Enterprise Wheel & Car Corp., 363 U.S. 593, 46 LRRM 2423 (1960).
[24] Notably, among others, Local 174, Teamsters v. Lucas Flour Co., 369 U.S. 95, 49 LRRM 2717 (1962); Drake Bakeries, Inc. v. Local 50, Bakery Workers, 370 U.S. 254, 50 LRRM 2440 (1962); Carey v. Westinghouse Elec. Corp., 375 U.S. 261, 55 LRRM 2042 (1964); Wiley, John & Sons v. Livingston, 376 U.S. 543, 55 LRRM 2769 (1964).
[25] Spielberg Mfg. Co., 112 NLRB 1080, 36 LRRM 1152 (1955).

fails to draw its essence from the collective bargaining agreement, is likely to undergo refinement in the future.[26]

The true philosophical impact of the Trilogy and subsequent decisions is in the written opinions, particularly that of the *Warrior and Gulf Navigation Co.* case. They have evoked much comment, including suggestions that the "current eschatology of labor law" represents "A New Theology" [27] with appropriate "canonization" [28] of the "philosopher-king"[29] arbitrator. There have also been vigorously stated opinions urging reinforcement of the judicial functions in collective bargaining agreements, championing jurists over arbitrators for performance of judicial functions, and suggesting reemphasis of the private, voluntary role for arbitration [30] (the latter suggestion has produced its own dissent [31]).

No doubt, the Supreme Court decisions amount to an encouragement to make arbitration effective in labor-management disputes. The courts do reserve the power to decide whether there is an agreement to arbitrate.[32]

> "But this is a small role, indeed, since the slightest hint of an intention to arbitrate, couched in the most amorphous terms, leads almost inevitably to a reference to the arbitrator. This stems from the principle 'if in doubt, arbitrate' and the subordination of common law principles governing the construction of contracts to the federal policy which elevates arbitration from the status of a technique for settling labor disputes to a philosophy." [33]

The philosophy is supportive of the harmony-promotion viewpoint. The labor agreement is "sui generis," not being a "generalized code" applying the "common law" of the plant or the industry involved in "a system of industrial self-government." Rather, an arbitrator should consider, in disputes under

---

[26] Myers, *Challenges to Labor Arbitration*, LABOR RELATIONS YEARBOOK—1967, at 54 (1968).

[27] Burstein, *Labor Arbitration—A New Theology*, 10 VILL. L. REV. 287 (1965).

[28] Seitz, *Grievance Arbitration and the National Labor Policy*, NEW YORK UNIVERSITY EIGHTEENTH ANNUAL CONFERENCE ON LABOR 201 (1966).

[29] Davey, *The Supreme Court and Arbitration: The Musings of an Arbitrator*, XXXVI NOTRE DAME LAW. 138 (1961).

[30] HAYS, *supra* note 2.

[31] Wallen, *supra* note 13.

[32] Burstein, *supra* note 27.

[33] *Id.*

the agreement, such factors as the impact of his award on productivity and morale. [34]

Arbitral Judgment

In his comments about the Trilogy,[35] Dean Smith pointed out that such bases for arbitral decision as productivity and morale (and/or the reduction of tensions) are not widely applicable insofar as negotiated agreements are concerned. He further noted that both the agreement and the arbitration function remain the product of agreement—between company and union—and that the court did not intend to rule that the parties were incompetent to make of their agreements what they would.

Arbitrator Davey, in what amounts to a restatement of the judicial philosophy of arbitration, stated:

"But it is vital to remember that the parties are living together *under a written agreement.* When they are unable to resolve a dispute over the interpretation or application of that agreement, they agree to use arbitration for final determination of the dispute as a preferable alternative to a strike or lockout. But, in the overwhelming majority of cases, the employer and the union make clear that the arbitrator in exercising his discretion is also under the agreement. He is constrained by the terms of the agreement as much as are the parties themselves." [36]

Since the article by Dean Shulman [37] was liberally cited in the *Warrior and Gulf* opinion, these particular comments therefrom are instructive:

"Despite all platitudes as to the inherent ambiguity of language, there are cases in which the language of the agreement appears compelling and leaves no room for consideration of other evidence of meaning; cases in which the dispute seems frivolous or captious, or patently designed to shift the onus of decision from the party to the arbitrator, or a desperate effort to recapture a concession made in negotiations and subsequently regretted. Assuming, however, a real difference of opinion, what criteria may the arbitrator look to for the choice between conflicting interpretations, each of which is more or less permissible?" [38]

Thereafter, the article contained these statements which, among others, undergird the *Warrior and Gulf* opinion:

---

[34] Smith, *Arbitrability—The Arbitrator, the Courts and the Parties,* 17 ARB. J. 3 (1962).
[35] *Id.*
[36] Davey, *supra* note 29.
[37] Shulman, *supra* note 20.
[38] *Id.*

"His choice from the more or less permissible interpretations of the language of the agreement, keeping the basic conceptions in mind, requires an appraisal of the consequences of each of the possibilities. Though all the parts of the agreement do not necessarily make a consistent pattern, the interpretation which is most compatible with the agreement as a whole is to be preferred over one which creates anomaly. The effects on efficiency, productivity, and cost are important factors to be considered. So are also the effects on the attitudes and interests of the employees. The two sets of factors are not always in opposition. An apparent increased cost may in some circumstances be more than repaid by the increased productivity resulting from the greater stimulus to voluntary cooperation. Practicality of the interpretation in its day-to-day applications is a related value. The interpretation, no matter how right in the abstract, is self-defeating and harmful to both sides if its day-by-day application provides further occasion for controversy and irritation." [39]

The answer to the question about criteria, above, was: "In the last analysis, what is sought is a wise judgment." [40] However, "[t]he beckoning star which guides the wise men of arbitration is the mutual intent of the parties, often obscured by the ambiguities of the contract language pertinent to the dispute." [41]

Much of Dean Shulman's career as an arbitrator involved a permanent umpireship wherein he handled certain cases as a mediator "able to exert the gentle pressure of a threat of a decision." [42] This has been termed "consensus" arbitration, with the arbitrator serving as "a mediator with a club." [43]

"Consensus arbitration still plays a useful role in a number of industries which retain an impartial chairman or umpire. The most prominent of these are, of course, the men's and women's clothing industries which have had a half century of experience with consensus arbitration. However, the great bulk of arbitrations today are judicial in nature and their awards are rooted in the provisions of the collective agreement and in the practices of the workplace." [44]

To this may be added comments by two arbitrators.

"The supreme test of the arbitrator's art is to read, interpret, and

---

[39] *Id.*
[40] *Id.*
[41] Prasow & Peters, *The Development of Judicial Arbitration in Labor-Management Disputes,* IX CALIF. MGMT. REV. 7 (1967).
[42] Shulman, *supra* note 20.
[43] Prasow & Peters, *supra* note 41.
[44] *Id.*

apply the cold words of the 'contract' and then to know when it is suitable to consider other unexpressed circumstances and conditions as appropriate to a determination of what the *reasonable expectations* of the parties might have been when they looked each other in the eye, struck a bargain, and signed a document." [45]

"Arbitration is not an inflexible procedure; it must be continuously tailored to the needs of the particular relationship. By its very nature, it is an instrument of the parties, created for the particular collective bargaining agreement. . . .
"There can be a substantial difference between the function of the impartial chairman in one industry, and that of an *ad hoc* arbitrator appointed in another industry. The same person may serve in both situations. In one he will act as a positive extension of the collective bargaining, and in the other, he will play a strictly judicial role. His conduct will reflect what the parties want." [46]

In the quotation relative to the arbitrator acting as mutual agent of the parties, *supra,* it was stated that the arbitrator was without jurisdiction to make a "contract of settlement" for the parties. Unquestionably today, given an arbitration clause (particularly of the open type) [47] with no specific exclusion, an arbitrator could fashion a contract of settlement; enforceability might be a question.[48] What is interesting to note is that, even in the absence of the Trilogy, an arbitration clause limited to questions of contract interpretation permits the resolution of a dispute in terms of contract language (it is not a violation, or it is a violation and the award is . . .). In such circumstances, the arbitrator has jurisdiction and the issue is arbitrable; a broader jurisdiction does not exist. However, even in these restricted circumstances, the arbitrator could propose a broader perspective—even though his jurisdiction would not enlarge save through the assent of the parties.

Responsiveness to Parties

The point is, there is merit in each of the philosophical perspectives on the role of arbitration, with primary emphasis upon responsiveness to the parties' wishes. The harmony-pro-

---

[45] Seitz, *Reply to Gross article—"Value Judgments in the Decisions of Labor Arbitrators,"* 21 INDUS. & LAB. REL. REV. 427 (1968).
[46] *How to Get Better Results From Labor-Management Arbitration: Benjamin C. Roberts and G. Allan Dash Exchange Views With Representatives of the Parties,* 22 ARB. J. 1 (1963).
[47] Davey, *supra* note 29.
[48] Myers, *supra* note 26.

motion viewpoint seems more readily applicable to consensus arbitration while the judicial viewpoint seems more readily applicable to *ad hoc* arbitrations, but not exclusively so in either case. In truth, each of the two divergent viewpoints is both erroneous and correct. Each arises from assumptions made about the nature of the arbitral process, most aptly stated as follows:

> "In the end, perhaps, there is no escape from the conclusion that both the leading proponents and the principal critics of the 'judicial process' theory of grievance arbitration have proceeded on the basis of false assumptions as to the nature of the process, the former holding it to exclude any encouragement of settlement, and the latter deeming it to require a mechanical and sterile approach to interpretation of the agreement." [49]

The most fundamental aspect of American arbitration is that it is voluntary and private,[50] a point emphasized by Professor Taylor[51] and stated in the Code of Ethics adopted by the American Arbitration Association.[52] The parties to a collective bargaining agreement do not generally restrict themselves in grievance procedures but they do circumscribe an arbitrator's jurisdiction.[53] The fact that an arbitrator must conduct himself within the framework set by the parties is a principal distinction from the role of a judge.[54] It certainly seems appropriate and even "highly desirable," in a given case, for the arbitrator to ask the parties if they desire mediation.[55]

"A proper conception of the arbitrator's function is basic. He is not a public tribunal imposed upon the parties by superior authority which the parties are obliged to accept. He has no general charter to administer justice for a community which transcends the parties. He is rather part of a system of self-government created by and confined to the parties. He serves their pleasures only, to administer the rule of law established by their collective bargaining agreement. They are entitled to demand that,

---

[49] Garrett, *The Role of Lawyers in Arbitration*, ARBITRATION AND PUBLIC POLICY 102 (1961).

[50] Justin, *Arbitration under the Labor Contract—Its Nature, Function, and Use*, 24 PERSONNEL 286 (1951).

[51] Taylor, *Arbitrating Wages and Working Conditions*, CURRENT PROBLEMS IN LABOR RELATIONS AND ARBITRATION 13 (1954).

[52] *Code of Ethics and Procedural Standards for Labor Management Arbitration*, THE PROFESSION OF LABOR ARBITRATION 154 (1957).

[53] Shulman, *supra* note 20.

[54] Fuller, *Collective Bargaining and the Arbitrator*, COLLECTIVE BARGAINING AND THE ARBITRATOR'S ROLE 8 (1962).

[55] Handsaker, *Grievance Arbitration and Mediated Settlements*, 17 LAB. L.J. 579 (1966).

at least on balance, his performance be satisfactory to them, and they can readily dispense with him if it is not." [56]

Thus, it can be said that both viewpoints about the proper role of the arbitrator are correct within all contexts of responsiveness to the wishes of the parties.

Rights and Limitations

Another area of philosophical differences detected in the cases concerns the status to be accorded the written collective bargaining agreement. This will be treated but briefly at this point since the ideas are closely related to those set forth in Chapter II.

One perspective is labeled the inherent- or reserved-rights view, under which the employer is said to retain all rights not expressly granted by the contract. This philosophy proceeds from the view that all the rights were originally management's and are restricted no more by collective bargaining than is provided in the express language of the contract.

In contrast is the viewpoint of implied limitations upon the employer's rights which arise because of and out of the collective bargaining relationship, usually stemming from a National Labor Relations Board certification. This view holds that a recognized union, certified or not, in its exercise of powers under federal statutes relative to wages, hours, and working conditions, is a kind of partner with the employer in various matters which arise out of the relationship. Frequently the implications of limitations are said to arise from the recognition clause in the contract.

Here, again, the differences are not always as sharply delineated as one might think. For example, the most outspoken of reserved rightists, in discussing the company's right to make a change in the work force, the job classifications associated therewith, or fundamental changes in manufacturing processes, will usually concede that such rights may not be exercised discriminatorily, in bad faith, in derogation of collective bargaining relationships, or the like. In contrast, the implied-limitations theorists will frequently uphold the right of the company to make technological changes in distress situations, in recogni-

---

[56] Shulman, *supra* note 20.

tion of the fact that the collective bargaining relationship would be tenuous or nonexistent if the company were not able to survive economically.

These two areas of philosophical perspective are important. Indeed, they may represent but two aspects of a single dichotomy,[57] except that the polarization with respect to an arbitrator's role need not necessarily be of the same direction or intensity. The influence of these perspectives can be detected in the cases but not so clearly as to permit ready classification. They do, however, aid in understanding aspects of this book.

3. THE BASIC PROBLEM

All arbitrators of whatever persuasion are aware of the deeper problem involved in the categories of this study. No documentation is necessary to characterize our American economy as one of dynamic change. And basically it is this change characteristic which creates labor-management problems for arbitrators to solve—at least and especially in industrial engineering areas.

Two Aspects of Change

This fact of change, the need for change, adaptation of methods, and other means for more efficient production constitute the essential rationale of management. While the change imperative also applies to organized labor, its essential rationale (at least for the areas of this study) is job stability, job security, emphasis on the familiar and customary. While these two opposing viewpoints have been explained by various commentators, the following, somewhat turgid language puts them in an interesting focus.

"Business is often a conservative force on social questions. But when it comes to production, it is as radical as it can be. To the enterpriser feeling the sting of the competitive lash, there is no such thing as the status quo in technology or in the organization of production. He hunts feverishly for new materials, for new machines, for new ways of organizing work. When he finds them, he does not hesitate to uproot the established way of making or doing things in order to replace it with a better way.

"On the other hand, trade unionists and trade unions are often the pioneers, the radicals, in changing social institutions.

---

[57] Fuller, *supra* note 54.

But they tend to be the conservatives in their approach to changes in the methods of production. The status quo represents, they think, job security and certainty; change, presented in terms of the promise of a glowing long-run future, is often accompanied by an uncomfortable, if not menacing, tomorrow." [58]

This tension between the forces for change and the forces for stability has seemed to be an even greater problem with the accelerating pace of change. More flexibility and adaptability for management are needed, and arbitrators should be cognizant of accelerated change.[59]

The point has been made [60] that accelerated change is not the special problem of arbitrators. Rather, the principal task of the arbitrator is to interpret contract language. However, these comments about change are relevant:

"Understanding the conceptual framework of the agreement presents particular difficulty—and is particularly important—in times of change. In stable situations, where neither management nor union is trying to upset the applecart, where the disputes mainly concern the application of accepted principles, conceptual problems do not give us much trouble any more. Over the last fifteen or twenty years, in the major industries, most concepts have been arbitrated and rearbitrated until they are now pretty well understood.

"Established concepts, however, are instruments of stability. Where there is pressure for change, there also tends to be pressure for the reexamination of ideas and of the meaning of words. Four concepts in particular, I think, are facing reexamination today; (1) the nature of a 'job'; (2) the reason why a man gets paid; (3) the relationship between seniority rights and work; and (4) the meaning of past practice, custom, and understanding. I want to touch briefly on each of these concepts and tell you why I believe they need the hard thought of all of us." [61]

There followed some interesting comments about the four concepts.

Adjusting to Change

Accommodation to change has taken a number of courses, as would be expected. The two opposing approaches of unions—

---

[58] Wallen, *How Issues of Subcontracting and Plant Removal are Handled by Arbitrators*, 19 INDUS. & LAB. REL. REV. 265 (1966).

[59] Chamberlain, *Job Security, Management Rights, and Arbitration*, WORK ASSIGNMENTS AND INDUSTRIAL CHANGE 224 (1964).

[60] Seward, *Reexamining Traditional Concepts*, WORK ASSIGNMENTS AND INDUSTRIAL CHANGE 240 (1964).

[61] *Id.*

resistance to change on the one hand and acceptance with appropriate benefits for and protection of workers on the other—have been noted.[62] Informative are the case histories in dealing with "demoralized" incentives;[63] many other examples of the effects of change are illustrated. That unions and management may grow to think alike, the way husband and wife are said to grow to think alike, has been suggested.[64] Arbitrators have, predictably, dealt with the problems arising from the change phenomenon in various ways.

> "The problem presented to the arbitrator in this case is one that is not uncommon in arbitration. On the one hand is the age old problem of American industry in which a Company, faced with the hard facts of competitive life, must constantly devise ways of improving its performance and adopt new techniques of production. On the other side is the concern of a union with the loss of jobs created by changes in operations. . . ." [65]

> "It is a fundamental principle in labor management matters, that jobs cannot remain static. . . . The interests of the few must necessarily give way to the interests of the many and it is the considered opinion of the Arbitrator that it was not the intention for a Union contract to stop the continuous development of new methods of efficiency in the development of industry." [66]

In discussing a strike in violation of a no-strike pledge, an arbitrator observed: "Aside from the illegality thereof and the financial loss suffered by all concerned, it is apparent that no industry can long survive such practices. The economic welfare of Company, Union and employees are inextricably interwoven." [67] Another arbitrator emphasized the union's and employees' stake in technological progress.

> "This history of the labor movement in the United States is replete with examples of unions that underwrote their own destruction by opposing technological change. The resistance of the cigar makers union to automatic machinery, of the flint glass workers union to the semi-automatic bottle machine, and of the stonecutters union to the stone planer are cases in point." [68]

---

[62] Brooks, *Unions and Technological Change*, 5 CONF. BOARD REC. 46 (1968).

[63] S. SLICHTER, J. HEALY & E. LIVERNASH, THE IMPACT OF COLLECTIVE BARGAINING ON MANAGEMENT (1960).

[64] Foegen, *Synthesis: Evolution of Industrial Power*, 33 ADVANCED MGMT. J. 75 (1968).

[65] 34 LA 365.

[66] 34 LA 226.

[67] 40 LA 199.

[68] 10 LA 535.

In an interesting case, [69] wherein the union claimed changes had affected some jobs and the company denied any change affecting the grievants—the problem having developed because of physical changes which yielded more production in existing operations—the arbitrator reasoned, in effect, that there had been at least a psychological change, deriving from the impact of changed prior operations, such as to justify consideration of grievants' claims for increased rates.

Effects of Collective Bargaining

Even while recognizing the need for change, arbitrators do sometimes hold that jobs under a contract are frozen for the duration of the contract (especially if there has not been substantial change in technology). Since the initiatory dynamics of management rights are not readily available in such circumstances, arbitrators develop other logics through analyses of the parties' negotiations and relationships, practices, or the language of the contract (and, no doubt, personal orientation). For example, a theory of contracting-out to employees was the rationale used in a case denying a company's right to combine two existing jobs into a single job:

> "The work, that is under and is the subject matter of said contract, has been let and contracted to employees in classified employments, each employee to be assigned and classified according to the work he is actually doing. Work that is peculiar to a classification within the bargaining unit is to be assigned and performed by employees under the contract according to job classification, subject only to noted exceptions, not here pertinent, as provided in Section 5." [70]

(There was nothing in the report of the case to indicate that the "contracting-out" to employees was contained within the collective bargaining agreement.) It is interesting to note, in this case, that union recognition of the need for change—modernization—in order for the company to be competitive was explicitly stated in the arbitrator's opinion.

Under a contract providing that the union could file grievances on any acts of the company under the contract which "it believes may be unjust to an employee . . .," an arbitrator—not illogically—concluded that the parties had agreed upon a contractual principle that the company's acts must be "just." This

---

[69] 27 LA 324.
[70] 39 LA 1058.

principle was applied in a decision which held that a freeze on wage rates in a particular department (through a negotiated progression system) required a balancing freeze on jobs and job duties and, as a consequence, the company was in error in eliminating a helper classification in existence at the time the contract was negotiated.[71]

Balancing Interests

Finally, there is the logical recognition of the need for change balanced by compensation adjustments to employees affected thereby. Thus, a "well-established generalization" was noted [72] under which, absent restrictive contract language, management could proceed to effect changes in operations (from single to dual machine assignments in the automatic-screw-machine department). However, a grievance seeking pay adjustments not only was appropriate but also was the basis for the arbitrator's decision awarding responsive wage treatment.

No doubt the balancing of interests is even more equitably accomplished in situations where a technological displacement allowance structure has been negotiated. As the arbitrator in one case observed:

> "The history over 18 years of close to three thousand employees receiving technological displacement pay for an aggregate of close to two million dollars, indicates stronger than words that the Union and Management both have worked together to solve the problem of reconstituting the job due to technological improvement. The Union, it would appear, has broadly recognized the right that management has to effect a consolidation of jobs, and transfer bits of work from one sub-division to another, if the rights of the employees adversely affected were recognized under the T.D.A. provision of the agreement." [73]

The phenomenon of change and the correlative resistance to change represent a unifying theme for the industrial engineering cases analyzed in this book. Because of the nature of the relationships involved, management initiates action and the employee/union initiates grievances in reaction. However, there are a few cases in which the action-reaction roles are reversed. In either event, the resulting disputes become matters for arbitral decision.

---

[71] 41 LA 268.
[72] 7 LA 943.
[73] 30 LA 705.

CHAPTER II

MANAGEMENT AND UNION "RIGHTS"

The basic problem of accommodation to change between the parties to a collective bargaining agreement, required by the dynamics of our economy, was briefly discussed in Chapter I. How the parties have sought to respond to this by contract provisions, practice, and policy/philosophy concepts—as interpreted by arbitrators in disputes settlements—is the subject of this and the next four chapters.

As stated in Chapter I, change pervades the entire book and is, therefore, intimately involved in Chapters VII through X as with these earlier chapters. There is a shift of focus in the later chapters, however, to reflect the specialized perspective of Chapter VII and to highlight industrial engineering problems in all four chapters.

This chapter is concerned with the interaction of the interrelated ideas of management rights and union recognition, both in expressed contractual language and as generalized concepts urged by the parties and evaluated by arbitrators. Notice should be taken of a practical suggestion for the use of the term "management functions" [1] to avoid the emotionalism of "rights." (There is, of course, the extreme view that management has no rights as such.) [2] However, since most of the cases refer to management rights and prerogatives, that terminology will be retained. The rights of labor have been pointed out; [3]

---

[1] Seward, *Arbitration and the Functions of Management*, 16 IND. & LAB. REL. REV. 2, 235 (1963).

[2] Young, *The Question of Managerial Prerogatives*, 16 IND. & LAB. REL. REV. 2, 240 (1963).

[3] Goldberg, *Management's Reserved Rights: A Labor View*, MANAGEMENT RIGHTS AND THE ARBITRATION PROCESS 118 (1956); Ostrin, *Reserved Rights in Labor Arbitration*, NEW YORK UNIVERSITY TWELFTH ANNUAL CONFERENCE ON LABOR 227 (1959).

reference here is not to the basic rights imbedded in the labor statutes, but to those related to the recognition clauses of contracts.

The sectional divisions used derive from the analysis scheme utilized, arranged for logical presentation and interest. Clearly, there is considerable overlap in the cases; an effort has been made to minimize this by using multiple categorization only to the extent thought desirable for content results.

The pattern of all the issues considered is pinpointed in Chapter I. More particularly, in this chapter, one or more changes are made affecting the way things have been done and, more or less, the accepted way of doing things. It is left to the arbitrator to decide what rights exist.

1. BARGAINING-UNIT WORK AFFECTED BY CHANGE

The dispute usually arises over some action taken by management as a result of or in implementation of changes in company operations. Automation efforts by the company [4] had resulted in the assignment of programming duties on tape-controlled machine tools to toolmakers in the bargaining unit. Later, when a new tape-controlled turret lathe was installed in the tool room, management decided, in the interests of efficiency, to assign the programming work to a non-bargaining-unit production engineer, citing the management-rights clause in defense of its actions. The arbitrator pointed out that programming had always been toolmakers' work, the classification was then performing programming duties, management had not abolished the function, and there was no change in methods or processes of manufacture—since programming was still being performed as before. It was suggested that management, by the procedure adopted, could nullify recognition and diminish the bargaining unit.

Programming of tape-controlled machines was also the issue in another case.[5] Here, the programming was performed initially by a salaried employee and the grievance represented the union's position that the work and job of programming should be in the bargaining unit. The arbitrator reviewed the programmer's duties and concluded that 80 percent or more of the work done by him had previously been jig work, which

---

[4] 37 LA 192.
[5] 50 LA 157.

had previously been done by non-bargaining-unit personnel. The arbitrator acknowledged the union's concern about erosion of the bargaining unit, but pointed out that the only applicable contract provision was the recognition clause. Since this clause contained specific exclusion of clerical, production and material control, and engineering employees, the jig-work analysis placed this job within the exclusions.

Pursuant to recommendations of consultants, the company [6] adopted what is known as short-interval scheduling and, to work the system, created a new managerial position of production planner. The union did not argue about the installation of the new system but did file a grievance to the effect that the system had resulted in improper reassignment of work duties in violation of the contract; a major claim was that the planner was taking over some of the duties of expediters, bargaining-unit personnel, who had previously communicated decisions to line foremen. The arbitrator concluded the planner had become supervisor of the expediters and, further, that no duties which were properly in the bargaining unit had been reassigned to managers—this last in accordance with the contract requirement that jobs would be assigned to bargaining-unit employees in accordance with work duties.

Other Transfers of Duties

Weigh-counting [7] of produced nuts and bolts was the regular responsibility of the bargaining-unit job of weighmaster. Installation of electronic sensors on the machines resulted in a company decision to eliminate the weighmaster job. The grievance alleged that bargaining-unit work was to be taken over by non-bargaining-unit operators in the control room where the sensors' signals were received. The company argued that the control-room function was primarily production scheduling and the replacement of the weighmaster's work was incidental, though important to the scheduling functions. Since the contract provided that a new job combining unit duties with nonunit duties was to be within the unit, the arbitrator concluded that the weighmaster duties were involved in the control room, even though they might not be a major function, and the particular job was to be in the bargaining unit. (He stated that the rela-

---

[6] 51 LA 293.
[7] 46 LA 730.

tionship to the bargaining unit of control-room scheduling duties was not being decided.)

Warehouse employees [8] had, for several years, thrown the switches and moved railroad cars within a steel mill's warehouse area. In his decision against the union's grievance on behalf of railroad crews, in which he considered the established practice and the efficiency of the arrangements, the arbitrator made this statement:

> "The principle is well established in industrial arbitration that a company may not arbitrarily change the duties of existing classifications during the life of an agreement; on the other hand, the duties of a classification are not unalterably frozen either. The propriety of changes made by management depends on the circumstances of each case and the pertinent contract provisions."

In one case,[9] the problem was the transfer of the specialized duties of a classification known as leader, banana room. The particularized duties involved care, count, cure (humidity control), and storage of bananas in a warehouse operation. Decision was that the recognition clause prevented transfer of the duties outside the unit, ". . . unless, perhaps, they are supervisory, or the *de minimis* doctrine applies"; neither was held to apply. In another case,[10] the contract recited the parties' mutual understanding that four employees classified as tester at the time of signing, and that this number could vary depending upon work requirements. Such understanding did not justify reducing the number of testers to one on the first shift, coupled with assignment, on a part-time basis, of testing to first-aid attendants on other shifts—there being no evidence of methods or process changes such as might make the management-rights contract provisions applicable.

In a decision [11] upholding management's actions, the arbitrator spoke about management rights and the recognition clause. Involved was the assignment of work previously performed by bargaining-unit production clerks to salaried, nonunion clerical employees, with the result that the jobs of three of 5,000 bargaining-unit jobs were eliminated. (While *de minimis*

---

[8] 50 LA 361.
[9] 33 LA 188.
[10] 41 LA 24.
[11] 42 LA 1025.

might have applied, this was not a principal part of the arbitrator's opinion.) The decision was based on the view that restrictions on management's right to assign work could not be implied from the recognition clause. No other contract clause restricted management's right, and the right was exercised in good faith and for sound economic reasons.

Especially interesting in this case was the arbitrator's detailed analysis of the "implied limitations" theory, that is, limitations on management actions implied by or inferred from the recognition clause. It is also interesting for its categorization of the recognition clause as the only "completely non-volitional" clause in a labor agreement; that is, recognition follows automatically from NLRB certification, and cannot be refused. Recognition was likened to a "verbal act," completed as soon as it is performed; it was contrasted with "scope" clauses, as found in some contracts, to indicate that it is not a "work jurisdiction" clause.

Elimination of Duties

One company [12] discontinued cement manufacturing at a plant and converted it to a warehouse. Bulk loading and unloading became a part of the packers' job, although not previously performed, and this was held to be a substantial change in job. While no objections to the conversion to warehouse were entered, a grievance was filed over the company's failure to negotiate rates pursuant to the contract's language calling for negotiations should a job be variously affected including, as here, "substantial changes in duties." The arbitrator held that the company's announcement of new rates did not constitute negotiations.

A contract [13] had a provision, relating to consolidations and mergers, aimed at preservation of union membership and protection of employees' seniority. It did not, however, contain anything about the rights of dairies to merge and/or consolidate. After acquiring another dairy, the company rearranged the routes of the acquired dairy, after an intensive study, combining 10 routes into five. The grievance was initiated by an employee

[12] 47 LA 601.
[13] 50 LA 157.

laid off because his route was eliminated. The arbitrator concluded there was no contract violation.

A company decision [14] to eliminate the operators after automating threading machines (for putting threads on bottle-closure caps) and to run the machines unattended after the machine setter started them (except for supervisory surveillance and trucker stopping of the machine when an order had been filled) was the issue before the arbitrator. It may be noted, incidentally, that the classification was not abolished since the decision applied only to unlined caps; machines producing seal-inserted caps were still attended by operators. The arbitrator concluded that the company had the right to take this action under the management-rights clause in the contract. He stated:

> "Arbitrators hold generally that, in the absence of provisions in the labor-management agreement relative to the hazards of job elimination through so-called technological advance, the management may proceed as its sound discretion indicates. These parties either have not had the occasion heretofore to negotiate such clauses or have not seen fit to do so. Therefore management's decision that it no longer needs Threader Operators on the threader machines when liners are not being inserted, is not subject to any modification in the agreement. The Company has the right, as a consequence, to eliminate the Threader Operators in these circumstances, if it so sees fit."

Addition of Duties

For several years, [15] nonunit laboratory workers had mixed and added color to calendar operations as needed. The arbitrator upheld the assignment of color adding to bargaining-unit personnel as an exercise of management discretion. He stated that the recognition clause merely listed categories of employees, without defining duties, and the references to duties in the job classifications were illustrative rather than exclusive. In contrast,[16] where a contract specified that the assignment to drivers of work other than route work was to be discussed between the company and union, the arbitrator concluded that the company could not unilaterally assign to drivers the duties of inserting and removing the charts for the tachographs installed in company trucks (for continuous recording of the truck's ac-

---

[14] 49 LA 874.
[15] 5 LA 304.
[16] 47 LA 547.

tivities while on the routes). It may be noted that the arbitrator rejected the company's *de minimis* argument (based on an average time of two minutes per day).

Even though there was a management-rights clause in the contract,[17] a union filed a grievance protesting dual assignments, the second consisting of various duties to be performed by glass mold makers "in cycle," that is, while machines were operating automatically. It was strongly argued that such dual assignments had not been made in the past. It also appeared that the union had attempted, unsuccessfully, to restrict such assignments during negotiations. In upholding the company's right in this matter, the arbitrator stated:

> "The important consideration in these proceedings is whether any limitation existed so as to prohibit the Company's right to institute such changes. Before such restriction may be found it must appear in clear and unambiguous terms in the applicable collective bargaining agreements or in a past practice which would leave no doubt but that it was to have operated as a limitation and that the Union, the Company and the employees so relied on it and construed it as such a limitation.
> "Neither the Master Contract nor the Supplemental Agreements contain any language which could be reasonably interpreted to require that the duties of the mold makers remain unchanged or that the changes had to be negotiated before putting them into effect. Accordingly, the Company in exercising its right to manage, was free to add to the existing duties of mold makers other work which was within their job classification."

Legally Imposed Changes

Substantial changes [18] were made in the company's job structure, with union concurrence, in order to comply with the equal-opportunity law. What brought the matter to arbitration was a grievance that the company had improperly refused to recall senior laid-off female employees. The contract had combined separate seniority lists into one. However, because of a state law specifying maximum weights which female employees could lift, the company prepared a list of jobs which women could fill, the union added one classification, and the arbitration considered and directed the expansion of potential female occupations—from those categories in which both men and women were then employed and from his inspection of jobs at the

---

[17] 43 LA 1006.
[18] 48 LA 819.

plant. He also retained jurisdiction of the grievance, for any determinations relative to application of guidelines he supplied to the parties.

The cases reflect arbitral belief that, absent specific, governing contract language, management does have the right to make changes affecting the bargaining unit—with several important provisos which collectively say that the changes must be logical and minimize the impact upon the bargaining unit. Included in the cases are illustrations of governing contract language.

The provisos include requirements of good faith, a sound business basis, and reasons not arbitrary or capricious. They involve the idea of less freedom to act if the action directly affects bargaining-unit jobs than if there was no prior history (the automated-machine tool cases). They often include the important requirement to negotiate with the union over the impact of the change upon bargaining-unit jobs, usually classifications and wages.

These provisos will, generally, not apply if the change involves duties jointly performed with supervisors (see next section) or are *de minimis*.

Finally, it is noted that extensive changes will take place, probably on a joint basis, when the impetus for change is outside the organization—federal employment requirements and state health regulations in the case noted.

2. BARGAINING-UNIT WORK PERFORMED BY NONUNIT PERSONNEL

The work [19] of operation planner, a job in the bargaining unit, was still "distinguishable or identifiable" after the company transferred it outside the unit to the industrial engineering department. The arbitrator held this to be a violation of a contract clause providing that production and maintenance work was not to be performed by personnel outside the bargaining unit, there being no evidence that the parties intended the clause to apply only to direct production work. The arbitrator commented that there was no freeze in the status quo, but the company had no right to make this move unilaterally absent

---

[19] 44 LA 840.

technological change or other basis for eliminating the need for this particular work.

However, there was nothing to prevent a company [20] from unilaterally abolishing what, in the circumstances, amounted to a sort of privilege of overtime work for certain production and maintenance workers. Bargaining-unit personnel had been utilized, on off shifts, as furnace watchers. They punched time clocks regularly to keep awake and reported suspicious occurrences to the county sheriff. The company decided to install an alarm system and contracted for guard service in the interim. There was nothing in the contract to inhibit subcontracting, so the grievance, essentially, hinged on nonunit personnel displacing bargaining-unit workers. The arbitrator found no displacement; there was, in fact, no production work performed during these off shifts. Involved in this case is the legal proscription against a production/maintenance unit's having jurisdiction over guard work.

In a move to centralize and regularize its quality-control function, a company [21] placed all inspectors on salary as management personnel. This impinged on one bargaining unit in a plant where the inspector's job was in the unit. Since he supervised no one, and no changes had occurred in previously performed duties, he remained in the unit. In fact, said the arbitrator, should the incumbent vacate the job, it was to be posted pursuant to the contract.

Nature of the Work

The recognition clause in a contract [22] covered "all hand cutters of window glass," and the arbitrator reasoned that this implied that hand cutting of window glass was bargaining-unit work—that is, "normal production work." The grievance involved small samples, taken every two hours, from randomly selected sheets by nonunit quality-control personnel, who tested the samples for flatness (customer complaints) and then threw them into scrap boxes. Since the arbitrator found that the samples were not production, a judgment reinforced by other considerations elaborated in the opinion, the grievance was denied.

[20] 49 LA 471.
[21] 48 LA 751.
[22] 46 LA 920.

"Be sure the 20 years of practice are on your side"—this is the essence of two other cases involving electric meters. In one,[23] the company unilaterally decided to have nonunit bill collectors disconnect meters when deemed appropriate, whereas bargaining-unit metermen had performed this function for 20 years. The union's grievance was upheld. In the other,[24] members of an electric cooperative read their own meters except during a three-week period each fall (when both bargaining-unit and non-bargaining-unit employees read all meters). The union's bid for an exclusive on meter reading failed because of nearly 20 years of practice.

Technological Changes

Drastic changes [25] were made in a company's cost accounting system which eliminated many job cards previously handled by timekeepers, and the timekeeping job was abolished. Residual timekeeper duties were assigned to supervisors and other employees outside the bargaining unit. The arbitrator ruled that the company had the undoubted right to make changes in its cost accounting and could eliminate the classification of time-keeper so long as it made no assignments of its job duties outside the bargaining unit. Since this had occurred, the union grievance was upheld.

A change to centralized machine accounting was involved in another case.[26] The arbitrator considered the question of transferring job duties outside the bargaining unit to be settled. However, a different result was reached in this case because the work involved was completely eliminated by mechanization. The contract did not bar mechanization; in fact, said the arbitrator, such a prohibition would violate one of the most basic rights and responsibilities of management.

Upholding the transfer of duties under a management-rights clause [27] from bargaining-unit workers to members of a different union because it was motivated by legitimate business considerations, an arbitrator commented that none of the provisions of the contract ". . . assures to the bargaining unit or any classification in it the ownership of work for all time to come,

---

[23] 48 LA 1192.
[24] 50 LA 194.
[25] 10 LA 143.
[26] 35 LA 72.
[27] 48 LA 563 (also reported at 49 LA 1083).

regardless of changed circumstances expectable with the passage of time. A labor agreement is not a trust indenture. It does not freeze the status quo."

A contract [28] did not freeze any particular kind of composing-room work, and the arbitrator upheld company elimination of a page-palming operation. The contract gave jurisdiction to the bargaining unit of all work and duties performed in the composing room; but after being eliminated, the particular operation would not be done by anyone.

The recognition clause of a contract [29] impliedly prohibited assignments of bargaining-unit work to nonunit employees for training purposes if, as here, the assignments (some 100 man-weeks of work) would substantially curtail work opportunities for unit members. In response to a company argument, the arbitrator stated that the recognition clause was, in fact, a limitation on management rights under the reserved-rights doctrine. (There was an earlier effort by the company to secure agreement with the union for the extensive training time.)

Work Locale

A contract provision [30] stating that technical equipment was not to be "operated in operational areas by persons other than technicians" was not determinative of a grievance filed when the company leased one of its studios to a broadcasting company which used its own technicians on the equipment involved. The arbitrator opined that ". . . the leasing of facilities as such does not violate the jurisdictional rights of the Union to have the work performed by employees under this contract, *so long as there is no foreseeable erosion of the bargaining unit.*" (Emphasis added by arbitrator.)

"It is commonly understood that a Union's jurisdiction as a bargaining agent is over the people in a bargaining unit not over the jobs in the bargaining unit, at least in the sense for which the Union contends in this case."[31] This was the arbitrator's reaction to a union's argument that the recognition clause barred the transfer of stocking and shipping of certain products from a national distribution center (bargaining

[28] 51 LA 1174.
[29] 48 LA 305.
[30] 51 LA 600.
[31] 50 LA 1165.

unit) to a regional terminal (non-bargaining-unit, salaried employees), both located in St. Paul, Minn. The company's actions, planned before a strike that occurred shortly before the arbitration, were found by the arbitrator to be for sound business reasons. A second major argument of the union was based upon a contract provision stating that "[s]upervisory and other salaried employees will not perform the work of hourly production employees except in cases of emergency." The arbitrator found that such a provision usually was taken to apply to work within the plant, rather than to a transfer of work as in the present case.

The concept of locale also was involved in a grievance [32] challenging the company's direct sale of imported frozen lamb products, some of the processing on which was done in New Zealand before export. There was an extensive scope or jurisdiction clause in the agreement, but it did not reach the particular processing involved and the grievance was denied. (Had the importation been similarly processed fresh lamb, for example, the New Zealand processing would have conflicted with the jurisdiction clause.)

The adoption of a new marketing system, in which the distributor received the product in bulk liquid form rather than in gaseous form contained in cylinders, resulted in a distributor's nonunion employees performing bargaining-unit work of filling cylinders (and one employee was laid off).[33] The arbitrator upheld the company's decision as economically necessary to stay competitive and not intended to undermine the union. (It appears that the union, in negotiations, had sought jurisdiction over such work at distributor locations, but the company had rejected the proposal.) A similar result [34] was reached in an arbitration concerning the adoption of a new (milk) distributing system.

Supervisors

One employee category which is often involved in questioned performance of bargaining-unit work is the supervisor. A typical contract provision is cited in the St. Paul case of a change from national to regional distribution, *supra*.[35] A similar prohibitory

---

[32] 51 LA 189.
[33] 51 LA 660.
[34] 51 LA 1159.
[35] 50 LA 1165.

clause,[36] but with an exception up to seven days for foremen to drive regular milk routes, was involved in an arbitrator's supporting a grievance in which a foreman drove in excess of the allowable time.

In a case,[37] discussed in the preceding section, involving the operation of automated threading machines without operators, the arbitrator noted that certain of the operator duties had been passed along to machine setters and, probably, truckers. Since these were bargaining-unit jobs, no problem arose with respect to them—except that he ordered, pursuant to the contract, joint reevaluation of the setter's job to assess the impact of the extra duties. The arbitrator did rule that it was improper for the foreman to make spot-check inspections of the threaders, since spot checking was a routine inspection duty, involving closeness of examination not compatible with the general surveillance usually associated with a supervisory job.

During a period of moving transmitter operations from one site to another, a company [38] scheduled a supervisor, in advance, to work as engineer on the graveyard shift on three consecutive weekends. It appeared that 14 additional engineers were hired to install the new equipment and the expanded work force worked substantial overtime; however, bargaining unit employees were not asked if they wanted to work additional hours on these weekend graveyard shifts. The arbitrator (tripartite) sustained the union grievance protesting this supervisor's performance of unit work, on the basis of the recognition clause—there being no other applicable provisions—and made these comments:

> "One of the basic and primary principles of construction of contracts is that there is an implied obligation on a party to a contract to do nothing which would prevent execution of the undertakings or which would prevent accomplishment of the objectives which the parties must have contemplated. To put it another way, a party to a contract is obligated not to render it without meaning or to frustrate its purposes."

Following this, the arbitrator reviewed some arbitration cases dealing with the extent to which a recognition clause prohibits supervisory work, including an earlier decision of his, and

---

[36] 50 LA 357.
[37] *Supra* note 14.
[38] 51 LA 1221.

concluded there was a discernible trend of prohibition implied from the recognition clause.

There was a vigorous dissent to this decision written by the company-appointed arbitrator and published at his request with the arbitrator's opinion and award. He expressed the management-rights philosophy, suggesting that the prohibition to be implied from the recognition clause should amount to a finding that supervisory assignment was an "excessive and unreasonable abuse" resulting "in serious and permanent consequence." He also reviewed the cases cited in support of the arbitrator's opinion and thought that all, save one, were distinguishable. (The opinion and dissent are particularly interesting on the subject of practice, discussed in Chapter VI).

A contrasting situation [39] is that of the sole office secretary, a member of the bargaining unit, who was properly terminated under the contract (reduction in force) but whose duties were split between the business agent and the assistant of the union employer. The grievance was based on the fact that the duties had not been eliminated but were being performed by supervisory personnel, contrary to the recognition clause. In denying the grievance the arbitrator noted that the contract provided that duties could vary in each individual office and that supervisors were excluded from the recognition clause. Consequently, office and clerical duties could be reassigned to supervisors, even though depopulation resulted.

Performance of bargaining-unit work by a supervisor may be sanctioned, even though there is a specific contractual prohibition upon his performing such work, on the ground that it is *de minimis*. Such a situation was noted.[40]

Practice and Practicality

In one case [41] a prior contract had contained a general waiver of violations of nonunit personnel performing bargaining-unit work. In the current contract the waiver was removed but provision was made for continuance of past practice in shipping. Consequently, the union grievance protesting the shipping department supervisor's performance of bargaining-unit work was denied. The supervisor was, in fact, performing all kinds of

---

[39] 47 LA 836.
[40] 48 LA 746.
[41] 47 LA 748.

work normally done by union members—but his activities were in keeping with past practice. The contract in another case [42] contained a recognition that, because of the branch size, the foreman would be "often expected to work," and this was acceptable provided regular employees did not involuntarily lose time as a result of his working.

In carrying out such duties, however, a foreman who is also a union member should not be charged with conduct unbecoming a union member. A contract,[43] which recognized that foremen could be union members, stated that "the foreman shall be responsible to the employer only." The arbitrator stated that misconduct charges brought by the union violated the contract and should be dropped. Passing upon a grievance [44] challenging the action, an arbitrator upheld the company's orders to certain department heads to withdraw from the union since they were, in fact, supervisors as defined in the law. Similarly, an arbitrator [45] upheld the company in changing a leaderman classification to supervisor, since this was more descriptive of the first-level management responsibilities.

Presumably, company management is empowered to create supervisory positions in its discretion. Problems arise when the positions include bargaining-unit work. In the short-interval-scheduling case,[46] discussed in the preceding section, the arbitrator upheld the company's action in creating a new supervisory job, which included direct transmittal of production decisions to foremen; this formerly had been done by expediters. The new position supervised the expediters, so that no duties exclusively reserved to the bargaining unit had been affected. In another aspect of the same case, the company was upheld in its assignment to foreman of clerical duties which had been performed, years earlier, by a clerk—the clerical work being minor and incidental. (Both of these issues tend toward *de minimis.*) Similar to the first of these issues is a case [47] wherein the arbitrator endorsed the creation of a salaried receiver-scheduler in place of a receiver-of-stores bargaining-unit job—the endorsement being primarily because of super-

[42] 46 LA 707.
[43] 50 LA 186.
[44] 49 LA 271.
[45] 51 LA 296.
[46] 51 LA 293.
[47] 50 LA 107.

visory responsibilities. It is to be noted that a bargaining-unit job was eliminated in this situation, which was not so in the short-interval-scheduling case.

Concurrent Duties

Somewhere in between is a decision [48] requiring some of the history of the job in question to be appreciated. A certain cost-reporting clerk was to do her job and also supervise typists and clerk-typists in her department. Later, she divided her time between two departments. Then she went full time with the second department. At that time, she was replaced for a short while, but when the replacement left, management stated the position was being eliminated because of the presence of a full-time department head, and an additional clerk-typist was hired. Denying a grievance alleging that this was a unilateral transfer of duties outside the bargaining unit, the arbitrator viewed it as a managerial decision to increase the amount of regular supervision, which eliminated the need for "secondary supervision" of the leadman type.

The case [49] of the employee whose nose was a unique "tool" puts concurrently held duties in clear perspective. The employee, who tested the company's natural gas lines for leaks, using only his nose, retired, and the company failed to post his job for bid. Involved in the grievance was a charge that the supervisor was performing this testing duty contrary to a clause stating that supervisors "shall not perform work of the same nature as performed by employees covered by this contract." The arbitrator pointed out the company had had three ways to test for leaks: (1) the employee, using his nose, (2) supervisors, using mechanical testers, and (3) outside contractors. The company had the right to eliminate the first method and the job involved, he said, and the supervisor's mechanical testing, supported by practice, was not of the "same nature" as that performed by the retired employee. The supervisor was not nosed out.

The concept of concurrently held duties is valid, however, only if analysis shows the concurrence. Thus, in the leader, banana room case,[50] discussed in the preceding section, the

---

[48] 33 LA 557.
[49] 51 LA 1269.
[50] *Supra* note 9.

arbitrator found that the activities performed by this man were integral to the proper care of the bananas and not supervisory in nature, so that the company's assignment of the duties to a supervisor was an error. He therefore upheld the grievance of the union requesting that the job be posted when the incumbent bid to another job. This preservation of a bargaining-unit job was grounded on the recognition clause, which applied, said the arbitrator, unless the duties were supervisory or *de minimis* (he decided they were neither).

The decision [51] of one arbitrator about a *de minimis* situation is of interest. The grievance protested the performance by a service crew of production work, in the course of cleaning a lime kiln. In connection with this there was an issue of a supervisor's doing bargaining-unit work—pushing buttons which started and stopped the motor to revolve the kiln, as necessary, for the cleaning operations. The arbitrator ruled *de minimis*, since it involved not more than five minutes per eight-hour shift. He also cited, with approval, the following comments by another arbitrator (35 LA 917), which are interesting since application of this language would mean that even *de minimis* is not applicable in button pushing.

> "The pushing of buttons to activate the automatic system might perhaps be regarded as a kind of physical work, but it would be wholly unreasonable to rule that this kind of task, under the circumstances present here, may be assigned only to bargaining unit employees. The button-pushing takes only seconds and is performed only a few times per shift. It is simply a signal or instruction to the machine. It is of the same character as the issuance of instructions to truckers, unit attendants, and other bargaining unit employees, perhaps by means of an intercom system on which a button must be pressed to talk. Such direction of work is essentially supervisory in nature."

The performance by supervisors of bargaining-unit work may be upheld when the arbitrator is convinced the circumstances amounted to an emergency. This was the case where there was provision for emergency situations in the contract.[52]

Two Unions Involved

No discernible difference exists where the personnel involved in disputed bargaining-unit work are members of another un-

---

[51] 47 LA 756.
[52] 48 LA 124.

ion. This is illustrated in a special way in the sole-office-secretary case, discussed above.[53] Other office clerical types of changes also involved a second union.[54]

A company's transfer of a moisture register from the laboratory to another department in the plant was the subject of a grievance.[55] The union contract covered employees in both departments, except that there was a separate agreement containing several general provisions applying to laboratory personnel. The arbitrator concluded there was but one union involved, the contract spelled out no jurisdictional (craft-type) separation, and the assignment was simply intrabargaining unit in nature.

Two locals of the same union [56] had separate NLRB certifications and separate contracts. In a dispute over which local should perform a certain job (removing a scrap overhead drive shaft), the parent district lodge stressed that this was not a general jurisdictional dispute but rather "a problem of appropriate work assignment." The company and the local that was involved in the arbitration proceeding stipulated to that effect and the arbitrator resolved the controversy.

Several of the cases herein reinforce the general conclusions stated in the preceding section. Where changes are made by a company and are judged to be for sound business reasons by the arbitrator, he will support the changes—even against claims that others are performing bargaining-unit work.

Where the issues are not so basic, company actions affecting bargaining unit work are circumscribed considerably. Absent controlling contract provisions jobs, duties are not frozen, but changes must make sense in terms of the union interests involved. When changes involve non-unit personnel doing bargaining-unit work, the tendency is clearly toward arbitral retraint on company action. Exceptions occur when the duties involved are supervisory in nature or the situation is *de minimis,* as well as in emergency situations.

Some contracts contain provisions restricting or precluding

---

[53] *Supra* note 39.
[54] 46 LA 1065, 48 LA 563.
[55] 46 LA 532.
[56] 47 LA 414.

performance of bargaining-unit work by supervisors. Violations are treated by arbitrators in accordance therewith—*de minimis* situations being recognized. However, in one case, absent explicit contract language barring the performance of unit work by supervisors, the recognition clause was volitional. Other cases were marked by waivers of the proscription against supervisors performing bargaining-unit work.

An analysis of a number of arbitration reports on supervisory performance of bargaining-unit work, including a box score on decisions, appears in *Arbitration Journal.*[57]

3. CHANGES WITHIN THE BARGAINING UNIT

Employees in the engineering department at one company for years had made necessary changes and adjustments in yarn-winding machines. The company, in good faith for efficiency reasons, reassigned this work to regular production workers. An arbitrator upheld the action. He considered that management had the right, if exercised in good faith, "to change, eliminate or establish new classifications" unless the agreement specifically restricted this right; any such restriction would have been in express language "and not left to any conjectural inference."[58]

The requirement of explicit limitations was also thought necessary to warrant a decision "to deny one of the most important and fundamental and inherent prerogatives of management."[59] At issue was the assignment to production workers of work previously done by skilled mechanics, the change occurring when the work was established on a production line basis.

An overall program to transfer certain testing work involving quality control to the quality control division at each plant, coupled with changes in and elimination of certain tests, was upheld by an arbitrator,[60] even though certain employees then working in various plant laboratories had their jobs eliminated and were forced to transfer to less satisfactory jobs. It was held that such transfers were normally within managerial discretion, and were not to be interfered with absent restraining language in the contract or a showing of bad faith by the employer.

---

[57] Harris, *Supervisory Performance of Bargaining Unit Work*, 20 ARB. J. 3, 129 (1965).
[58] 30 LA 705.
[59] 21 LA 424.
[60] 33 LA 169.

Effects of Job Descriptions

However, a different result occurred in a case [61] where material-control clerical work, involving the typing and distributing of reports of materials received, was eliminated by the installation and use of a telautograph transcriber. In ruling on a grievance protesting the layoff of the clerk-typist involved, the arbitrator held that management clearly had the right to eliminate a job, provided it acted in good faith. The evidence was, however, that this employee had been operating the transcriber for about 18 months. This fact resulted in a conclusion that the transcriber work had been added to her job description even though formal revision had not taken place.

Job descriptions figured even more prominently in another case.[62] Here the arbitrator concluded that the fact the parties had negotiated job descriptions had a direct impact upon managerial assignment rights; indeed, mutual action was required. This case involved the reassignment to assembly workers of disassembly and repair of defective gyros, work that previously had been done by higher skilled employees.

An even more direct impact was found in a case [63] where the company reduced the classification of a job although the job had not been changed and had not previously been classified at a lower level. The arbitrator ruled that the company had acted unilaterally in violation of the recognition clause; the company was bound to negotiate with the union on this matter. Involved were the reclassications of certain employees from welder, first class, to welder, second class, after World War II. During the war they had performed high-skilled welding; but thereafter they did relatively unskilled and routine welding work on the company's commercial products.

An arbitrator upheld, as exclusively within management direction, the transfer of the operating responsibility for a fuel-oil system and air compressor from a fireman to treating-room personnel. There were no agreed upon job descriptions, and the arbitrator characterized the duties as a combination of semiskilled and unskilled work, not highly skilled work. He reviewed a number of arbitrations upholding transfer of semiskilled and un-

---

[61] 35 LA 367.
[62] 23 LA 829.
[63] 6 LA 156.

skilled duties from one group to another, for convenience and economy, as management rights.[64]

Operational Requirements

In another case,[65] management had good reasons—serious material shortages affecting the handling of back orders—for taking some of the duties of a particular classification and forming them into a new classification. The contract's management rights clause permitted the company to alter, add to, or subtract from employees' duties. The arbitrator upheld the company's right to form the new classification, but he also upheld the union's grievance because the company had acted unilaterally and without collective bargaining.

In sharp contrast was another arbitrator's holding.[66] He expressed the conviction that the recognition clause did not give the union the right to insist on prior negotiations with respect to changes from skilled journeymen to semiskilled production workers when the work had become repetitive in nature. He felt this conclusion was buttressed by the language of the management-rights clause.

An employer's unilateral elimination of a fireman's classification and assignment of the functions to the engineer classification, where both were involved in boiler room operations, was upheld by an arbitrator.[67] There was, he stated, no explicit limitation on the company's right to take the actions, and they were for economic reasons, without evidence of bad faith. (An analysis had indicated that the engineer could reasonably assume the functions within his work schedule, and that safety regulations would not be violated.)

Because of improvements in wire-splicing techniques that permitted the lineman and his helper to splice wires at the same time, a company required helpers to splice regularly along with linemen.[68] There being no job descriptions, the arbitrator looked to practice and found that the company could not require such splicing as a regular duty—since it was contrary to the established pattern for helpers—without compensating the individuals in-

[64] 45 LA 557.
[65] 7 LA 368.
[66] 6 LA 200.
[67] 48 LA 24.
[68] 43 LA 651.

volved at the higher rate of lineman. In a contrasting case,[69] a maintenance helper was told to perform certain duties by the journeyman to whom he was assigned. The helper performed some tasks which could be classified within the journeyman skill and filed for the higher rate. The grievance was denied. There was a job description, specifying that the helper would perform as assigned under close direction, and in the arbitrator's opinion that is what the helper was doing in this case.

In an assignment situation,[70] a grievance alleged that work of general hands (unskilled labor) was being done by screw machine operators. The work in question was the movement of the screw machine department to a new location. The arbitrator denied the grievance, finding that the movement of machines and equipment was done by several classifications as well as by general hands. Also, knowledge of the operations was needed in the move in order to locate properly such things as tools and cams as well as for correct positioning of the new materials. Similarly, an arbitrator denied a maintenance mechanic's claim for call-in pay when night-shift production employees moved and installed a portable compressor.[71] This had simplified (and was identified by management as a technological improvement) the former procedure, which involved the use of a maintenance mechanic when a building's compressor went out.

An arbitrator upheld the disciplinary suspension of chemical production operators who refused, on second and third shifts where there were no fork-lift operators, to operate fork-lift trucks as needed for production operations.[72] It appears that manning of the fork lifts on these shifts had been discussed but not resolved in negotiations. One of the contract provisions stated that employees' duties were flexible, so that the interchanging of jobs and performance of assigned work was expected. The arbitrator thought the employees should have followed the maxim "work now and grieve later." An arbitrator thought the same in a similar incident in which an oiler refused a cleaning job when directed to perform it.[73] Here the job description included cleaning, but practice had been otherwise.

[69] 26 LA 114.
[70] 48 LA 941.
[71] 50 LA 677.
[72] 48 LA 124.
[73] 28 LA 394.

Skilled Trades

A few cases involving jurisdictional problems of skilled trades were noted. Thus, arbitrators found that the questioned assignments were proper where pipefitters thought millwrights were improperly loosening and removing bolts and removing an obstruction from a digester;[74] where heat treaters thought a portable electric oven used for drying in small-parts assembly should not be operated by assemblers;[75] and where welders protested an assignment to clean welds (both chippers and welders were in the same craft jurisdiction).[76] However, the company's action in reclassifying a female welder's job to include inert-gas welding was improper, since such welding was already a significant part of the higher rated male welding classification.[77]

Under a contract,[78] production workers did not have a jurisdictional right to their jobs as did the skilled trades. In a grievance in which a pipefitter alleged that a production worker should not clean a spinning machine tub since pipefitters had done this in the past, the arbitrator stated that skilled tradesmen's jurisdictional right did not extend to unskilled work—work which, by its nature, could not properly be considered as belonging to any craft. An interesting case [79] involved a shop repairman who worked regularly from 7:00 a.m. to 3:30 p.m., and departmental shift repairmen who worked around the clock. There was almost complete overlap of duties and both joint and intermixed assignments. The grievance of one shift repairman for overtime was denied. The absence for illness of shift repairmen of the shift following his was properly handled by using the shop repairman.

Welders filed a grievance, the gist of which was that pipefitters and a millwright at different times were performing welder's work by using an acetylene torch.[80] The arbitrator stated that this torch was not a tool limited to the welding craft but was a tool that other maintenance classifications could use. Although the contract provided for the integrity of the various maintenance skill classifications, he thought that a rule of reason should apply.

---

[74] 47 LA 761.
[75] 50 LA 1048.
[76] 50 LA 1001.
[77] 46 LA 62.
[78] 47 LA 609.
[79] 48 LA 52.
[80] 45 LA 201.

The cases herein stand for a general rule that management may accomplish changes within the bargaining unit, absent restrictive contract language, so long as the action is motivated by the needs of the business and is accomplished in good faith (meaning minimization of the impact on employees, to the extent possible). Good faith is not shown by a statement that a job is the same when it has changed in fact, even though the job description has not been modified. Also, reducing a job unaccompanied by changes is unwarranted unilateral action in violation of the recognition clause.

Where jobs and job descriptions are negotiated, changes therein must also be negotiated. When mutuality is not so explicit, management may be supported in its right to make the changes but required to negotiate about them, although one ruling was that negotiations need not precede the changes. Impliedly, negotiations are necessary with respect to resultant rate changes whenever such rates are not within an established structure (*i.e.,* one which has already been negotiated).

It will be observed that changes from higher classifications to lower classifications are approved by arbitrators when these are consistent with progress toward rationalized and standardized production or otherwise reflect economic reality. If not so justified, changes will not be supported by arbitrators.

Generally, arbitrators view less permanent assignments by management even more liberally if the aim is to keep the work going, if not discriminatory, and if not governed by specific language. This is not so with skilled trades, where jurisdiction is recognized and protected within the accepted parameters of the skills. Efforts of skilled tradesmen to extend jurisdiction beyond these parameters are not endorsed by arbitrators.

4. PROBLEMS OF SEX

Some of the more recent of the cases analyzed involved problems arising from the separate classification of employees by sex. These cases are separately considered because the area will become more generally significant to parties involved in arbitration.

A relevant case [81] has already been discussed in Section 1. It is important because it reflects major activities by the parties to

---

[81] *Supra* note 18.

the agreement—in response to civil-rights regulations and legislation—as well as the determinations of the arbitrator, in which he seeks to extend the parties' implementation of a nondiscriminatory structure. The case also illustrates the problems which developed with respect to state regulations governing weights which can be lifted by female employees. Another case previously noted in Section 3 [82] illustrates a problem to which civil-rights criteria were not applied (but possibly could become a factor in other circumstances).

Seniority Considerations

There was an interesting provision in one contract under seniority rights.[83] It provided that, effective at the signing of the agreement, male employees would not be allowed to replace female employees permanently or to bid for jobs held by female employees. Similarly, female employees would not be allowed to replace male employees permanently or bid for openings held by male employees. It further provided that any new job classification established after the date of the agreement would be open to bid by both male and female employees, and the prohibitions in the preceding parts of the paragraph would not apply to such new jobs. The company eliminated a female classification called weight checker. The arbitrator noted that, while such elimination could be justified if the duties had terminated, all the company had done was to abolish the title and transfer the duties to male employees. The same arbitrator concluded in another case [84] that there was no evidence of an intent to segregate female employees for the purpose of evading equal payment under the law. The contract permitted the company to eliminate job classifications, where reasonable and warranted by circumstances. The company did eliminate a job, and one of the claims of the union, in support of its grievance, alleged that the company was trying to avoid paying equal wages to female employees.

A new classification was created specifically for females, at a lower rate.[85] The contract provided that classifications and rates would be maintained unless changed by mutual consent of the parties. The company furnished information and all the relevant data concerning reasons for the new classification to the union,

---

[82] *Supra* note 77.
[83] 46 LA 396.
[84] 46 LA 572.
[85] 48 LA 339.

but the union did not undertake to challenge the correctness of the new classification pursuant to the contract. Consequently, the arbitrator concluded that the company was justified in creating the new classification.

After instituting more efficient ways of performing the work, a company removed certain duties from the jobs of male employees and assigned them to female employees working in the same area.[86] The action was challenged in a grievance alleging overload of the female employees. The arbitrator viewed the operation and the surrounding working conditions and concluded that the revised job appeared not to represent a specific health hazard. He upheld the company's action on the ground that it was within the discretionary power of management under the contract. However, the arbitrator did note that an employee could request transfer—rather than face discharge—where the work was found to be particularly burdensome.

Discrimination

The parties [87] had established a single seniority system in order to overcome possible discrimination with respect to sex. It developed that female employees were often unable to perform their assigned jobs under the single system. As a result, the company worked out a three-classification job plan, with the consent and approval of the employees affected, to avoid the jobs which females were not able to handle. The union challenged this arrangement. The arbitrator concluded that the company could not unilaterally change the job classification plan in this manner, since the contract was with the union and not with the employees.

A "feeling" of discrimination has been held not to be an arbitral issue.[88] The contract precluded upward bumping, and in practice this meant that female employees could not bump males. It was this that had led to the so-called feeling. The parties corrected this problem in negotiations and permitted upward bumping (they also eliminated male and female job separation). However, absent such action by the parties, it would appear that the effect of a proscription against upward bumping, where there are separate male and female classifications, is potentially discriminatory.

---

[86] 50 LA 871.
[87] 51 LA 970.
[88] 47 LA 1045.

In order to comply with federal legislation on equal-employment opportunities, a company [89] unilaterally changed two classifications bearing female and male designations to light and heavy designations. The union protested this and the arbitrator upheld the union grievance, stating that the company did not have this right under the contract. In another situation,[90] the grievance claimed the company had violated the contract by hiring a male employee to fill a job which had always been filled by female employees. The arbitrator stated that there was nothing in the contract relative to sex of employees and upheld the company's action.

Practical Considerations

Prior to the time when two girls were promoted to jobs in the starter assembly department, work in the department had been performed exclusively by men.[91] After six months on the jobs, the company demoted the female employees because they were making only 40 percent of the established production standards. An arbitrator upheld the company action. One of the issues in this case concerned the application of a seniority clause under which employees, after promotion, were allowed only three working days to demonstrate ability to perform the job properly. These girls had been on the job for six months. The arbitrator said the production standards, properly established by the company, should be met; he further thought the girls had been given an extensive trial period, well beyond the usual three days.

The welder B classification in a company [92] was occupied by female employees. When welder A employees (male) were absent, a welder B employee was assigned to weld light parts on an automatic welding machine. As the arbitrator noted, had welder A men been present, this assignment probably would not have been given to the female employee. The arbitrator reviewed in detail the requirements of welder A and welder B classifications, finding that the "core elements" of the welder A job involved layout and setup as well as operation of the machinery; welder A men also did the heavier jobs. The welder B female employes did not perform layout or setup and, al-

---

[89] 45 LA 923.
[90] 43 LA 1181.
[91] 49 LA 669.
[92] 51 LA 35.

though they usually did not operate the automatic welding machine, the work assigned was well within their classification.

Hospitals involved in one arbitration [93] had promoted male orderlies to Licensed Vocational Nurses (LVN). Later on, the hospital demoted these employees, saying it would be improper for them to attend female patients. This posed a problem of discrimination in an acute form, inasmuch as some form of discrimination would result no matter how the issue was resolved. The arbitrator put this in clear focus:

> "It is reasonable to conclude that neither the collective agreement nor the Civil Rights Act proscribes all instances of discrimination based on sex. The evil arises when the discrimination is invidious, when it derogates from the dignity of the man or woman affected. No one is apt to argue that a regulation is proscribed under either agreement or Act which accurately assesses the physical strength of women to be typically less than that of men and therefore bars utilization of women to perform work which foreseeably would be harmful to them. That is protective rather than invidious discrimination. Thus reasonableness of the act or omission to act may privilege the discriminaton effectuated. . . ."

The arbitrator pointed out that the hospital administration had adopted a policy of discrimination based upon its expectations as to the desires or revulsions of its female patients with respect to male LVN attendance. He thought this was not "invidious" discrimination. His award was that males already classified as LVN's could not be demoted, but that the hospitals could discriminate by refusing future promotions wherever, in the system, "intimate care of female patients is a routine requisite of employees working as an LVN."

It is apparent that there are problems of arbitral concern, within the subject area, which are related to the sex of employees—a conclusion unlikely to startle many people. What may be of interest is the insight these cases give of special sex-related issues, present and future.

5. CLASSIFICATION CHANGES FOR EFFICIENCY

One company [94] established a new job classification, met and discussed a rate with the union, and, when unable to reach agreement, put the job into operation at a unilaterally determined rate. In the resulting arbitration, it was held that this was

---

[93] 48 LA 1138.
[94] 12 LA 676.

proper action under the management-rights clause; in fact, even in the absence of such a clause," such rights are generally recognized as being inherently vested in management, where not otherwise expressly limited in the contract." The arbitrator took testimony and decided upon the rate he considered proper for this new job.

This same arbitrator resolved another dispute differently.[95] The company combined two existing jobs into a single job, pursuant to a modernization study; the union claimed this violated the contract. In upholding the grievance, the arbitrator apparently was in general agreement with the union's "scarlet thread" theory—that job classifications ran like such a thread through the whole fabric of the contract. The arbitrator noted that, in most instances, a union seeks only to preserve its bargaining position on pay rates in circumstances involving classification changes; a different result obtains where it is found that job classifications are "built into the entirety of the contract, so as to become the arch or cornerstone of same."

New or Combined Jobs

When a new industrial starter was designed, the company[96] decided to adopt a new production system for it. It broke up a combined job into three component jobs, one of which, testing, turned out to be simpler for the new starter than for earlier models. The company established a lower rate for testing, and the union filed a grievance protesting the classification. The arbitrator reviewed the arguments and concluded that there was nothing in the contract to preclude the company from making the change. He reached his decision on the basis of management rights.

When a company[97] brought in a new tape-controlled profiling machine, it followed its established practice of slotting machines into three broad classifications (this was to the middle classification). The union filed a grievance, claiming the contract required negotiations on wage rates for new job classifications, despite its past acquiescence in the practice followed by the company. The arbitrator concluded that the contract did so provide, and ordered negotiations. In another company[98] having

---

[95] 39 LA 1058.
[96] 46 LA 39.
[97] 48 LA 518.
[98] 50 LA 823.

the same general kind of practice, a new tape-controlled machine was slotted into an established classification. Here, in response to the union grievance, the arbitrator upheld the company action. In still a third case [99] on this type of machinery, the union agreed to the description prepared by the company but disputed the evaluation. (The case involved the determination of the evaluation dispute.)

The elimination of a skilled-trades classification was involved in another case.[100] The contract gave the company the right to change the work content of classifications as well as the right to create new classifications. The arbitrator determined that the right to change the content carried with it, in some circumstances, the right to eliminate all the work. It was on the basis of this analysis that he upheld the company's elimination of the classification of carpenter and assignment of the duties to a general classification of maintenance mechanic. It may be noted that several other skilled trades categories had previously been combined into the maintenance mechanic classification.

As a result of negotiations [101] the parties listed certain skilled-trades classifications in the appendix of the contract. The union had proposed an apprenticeship program for the skilled trades, but the company had refused. Subsequent to negotiations, the company established eight new jobs in the departments in which the skilled-trades classifications worked. Typical of these new jobs were millwright C and millwright trainee. There were provisions in the contract for company establishment of new jobs, and for union grievance after a trial period. The arbitrator stated that the management-rights clause of the contract supported the company action on the eight jobs. The arbitrator in another case [102] determined that the company did not have the right unilaterally to establish a new position of learner-maintenance man. Here the learner progression schedules were contained within an appendix to the agreement.

As a result of layout arrangements of the plant,[103] a company decided that the work could be done more efficiently if three jobs were combined into one job classification. The arbitrator upheld this action on the basis of a wages clause of the contract

[99] 48 LA 957.
[100] 44 LA 33.
[101] 50 LA 997.
[102] 50 LA 624.
[103] 47 LA 282.

which began "in case of creation of any new job." In another case,[104] the company upheld the combination of two classifications into one as an exercise of the management-rights clause and on the basis of a finding that the combination was necessary for efficient and economical production. The right to combine jobs was also upheld, as a matter of company discretion, in another situation.[105] Here the grievant (who was a female employee) argued that the jobs could have been so combined as to permit her job to continue without change. The arbitrator thought that this amounted to a requirement, not so stated in the contract, that the company prove that its action was the most efficient. He felt that the company was not obligated to demonstrate efficiency so long as it sincerely believed (and could establish such belief, presumably) that it was acting in the best interest of efficiency.

Job or Duties Eliminated

Declining prices, a severe recession in the industry, and a sharp drop in profits formed the background for substantial changes in the work flow, resulting in consolidations and eliminations of job assignments.[106] The grievance challenging these acts alleged that the changes were subject to negotiations. The arbitrator ruled that industry and plant custom was for management to make such changes and that the negotiations requirement pertained to wage rates. He concluded the company had not exceeded its "inherent prerogatives" or violated its contractual obligations.

A contract [107] included this language: "Work processes, methods, routing and scheduling production are the Employer's job exclusively, and the union and its members agree that they will not in any way interfere therewith." An arbitrator decided that this validated the company's elimination of a particular job, which was said to be no longer necessary because of a manufacturing change. He found no evidence that some of the work of the eliminated job was being performed by a foreman.

Elimination of threader operators, with machines to run automatically, was upheld as an exercise of management direction.[108] Part of the arbitrator's opinion is quoted in Section 1.

---

[104] 51 LA 1051.
[105] 50 LA 287.
[106] 34 LA 209.
[107] 4 LA 136.
[108] *Supra* note 14.

The elimination [109] of a gateman's job because most of the duties were automated was also upheld as a management right. It was alleged that supervisors were performing residual duties; the arbitrator considered this work *de minimis*. However, unilateral discontinuance of a job classification accompanied by distribution of the major portion of the duties to other job classifications was held to be a violation of contract provisions (one of which was to give written notice of a job shutdown). [110]

Also, a company's elimination of a job and adding some of its duties to another job was held to be a violation. [111] The contractual requirement to "advise and discuss" with the union was mandatory, said the arbitrator. The company argued this was a temporary job, but the arbitrator pointed out that it had existed for 15 months and, therefore, the contract requirement applied. The arbitrator ordered the company to reinstate the eliminated job for a period of 40 days during which it was to hold discussions with the union in accordance with the contract.

In one case, [112] the decision upheld the company's elimination of certain clerical work. Here the clerical duties were transferred out of the bargaining unit to nonunit employees in another city. In contrast the elimination of a job coupled with subcontracting of the work involved therein was held to be a violation of the contract. [113] A special transfer agreement, [114] having to do with relocation to a new plant, was held not to affect the basic contract provisions which supported management's actions in not manning certain jobs not needed at the new location. The elimination of a branch plant which distributed dairy products affected both the union's jurisdictional scope under the contract and job duties. [115] The arbitrator held that the decision to discontinue the branch was a managerial right that had been exercised in a reasonable and normal business manner.

Added Duties

A different factual pattern appeared in a case [116] where the right of management to require a drill-press operator to perform

---

[109] 48 LA 746.
[110] 47 LA 396.
[111] 50 LA 344.
[112] 50 LA 322.
[113] 51 LA 842.
[114] 51 LA 1031.
[115] 51 LA 1159.
[116] 27 LA 784.

his own layout work was challenged. A significant union argument was that, for long periods of time, the company had had higher classification machinists perform this work. This, said the arbitrator, was an exercise of management's right to secure a higher volume of production, but it did not preclude asking the operator to do his own layout work. Moreover, nothing in the job description or the contract otherwise forbade this action.

The installation of new precision-type bars effectively simplified the job of assembling die bars, work which had been performed by millwrights.[117] The simplified work was primarily a cleaning operation, and, as a consequence, it was assigned to production workers. While it appeared that management rights were involved, the decision turned on the arbitrator's interpretation of the operator's job description. This required the cleaning of die components, and he considered that the die bars, as modified, were essentially such components.

In a case discussed in Section 3,[118] the issue was the transfer of certain semiskilled and unskilled work from a fireman classification to treating-plant personnel. This was held to be an appropriate and proper exercise of management rights.

Another situation [119] involved unilateral changes in duties of certain classifications. The arbitrator reviewed the contentions of the parties and also a prior arbitration which was somewhat in point. He pointed out that the contract did not call for bilateral staffing, although the union had sought for some time to develop this through negotiations. The contract actually permitted the company to make changes in job duties as the need arose. However, in the last negotiations between the parties it was spcified that past practice might not be ignored in the modifying of jobs. The arbitrator concluded that the inclusion of the jobs in a report sent to the union several years earlier, which reflected the union's views of duties of the jobs in question, constituted practice—because this report had been followed, effectively, from that time forward.

These cases establish that arbitrators usually support management changes in jobs as an appropriate exercise of management rights (contractual or inherent), when the changes are

---

[117] 48 LA 1000.
[118] *Supra* note 64.
[119] 44 LA 1230.

undertaken for efficiency—unless restrictive contract language, past practice, or the absence of good faith intervene. This applies to new jobs, splitting of one job into multiple jobs, combining multiple jobs into a single job, including a skilled-trades job in one case, eliminating jobs, and transfer of duties (including transfer out of the bargaining unit in one case).

The holding that the test of efficiency is not necessarily one of absolute efficiency, so long as the actions were taken in the belief of efficiency, is significant. Also noteworthy is the good-faith requirement involved in the case of job elimination coupled with subcontracting of the same work. Although not reported above,[120] the company had been subcontracting similar kinds of work in other parts of its plant, and it is not illogical to assume that subcontracting could have been utilized here, given other circumstances. However, the pattern of company actions, as reported, certainly gave rise to implications of bad faith, which inhere in the opinion and award.

6. WORKLOAD AND CREW SIZE

Pursuant to contract procedures, a company [121] advised the union of changes in workloads and job assignments for certain weavers, but did not change piece rates until five weeks later. The union claimed this was a contract violation—refusal to bargain on the new rates. The arbitrator concluded that the contract permitted arbitration only by mutual consent on matters involving wages, except for the impact of workloads on job assignments. On this point, the contract made provision for arbitral review, including the effect on hourly wage guarantees, but was silent as to possible changes in piece rates. Consequently, the union grievance was denied as to this issue. The arbitrator reasoned that explicit procedures, such as those before him, would logically have to spell out obligations said to be incumbent on management.

Workloads

The same rationale for decision was used by another arbitrator.[122] The fact that the contract was silent as to a specific point— that is, workloads—raised a presumption that it was a prerogative of management. But if, by reasonable implication, a point is as-

---

[120] *Supra* note 113.
[121] 14 LA 802.
[122] 17 LA 268.

sociated with other aspects of the contract, then its reservation to management needs to be spelled out.

In a case [123] where management increased workloads substantially because time studies had indicated more than 50 percent of a machine operator's time was idle time, there was no disagreement about the company's right to make the workload changes. However, the union alleged that the company was obligated to negotiate a new rate because of the workload increases. The company refused to negotiate on the ground that rates were fixed by the contract, but conceded it would be proper to discuss with the union whether or not the increased workload was "just and reasonable." The majority opinion of the board of arbitration contained these comments:

> "But the job rates have been established for existing jobs, jobs as they existed at the time of the signing of the Agreement, and it does not follow that job rates are frozen for established job titles regardless of what changes might occur in the jobs. It may happen and does happen, that changes in a job may be so substantial that, while the job may retain the title of the job negotiated by the parties, the changes made make the job a substantially different job."

Thereafter, in discussing the company position, it was said: "It is difficult to say how practically in the circumstances of the substantial change admittedly made in this job one can be discussed without the other. It does not necessarily follow that an increase is warranted and that question does not concern the Board." The board ordered the company to bargain on the rate.

The opinion of the dissenting board member is of interest. He considered it unfortunate that workload was not an issue; since it was not logical to expect the union to accept an unreasonable workload, there should be no rate question involved. Hence, what the situation represented, in his opinion, was a recognition of the principle that management could expect "a fair day's work for a fair day's pay."

Multiple Assignments

A union argued that a company's proposed machine grouping was not practicable because of the variety of parts in the department; it alleged also that the grouping imposed such loads on the operator that he would have no idle time. As to the first

---

[123] 23 LA 782.

point, ruled the arbitrator,[124] practicability was a matter for the company alone to decide. "As long as the decision is honestly made," he stated, "it should not be disturbed by the Arbitrator." Excessive workload might be a reason for upsetting the company's actions, but the union had not established this point. Finally, the arbitrator noted that increased workload, while not barring the company's actions, might be a basis for wage adjustment.

A succinct statement that management may increase workloads on the basis of a management right (sometimes to be implied, as one case above [125] indicates), but that the resulting impact is subject to judgment critiques (and possible wage adjustments, as in the preceding case) is contained in this statement: [126] "Under contract which vests direction of working force and scheduling of production exclusively in management, employer has right unilaterally to increase work load of hourly-rated employees so long as increase is not unreasonable or unduly burdensome."

One arbitrator's views [127] that the exercise of management's rights in this area was not unreasonable or burdensome involved the unilateral assignment of one tool grinder to the simultaneous operation of two grinding machines. The arbitrator felt that no safety hazard was created and that the additional machine did not create an undue workload for the operator. He commented that the work assigned was identical to that which had been previously performed and, consequently, the only change was in job content (workload, that is). Similarly, where a contract [128] stated that adequate manpower would be provided in all departments, it was ruled not a violation when the company removed a second can filler in a brewery, reducing a two-man crew to one. The second job concerned primarily the keeping of a watch on the filler, and this was not so critical subsequent to technological changes. In a case [129] described in Section 4—relating the demotion of female employees for failure to meet production standards—the arbitrator held that the company had the right, under the management-rights clause of the contract, unilaterally to set production standards—always assuming that they were fair and reasonable.

---

[124] 33 LA 537.
[125] *Supra* note 122.
[126] 20 LA 309.
[127] 49 LA 487.
[128] 50 LA 458.
[129] *Supra* note 91.

The contract in one situation [130] provided for a 7½-hour work day, but in practice the day had been shorter—6½ hours including wash-up time. The company posted a notice that the workday was to be the contractual 7½ hours and included working schedules in accordance therewith. The union grievance covered several areas, including the question of workload occasioned by the reduction of the force by six positions, which reduced crew sizes. The basis of the force reduction was efficiency studies which established that better manpower utilization was possible. The arbitrator concluded that, in the absence of evidence to the contrary, this was an appropriate exercise of management rights.

"There is nothing in the contract that prevents the Company from deciding to operate with a two-man crew instead of a crew of three men if in its opinion this will improve the efficiency of operation. It is the Company's function as well as prerogative to direct the working force according to its best judgment and that is what happened in the present situation." [131] In so deciding, an arbitrator also upheld a company argument that this crew-size change was an indirect result of changes in operational methods, and thus did not run afoul of the contractual interdiction of unilateral changes of established work practices.

Similar views on management rights were expressed in another case.[132] It was further stated in that case that such rights could be denied only by a specific contract provision. "An arbitrator must recognize this right as long as its use is not to undermine the wage structure, discriminate against certain employees, or result in such a burdensome or unreasonable assignment of duties to employees as to constitute a violation of managerial obligations of an employer to its employees."

Crew Size

Management's right to direct the work force was confirmed in a case involving crew size.[133] The arbitrator decided that the company's actions in reducing crew size were reasonable in the circumstances of the case.

In upholding a company's unilateral reduction of the crew on a lithograph press from five men to four, an arbitrator [134] noted

---

[130] 51 LA 549.
[131] 29 LA 687.
[132] 34 LA 365.
[133] 12 LA 865.
[134] 46 LA 70.

that a manning table had been proposed by the union during negotiations but not accepted by the company. A principal argument of the union was that such unilateral changes would undermine the classifications on which the wage structure was built. The arbitrator agreed that this was a possibility; however, he said: "But there is no proof in this case that this happened. The mere fact that the size of the crew was reduced does not prove any change in duties or responsibilities, nor does it prove any increase in the work load of the remaining crew members." One arbitrator [135] made a specific ruling that an operator and his helper constituted a crew. However, he reviewed the number of changes which the company had instituted in the yard where these employees worked and decided that conditions had so changed that the company was justified in reducing the crew by eliminating the helper.

Two cases involving the same parties but different arbitrators were concerned with the interpretation of a clause stating that full crews, determined by the company, would be maintained. In one,[136] the arbitrator upheld the company's reduction of a crew by one man per shift. In the other,[137] the argument was made that the right to reduce crew size did not include the right to eliminate a classification. However, the arbitrator disagreed with this and supported the company's position.

Two other cases are interesting as a pair. In one,[138] the parties' practice had been to assign mould dipping laborers in accordance with workload determinations, not on the basis of any given set of working conditions. Consequently, the company's reduction in the number of these laborers was not a violation of the contract provisions on protected crew size. In the other case,[139] the practice had been to assign maintenance crews in relation to the numbers of lines operating, not actual workload determinations. On this basis, the action by the company in reducing maintenance crews was held in violation of the protected crew-size provisions.

It developed in another case [140] that a company could put itself into a position akin to estoppel with respect to crew-size reductions. In this situation, certain duties had been removed at various

---

[135] 43 LA 770.
[136] 46 LA 140.
[137] 50 LA 752.
[138] 46 LA 733.
[139] 45 LA 104.
[140] 44 LA 353.

times from one classification involved in a crew, but without change in crew complement until the time of the grievance. For this reason, and also because the job description for the classification was quite out of date, the arbitrator upheld the grievance protesting elimination of the classification.

In one [141] of three quite similar situations, the arbitrator held that the agreement specifically required the company to negotiate crew size following installation of bulk mailing for newspapers. In the second case,[142] involving improvements in printing presses, the company was obligated to negotiate manning practices after making the improvements, with the criteria to be the changes in workload and responsibilities. In the third case,[143] the arbitrator ruled that, during the interim period provided by the contract for manning experimentation when technological improvements were made, the temporary manning must be reasonable. Manning below that provided in the contract was held to be unreasonable.

Shirt pressing in a laundry operation [144] was performed by two women who were paid an hourly rate plus a two-cent premium for shirts pressed in excess of 96 per hour. When the company, with the concurrence of the union, added a third pressing machine and a third operator, it increased the standard from 96 to 105 shirts per hour before the two-cent premium per shirt applied. In subsequent negotiations, the union tried to change the standard and to increase the bonus, but it was agreed that the existing bonus would continue until an updated incentive could be inaugurated by management with the consent of the union. Thereafter the company unilaterally reduced the crew to its former size, and this led to a grievance which was upheld by the arbitrator.

In the absence of a contract provision relative to the size of furnace crews an arbitrator [145] ruled that company actions in reducing such crews should be in good faith. The crew size before reduction had been static for a period of 27 years, and no changes had been made in the operation of the furnaces which had any impact upon the workload. The arbitrator's comments are of interest:

"Except to the extent that its power to direct or manage the

[141] 50 LA 186.
[142] 49 LA 1018.
[143] 49 LA 521.
[144] 50 LA 804.
[145] 51 LA 37.

work force has been circumscribed by the Contract or by binding past practice, the Company may eliminate a job, reassign job
duties, and reduce crew sizes so as to achieve more efficient or
less expensive operations, provided the Company does so in good
faith, does not discriminate against Union membership or transfer significant work out of the bargaining unit to supervision,
and observes the seniority, job classifications, and other obligations of the Contract. Good faith requires that such changes or
reductions in crew sizes be for authorized and justifiable reasons."

Workload and crew-size problems which reach arbitration are,
by the cases analyzed, handled about the same way as classification changes (Section 5). Management is free to make changes
in workload and crew size except as limitations appear in the
contract or as practice may have evolved. Exercise of this right
of management must be reasonable and not discriminatory or
unduly burdensome. While some cases indicate that workload
may be increased or crew size reduced without rate adjustments,
the more general rule is that negotiations, or grievance arbitration, should measure the impact of the changes on wages. Logic
suggests that this impact is, usually, at least a relative increase in
workload—although this is a rebuttable assumption.

It is of interest that the same idea, as expressed in Section
5, of management expectations that the changes are appropriate, rather than hindsight, governs the arbitral decision—subject
to such requirements as reasonableness, stated above.

7. PRODUCTION STANDARDS

The "rights" issue in cases involving production standards is
often stated in rather direct terms. Thus, an arbitrator [146] held
an employer could establish such standards "as a measure of
skill and efficiency of employees" both under reserved prerogatives and the specific right to manage the plant and to direct
the work force (both in the contract). Having retained the "sole
right to manage its business," a company [147] had the right to
combine grinding and marking operations on tools (and allow
setup time only once, rather than twice as sought in the union
grievance).

The same conclusion [148] was reached where the circumstances (loose practices) and the management clause led an

---

[146] 33 LA 913.
[147] 38 LA 1068.
[148] 41 LA 1038.

arbitrator to uphold the company's actions in formally establishing production standards. The case is noteworthy in its indication that management could not make its changes "arbitrarily or unreasonably"—although no claim was made, nor did the evidence show, that it had done so.

In another situation,[149] the contract did not deal specifically with production standards. The company unilaterally established standards on the assembly of certain power lawn mowers because the assembly work had become inefficient and too costly. The resulting line balancing caused a reduction in the number of people on the line; the rate finally determined upon was 32 units per hour. It was not claimed that this was an unreasonable rate. There was much discussion between the remaining employees on the line and the foreman, including a specific meeting on the standard, but actual production was only about 65 to 70 percent of the standard. People on the line were thereupon laid off for two days without pay. Production then increased, though not immediately, to 32 units per hour. The grievance challenged the discipline and also brought the standard into question. The company's setting of the standard and the balancing of the line were held to be appropriate by the arbitrator.

Constraints

A contract [150] provided that production standards for all operations were to be set so that a qualified, competent operator working at "normal incentive effort" could earn approximately 30 percent above base rate. It also provided that operations on incentive would be those which, in the opinion of the company, should be performed on an incentive basis; the company would also decide on the methods to be used on these incentive operations. Finally the contract provided that the production standards could be changed when there were changes such as in equipment or methods.

A company [151] agreed by contract not to adjust any standard task, once set, unless the operations had changed by an accumulation of changes totaling at least 5 percent, or unless an error in computations had taken place. As a result of check studies, the company changed the standard task on some of the operations, for two different reasons, and the arbitrator found the

---

[149] 50 LA 888.
[150] 50 LA 882.
[151] 49 LA 912.

company wrong in both cases. One involved a company claim of error in the original studies; the other involved a question of allowed dwell time on a specific machine.

One company [152] was permitted by a memorandum of understanding between the parties to review and reestablish various incentive standards in order to assure their accuracy and thereby carry out a contract provision requiring that standards be fair and equitable. The union charged that the company was not setting rates properly, but the arbitrator determined that the company was not in violation of the contract or the memorandum of agreement. However, he did conclude that the application of allowances was not in accordance with the contract, and he ordered a review of operations to determine proper allowances.

"The right of the Company to establish and determine and to maintain and enforce standards of production is fully recognized." [153] The contract containing this language also provided for discipline of employees who failed to produce to established standards. But, said the arbitrator, this contract provision "is not a right to make a final and binding determination." Such finality did apply to such management rights as determining the number and location of plants, the product to be produced, and schedules. With respect to production standards, however, the right was "more in the nature of a right to initiate." That is, the union had the right, upon written notice, to strike over a disputed standard or, alternatively and if mutually agreeable, to have the matter decided by an industrial engineering consultant.

Discipline and Standards

A test requiring that the time allowance per piece be "reasonable and realistic" was applied and determined by an arbitrator to have been satisfied.[154] The time allowance was developed by a measured-day rate system, instituted by the company without negotiations with the union. This omission, said the arbitrator, was not ground for negating the discharge of an employee for inefficiency, since the system did not affect wages or hours but "merely provided objective method of evaluating employees' work performance." (The discharge was invalidated, however, for procedural defects in dealing with the employee.)

---

[152] 49 LA 320.
[153] 12 LA 949.
[154] 36 LA 1442.

Another case [155] was similar to the above in that a particular system was used for setting production standards; the issue, however, was discipline rather than discharge. The arbitrator thought there was justification for "discussion and/or agreement" as to what system was appropriate. However, he found that the union had accepted, through its past actions, the particular system used by management. He upheld the company's disciplinary action.

Another case [156] involving the same two parties was concerned with the discharge of the employee who had been disciplined in the earlier case. The arbitrator concurred with the general proposition, expressed thus: "The right to set production standards unilaterally and to use them as a general measure of output has generally been upheld." However, he observed that this did not give the company "carte blanche authority" to discharge employees for failure to meet established standards. The reason was that the company's efficiency objectives conflicted with job-security provisions in contracts and, particularly, good-cause requirements for discharge. As to the union's actions with respect to the company's system, this arbitrator concluded that they did not add up to acceptance. He overruled the company's discharge action.

A contract [157] gave the company the right not only to fix work-output standards but also to impose demotion for just cause. The company demoted a girl from an inspector classification for failure to meet output standards, but the arbitrator ruled that the demotion was not for a just cause. The girl had reached 85 percent of the output standard after 10 weeks on the job, while top-paid inspectors who made the full standard had 40 weeks' experience or more. The arbitrator thought she had made good progress since assuming the job. Moreover, this girl was a particularly capable employee, having risen from the lowest labor grade. This may be compared with another case [158] in which the company contended, and the arbitrator agreed, that an employee's progress towards the production standard should be commensurate with his progress along the automatic rate range. The union had successfully persuaded the company in negotiations to change its rate ranges from 50 percent automatic

---

[155] 40 LA 33.
[156] 40 LA 866.
[157] 51 LA 1280.
[158] 50 LA 136.

and 50 percent merit to fully automatic. The arbitrator reasoned that relating performance to pay was not practicing merit rating in disguise, but a reasonable expectation of progress toward meeting a production standard properly established by the company.

Administration of Standards

Finally, two cases may be noted relative to bilateral problems of administration of production standards. In one,[159] the right of union representatives to have access to time-study data was discussed in some detail and affirmed by the arbitrator. In the second case,[160] the contract provided both that an employee would be permitted to leave his job for investigation of a grievance, and that a union international representative (presumably a time-study expert) would be accompanied by a company industrial engineer when an investigation of a time study was requested by the union. The issue arose when the union president wished to leave his job, in order to acompany an industrial engineer and an international representative on a time-study investigation. The arbitrator held that this was appropriate since the contract stated that permission to leave work to investigate a grievance "shall not be withheld unreasonably."

The cases support management actions in setting production standards on the basis of right or contractual provisions. There is reasonably solid agreement that the right to initiate standards is a qualified one. The qualification is but another way of expressing the requirement, explicit in some of the cases, that the exercise of the right must be realistic, reasonable, and not arbitrary.

Paralleling the right to set standards is the right to enforce standards. Arbitrators recognize this right but demand full protection of the employee—as to both application of the plan and procedural matters—in disciplinary situations, particularly discharge.

8. METHODS AND INCENTIVES

The last group of cases dealing with "rights" concern two industrial engineering areas which are treated together because of interrelationships indicated in the cases.

---

[159] 49 LA 922.
[160] 48 LA 524.

First may be noted what was described as an unusually strong management-rights clause whereby the employer was enabled to alter the character of the work or type of equipment used, "whatever might be the effect upon employment when in its sole discretion it may deem it advisable to do so." [161] Exclusive reservation in the wage section of the right to introduce new or improved facilities or methods of production was indicated in one of the cases.[162]

Methods Changes

The management article in a contract [163] contained these two somewhat unusual sections:

"(a) The management's policy of expansion of output and cost reduction through improved methods and better equipment is of vital importance to employees and the Employer. The elements of methods, equipment, etc., are the exclusive responsibility of Management for the production and sale of their services and must be produced at a cost free of disadvantages in a competitive market with other kinds of advertising media.

.   .   .   .

"(c) There shall be no restriction placed upon the amount of work performed by any individual or group of individuals, nor shall production be limited in any manner."

The right of management to make studies of company operations for efficiency purposes was stated by one arbitrator [164] in this fashion:

"The rule applicable in the case of this type is clear and simple. The Company has the absolute and untrammelled right to conduct the management studies of its own operations, of both men and machines, including time studies, to ascertain whether or not the machines alone are operating at maximum efficiency, whether or not better design is indicated, the relationship between machine and man, and the potential, if any, for improvement, in accordance with accepted industrial engineering practices. This is precisely what it is doing.

"Indeed, the right to conduct such studies, as are here being made by the Company, has apparently never been questioned heretofore either in this industry, nor in any other industry, as far as diligent search of the reported labor arbitration awards discloses."

A management-rights clause [165] permitted the company to take

---

[161] 41 LA 651.
[162] 41 LA 1169.
[163] 46 LA 1196.
[164] 40 LA 199.
[165] 12 LA 1084.

such action as was "not in conflict with the law or specific provisions of this Agreement." In a dispute over a piece-rate reduction following what the company considered to be a methods change, the argument was made that this language permitted the rate change even if there had not, in fact, been a methods change. The arbitrator decided, primarily on the basis of past practice, that the reduction in rate was unwarranted. Implicit in the decision was an apparent conclusion that the methods change was not significant.

In another case,[166] incentive rate changes not based upon methods changes were okayed. There was nothing in the contract on this point, said the arbitrator; there was only a requirement that rates be set according to enumerated "sound time study methods." Since nothing in the contract proscribed it, the company's action was validated on the basis of inherent management rights.

Economic Changes

In a decision [167] on a grievance alleging violation of the contract—which permitted the company to set incentive rates which would remain in effect unless there were changes in methods or the like—the arbitrator concluded that the company had the right, under the circumstances of the case, to institute any cycle or method it wished. The arbitrator found that the history of the rates on this work had been one of successive estimations and adjustments and that the rates were, therefore, not measured. Part of the problem, he stated, was that the employees in the activity in question—alignment in typewriter manufacture—had come to think of their work as a sort of craft work because of the special skills needed, which differentiated them from other production and assembly workers in the plant.

A problem in one case [168] evolved because of a change in demand for certain of a company's products, identified as VF and PDI rings. When a new series of PDI rings was initiated, these rings constituted between 5 and 10 percent of the total of VF and PDI rings being polished. Since the PDI rings were such a small percentage of production, the company merely applied the VF polishing rates to PDI rings without making new time studies. The union was informed of this action, but there was

---

[166] 14 LA 490.
[167] 45 LA 996.
[168] 50 LA 882.

nothing to indicate that the company sought union agreement to have the application of VF rates be considered temporary or preliminary.

Later on, the production percentages changed to the point where 85 percent of the combined volume were PDI rings. The company thereupon proceeded to revise all of the PDI rates, which led to the grievance. Two main arguments were advanced by the company, one based on past practice and the other having to do with the so-called "product mix" doctrine. The arbitrator stated that this doctrine might be applicable to some cases, but not this one. He reasoned that the application of the VF rates to the PDI rings meant the company considered there was only a single product and not a product mix.

In 1953 a company [169] unilaterally established for certain classifications an indirect group incentive related to regular production operations. It appears that this was not discussed with the union at the time, nor was there agreement on the incentive.

In 1959 the company unilaterally adjusted the incentive for the conditions then existing, but there was no clear evidence to indicate that the revised plan was formally transmitted to the union. At this time, if not earlier, the contract provided that existing incentive plans would remain in effect unless replaced by mutual agreement.

In 1964 the union filed a grievance alleging violation of this provision. On the merits, the arbitrator concluded that the modification of the earlier plan was not mutually agreed upon and was therefore a violation of the contract. It is interesting to note that the contract contained another provision relating to new or changed incentives whereby the company could, at its discretion, establish new incentive plans to cover "changed jobs when existing plans require revision or replacement because of new or changed conditions." The arbitrator discussed this language in his opinion, but apparently it was not controlling.

Incentive Changes

A contract [170] provided that piecework prices might not be changed except when "a change in process occurs." The company changed a particular job from incentive to a day-rate basis. When a grievance was filed, the company argued that the action

---

[169] 45 LA 812.
[170] 27 LA 758.

was a change in method, not process, and therefore was within management prerogative. The arbitrator decided the company's action was a violation of the contract.

A change from day rate to incentive was involved in another case,[171] in which the union argued that the company had violated its duty to bargain on wages and conditions of employment. (There was a contract clause stating that work would be on incentive, whenever practical.) The arbitrator ruled that the recognition clause did not preclude the company's converting from day work to incentive, provided this was practicable. However, should the company attempt to set incentive rates so as to yield more or less than the 15 percent above day work provided for in the contract, the recognition clause would require negotiations with the union.

In another situation,[172] the parties argued about management's right to determine manning and the union's right to negotiate concerning crew size. The arbitrator said neither concept was involved; the sole question was whether the company had developed "an appropriate incentive plan," as required by contract. His answer was in the negative.

A company and a union agreed that the management-rights clause permitted the company to introduce new equipment and processes.[173] However, the union argued that the wage section of the contract, which stated that rates were to "remain in effect without change" for the contract term, prevented the company from unilaterally changing piece rates after methods changes. The arbitrator concluded that the jobs involved were so changed in content that they were, in fact, different jobs; thus the freeze did not apply.

Employee Problems

An association [174] invoked federal conciliation because employees of member companies were refusing to work at a proper rate on new equipment but were maintaining about the same rate as on the previous equipment. Arbitration was recommended, and the parties agreed.

The arbitrator noted that the contract gave the individual companies the "sole right" to decide on processes, machinery,

---

[171] 26 LA 3.
[172] 42 LA 944.
[173] 17 LA 472.
[174] 10 LA 535.

and equipment. Hence resistance to the new equipment was bad faith on the part of the workers since, when agreement was made on management freedom to introduce new machinery, it was intended that "those machines would be operated in good faith by workers up to the level of their productive capacity. To permit them to maintain output at the rate of the old machine would negate the purpose of the clause." The arbitrator thereafter awarded new rates 39 percent below the old rates.

In the case from which the contract language is quoted above,[175] the particular issue was that of the disciplinary layoff of an employee because he had failed to meet established production standards. The union alleged that the company had improperly used time studies to set standards. The arbitrator commented that there was nothing in the contract to preclude unilaterally initiated time studies as a basis for minimum standards —so long as the establishment and enforcement of the standard were reasonable.

In another situation,[176] company rules issued to all employees stated that deliberate restriction of production or failure to meet standards was cause for discipline. A grievance was filed over a disciplinary layoff. The product was a toy fire engine which had been produced under a time-studied standard in the past, and the employees had met the rate of about 13 per hour. Later, when this was again put into production, a slight change in packaging was made because of marketing considerations, and this changed the standard slightly. A new standard was set, but employees produced only about 60 percent of it; they asked for and were given a restudy, which validated the standard. The employees continued to produce at less than the standard and were given a warning. When performance did not improve, the company gave them a three-day disciplinary suspension. By the end of the week following this action, production was still below standard, and the employees were given a five-day disciplinary suspension. The arbitrator concluded that, for reasons not discernible, the employees had lost interest in the particular product inasmuch as they had produced at standard in the earlier production run. He therefore upheld the company in its position that the employees were unduly restricting production, though he decided that the suspensions were excessive.

---

[175] *Supra* note 163.
[176] 49 LA 581.

Finally, reference is made to a case [177] in which a company-initiated grievance was not arbitrable since no violation of a contract clause was claimed. An important aspect of the arbitrator's decision was his determination that the company had not "utilized its rights and prerogatives, expressed or implied, to remedy the situation." That is, the company could have put a rate into effect, thereby resolving the problem, either directly or by arbitration, had the union filed a grievance protesting the rate.

A general rule emerges from these cases—that management initiative with respect to incentives will be supported by arbitrators. The exception occurs when such right is restricted by contract provisions (including limitations implied from the recognition clause or the bilateral relationships). The same rule applies, by and large, to changes in established incentives as long as they are based upon methods changes.

Implicit in the above and in the cases—explicit in some—is universal recognition of the management right to make changes in methods, with proviso for good faith, if the changes are efficiency related and not capricious.

Changes in the type of incentive plan or from day work to incentive and vice versa, as opposed to other aspects of incentives, tend to be restricted, if not by contract then through arbitration.

In all circumstances of change, there is recognition of the need to determine any impact on wages—through negotiation or through established contractual procedure culminating in arbitration.

The requirement that employees follow established work methods and the penalty of discipline for lack of reasonable effort in so doing are recognized in the cases.

9. WHAT ABOUT "RIGHTS"?

It has been pointed out [178] that management needs the discretion and the ability to make choices to fulfill its function. On the other hand, a basic function of a union is protection, "establishing limits on, or guideposts for, the exercise of management's discretion." [179] The issue, and the conflict, is of funda-

---

[177] 28 LA 132.
[178] Seward, *supra* note 1.
[179] *Id.*

mental importance since American industry must be efficient, productive, and competitive.[180]

These generalizations will have general concurrence. For example, it has been pointed out [181] that management must take action on product determination, prices, machinery, methods, plant layout, organization, and "innumerable other questions," albeit within a status quo/negotiated change structure. The problems of particularization remain—what are the "areas of predictability" [182] of arbitral decisions on rights issues.

Clearly, "the job of management is to manage." [183] Attempts to classify management rights as between those final with management and those initiatory in nature,[184] or the "normal and customary rights," [185] are helpful in circumscribing the area of predictability, but not conclusively so. A somewhat broader conception of management's initiatory status [186] perhaps points to even clearer predictability.

The parties to a contract sometimes recognize and circumscribe the problems involved in this basic issue, as in this example: [187]

> "The Union recognizes its responsibilities as exclusive bargaining agent of the employees covered by this AGREEMENT, and realizes that in order to provide maximum opportunity for continuous employment and reasonable wage rates, the Company must be in a strong marketing position, which means it must produce at the lowest possible cost consistent with fair labor standards. The Union agrees that it will not oppose the efforts of the Company to obtain a fair day's work from all employees, or institute technological improvements. The Union further agrees that it will not oppose the efforts of the Company to conserve material and supplies, and improve quality of workmanship; prevent accidents and strengthen good will between the Company, the Employees, the Customer and the Public."

The fact that the above quotation appeared in the report of

---

[180] *Id.;* Chamberlain, *The Union Challenge to Management Control,* 16 IND. & LAB. REL. REV. 2, 184 (1963).

[181] *Supra* note 3.

[182] Phelps, *Management's Reserved Rights: An Industry View,* MANAGEMENT RIGHTS AND THE ARBITRATION PROCESS 102 (1956).

[183] *Supra* note 3.

[184] 12 LA 949.

[185] Wolff, *Management's Reserved Rights: Discussion,* MANAGEMENT RIGHTS AND THE ARBITRATION PROCESS 130 (1956).

[186] Chamberlain, *Management's Reserved Rights: Discussion,* MANAGEMENT RIGHTS AND THE ARBITRATION PROCESS 139 (1956).

[187] 50 LA 677.

an arbitration case indicates that such a policy statement does not eliminate disputes. It does clarify predictability, however (in a general sense, not necessarily with respect to the cited arbitration).

Role of Reason

A review of the foregoing cases in this chapter gives some indication that arbitrators differentiate between operational methods and working conditions [188] when deciding upon management rights, but clear lines of demarcation are not established. It is significant, that the issues develop considerably more often as challenges to management rights than in defense of union recognition. The commentators and the cases taken as a whole—at least within the scope of this book—appear, on balance, to stand for some fairly straightforward propositions.

Where an issue arises within contractually specified management rights, arbitration will proceed to decisions interpreting the stated rights, within the structure of the contract's provisions and other criteria necessary to determination of the issue. In some manner, the arbitrator will apply a rule of reason to management's actions. (Are they just, in good faith, realistic, not unduly burdensome?)

The situation where the contract is silent as to rights is only slightly less clear. True, the arbitrator may bring a basic orientation into the dispute settlement—believing either in reserved, inherent, exclusive,[189] or residual [190] rights, or in an implied-limitations theory. Whichever it is, the issue proceeds to settlement, again on a rule of reason. Reasonableness applies as well to limitations sought to be implied in or inferred from the union-recognition clause, as the cases reviewed herein illustrate. On the other hand, the suggestion that the doctrine of implied limitations is sometimes referred to as a "covenant of good faith" [191] is significant.

The area of unpredictability of arbitral decisions on management rights is, therefore, quite narrow. In the nature of the labor-management relationship, management acts, the union reacts. Resulting disputes will be resolved by arbitrators in terms of contract provisions, history of relationships, past practices,

---

[188] F. ELKOURI and E. A. ELKOURI, HOW ARBITRATION WORKS (2nd ed., 1960).
[189] *Supra* note 3.
[190] M. STONE, MANAGERIAL FREEDOM AND JOB SECURITY (1964).
[191] *Id.*

and other applicable criteria, including reserved rights v. implied limitations where applicable, and within a framework of judgment as to whether or not management's act is "reasonable under the circumstances." [192] Consequently this unpredictability relates to the judgment about reasonableness; that there will be some variability in such judgment can be expected.

However, such judgment, including the variability, inheres in every labor-management dispute which culminates in arbitration. Consequently, it would seem that rights issues in arbitration are not markedly different from any other grievances submitted to arbitration, except for the "emotionalism" [193] associated therewith.

Implied Obligations

This summary and analysis of the rights issues is believed to reflect, reasonably accurately, the views of arbitrators on such issues—particularly with reference to the subject matter of this book. However, it is not the complete picture; indeed: "One thing we do *not* need . . . is much more of the sterile, dried-up, and useless argument between the 'Management's reserved right' theory, on the one hand, and the 'implied obligations' theory, on the other." [194]

The use of implied obligations in this quotation is significant. Comparison of the literature a few years back with more recent publications generates the impression that what was viewed as implied limitations on the management right to act is becoming implied obligations—presumably, not to act except within explicit contractual limits or to act only collectively.

The trend represented by this change in labels undoubtedly is founded on the opinions of the U.S. Supreme Court and the developing national policy with respect to the role of arbitration. NLRB views on management rights, expressed and reserved, are also involved.[195] The general orientation is presented concisely in a recent article.[196]

---

[192] *Code of Ethics and Procedural Standards for Labor Arbitrators*, THE PROFESSION OF LABOR ARBITRATION 154 (1957).

[193] Seward, *supra* note 1.

[194] Seward, *Reexamining Traditional Concepts*, WORK ASSIGNMENTS AND INDUSTRIAL CHANGE 240 (1964).

[195] Platt, *The Duty to Bargain as Applied to Management Decisions*, LABOR RELATIONS YEARBOOK—1968, 145 (1969); American Bar Association, Labor Law Section of, *Report on Developments in Labor Arbitration*, LABOR RELATIONS YEARBOOK—1967, 113 (1968).

[196] Prasow & Peters, *New Perspectives on Management's Reserved Rights*, 18 LAB. L.J. 1, 3 (1967).

The starting point is the bargain between the parties whereby the union foregoes its right to strike in exchange for pay and working conditions, thereby affecting employee rights. *"The grounding of employee rights in this bargain is the key to the workability of the reserved rights theory."* [197] Therefore, this "bargain" concept of employee rights coupled with reserved rights of management gives a pragmatic frame of reference for arbitrators. "The 'Doctrine of Implied Obligations' is an important corollary to the reserved rights theory of management." [198]

It is interesting that the illustrations given in the referenced article [199] seem to reflect application of the somewhat less dynamic and historical implied-limitations approach, whereby management's right to act is generally not limited when the actions are for sound business reasons, neither arbitrary nor capricious. This view is reflected in the cases considered herein, and noted elsewhere.[200]

The insight into some critical problems given in one of the references,[201] and the fundamental issues raised in another,[202] indicate that the present ideas about rights, as expressed by arbitrators in their awards and opinions, are unlikely to remain static.

---

[197] *Id.*
[198] *Id.*
[199] *Id.*
[200] American Bar Assn. Sec. of Labor Law, *Report on Developments in Labor Arbitration*, LABOR RELATIONS YEARBOOK—1967, 113 (1968).
[201] Seward, *supra* note 194.
[202] E. GINZBERG & I. BERG, DEMOCRATIC VALUES AND THE RIGHTS OF MANAGEMENT (1963).

Chapter III

A FAIR DAY'S WORK

One of the judgment areas faced by arbitrators in industrial engineering disputes involves management concern with securing sufficient production and union concern with insuring that employees are not required to expend excessive effort in so producing. These divergent views of the parties are integrated into the expression "a fair day's work for a fair day's pay." Comparable expressions include "reasonable day's work," "fair share," "reasonable effort," and even "equal pay for equal work."

The interest here is in the first half of the slogan; "a fair day's pay" will have explicit quantification in the wage bargain. In a very real sense, the idea of "a fair day's work" is implicit in all of the cases considered in this book. However, this chapter will consider those cases in which the concept is highlighted, usually because of contract language but also because the arbitrator indicates it to be his rule for judgment.

It should be noted that the concept of a fair day's work is intimately related to the idea of pace, at least in the sense of the slogan most important in industrial engineering applications. Pace is discussed in Chapter X.

1. DEFINITION

The concept of a fair day's work is used in two senses, albeit the distinction is not very sharp. It is, in one sense, a sort of proverb or maxim, to which all right-thinking persons can subscribe (inasmuch as the other aspect—a fair day's pay—is involved in a full statement of the slogan).

It is in this sense that the answer to the question of what is a fair day's work is, by its nature, unanswerable.[1] Unanswer-

---

[1] Halperin, *What is a Fair Day's Work?*, 39 Personnel J. 91, 97 (1960).

ability relates to the orientation or bias of the person seeking to answer. While people may be created equal, they vary greatly in physical, psychological, mental,[2] social and political terms.

This sense of the concept probably finds one expression in a general productivity clause recognizing the principle that more production with the same amount of human effort is a sound objective. Such an expression was quoted [3] in Chapter II, Section 9. Similar statements appeared in other cases.[4] It also finds expression in the somewhat quixotic statement that appears in one contract: "It is the intention of the Company to secure and sustain maximum production and efficiency, based on a fair day's work for a fair day's pay, which is the rightful duty of the Union to gratefully accept this rightful expectancy of the Company." [5]

The other sense is more explicit in that the general rule finds expression in a production or work standard. A fair day's work is a fair, reasonable, acceptable, and understood production standard. Thus, one means of determining a fair day's work was identified as "Normal Performance," described as the work performed by a normal operator, with normal skill and training, working at a normal rate of speed and exerting a normal effort for the entire work period. It was further observed: "Yet this normalcy itself is not a balanced formula." [6] The plethora of adjectives to objectify a subjective phrase indicates that this sense of the concept is not much more explicit than the other, although a production standard, once established, is very definite.

It was argued [7] that the company's unilateral establishment of production standards was inconsistent with the hourly rates negotiated in the contract. The arbitrator stated that the standards were intended to determine not compensation but "whether the employees were producing a normal day's work for a normal day's pay."

The problem of definition is identified as follows in an excellent study of management and union views about the subject in the automotive and automotive-parts industries:

"Workers view a fair day's work in terms of effort. 'How weary

[2] Id.
[3] 50 LA 677.
[4] 43 LA 353, 47 LA 577, 48 LA 339.
[5] 5 LA 247.
[6] Supra note 1.
[7] 50 LA 888.

is a fellow at the end of the day?' is one such index of fairness. The manager takes a different point of view. He bases his evaluation upon results obtained from effort. To him, the payoff comes from completed tasks, not from burning up energy on vitality-sapping, unproductive projects. When results and efforts expended are not directly related, friction often occurs." [8]

The same author observed: "The quantitative side of the 'fair day' phrase is the essence of the administration and setting of production standards." [9] Most of the cases used in the following sections reflect this perspective, although maximum application is also noted.

2. MEANING AND MEASUREMENT

As a preliminary to the main issue,[10] an arbitrator discussed the initiation of a time-study program by the company, undertaken as a means to secure "a fair day's work and an efficient allocation of work assignments and manpower."

Each operation was studied and the time determined for its performance "by a normal experienced operator working with normal effort and without undue fatigue." The use [11] of time studies as a basis for employee performance, in a situation where the union endorsed the concept of a fair day's work for a fair day's pay, was upheld by an arbitrator. However, he cautioned the company to be certain its standards exemplified the concept and advised better communications with the union about its efforts to achieve a fair day's work.

Another arbitrator,[12] in discussing a company's removal of minor duties from a particular classification, stated:

"The Company is entitled to make reasonable alterations in respect to any and all jobs from time to time so as to provide that the incumbents of the same shall do 'a fair day's work for a fair day's pay.' Management, however, is not entitled to load up any job with additional duties to such an extent as to make it unduly and unfairly onerous to the incumbents of the same."

That the principle of equal pay for equal work has great importance was the view expressed in one case,[13] wherein it was noted that arbitrators had given the principle two main applica-

---

[8] Hutchinson, *Managing a Fair Day's Work*, Bureau of Indus. Rel., U. of Mich. Rep. 15 (1963).
[9] *Id.*
[10] 12 LA 949.
[11] 46 LA 1196.
[12] 18 LA 827.
[13] 33 LA 725.

tions. In one of these, they have held that "the pre-existing ratio between effort and earnings should be preserved." (The idea of maintaining and/or guaranteeing earnings or earning opportunities is a part of Chapter V.) The other application noted was the necessity for "parity or comparability" between operations or departments within the same plant. "In other words, the concept of 'normal' should be reasonably consistent."

Workloads

In a dispute involving increased workloads for certain employees in a group,[14] the arbitrator commented that a search of the various agreements between the parties failed to disclose any firm definition like "a fair day's pay for a fair day's work." The nearest to a prescription thereof was found in the agreement relative to the incentive plan, wherein it was declared that the success of the plan was based upon

> "the employee doing *his or her fair share of the work*" (emphasis added by the arbitrator). "This suggests that where there is unevenness in the effort required among the jobs in a group, it would be possible and reasonable under the principle of requiring a 'fair share of the work' of all group members to equalize their effort requirements through re-definition of workloads, when changes in methods make such re-definitions defensible."

The arbitrator also pointed to a provision in the basic contract prohibiting changes unless there had been methods changes (he found there had been), as protecting the union against arbitrary changes in standards.

An interesting view[15] about workload in relationship to this subject was expressed in the dissenting opinion to a case discussed in Chapter II, Section 6. This particular analysis reflects a very pragmatic measurement.

Methods of Measurement

One company[16] hired an outside industrial engineer to make time studies, on the basis of which a system of production standards was set up. After some experience with them, the company announced that employees were to maintain "normal efficiencies." Those who did not were interviewed, and certain standards were revised or adjusted. Thereafter, the company

---

[14] 33 LA 29.
[15] 23 LA 782.
[16] 33 LA 913.

announced that employees would be disciplined for failure to meet standards. Arbitration resulted over protest of the disciplinary layoff of an employee who failed to meet production standards; it was alleged that the standards were a "form of piecework," which the contract prohibited. In the arbitrator's view, the establishment of production standards "to measure skill and efficiency of employees" was not a method of determining compensation, which would be the piecework proscribed by contract, but a means of determining if employees were producing "normal day's work for normal day's pay." He observed that the parties had conducted contract negotiations after the standards were established but that the union had not raised the question of standards at that time.

Much the same result as to what yardstick the company may use in setting production standards was reached in a particularly instructive case.[17] The company had developed a number of standards under a new incentive program, which, however, was later abandoned. Subsequently the company used the output standards developed during the program, where available, as the measurement of a fair day's work; the union objected to the use of these or any standards. A welder who refused to produce at a rate of 47 pieces, base output under the abolished system, was suspended, and a work stoppage occurred. This was resolved by company agreement to void the suspension and employee/union agreement that production be at the 47-piece rate, pending arbitration. The issue posed in arbitration was: "What constitutes a 'fair day's work' under the new Agreement?"

The arbitrator first decided that the contract contained commitments from the union to support company efforts to maintain "recognized rates of output." Such being the case, it did not matter what particular method for measuring productivity was used, if it were properly constituted. "What is important is that there exists a generally accepted method of obtaining the quantitative value of output at a normal pace, or as we will refer to it, at 100. The value at 100 is arrived at when the employee works at a normal pace, without unaccounted-for interferences and when he utilizes whatever (personal-fatigue-process) allowances the work-day and the work call for."

It was pointed out that, while all incentive systems need a "yardstick of the '100' type" to function properly, the yardstick

[17] 40 LA 875.

as such is not the incentive system any more than are production records or the product being produced. The system is a method of payment while the yardstick is a device for measuring output under predefined conditions. It would be appropriate for the union to claim that the 100 value for the welding job should be 46 or 45 instead of 47 but, except for such a challenge to correctness, the old 100 values "are fully acceptable measures of productivity."

The arbitrator thereafter concurred with a union argument that the company was in error in its views about high productivity. "In an incentive-based system for example, 'high' productivity refers to output at high incentive rates, at 130 or perhaps even at a higher average rate." Also the following comments:

"In a non-incentive-based plant, normal productivity may vary from below 80 to over 100, the higher value usually being the result of conveyor-controlled output. It is your Arbitrator's experience that 'high' in day-rated industries approximates 100. Anything consistently above 100 belongs to the realm of incentive-based wages. This position runs counter to the Company's claim that 100 is the *minimum* expected of the employee. . . ."

Finally, there were these additional comments about day-rate standards:

"[U]nless the standard hour system is used and there is agreement to the effect that output must be confined to a single point on the incentive curve (i.e., 100), the rigidity of the '100' concept ceases to exist under the day rate system. Short of a conveyorized job or one that is actually of the fixed task variety (patrolmen), the to-the-point control ceases and for it is substituted a range control. Considering the type of yardstick used in this plant, your arbitrator would consider a 90-110 spread as a practical output range. . . ."

Specifically, the arbitrator found that the 47-unit output for the welder yielded an average productivity of 101, and that this output rate had been maintained for approximately a year without objection by either company or union.

In another contract,[18] this output range measurement narrowed to a single-point measurement of a fair day's work. This contract provided that rates be set on the basis of "fairness and equity," a union agreement on the principle of a fair day's work, and a company policy statement that employees were ex-

---

[18] 41 LA 953.

pected to approach 100 percent of established standards but with a commitment that no disciplinary action would be taken on performance between 83 percent and 100 percent.

Argument arose as to whether or not 83 percent of standard constituted a fair day's work. The arbitrator pointed out that if 83 percent did meet this criterion then employees would actually be expected to approach 120 percent (100/83) which would be a violation of the union agreement to the "fair day's work" principle. However, it was found that 83 percent performance merely represented the minimum performance to escape disciplinary action; therefore:

> "Consistent performance at or slightly above 83% of standard does not meet the requirements of a 'fair day's work'. The Agreement calls for 'approaching 100% of standard' with the clear implication that less is looked upon with concern although 'discipline' may not be administered."

In commenting about employees' reactions to standards set by a predetermined time method (the administration of which was criticized in the decision), the arbitrator noted the natural tendency of employees—who in this situation had 20 or more years of experience on their jobs—to compare production requirements before and after standardization and measurement. He stated that such comparison, "unsupported by objective data," was not a reliable measure of a fair day's work.

Comparisons

A case [19] from which quotations are set forth in Chapter I also concerned the issue of comparisons. The grievance claimed that a particular rate set by time study should not apply, but rather that an earlier rate, on an almost identical part number, should be applied. After examining possible reasons why there should be discrepancies between the two rates, the arbitrator concluded that comparison would have violated the "ideal" contained in "equal pay for equal work."

However, in a somewhat unusual fact situation,[20] an arbitrator ruled that comparison was a valid way to measure a fair day's work—in the absence of production standards. The basis for comparison would be "average output over a reasonable period in the past" of the same and other employees—with reasonable

---

[19] 6 LA 979.
[20] 12 LA 1126.

adjustments for relative speeds—working at the same or similar positions along the conveyor belt and filleting the same size and type of fish. Also needed, said the arbitrator, was credible evidence that failure to produce more was directly related to an intent to limit output. He also made these statements:

> "Implicit in the Agreement is the obligation to give a fair day's work in return for a fair day's pay. In return for his wages an employee should work at a normal and reasonably consistent pace which will neither undermine his health nor deprive Management of the benefit of his capacities. The deliberate failure of employees to give a fair day's work is a breach of discipline subject to Management's normal disciplinary powers."

The contract in one case [21] stated the principle as a limitation on management: "The employer agrees to carry on his his operations without demanding or requiring more than a reasonable day's work from any member of the Union." The net effect of a new layout of production equipment and reassignment of duties amounted to, the arbitrator ruled, an unreasonable day's work for certain classifications.

There were two cases involving female employees. In one [22] the assignment of female production workers to previously male production jobs, at lower rates of pay (on the basis the ladies did not do all the work that the men had performed) was held to be a violation of the contractual agreement of "equal pay for equal work." In the other,[23] the creation of a new job classification of operate-only, from the setup-and-operate male job, to be performed by female employees was upheld. In this second case,[24] the general productivity clause contained an undertaking by the union to ". . . cooperate in the determination of what constitutes a fair day's work . . . ."

The meaning of a fair day's work can thus be seen in a variety of situations. Aside from maxim application, the essence of the principle has to be that of measurement—or, much the same thing, the quantification described in the next Section.

Arbitrators support job alternations and increased workload pursuant to the principle, including the indirect endorsement of

---

[21] 23 LA 188.
[22] 42 LA 638.
[23] 48 LA 339.
[24] Id.

increased workload by a union. Use of time study, directly or from an abandoned incentive plan, to establish production standards as application of the principle is supported.

Comparisons of before and after the installation of standards are considered invalid. In the absence of standards, the history of output is thought to give meaning to the principle. Arbitrators will make interjob comparisons, particularly under equal pay for equal work.

The principle operates to restrain management from unduly or unfairly loading the content of jobs, and to give meaning to yardstick efficiency designations in nonincentive, time-studied standards.

3. QUANTIFICATION

The key aspect of a fair day's work is, of course, quantification—the output level which will satisfy the apparently disparate views of managements and unions (employees). Indeed, the cases discussed above deal with quantification. The cases considered hereunder are not markedly distinguishable; but they give further insight into arbitrators' views about output levels.

Reasonable Effort

The first case [25] deals with a company effort to quantify "reasonable effort" on off-standard conditions, as required by the contract. Involved was a truck tire with a wire-loaded tread, the same size and construction as a regular production tire except for the tread. When the tire first was put into production, builders were assigned to the job at 90 percent of job wage level for the first week and 95 percent thereafter. Production averaged 1.8 tires per shift, as compared to the 4.85 job wage level rate for the regular production tire and the 4.3 job wage level ultimately set for this job.

Management, thinking this was not "reasonable" effort, instructed foremen to seek 3 to 3.5 tires per shift. Certain employees, after warnings, increased to 2.2 to 2.7 per shift. Thereafter, not increasing further, they were given disciplinary layoffs, which brought on the grievance. The arbitrator ruled that the company's efforts to establish 70 percent of the ultimate standard as quantification of reasonable effort were not supported by the contract; the unilateral imposition of a quota by

---
[25] 35 LA 575.

the company, whether by measured-day work or otherwise, could not be used as a sole criterion in such a situation nor was merely being on the job sufficient under the contract. Also, he noted, employees on off-standard jobs do not have the same opportunity to be away from their jobs as employees on self-policing incentive jobs. A number of criteria must be used in determining reasonable effort, said the arbitrator; these criteria were not spelled out in detail in the arbitral decision.

In a case [26] involving the equal-pay, equal-work concept—the idea of a fair day's work is frequently expressed in these terms—the company removed employees in a helper classification from the second and third shifts for economic and competitive reasons. The helper remained on the first shift; his duties were transferred to journeymen on the other shifts, which led to the grievance. The arbitrator concluded that the company's action resulted in a substantial increase in duties, without corresponding pay adjustment, as could be seen by retention of the helper on first shift. (In fact, the arbitrator observed, there was actually more need for helpers on the other two shifts.)

Employees on a particular operation had been producing about 950 pieces per day.[27] After time studies, the company set and announced a production standard of 1,200 pieces per day. There followed some six weeks of explaining the new standards and the need to meet them. Seven-day warnings were then issued; one employee improved at first (but later fell off), while two did not. All three were given 30-day disciplinary suspensions, which resulted in a grievance.

The union argued that the imposition of standards was essentially a task system which was prohibited by a contractual ban upon the introduction of incentive, task, bonus, or piece-rate system without joint agreement. The arbitrator observed that the dispute involved the question of the company's right to insist upon a reasonable day's work for a reasonable day's pay. He differentiated the setting of production standards from a task system, concluded that nothing in the contract prevented the company from setting standards, and pointed out that the standards were challengeable through grievance arbitration. Finally, he thought the discipline too severe in the circumstances (long-service experienced operators were given too short a pe-

---

[26] 41 LA 268.
[27] 37 LA 758.

riod to raise production to the new standards) and reduced the suspensions to five days.

Bases of Quantification

Two cases already discussed in Chapter II bear on quantification. In one,[28] the arbitrator stated that the fundamental question was what constituted a fair day's work, regardless of the yardstick used. In terms of the standards instituted by management, he asked: "Is it 100, 80, 60, or what?" Factors to be considered in determining this question were ". . . mechanization, degree of automation, elimination of useless work elements, balance in work elements to avoid forced idleness, etc." It was also noted that an individual's "work-pace" was involved and that it was primarily the relative absence of this factor which resulted in the disciplinary layoff for an employee. The layoff was upheld by the arbitrator on the basis of the employee's poor personal record, his general tendency to work in the 30-40 percent productivity range (although he worked at 65 percent for one four-week period), and the employee's poor output as compared to other employees in the plant. (Also, it was noted that the union did not seriously defend the employee, although it attacked the yardstick used.)

Implicit in the above is that there is no specific productivity percentage figure that equitably quantifies a fair day's work. It is entirely possible that a percentage range of 65-75 percent might represent a fair day's work in the given situation. Also to be considered is that performance can be specified from actual time values, unadjusted for fatigue, delays, and personal time; in such case, a fair day's work would never be pegged at 100 percent.

In the other case [29] involving the same employee, the arbitrator pointed out that he was dealing with discharge, not disciplinary layoff, wherein ". . . the basic issue is not the same." Having reached a different conclusion about union "acceptance" of the production standards and dealing with the question of discharge and not lesser disciplinary action, the decision proceeded within its own rationale. On the subject of quantification within the company's standards system, the arbitrator observed:

---

[28] 40 LA 33.
[29] 40 LA 866.

"Questions which remain unanswered in the record of this case concern the wide discrepancies between the production standards set on the basis of the standard time data and the actual performance in many of the departments of the plant. It does not appear that anyone in the metal department has ever been able to achieve 100% of standard, at least over any extended period of time. In most instances shown by the record, involving other employees as well as the department as a whole, actual attainment has been far below the standards set. The Arbitrator cannot comprehend how standards of this kind can be fairly applied as a basis for discharge action. If they are to be used for this purpose, the standards should be set so that any employee with training and experience, the naturally slow as well as the swift, can meet them with normal effort."

Consideration of a fair day's work for some of the employees in a group was discussed in the preceding section. In his ruling,[30] the arbitrator concluded that no hardship had been imposed upon employees in two classifications when their workloads were adjusted to a higher but still below-normal work pace.

In another workload situation,[31] involving yarn winders' being assigned two machines to operate, the arbitrator commented about the quantification problem:

"The Agreement's expression of the principle of the fair day's work for the fair day's pay is necessarily the fulcrum on which the Company may secure and sustain full productivity. However, the level of productivity expressive of the fair day's work is not expressed in the Agreement, nor evidenced as fixed in practice. Absent any evidence indicating otherwise, the principle of a fair day's work does not fix the work loads existing at the time of the effective date of the Agreement, subject only to bilateral change. The Agreement itself, as well as general industrial practice with regard to day work—without incentive—sets forth the framework within which the Company can maintain and even increase the efficiency of its operations without onerous, burdensome or unreasonable imposition of work loads."

The same question came up in another case [32] in connection with incentive rates. The arbitrator decided that production increases resulting from the rebuilding of a furnace were appropriate under contractual relationships. Such changes had the effect of increasing work occupancy from about 60 percent to not more than 90 percent. The company argued that it was entitled to increased incentive performance without providing increased

[30] 33 LA 29.
[31] 47 LA 577.
[32] 8 LA 846

incentive earnings, up to the point of reasonable occupancy at incentive-level performance, within the limits of "a fair day's work."

The arbitrator stated that this view would have been correct if there had been an understanding that incentive rates presupposed incentive performance for a full shift, even though actual incentive performance was for less than the full shift because of machine limitations. However, as there had been no such understanding, the conclusion had to be that the rates were based upon the incentive performance actually required. Thus, if higher performance were to be required, it should be reflected in incentive earnings.

These principles had previously been set forth by the same arbitrator in another case [33] to which he referred in this decision.

Finally to be noted is a case [34] wherein quantification is explicitly grounded on time study. This appeared as the company's time study manual, discussed and quoted in the opinion, entitled "Procedure Guide To A Fair Day's Work."

It seems clear that quantification of the principle is difficult because of varying views of employees and unions, managements, and arbitrators. Illustrations are the arguments about standards being a task system, the overassignment of work to a classification (best illustrated in a case discussed in the preceding section [35]), and the significance to be attached to the 100 percent figure in production standards.

4. EMPLOYEE REACTIONS

It is entirely predictable that employees will not cooperate fully when management seeks to adjust previous understandings about the meaning of a fair day's work. (However, this does not imply that conflict is inevitable.) The idea of comparisons is evident in the cases already discussed. Also implicit is resistance and even hostility to change.

More specific are some comments by the arbitrator in one of the cases discussed in Section 2.[36] He noted that the employees had strongly resisted changes in methods and were

[33] 5 LA 712.
[34] 51 LA 101.
[35] *Supra* note 21.
[36] *Supra* note 18.

"somewhat hostile" toward the established standards because they required more work than had previously been performed. He suggested that the employees work on the standards, to the best of their abilities, in order to determine if they were equitable. He further commented: "Claims of the operators that 'the job isn't like it used to be,' 'we don't work as a team any more,' 'we haven't any time to talk now,' and similar observations by the union witnesses are not persuasive."

In another case,[37] the arbitrator commented that the employees had not realized the significance of the contract terms they had approved, that is, incentive standards under a newly instituted program. Prior to the new standards, an output of 50 units per day, commonly referred to as the quota, represented a fair day's work. Therefore, in general, employees considered that all incentive standards calling for more than 50 units at 100 percent unfair.

In another situation,[38] management leniency had led to abuse of lunch and rest periods. The company undertook major equipment and methods changes, adopted a measurement system for determining production standards, established specific lunch and rest periods, reduced the crew from seven to six, and granted a 3-percent pay adjustment. A grievance resulted which related in part to the changes in working conditions. The arbitrator upheld the company's actions, holding that they were neither arbitrary or unreasonable, and determined by personal observation that the increased workload was not burdensome. He also commented:

> "The method of obtaining a reasonable or fair day's work is not specifically limited by the existing Agreement. It may not be inferred or implied that the parties ever contemplated or intended that loose, imprecise and informal methods of obtaining or measuring a 'reasonable day's work' would become rigid and inflexible. Laxity in enforcing a reasonable rule is not tantamount to establishment of a binding local condition or practice."

That resistance to company changes continued is evidenced by another arbitration,[39] about six months later, between the same parties but before another arbitrator. The employees involved here were in another department of the company; other-

---

[37] 37 LA 279.
[38] 41 LA 1038.
[39] 42 LA 1127.

wise, the factual pattern and the results were not sufficiently different for further review here.

Two other cases further illustrate the importance of employee attitudes and/or work behavior in the fair-day's-work context. In one,[40] in a day-work situation, the arbitrator observed that:

> " . . . [T]here is a 'truism' or a sort of Parkinson's Law—that most workers have a tendency to fill up their working hours with activity so paced as to fill out the elapsed time. In other words, a worker will seldom, when hired for eight hours and able to do the work in four, complete the job in four hours and then sit around for the other four. He would probably pace himself to more or less fill out the eight hours with activity. Therefore, lacking any standards or measures, discussion regarding the numbers assigned to the work in the past, would be inefficacious."

The arbitrator in the other case,[41] involving an incentive situation, commented:

> "It is well known that workers start to work at 7 A.M., start slowing down in mid-morning, say at 9:30 or 10:00 and pick up their pace again following a coffee break or lunch period, and again slow down in the afternoon, perhaps about 1 or 1:30 when a break again revives them. This slowing down is never thought of as a 'slowdown' in the sense we are referring to.
>
> "To get closer to the subject matter, it is well known in the rubber industry that men often informally agree on a production limit. If tire builders decide that to build 35 of a particular tire is a fair and full day's work, then *all* the tire builders will build that number, or perhaps one less or one over, and will stop work when they have produced that quota and do nothing for the balance of the shift. If the shift ends at 3 P.M., some will have built the limit by 1 P.M., others by 2 or 2:30. A really fast worker, if he really tries, may get 35 built by noon. I have sometimes asked management people in tire plants why they permit this and have been told that if the Company required them to work till 3 P.M. they would take it a little easier and still produce only 35 tires."

The situation leading to the foregoing comments concerned a management effort to secure higher production by employees under the established incentive standards. The error in management's case, said the arbitrator, was that there was no dispute. Consequently, penalties which had been assessed against employees were unfair.

---

[40] 42 LA 125.
[41] 42 LA 1162.

5. UNDERSTANDING

"Plainly, a fair day's work is any reasonable amount the employer can enforce . . ." [42] Such a pragmatic assessment makes considerable sense, particularly in view of the adversary nature of arbitration.

However, the specific illustrations of employee lack of understanding and resistance indicate that better understanding of the processes of change and adaptation to it might lead to more harmonious labor-management relations and some deemphasis on the application of power. While the concepts and practices involved in better understanding are not within the scope of this book, the thinking appears to be set forth in the following: "In essence, the fair day's work seems to come from setting realistic standards which the parties understand and accept, from administering these standards faithfully and consistently over time, and from obtaining a working agreement on the adjustment and control of the process for determining the fair day's work." Also in point is the comment that ". . . acceptance of the concept of a fair day's work must be paved with explanation, objectivity and fairness, and though this road is hard, costly and time consuming when it is travelled, it offers the safest, most pleasant journey over the 'long haul.' " [43]

---

[42] M. STONE, MANAGERIAL FREEDOM AND JOB SECURITY (1964).
[43] *Supra* note 8.

CHAPTER IV

CLASSIFICATION AND EVALUATION ISSUES

Express contractual provisions dealing with some of the subject areas of this study are reflected in arbitrators' decisions and opinions. If nothing more appears, there is usually language dealing with wages. Details of classification, evaluation, work standards, and incentive applications were found to be in the basic contract, in supplemental agreements, and/or in separate plans—not necessarily grounded in mutual concurrence. As Chapters I, II, and III indicate, arbitrators, perforce, supply bases for decision in the absence of contractual language, or in explication thereof.

The principal focus here is on interpretations of explicit provisions as they apply to problems presented through grievances. Included are problems concerned with techniques, procedures, and elements of various plans and programs. Presentation is representative, to show the types and variety of contract provisions, plans, and administrative problems reflected in the cases—together with a more detailed examination of the situations which seem to warrant such treatment. The materials generally are presented in two chapters because they group logically into two segments—classifications and evaluation issues in this chapter, work standards and incentives in the next chapter.

Some note should be made here of the complications and perplexities faced by an arbitrator in dealing with classification and evaluation issues. These particular comments are also applicable to later chapters; they are pertinent, in a general way, to standards and incentives cases.

The parties to a contract carry on a continuing two-way educational process with respect to technical matters of interest to them,[1] in addition to actual changes on such matters which oc-

---

[1] Simkin, *The Arbitration of Technical Disputes*, NEW YORK UNIVERSITY SIXTH ANNUAL CONFERENCE ON LABOR (1953).

cur, over time, through negotiations, grievance settlements, and arbitrations. These ongoing, progressive patterns of mutual education are what the arbitrator must come to understand in order to perform his services equitably.

Sometimes the situation between the parties engenders misunderstandings which inhibit this process of mutual education, and this, too, the arbirtator must come to understand. The impact of misunderstanding was a matter of the following comment: [2]

> "One of the major blocks to the bilateral settlement of job evaluation disputes is rooted in the fact that the parties concerned do not have a common basis for their discussions. In this case, for example, the grievant is strongly influenced by what he knows he brings to the job while the Company insists that only those characteristics listed in the job's description and only to the degree that they are detailed, are of value. In actual application, neither position is wholly correct . . . ."

Understanding the Issue

In a discussion of job evaluation cases,[3] the first problem was that of arriving at a knowledge of job content. Job descriptions vary from much too sketchy to overly comprehensive statements. Content can be developed, however, from these descriptions plus testimony from the parties plus observations of jobs being performed in the plant.[4] The specifics of the job evaluation plan itself are important: What is the system, was it unilaterally or mutually installed, what special principles apply to particular groups (*e.g.*, skilled trades), how old is the program, has it been updated? [5]

The question of updating was an ancillary issue in one case.[6] The company had unilaterally updated dollar values in the degree definition of the responsibility factor in job evaluation. The union contested the action, claiming such a change should be negotiated. The arbitrator concurred in this view but declined to assess a penalty. Adjustment of monetary definitions to reflect current economic levels, he said, was common practice; the change was "fair and most meaningful," and he

---

[2] 48 LA 957.
[3] Unterberger, *Arbitration of Job Evaluation Cases,* 17 ARB. J. 219 (1962).
[4] *Id.*
[5] Sherman, *Arbitrator's Analysis of Job Evaluation Disputes,* 43 PERSONNEL J. 365 (1964).
[6] 31 LA 121.

believed that "undoubtedly a bilateral acceptance of the change would have resulted."

In determining disputed factors in the application of a job evaluation plan, the arbitrator will want to know the specific premises underlying the program being applied. If job comparisons are to be made, what comparisons—benchmark jobs only, a pattern of nonbenchmark jobs, or a combination of the two? [7] The need for the arbitrator to seek out and apply the criteria already used by the parties was emphasized.[8] Where the company had a job-evaluation committee but the evidence indicated the parties had on previous occasions ignored the conclusions of the committee, the arbitrator thought the approach to the particular issue involved

> ". . . must not be that of technical, point job evaluation but rather the approach which the parties themselves, in their *joint* dealings, seemed to have adopted. To the extent that the latter may coincide, in particular cases, with the principles or results of a proper, technical job evaluation, there will, of course, be no conflict. Where they do not coincide, however, it seems clear that the Arbitrator cannot be bound by the latter." [9]

Also noteworthy is this quotation:

> "Thus, to make a satisfactory judgment, the arbitrator would have to be familiarized with the special idiosyncracies of the establishment in which the issue arose and be able to appreciate how they affect the application of the plan. Among these might be the relationships between key jobs which have become conventionalized and, thereby, acceptable to the parties, so as to be sure that his award will not impair a stabilized relationship." [10]

The special idiosyncrasies of the establishment become even more significant when classification problems are not governed by formal job evaluation. It has been noted that a major problem with classification grievances is that, so often, only job titles exist, without written, detailed job descriptions.[11] The view also has been expressed that, after analyzing a disputed job and comparable jobs, the arbitrator could proceed to slot the disputed job "by a process of job evaluation." [12] The arbitrator in

---

[7] *Supra* note 5.
[8] *Supra* note 3.
[9] 29 LA 123.
[10] *Supra* note 3.
[11] Handsaker, *Classification Problems*, MANAGEMENT RIGHTS AND THE ARBITRATION PROCESS 54 (1956).
[12] *Id.*

one of the cases studied adopted this approach, using a "standard system" of his own selection for assessing the relationship of a disputed job to the jobs suggested for comparison.[13] Another arbitrator, "to be doubly sure in his own mind," applied the information from testimony and his own notes to "factors ordinarily used in evaluating jobs."[14]

Finally, note should be taken of the comment [15] that few job evaluation awards are published (and those, as indicated above, are not too useful as guides). No doubt this reflects the tendency of the various arbitration reporter series to publish awards considered interesting and instructive.[16]

1. EQUAL PAY FOR EQUAL WORK

A somewhat specialized meaning of the concept of equal pay for equal work appeared in the preceding chapter. In its more generalized meaning, the concept undergirds wage structures of every kind, no matter how developed. Thus, when wages are set by negotiations only, without the reference guidelines of, say, an evaluation plan, the structure must effectively reflect this equity. Otherwise, union leadership will face a revolution within the membership. True, distortions from the ideal can and do exist—as when some segment of the employee group is articulate and vociferous enough to tilt the structure—but any structure will be unstable, in the long run, if it fails to adhere substantially to the principle.

When job evaluation and/or standards, properly conceived and properly administered, are used as bases for the wage structure, the principle is much more closely realized in practice. Comments from a case on this point specifically have been quoted already, in Chapter I, Section 1.[17]

A contract clause in one case [18] provided that, when a new job was created, the rate thereon was to be determined by the principle of equal pay for equal work. In a case noted in the last chapter, wherein the idea of a fair day's work for a fair day's pay was stated, there was also reflected in the procedure guide the principle of "extra pay for extra effort"—extending

---

[13] 30 LA 290.
[14] 35 LA 113.
[15] *Supra* note 3.
[16] Benewitz & Rosenberg, *The Arbitration Reporters as a Reflection of Arbitration Issues*, 18 ARB. J. 162 (1963).
[17] 6 LA 979.
[18] 2 LA 572.

the equal-pay concept to incentive applications.[19] The problems involved in incentive applications of the principle are succinctly explained in one of the references.[20]

"There shall be equal pay for equal work for all employees covered by this Agreement."[21] This clause was to be interpreted by the arbitrator in a case wherein an employee in a welder B classification was assigned to do some welding on a machine usually operated by welder A employees. The conclusion of the arbitrator was that the work performed was of the B category and, as a consequence, the higher wage rate was not applicable. Said the arbitrator: "Then, having not performed 'equal work' she was not entitled to 'equal pay'. . . ." This concept was noted in other cases and, of course, is implicit in all of them.

2. VARYING VIEWS ABOUT JOB CHANGES

Contract provisions, especially as they are interpreted by arbitrators, reflect a variety of ideas about the status of a negotiated structure and individual jobs and associated wages during the term of the contract.

Changes by Negotiations Only

That jobs and wages are considered to be set and changeable only through negotiations appears as a straightforward proposition in five of the cases.[22] In one of these, the arbitrator stated that the issue should have been negotiated, but he decided not to return it to the parties in order to assist them to a prompt and equitable decision.[23] The "scarlet thread theory" case[24] referred to in Chapter II, Section 5, is within this category. So is another case[25] where the contract principle was held to apply even though the union president had signed new job descriptions to cover the splitting of an existing job into two. The arbitrator stated that union agreement under the contract was necessary but was not forthcoming here, even though the established procedure of presidential signature had always indicated union agreement in the past.

A provision appeared in one of these cases that job classifi-

---

[19] 51 LA 101.
[20] Presgrave, *Grievance Arbitration and the Industrial Engineer*, XVIII J. OF INDUS. ENG'R 605 (1967).
[21] 51 LA 35.
[22] 10 LA 812, 22 LA 785, 30 LA 290, 48 LA 339, 48 LA 901.
[23] 30 LA 290.
[24] 39 LA 1058.
[25] 39 LA 11.

cations and wage rates were to be maintained "unless changed by the mutual consent of the parties." [26] The provision in another case required that a job classification was to be continued unless the job were terminated.[27]

A contract made reference to a job classification plan "as the same may be amended by agreement of the parties hereto." [28] When the company combined two jobs, the union protested on the ground that mutual agreement was required. The arbitrator concluded that the language referred to the number of labor grades and rate ranges assigned thereto, reasoning that "classification does not presuppose any limitation on the number, types or combinations of jobs." He further pointed out that the purpose of a classification system was to insure equitable wage treatment of employees and that proper slotting was necessary to insure that equity. It appears that similar reasoning was implicit in a case just noted.[29]

In another case [30] the contract contained job classifications for which the specifications had been negotiated. Nonetheless, the arbitrator ruled that this did not impede management's action in transferring duties from outside the bargaining unit to employees within the unit. (It may be assumed from the reasoning used that there would also be no impediment to transfer of duties within the unit—although such was not decided in the case.)

Somewhat similar was a situation [31] in which a tool room heat treater was instructed to perform grinding whenever he had time from his primary duties; however, the employee was not qualified to perform the listed secondary functions for his classification, which included the grinding. It was claimed that this was a permanent addition to the employee's classification, contrary to the contract. Concluding that this amounted only to idle-time assignment, not a permanent classification change, the arbitrator upheld the company action.

A contract provided that classifications and rates "shall be effective during the term of the Agreement." [32] However, there was also explicit language giving the company the right to es-

---

[26] 48 LA 339.
[27] 48 LA 901.
[28] 10 LA 94.
[29] *Supra* note 26.
[30] 5 LA 304.
[31] 23 LA 206.
[32] 32 LA 115.

tablish new jobs and to leave jobs idle for legitimate reasons, and there were seniority procedures for handling employees demoted when a job was eliminated. The total effect of these provisions was held to support company action in creating new classifications for good business reasons and not in derogation of union interests.

Compare this with the arbitral reasoning on an issue involving a company's unilateral change in job titles. The company argued that, since it could unilaterally establish new job classification titles, it had the right to change job titles. The arbitrator disagreed, stating: "Once a job classification and its title become the *res* of collective bargaining, it may not thereafter be changed unilaterally, regardless of the fact that the genesis or origin of the job classification and its title were unilaterally established. There is a qualitative change in the *res* once it has become the subject matter of collective bargaining." [33]

The contract language in another case [34] stated that, when job descriptions were changed, the job description and evaluation would be reviewed by the company and the union. This language did not, however, in the arbitrator's opinion, require the company to negotiate or to secure agreement from the union with respect to changes in job descriptions.

A company and union agreed upon a system of progressive promotion, within a particular department, specifically freezing the job rates therein for the duration of the contract except as they might be changed by direct negotiations.[35] This was contrary to the general practice in the plant, which was to reevaluate jobs by an established procedure. Pursuant to this general procedure, the company unilaterally eliminated a job and merged its duties into another job. While such action was permissible in other departments, the arbitrator ruled, the progessive promotion scheme showed the parties' intent not to apply the regular procedure to this department.

In contrast, an arbitrator upheld the combining of three jobs into one, ruling that job progression charts for promotion by seniority did not freeze job classifications, nor did other provisions in the contract.[36]

A contract that was intended to "dispose of all bargainable

---

[33] 45 LA 923.
[34] 41 LA 510.
[35] 41 LA 120.
[36] 35 LA 434.

matters" included a list of the job classifications.[37] The company was held not to be privileged to hire a finisher trainee since there was no such classification in the contract.

Right to Make Changes

A second category represents the viewpoint that, as a general proposition, management can proceed to make changes in the job structure.[38] Limitations thereon will, at least, be implied; management actions must not be arbitrary nor capricious [39] and must be accompanied by reasonable rate adjustments thoroughly discussed with the union.[40] One contract provided specifically that jobs could be combined.[41] The arbitrator held that combination was not restricted to classifications within a single department, as was argued by the union. However, where the contract clearly gave management discretion, particularly with respect to the elimination of a job by combining its duties with another, de facto modification of the job—even though the job description had not been changed—operated to prevent layoff of an employee on the basis of job abolishment.[42]

The right to change jobs was present in two cases, but it also had limitations. In one case,[43] the contract stated that, when a machine was set up for production work not requiring a skilled operator, a less skilled worker could be used by joint agreement. The union grievance was upheld because such agreement was not had. In the other case,[44] the company's right to combine jobs was held not to include the right to abolish the craft component of the job structure by combining five skilled jobs in the maintenance department into one collective classification.

> "The right of a Company to eliminate and combine jobs, which is well recognized as one of its most basic, inherent powers, is subject to three principal limitations. First, the action cannot offend any express provision of the contract. Second, it cannot depart from any binding past practice. And third, it cannot be taken in bad faith; or expressing it another way, the action cannot be arbitrary, capricious, or discriminatory." [45]

---

[37] 46 LA 1208.
[38] 22 LA 336, 33 LA 421, 35 LA 664, 42 LA 945, 44 LA 33, 46 LA 1027, 48 LA 24.
[39] 33 LA 442.
[40] 22 LA 336.
[41] 42 LA 643.
[42] 35 LA 367.
[43] 41 LA 1140.
[44] 41 LA 285.
[45] 43 LA 353.

A case [46] which seems to fit into this category, as well as the next one, contained this contract language: "A change in methods, materials or functions, or addition or deletion of a job, may, among other things, constitute a change in duties or requirements." The arbitrator thought this supported company action in combining duties, as well as the union's right to review earnings of those affected.

The Right Restricted

In a third grouping of cases, the right of management to make job changes is restricted. Certain conditions must pertain (*e.g.,* as with methods, noted in the preceding case) before changes can be made, but as the cases show, once the arbitrator concludes that specified conditions have occurred, the changes by management are upheld.

Conditions presented in the cases include changes "in the amount of work done or in working conditions," [47] changes in operation or the installation of new equipment,[48] and changes only for efficiency or economy.[49] One interesting provision [50] permitted the company to change "a woman's job into a man's job or vice versa" if the company's actions involved a change in job content, monetary savings, production gains, or increased flexibility. Change in job content was enough in another case,[51] if content changed "significantly." In still another,[52] "substantial, material and significant" increase in the skill or labor of a job was the test applied.

In the last case,[53] while the company was permitted to act under the specified conditions, there was, apparently, contract language providing for joint study and negotiation of the rate as well as a 30-day trial period before final rate determination. Noting that the sequence of these procedural elements was not clear, the arbitrator included in his award a directive establishing a clearer pattern.

A company [54] could, under the contract, eliminate or combine jobs "as the result of changes," but was to advise and discuss the

---

[46] 33 LA 300.
[47] 6 LA 695.
[48] 33 LA 296.
[49] 41 LA 997.
[50] 32 LA 888.
[51] 27 LA 906.
[52] 17 LA 268.
[53] *Id.*
[54] 46 LA 36.

circumstances with the union committee and to consider the committee's recommendations. Failure to advise and discuss was held to be a contract violation. An arbitrator in another case [55] decided the company had complied with the contract requirement to "review and explore" with the union. Similarly, a contract [56] provided that, "when the installation of mechanized equipment or changes in production methods will have an effect on the job status of employees . . . ," reasonable advance notice was to be given to the union and the parties were to meet to review the effects upon employees. Another contract [57] had a provision that, when there was "substantial change" in an occupation, this changed occupation would be evaluated and slotted into the proper labor grade.

A case [58] which relates both to the first category, that jobs and wages are considered to be set and changeable only through negotiations, and to this one contained the following contract specifications: "The parties shall work out through negotiations the placement of new jobs in labor grades. It is not the intention of the company, during the life of this agreement, to reclassify any job downward without the approval of the union, except where it is warranted by a sufficient change in the job content."

The "Standard Relationship"

A final category may be, as one arbitrator [59] put it, the "standard relationship" between parties to an agreement. That is, the company establishes jobs and modifies jobs, but may not act capriciously or with an intent to subvert the contract. The union's role is to bargain on rates to be paid for new or changed jobs, and to protect the rights of employees. By so doing, the union normally would not interfere with changes in job duties—having the principal function of negotiating a rate once the duties have changed. However, the arbitrator commented, this does not preclude union questioning of the content of new or changed jobs.

Other cases are substantially to the same effect.[60] Unilateral right to make permanent changes sufficiently large to justify new job descriptions implied the unilateral right to make lesser

---

[55] 48 LA 72.
[56] 41 LA 1161.
[57] 43 LA 318.
[58] 11 LA 822.
[59] 25 LA 44.
[60] 30 LA 31, 34 LA 209, 34 LA 827, 47 LA 716.

permanent duty changes not requiring new descriptions.[61] A sort of a reverse twist developed in one situation.[62] The company made changes in the duties of a job, and the union demanded that the job be reclassified. The contract provided that the company would create new job classifications when this became "necessary or desirable"; hence, said the arbitrator, in effect, classification changes were optional with the company, and union's role with respect to wages did not arise until the company had made a determination of "necessary or desirable." Removing duties was upheld [63] where they overlapped duties performed by non-bargaining unit personnel (in contrast to an earlier case [64]).

Where the company's right to establish new jobs was recognized in the contract,[65] the union protested when management created a "new" job by removing duties from an existing job. The arbitrator concluded that this splintering process was supported by the contract; however, he found that the company had failed in its commitment to notify the union "as far in advance of such changes as possible."

Six months' advance notice was required by a contract [66] if "technological changes or improvements" were to be introduced. Mechanization of the methods for loading and delivering color sections of newspapers did constitute a technological change, as the arbitrator interpreted the parties' negotiations on the subject. Where a company eliminated the only job therein, without intent to fill it again, the arbitration found that this constituted a violation of a clause requiring a 10-day advance notice to the union of planned discontinuance of a department.[67]

The same sort of company-initiated action on job-structure changes occurred under another contract.[68] However, the contract here had specific provisions for a temporary rate to be put into effect, followed by negotiations and grievance arbitration if negotiations were not mutually satisfactory. Another approach is reflected in the following clause:

"When the Company changes equipment design, alters process-

---

[61] 33 LA 357.
[62] 24 LA 665.
[63] 43 LA 364.
[64] 5 LA 304.
[65] 17 LA 361.
[66] 45 LA 860.
[67] 46 LA 4.
[68] 18 LA 166.

ing methods or installs new or different operating equipment, the matter will first be discussed with the Union. Operations shall proceed as directed without alteration or slowdown pending agreement between the Company and the Union on any change in rates or manning. In the event that the Company and the Union fail to agree, the matter may be submitted to arbitration." [69]

An unusually complicated case [70] involved the creation of a new bowling-ball-repairman classification, because of a sharp increase in production, at labor grade 4. Previously such repair had been accomplished by assignment of available employees from various (enumerated) classifications, all of them at the higher labor grade 6. One of these classifications had language describing the patching of balls needing repair, which was the basis of the union grievance. The arbitrator, however, upheld the company's right to create the new classification.

The union thereupon challenged the company's evaluation of the new job on several grounds. It was apparent, however, that the actual disagreement concerned the regular assignment of the repairman, as part of his job, to relieve grinder and polisher operators. Because of the regular nature of the assignments, the union argued that this feature of the job should be reflected in the evaluation. The company argued that the assignments were temporary and that it was contrary to good engineering principles to evaluate the duties of one job into another.

It should now be noted that the repairman classification was labor grade 4, day work; also, the arbitrator agreed with the company evaluation of such work at labor grade 4. However, grinding and polishing had an established evaluation at labor grade 6, incentive. Thus, the dilemma: If the basic job were raised—to labor grade 5, say—payments to the repairman when he performed his relief duties would be inequitable. However, a classification at labor grade 6 would be inequitable for the main part of the job since, under the evaluation plan, the repairing of balls was at a lower skill level. The arbitrator concluded the best decision he could make was to continue the company-established practice—labor grade 4, day work, on repair, and labor grade 6, incentive, on grinding and polishing. He concluded with these comments:

"Therefore, though differing with the company in its treatment of the relief as a transfer and its policy of not evaluating

[69] 46 LA 1203.
[70] 36 LA 740.

the same function in more than one job as applied to this issue, the demands of practicality and feasibility in the recognition of the equities held by the employees and the Company, while conforming with the basic purposes of rational wage administration as expressed in a job evaluation system, require my holding that the present means of compensating the Bowling Ball Repair Man is in closest compliance with the contract."

It will be seen that the cases fell into four general categories: jobs and wages frozen for the contract term and changeable only through negotiations; jobs may be changed by the company during the contract term, generally without restrictions but within circumscribed limitations; jobs may be changed but only as a derivative result of operation or equipment changes or other conditions precedent; and, finally, changes may be made by the company—again within circumscribed limitations—with the resultant impact on wages negotiable and/or subject to the grievance procedures. (As is true of any categorization within this study, categories are not mutually exclusive) It will be observed that the right to have the wage question examined is almost always present in contract provisions for job changes, by grievance where direct negotiations would seem not applicable. If the contract is silent on the point, it may be expected that an arbitrator will see that equity prevails.

Consequently, giving consideration to the exceptions appearing within each of the above categories, the citation given earlier[71] is a reasonable summary of the matters herein, if the first limitation therein is understood to include specific freeze situations.

3. EVALUATION PLANS AND EVALUATION CONCEPTS

A number of evaluation plans were at least identified in the cases analyzed, and some of the details of the plans were included in many of the reports. The variety of evaluation plans used is interesting.

Plans with various numbers of factors, from five to 15, were noted.[72] Also noted was the steel industry CWS plan[73] and the rather widely used NMTA plan.[74] Some of the first-noted

---

[71] *Supra* note 45.
[72] 6 LA 304, 11 LA 703, 33 LA 296, 36 LA 740, 46 LA 295, 48 LA 901, 48 LA 957, 49 LA 1014, 51 LA 494, 51 LA 1194.
[73] 31 LA 111, 41 LA 285, 49 LA 1036, 50 LA 823.
[74] 21 LA 461, 30 LA 194, 31 LA 121, 48 LA 339.

cases may fit within these two more-or-less standardized plans or, more likely, are adaptations of them. Some of the cases reflect arbitrator-adopted plans used as an aid in resolving the issues presented; illustrations were given in the introduction to this chapter.

In many of the cases referenced with respect to evaluation plans, the reports frequently state, in detail, the company and union arguments about the application of various factors to the job or jobs in question. They also reflect the arbitrators' appraisal of these arguments, their judgments about manual applications (when available), their personal observations of the job or jobs involved, and of course, their decisions.

While the foregoing listing of references is not necessarily exhaustive, it is representative of the use and application of job evaluation plans within the cases studied. It is important to realize that the "special idiosyncrasies of the establishment" [75] must be searched for in the parties' evaluation plans. This was reflected in the cases, sometimes only through notations that a nationally recognized plan (such as NMTA) had been adapted. Also, it may be noted that cases involving the application of fully developed evaluation plans are relatively straightforward and uncomplicated ones to arbitrate [76]—at least, to arbitrators knowledgeable in this field.

Consequently, the handling of issues of evaluation and related matters in circumstances where fully developed, ongoing plans are not in use will have more interest, and may be more instructive; this can, in fact, include job-evaluation situations where direct application of a formal plan is not the major issue. Such will be the concern of the balance of this section, all of the following section, and, indirectly, some of Section 5.

An early case [77] illustrates the effect of historical relationships upon evaluation. The problem in arbitration was a request by operators in a certain classification in a woolen mill for an increase in base rates; they argued that skill and judgment had not been given sufficient weight in slotting their jobs. The arbitrator agreed that these and many other factors (such as might appear in a job evaluation plan) were legitimate bases for comparison. However, he found that, for an extended period of some 50 years, adjustment of wages in the disputed

---

[75] *Supra* note 3.
[76] *Id.*
[77] 2 LA 478.

classification had kept pace with three other classifications, and refused to disturb this clear evidence of the parties' views about the questioned classification.

By Location

The established pattern in another case [78] was to assign new, experimental work to a sample room where there existed a special inspector's rate. Once the bugs were smoothed out and a job became regular production, according to regular practice it was transferred to a production department. The rate for inspectors on regular production was five cents per hour less. At the time a particular job reached the regular production stage, the company decided to produce it in the sample room because of crowded production conditions. The grievance arose from these factors. The arbitrator's decision was that production inspectors, working side by side with experimental inspectors, were to receive the higher rate "so long as this job was being run in the sample department."

Such evaluation by location was not endorsed by another arbitrator.[79] The model shop, producing prototypes of new products, was normally manned by experimental machinists who ran a variety of machine tools and also performed assembly operations on prototype models. Because of a substantial backlog, the company transferred three assemblers from a regular production department into the model shop. They were to perform assembly operations there, the expressed objective being to increase machine tool utilization in the model shop. The main thrust of the grievance was a protest over the assemblers' doing the work of experimental machinists. Implicit in the dispute was the issue of locational evaluation.

By Commodity

A principle of evaluation by commodity was urged in another case.[80] Various leather packings had been produced on small power-driven lathes. The operations were simplified by installing a new machine—a variation of a drill press—which automatically trimmed and punched one of the packings, formerly trimmed and punched in hand operations on the lathes. In a dispute over the lower rate for the new operations, it was

---

[78] 2 LA 225.
[79] 18 LA 462.
[80] 4 LA 716.

argued that two people producing the same commodity should receive the same rate of pay. (Lathe operations had continued.) The arbitrator examined the proposition in some detail, then proceeded to a determination through evaluation of such factors as relative skills and experience. (There was, apparently, no formal evaluation plan in use by the parties.)

Variations of the same general idea were noted. In the zoo keeper's case,[81] the grievants sought essentially the reverse of the foregoing situation, in that they wanted segregated classification (and identification) by product. The sense of this problem is conveyed by a partial quotation from the opinion: "If indeed birds are for the birds when a keeper prefers mammals . . . ." What constitutes a new product was the issue under a contract [82] which stated that, in the event any new product was started in the plants involved, "there shall be a wage negotiation on those new jobs only." Salvageable waste was determined by the arbitrator to be a new product.

While a company [83] had a right under its contract to combine jobs, its reason for making certain combinations was more efficient utilization of equipment and personnel for the production level then prevailing. This appeared to be a concept of classification by production requirements.

The commodity/product idea was seen in another variation in two cases [84] involving the slotting of a new tape-controlled machine. In one case the arbitrator concluded [85] that negotiations on the slotting of a new machine were required despite the three-classification system for machinery utilized in the company. Part of his reasoning was an earlier decision by the parties, during negotiations, to establish a new classification and a higher wage rate for the operators of two new machines having profiling capacity. This was done to reflect the increased responsibility of the operators because of the large amount of work and dollar investment in each piece produced by the machines by the time it was completed. Thus, economic value of the part produced was an aspect of this particular variation of evaluation by commodity.

A clear issue under a job evaluation plan was presented in a

---

[81] 50 LA 1.
[82] 49 LA 544.
[83] 50 LA 287.
[84] 48 LA 518, 50 LA 823.
[85] 48 LA 518.

dispute over the slotting of a leader classification.[86] The arbitrator was impressed by the fact that the leader classification, which had supervisory responsibility, was in a lower labor grade than another job on the floor with no supervisory duties; and he supported the union grievance. "It is believed that the result of job evaluation should be considered on an overall basis as well as upon the basis of the relative ranking of specific jobs. In other words, the relationships should be considered on a horizontal basis as well as on a vertical basis."

The concept of evaluation by comparison is, of course, widespread; it appears in most cases. (To a degree, in fact, it is inherent in all evaluation plans.) Noted in this connection was comparison to a closely similar timekeeper's job in another subunit of the company.[87] Also noted was a contract provision giving the union jurisdiction whenever a new job was established because of new work "of a nature comparable" to the work covered by existing job descriptions.[88] When this occurred, the contract required the company to develop an appropriate job description.

On the other hand, it was pointed out [89] that comparisons may not be very useful where a specific evaluation plan is being used by parties. That is, the evaluation of the work being done on a given make and model machine tool in one plant is not a good basis for comparison with the work being done in another plant, since the actual work can vary so substantially from one plant to another.

By Size

A sort of classification by size was involved in one arbitration.[90] Work inside the second-stage motor case of the Polaris missile required small-statured men because of the small diameter of the case. Men who were small enough to work inside the case were bidding for better jobs; in an effort to hold them on the motor-case job, the company decided to pay second-operator rates rather than the third-operator rates appropriate to the work. The problem arose when the company sought to return to the lower rates for work on the motor case for the

---

[86] 7 LA 467.
[87] 43 LA 380.
[88] 46 LA 870.
[89] 48 LA 957.
[90] 49 LA 294.

Poseidon missile, which is larger in diameter. The arbitrator concluded the "small worker premium" should be continued.

By Union

Finally, what can be designated as classification by union should be noted.[91] This appears in a clause in the parties' contract: "The Union herein reserves the right to determine classifications of all workers employed by Employer, and the Employer reserves the right to determine the number of employees in each classification."

4. PRECEPTS AND PRINCIPLES

The special circumstances reflected in two cases emphasize the importance of the parties' approach to job evaluation. New owners of a company [92] proposed use of an evaluation plan to rationalize the plant's wage system, and the union, which had recently organized the plant, apparently agreed; the parties did agree upon job descriptions for all jobs in the plant.

The company evaluated all 130 jobs, pursuant to the plan, and gave the evaluations to the union. The union filed 76 grievances challenging various slottings in the evaluated jobs. The company stated that, in view of the large number of grievances, the entire evaluation plan was in dispute, so the arbitrator should hear and determine the evaluation factors on all 130 jobs. The union believed that the unchallenged jobs had been accepted and that the arbitrator should hear and determine only the 76 challenged evaluations. The arbitrator endorsed the company view, giving three reasons. One was the logic of the case: The company gave the union the evaluations as a package which was rejected; the 76 grievances amounted to a counteroffer, in turn rejected by the company. A second reason was that the 76 challenges were not really grievances but "bargaining expressions," the effect of which would change the underlying premises of the evaluation. That is, some 55 percent of the jobs (those challenged) could not be judged in terms of the 45 percent accepted jobs without altering "the basics of the original interpretation," thereby affecting the unchallenged jobs as well.

The third reason stated the arbitrator's opinion that the large number of grievances meant there was lack of mutual understanding and agreement between the parties about the

---

[91] 50 LA 1186.
[92] 47 LA 929.

evaluation system they had adopted. The significance of such mutuality was emphasized by reference to the fact that the value relationship between factors of the system had been established by agreement and not by measurement.

The follow-up report [93] outlines the arbitrator's handling of all 130 evaluations (finding the company slottings to be proper for all but 22 jobs, variously handled by the arbitrator). The report is instructive, in terms of the stated criteria used, the limitations perceived, and the dispositions of the 22 erroneous evaluations.

Company action [94] in combining two existing jobs, following methods changes, into a single classification was the genesis of a union argument that, since the job was a combination of two other jobs, the total numerical classification of the combined job should equal, at least approximately, the numerical classifications of the two jobs. While such a principle might apply where different skills were combined, the arbitrator held, a better approach was to evaluate each factor of the composite job as though it were a newly created job, giving effect to such factors as the highest skill and responsibility represented in either of the jobs being combined.

The arbitrator noted that the same combined job had been evaluated at job class 10 in several other plants of the company. This interplant horizontal-evaluation concept provided weighty though not conclusive evidence to the arbitrator. It should also be noted that the parties had originally agreed upon job class 10 for this combination job. The grievance challenging this evaluation was founded upon an explicit contract provision stating that the correctness of an evaluation could be questioned for any job not occupied for a period of a year.

An interesting case [95] to be compared with the preceding case concerned an employee who had what amounted to a double classification. That is, the man's regular classification was production painter, hourly rate. He also had regular assignments to piecework jobs, filling in for absent employees. The individual usually "made out" on piecework jobs; but when he did not, the company paid him the guaranteed hourly rate for piecework rather than his higher, nonincentive hourly rate. The grievance claimed the latter rate should apply since the man

[93] 47 LA 930.
[94] 20 LA 370.
[95] 21 LA 449.

was not a regular pieceworker. The arbitrator found that the contract contained nothing directly in point on this issue. But he did find a principle of "whichever is greater" in contract language dealing with other wage matters, and he applied this principle for an equitable solution to the grievance. In support of his decision, the arbitrator referred to the company practice, applicable to combination jobs, of compensating at the rate for the highest skill involved, unless use of the higher skill was clearly minor and incidental.

Job Descriptions

Requiring a drill press operator to perform his own layout led to a grievance.[96] It was argued that the word "layout" did not appear in the job description. The arbitrator thought the real questions were whether or not the description specifically forbade layout work (it did not) and whether it could reasonably be inferred that layout was contemplated by the parties (he thought so). The absence of the word was "not conclusive or controlling." The arbitrator thereafter referred to the difficulty of writing a job description in complete detail, commenting that about all that "can really be done is to indicate the level of difficulty of the work to be performed as well as the major functions" of the job.

Another arbitrator [97] noted that in the absence of job descriptions—and a formal job evaluation plan—"comparisons between same and/or similar jobs must of necessity be broader." Therefore, to secure a rate change for a job, "the fluctuation must obviously be more substantial than under precise plans."

In a dispute [98] about the effect of changes in production methods and a move to a new location, the arbitrator considered it "unreasonable" to insist that a new job be created unless the duties and responsibilities were so "significantly different" that they made the established description obsolete. To be compared with this is a situation [99] resulting from the introduction of incentives in certain departments, increasing the duties of timekeepers. The union requested establishment of a new job to cover timekeepers in incentive departments. This was done. In the resulting evaluation, the company allowed three points

96 27 LA 784.
97 35 LA 113.
98 31 LA 111.
99 5 LA 290.

for the physical-demand factor, whereas the evaluation of time-keeping prior to the change allowed six points for this factor. The arbitrator thought it "quite obvious" that physical demand for the new job was not one half of that for the old job.

In the absence of job descriptions, an arbitrator stated [100] that the titles of job classifications were significant, "usually invested with considerable solemnity and importance by the parties," and "an integral part of the past." At issue was a company change, held to be a violation, of certain job titles to remove male and female designations. The contract in another case,[101] stated: "The job title shown indicates the principal duties of the job." This language permitted minor changes in the "miscellaneous duties" of a job, but not a major redistribution of duties.

One of the issues in a case discussed in the preceding section [102] led the arbitrator to state that "the principle that the job and not the man carries the rate is so well-established that further comment is unnecessary." He pointed out that it is the work to be performed which is evaluated, not that which the man is qualified to do. This principle was involved in a grievance [103] challenging the evaluation of a job entitled "Numerical Control Milling Machine Operator." One of the claims was improper assessment of the grievant's educational attainments (he held an MA degree). Said the arbitrator:

"The grievant's chief difficulty is rooted in his opinion that it is he who is being evaluated and in consequence he applies skills, responsibilities, etc., which the job does not require. It is of course the job that is being evaluated, not the man and the only recourse the man has to better himself is to bid up into jobs which carry requirements more suitable to his personal capacity . . ."

Very close to this idea was the conclusion [104] that the excellence with which an employee performed his job was not determinative of its evaluation.

Red-Circle Rates

Related to the preceding issues is the question of personal and "red circle" rates. In one situation,[105] a job was no longer

---

[100] 45 LA 923.
[101] 44 LA 1230.
[102] *Supra* note 86.
[103] 48 LA 957.
[104] 6 LA 119.
[105] 42 LA 945.

needed and the incumbent was permitted, through the seniority provisions, to secure another job in the plant. The union argued that, having once attained a higher rate, he should retain it on the basis it had become a personal rate. The arbitrator noted that contract arrangements providing for personal rates were not unusual, but he found no such arrangement here.

Employees in a particular classification had attained personal or red-circle rates through job changes. The grievance [106] sought such rates for employees who were new to the classification. As the arbitrator put it, "the contract does not provide for hereditary transmission of what has come to be personal rates or 'red circle' rates." The real cause of the problem in another case [107] was the red-circle rate. As the arbitrator noted, most plants having such rates apply them to employees as personal rates, but the plant involved had applied its red-circle rates to jobs.

Use of High Skill

Contrasting with the ideas of evaluating the job, not the man, and personal rates is the very explicit principle that an employee is to be compensated accordingly if higher skills are utilized except where job changes are insubstantial or the use of higher skills is incidental. In one case [108] dealing with the principle the following appeared:

> "Job content, although apparently described in a job description, is usually broader than the written work requirements. The job duties are fluid and are affected by changes in procedures, organization, acquired skill and experience of the employees involved, etc. The margin of difference between a substantial change and one that cannot be considered substantial is often quite narrow and may be composed of numerous minor changes which when considered in their totality are sufficient to bring the matter within the area of a substantial change."

A substantial change upward in skills utilization, either directly or through this described accretion process, should be reflected in classification and compensation.

The insubstantial changes discussed in the above quotation reflect the view that minor changes in jobs do and will occur over time. As one arbitrator [109] put it: "Job classifications do

---

[106] 21 LA 244.
[107] 46 LA 295.
[108] 11 LA 490.
[109] 46 LA 70.

not by themselves freeze the content of a job *precisely* as it was at the time of the negotiation of the contract." In a problem involving the reassignment of duties among job classifications, wherein seniority was established by "Job Family," the arbitrator held that company reassignments had to involve "congruous," not "incompatible" classifications.[110]

In the dispute [111] involving experimental machinists in the model shop, noted in the last section, the arbitrator discussed the effect of job descriptions at some length, pointing out that descriptions were not necessarily mutually exclusive. None of the machinists spent full time on assembly work, and the fact that assembly work was included in machinists' description did not establish exclusiveness. Nor was the fact that the machinists' description was mutually agreed upon, while that of assemblers was not, considered to have established exclusiveness. The same kind of thinking occurred in a layoff case [112] where shaping work was covered in two job descriptions, those of tool and die maker and shaper operator. The arbitrator upheld the layoff of shaper operators and assignment of the work to the other classification, there being insufficient work for both. In the circumstances, the arbitrator observed, the decision was within management discretion.

A particularly instructive case [113] considered work jurisdiction of various skilled trades within a company where the parties had continued the craft concept within an overall production unit. The various grievances were concerned with assignments to tasks not clearly within the scope of the central skills of one particular trade. The arbitrator set forth two major categories of such borderline cases—those involving "overlapping" capabilities and those involving "incidental work." "The term 'overlapping' refers to a task or series of tasks which are of such a nature as to fall reasonably within the normal and proper scope of two or more trades." Bases for judgments in cases of this type include type of tools required, material worked on, apprenticeship training, "generally accepted features" of the trades involved, skill levels required, and other criteria—none of which is necessarily controlling. A major criterion, entitled to

---

[110] 47 LA 716.
[111] 18 LA 462.
[112] 21 LA 814.
[113] 30 LA 46.

"great weight," was the "clearly established practices" of the parties.

> " 'Incidental' work refers to a relatively minor task—not just trivial or insignificant—which is complemental to a major job and which is within the capabilities of and can be safely performed by the tradesman assigned to the principal job, whether it falls within the normal and proper scope of his trade or not. The incidental task is distinguished from the overlapping one by the fact that the latter is an entire job within itself rather than a minor segment of a major job."

The arbitrator discussed this definition in terms of the parties' views and various criteria for judgment. He concluded that the best criterion was the amount of time taken on the incidental task, pointing out that a series of minor tasks—performed sporadically over several days, each one requiring but a small amount of time—would classify as incidental even though total time would be fairly large. He also noted the management need to have other tradesmen available for sporadic and sometimes unforeseen needs; to require that all trades be present at any given time would be inefficient.

> "My conclusion on this phase of the matter is that a relatively minor task which is complimentary to a principal job but which does not require a long period of reasonably continuous work and which is within the capabilities of the principal tradesman and can be performed by him with safety, is incidental work which can properly be assigned to the principal tradesman on the job. On the other hand, a task which is outside the principal tradesman's skill may not be regarded as incidental."

The concept of overlapping duties applies also to overlap between skilled and unskilled jobs and between unskilled jobs. Several cases [114] involving the concept were noted. In one case [115] involving repairman classifications, the overlapping of duties was almost complete. Overlapping duties between an Operator 1 classification, with supervisory responsibility, and an Operator 2 classification appeared in one case.[116] And, finally, there was the case,[117] noted in Chapter II, Section 2, wherein the method of gas detection used by a supervisor overlapped with an outside contractor's method, both of which over-

---

[114] 43 LA 364, 43 LA 491, 48 LA 941, 51 LA 35, 51 LA 411.
[115] 48 LA 52.
[116] 49 LA 445.
[117] 51 LA 1269

lapped with the bargaining-unit member's method of following his nose.

The first cases cited in this section stand for the fundamental concept that classification systems, and particularly evaluation plans, rest on the mutual understanding and agreement of the parties about the general frame of reference of their system.

Other cases indicated a general rule that the designation of job duties, particularly where job descriptions are utilized, must be considered as general, designating scope and skill level, rather than as rigid delimitations. Therefore, a particular duty will be held to be within the job designation on the basis of what is reasonable in the circumstances. Nonexclusiveness is sometimes a part of these circumstances.

Demarcation between jobs will be less precise where no descriptions exist. However, while job titles do not freeze job duties, they mark out the general scope and skill level of the jobs they represent—albeit with less precision than job descriptions.

It seems clear that, whatever the mode of designation, reason in the circumstances will prevail in adjudging comparability and content. There are, also, criteria for determining tasks overlapping or incidental—both skilled-trades jobs, and otherwise.

Clearly, jobs are to be compensated in accordance with skills utilized. However, it is the job and not the man to which job evaluation applies. Red-circle rates are personal and not hereditary, except where they attach to the job.

5. PROCEDURES AND PRACTICES

A rule of reason [118] is applicable in dealing with classification matters, as with other aspects of the collective bargaining relationship. This is well illustrated by a case [119] in which, certain duties having been removed from a classification, the company added new duties. This, said the arbitrator, was proper management action in such circumstances. However, he considered the specific action unreasonable because the added duties were dissimilar in nature from the main duties of the classification, of far more strenuous character, and at a considerable distance from the usual work place (and involved hurrying up several flights

---

[118] Shulman, *Reason, Contract, and Law in Labor Relations*, MANAGEMENT RIGHTS AND THE ARBITRATION PROCESS 169 (1956).

[119] 18 LA 827.

of stairs each time an emergency signal was given). This all added up, in the arbitrator's view, to an "undue burden"; he ordered replacement of these duties by other work which would not "unduly burden."

The foregoing case was an "interests" arbitration; however, the issue originally arose out of an employee grievance and is included here for that reason. Another interests case [120] is included because the arbitrator specifically limited himself in his decision to "rights" criteria. There had been negotiations, pursuant to a wage reopener, and a general increase was agreed upon. However, an additional wage increase was granted to one classification, and this was referred to arbitration. The arbitrator stated that a distinction should be made between a plant-wide adjustment, to which interests criteria would apply, and an adjustment for a single classification, to which rights criteria were applicable. The latter criteria included changes in job content and their impact on various evaluation factors, e.g., skills and hazards.

To the same effect was a case [121] where the arbitrator was asked, as a part of the settlement of contract negotiations, to arbitrate differences of opinion about the evaluation of certain classifications.

The concept of reasonableness seems implicit in a decision [122] relative to the effect of having job descriptions and classifications. The union, opposing the abolition of a classification following methods changes had argued that the existence of a classification implied that the duties covered were to be performed by the incumbents of that classification. That arbitrator ruled that the contract supported no such implication under circumstances of change.

Element of Time

To be compared with this case is a situation [123] involving a rather large-scale reshuffling of personnel, during which it was discovered that a higher rated classification had performed certain work which was clearly within a lower rated job description. It was argued that the higher rate should apply to new employees coming into the department (it appeared that those

---

[120] 40 LA 565.
[121] 50 LA 927.
[122] 30 LA 1014.
[123] 23 LA 804.

in the department who had enjoyed the higher rate continued to do so). The arbitrator thought the job description which was jointly approved, was clear and specific; therefore, the assignments in question were appropriate despite "historical precedent."

Errors in payroll practices sometimes lead to grievances. Subsequent to the installation of a new evaluation plan, a company started paying a certain classification at the job class 3 rate, due to an erroneous entry onto payroll records.[124] When the error was discovered 18 months later, correct payment at job class 2 was initiated, and this led to a grievance. The arbitrator supported the error correction, since the contract provided for such action and it was not barred by the doctrine of laches.

That job descriptions should be kept up to date would seem to be a general rule. However, lack of currentness figured in two arbitrations,[125] both of which were decided against management. An argument was made in the first of these cases [126] that the parties had jointly "signed off" the job description during their last negotiations. However, it was clearly out of date at the time of and with respect to the issue in arbitration.

The fact that there is a classification, current or otherwise, with an appropriate rate, however, does not amount to a guarantee that one or more employees will always be employed in it.[127] Similarly, the existence of an established job does not mean it has to be filled.[128]

Changes in Procedure

Part of the argument in one case [129] concerned the adoption by the company of a new procedure for evaluating jobs. The arbitrator found that there was no prohibition against such action. However, he ruled that the new evaluation method had to be consistent and comparable with the old method of applying the scale of values; otherwise, jobs could be modified and rates reduced, although no real decrease in qualifications for the job had occurred.

Similar in effect is a case [130] where it was said that the old

---

[124] 49 LA 1036.
[125] 43 LA 380, 44 LA 353.
[126] 43 LA 380.
[127] 16 LA 252.
[128] 32 LA 115.
[129] 33 LA 296.
[130] 38 LA 584.

job evaluation plan had been eliminated in the new contract, thereby making negotiations the appropriate procedure for job slotting. The arbitrator stated that the substitute language in the new contract, while not using the term "job evaluation," added up to the same thing; for example, "[t]he analysis of job content will be based on skill, responsibility, working conditions and effort." Since the overwhelming majority of jobs in the plant had been evaluated by a specific system, observed the arbitrator, jobs thereafter had to be assessed under the same system, whether directly by use of the manual or indirectly through job comparison. He specifically ruled that he considered himself committed to the old system in his determinations.

During negotiations,[131] the parties agreed to abolish a certain classification and establish a new one. When the new classification was not established, the union filed a grievance. The arbitrator found that the union's view was that the new classification would be posted, if not filled by the incumbent of the abolished classification. The company's view had been that the new classification would be filled by a particular skill, which happened to be represented by another union in the plant. The arbitrator ruled there had been no effective agreement and ordered reinstatement of the abolished classification—if the new classification had not been properly established, the old one was not properly disestablished. This left the parties where they were; new negotiations for an effective understanding could be initiated, if desired.

An office girl was sometimes assigned to do labeling work, which was in the bargaining unit.[132] At the union's insistence the company transferred the girl into the bargaining unit. She continued to do both office and labeling work and was paid a special rate, agreeable to the parties, because she was particularly efficient and had long company service. When she left, the company refused to pay her replacement the special rate, contending that the established labeler's rate should apply. An arbitration board decided that, since the replacement was performing the combination of duties but the rate before had been special, the parties should negotiate a proper rate.

Absence of "effective agreement" was the pivotal aspect of another, rather unusual case.[133] The negotiated agreement pro-

[131] 20 LA 362.
[132] 14 LA 487.
[133] 9 LA 239.

vided for joint classification of jobs in the plant, after which the agreed-upon classifications would be paid rates "comparable to average rates [paid] by other concerns engaged in the industry." It developed that virtually all other concerns in the industry, at least within the area, had incentive systems of compensation (whereas the plant structure in arbitration was a day-rate system). The parties disagreed as to what was average for the incentive plants. Finding lack of effective agreement, the arbitrator returned the issue to the parties for immediate negotiations to determine a "fair and equitable method" for fixing rates for the agreed classifications.

Possibly the other end of the procedural spectrum is represented by another early case.[134] Since initiation of a job evaluation plan by order of the War Labor Board, the parties had often used technical commissioners (at that time available) of the U. S. Conciliation Service. The recommendations of the commissioner had always theretofore been followed by the parties, based upon a belief in his competence and impartiality. For the two jobs in question, however, his recommendations were not followed. As was pointed out for the two jobs in question, the company evaluated both at 326 points (under the evaluation plan), the union rated them at 390 and 344, while the conciliation expert rated them at 338 and 332. The particular plan provided that 340 points was the bottom value for the next higher labor grade, which would mean a three-cent-per-hour higher rate for the jobs in question.

The arbitrator discussed the company's arguments in the case, and pointed out his responsibility to make a decision in view of the submission of the case to impartial arbitration. These comments are pertinent:

"[O]n the whole, however, the testimony for the company emphasized chiefly the unwisdom of a policy which would permit an arbitrator to decide issues of a technical nature such as workloads, job evaluation, etc. without making a technical study of the job in operation. I am inclined to agree with this point of view, but, for reasons suggested above, I believe that this should not prevent a decision at this time on the basis of the evidence and arguments presented."

These suggested to the arbitrator that there had been sufficient increase in the duties and responsibilities of the two jobs "to

---

[134] 3 LA 855.

require an assignment of additional points to these jobs in order to increase the total points to 340 or more." He noted that company assessments indicated a belief in direct parity of the two jobs, and that the technical expert's evaluations were not too far from the 340-point total.

Note should be taken of some special procedures in job evaluation disputes (aside from, or in addition to, those utilized by an expert arbitrator).[135] One was a contract requirement that the arbitrator consult separately with the parties, observe the job in operation, and then make an award without any joint meeting. Another was agreement by the parties that neither side may be represented by a lawyer. The last was an agreement that each side would submit descriptions and classifications to the arbitrator without giving the other side opportunity to examine these exhibits.

Job Evaluation

A substantial number of the cases in the study illustrated effective handling of job evaluation problems. For an instructive view of arbitral handling of such problems, one report [136] is noteworthy—both because the evaluation plan is brief and because the essential aspects of what the arbitrator did and considered are reflected. Included in the report are the details of the evaluation plan, the evaluation factors of jointly selected comparison jobs, and the company and union evaluations of the disputed jobs. Also, having inspected the disputed and comparison jobs in the plant, the arbitrator discussed his assessment of the disputed jobs.

The practice of personal viewing by arbitrators of jobs and operations in dispute is often reflected in the cases, and emphasized elsewhere.[137] An unusually long period of observation (nine days) was required in one case;[138] involved were all of the jobs in the plant.

Of interest is one arbitrator's technique [139] of photographing specific operations in dispute. This, of course, gives the arbitrator pictorial notes to use with his other notes when he reflects on the case after the hearing. (Some of the photographs taken in

[135] Supra note 5.
[136] 11 LA 703.
[137] Supra note 3.
[138] 47 LA 930.
[139] 21 LA 461.

the particular case are presented in the report on it.) Two short articles,[140] describing and illustrating the technique, indicated that the arbitrator took close-up photographs of every job in dispute. Along with this, he made it a rule to question every operator on a disputed job, when practicable, and with the union and management representatives present.

The cases reviewed herein bring into play a rule of reason with respect to the several issues involved. Such a rule applies not only to a combination of duties, but also to the meaning and application of job descriptions, evaluation procedures, and errors. Where the parties have failed to attain bargained results, or the agreement was only apparent, new negotiations will be directed—unless the arbitrator's reactions to the facts of the controversy result in a decision contrary to that of a technical expert.

---

[140] *New Tool for Arbitration,* BUSINESS WEEK, Dec. 26, 1953, at 78; *Candid Camera Helps Solve Labor-Management Disputes,* 112 FACTORY MGMT. 106 (1954).

CHAPTER V

STANDARDS AND INCENTIVE ISSUES

Managements almost universally favor work standards and/or incentives, interest in them diminishing only because of an unacceptable amount of union resistance. Union views vary from active interest in such programs to aggressive opposition.[1] The resulting joinder of management and union interests, whatever it may be, finds expression in contractual agreements and in plans and procedures, all requiring administration.

One commentator [2] classified and quantified contract clauses on procedures for establishing incentive rates into three types: (1) 60 percent provided for company control of rate determinations, subject to the grievance procedure after issuance; (2) 25 percent provided for union consultation on rates but with company right to issue rates thereafter, without union approval but subject to the union right of grievance; and (3) 15 percent required that rates be negotiated and agreed upon prior to issuance. It was also noted, as would be expected, that contractual provisions on rate-setting procedures varied from great detail to as little as a passing reference that established practices would be followed.

The same article [3] identified "incentive creepage," the result of a progressive series of relatively minor changes which affected standards and incentives. The author commented that a few, but not very many, contracts provided for review and/or

---

[1] Hutchinson, MANAGING A FAIR DAY'S WORK (1963); Lasser, *Labor Looks at Industrial Engineering*, XXI ADVANCED MGMT. 14 (1956); Hutchinson, *Stiffer Battles Ahead over Work Standards*, 40 PERSONNEL 47 (1963).

[2] Werner, *Industrial Engineers, Incentive Systems, and the Contract*, XI J. OF INDUS. ENG'R. 231 (1960).

[3] *Id.*

restudy of incentives every six months. This idea is a part of one of what have been identified as two major problem areas with respect to incentive administration—restrictions on retiming jobs and requirements for payment of average earnings.[4] (It should be noted that the second reference identifies other "trouble spots" in union contracts, including arbitration.)

It appears to be a quite general rule that standards and incentives may be changed when changes in such things as methods and equipment occur. The content of such changes is reflected, to a limited extent, in the sections which follow; however, methods are the subject of Chapter VII.

What do appear herein, as major contractual provisions of interest, are those dealing with establishing and maintaining earnings opportunities and, to a lesser extent, those dealing with earnings guarantees. These concepts and a variety of questions involving incentive plans and their applications, administration, procedures, and techniques constitute this chapter. It will be noted that ideas of workload and crew size become involved in the cases considered; however, Chapter IX considers these topics more directly.

Quantification of earnings opportunity and/or guarantee is very often specified in contracts. When not so specified, the appropriate level of earnings—for the particular incentive job in issue before an arbitrator—was identified as one of "two great areas of doubt in our minds" by John W. Seybold in his discussion of a paper presented to the National Academy of Arbitrators.[5] The other area concerns the rate which will yield that level of earnings, considering such uncertainties as familiarity of employees with the job, whether or not they are holding back, and continuity of production runs.[6]

It is clear that "equal pay for equal work" is the essential rationale underlying contract clauses providing for maintenance of earnings opportunity. This was explicitly stated by the arbitrator in one case;[7] it was a provision of the contract in another.[8]

---

[4] Northrup, *Plain Facts About Featherbedding*, 35 PERSONNEL 54 (1958); Deloff, *Incentive Clauses: The Costly Clinkers*, 36 PERSONNEL 52 (1959).
[5] Waite, *Problems in the Arbitration of Wage Incentives*, ARBITRATION TODAY 25 (1955).
[6] *Id.*
[7] 33 LA 725.
[8] 2 LA 572.

Full meaning of this underlying concept is seen in an arbitrator's ruling [9] that a contractually specified 25 percent (above base rate) earnings opportunity did not mean that earnings were to increase in proportion to production irrespective of the impact of progress changes on elemental time per standard unit. That is, some idea of workload is intimately intertwined in the earnings-opportunity concept.

The basic rationale, of course, does not necessarily explain provisions for earnings guarantees. It does, however, where the guarantee is tied directly to workload. The contract language in one case [10] did just that, in providing that "the new standard shall be set on the basis that the employee with equivalent previous incentive effort shall be able to earn no less than his previous straight time average hourly incentive earnings." Thus, the language explicitly required that opportunity be present in the new standard for employees to make out as well as on the previous standard and, if the employee's effort corresponded to his previous effort, his previous earnings level was guaranteed.

1. EARNINGS OPPORTUNITY

Earnings opportunity is frequently expressed in terms of a percentage of incentive base rate or day rate (the two terms are not necessarily synonymous, of course). This percentage is usually the target earnings under the incentive plan; that is, rates are to be set so that employees who perform with incentive effort should normally expect to earn within only a small deviation from the target. Extraordinary effort, of course, would produce above the target-earnings percentage.

A variety of such percentages were indicated in the cases. Contracts provided for earnings opportunities of 15 to 40 percent.[11] Other cases state the earnings opportunity in terms of being able to maintain previous earnings and/or not have them lessened, the comparison standard being either the employee's own previous earnings or the general level of earnings.[12] Implicit in the commitment is that employees will perform at the

---

[9] 31 LA 662.
[10] 42 LA 661.
[11] 3 LA 309, 12 LA 1084, 21 LA 755, 26 LA 3, 28 LA 259, 31 LA 20, 31 LA 662, 33 LA 916, 41 LA 1053, 49 LA 320, 50 LA 882, 51 LA 101.
[12] 6 LA 218, 12 LA 273, 15 LA 195, 33 LA 29, 39 LA 102, 47 LA 170.

same skill and effort on the new incentives; thus, in one case,[13] the contract requirement was that new rates be set so as to "enable the operators to maintain their established level of earnings for the same skill and effort."

In this case the arbitrator concluded that the company had not met its obligations under the cited language and awarded a change in the piece rate involved. This was after consideration of allegations that skill and effort were markedly different in the new job and that the rates permitted full earnings opportunity if viewed in such context rather than judged in terms of skill and effort on the old job, as the union urged. In the case [14] where target earnings of 40 percent were indicated, there was evidence of a rising curve of earnings over a period of two years under the new rates. After that, earnings failed to continue the rise so that, at all times, earnings were below target expectations. The arbitrator's conclusion was that the incentive plan was the cause of the less-than-expected earnings, rather than employee resistance and slowdown as charged by the employer.

Meaning of Opportunity

The idea that earnings-opportunity language does not automatically require that earnings increase proportionally to production was noted in the introduction to this chapter.[15] The argument there concerned the effect of increased machine speed, together with engineering changes in the method of manufacture. The arbitrator pointed out that the essential question was not whether change of speed was a methods change, as argued by the union, but whether the result of increased speed was to be increased earnings for employees despite the fact that production was easier for employees. He thought not. Incidentally, this arbitrator observed that the 25-percent-earnings-opportunity provision did not mean the company could review incentive rates frequently so as to balance them out at 25 percent.

In contrast to the ruling in the above case, another arbitrator [16] considered that the impact of an employee-initiated speed-and-feed increase permitted increased earnings to the employee,

---

[13] 21 LA 550.
[14] 31 LA 20.
[15] 31 LA 662.
[16] 27 LA 389.

under somewhat unusual contract language. The contract provided for no change in incentive standards, except pursuant to methods changes. It also provided that no change would be made in the standards for certain listed equipment, should feeds and speeds be increased by employees and "approved" by the company. While this arrangement permitted the initiators to increase their earnings, it enabled the company to make appropriate adjustments in the standards on similar jobs. The grievance was argued largely on the basis of a technicality of language in the contract; however, the union position was upheld in full application of both earnings-opportunity and equal-pay concepts, although these concepts were not explicitly stated.

The provision of earnings opportunity, however, does not guarantee individual piece rates of individual employees.[17] Furthermore, the fact that an employee's earnings are down in comparison with previous earnings is not *per se* proof that the company has failed in its earnings-opportunity commitment.[18] The requirement that the new rate be in line with other rates in the plant did not mean the new rate was automatically incorrect when challenged, in a grievance, as too tight.[19] The arbitrator concluded that the circumstances of the new job were markedly different from those of the previous job, in contrast to a previously noted case,[20] so that application of the requirement was to be judged more generally than strict comparison with the predecessor job.

A "mongrel" type of rate was held not to be subject to an earnings-opportunity provision requiring that rates be set so as to yield 15 to 30 percent above base rate.[21] Employees in an electro-melting department were paid a certain base hourly rate whether or not they produced any steel tonnage. There was also a formula whereby tonnage produced was translated into an amount uniformly applied to each of the rates in the department. The arbitrator pointed out that incentives in other departments were "pure piecework," under which employees were compensated in direct proportion to output. This mongrel combination system, the arbitrator concluded, was not the

---

[17] 33 LA 916.
[18] 37 LA 279.
[19] 6 LA 218.
[20] *Supra* note 13.
[21] 3 LA 309.

type of incentive the parties had in mind when the earnings-opportunity provision was negotiated.

Workload and Crew Size

That workload has a relationship to the application of earnings-opportunity clauses is indicated in the previous cases. In a case [22] in which increased machine speed was involved, the arbitrator stated that an essential test—albeit not the sole criterion—was whether or not a substantial amount of scrap resulted when the machines operated faster. He concluded there was additional scrap but not enough to be significant. In another case,[23] gussets had been cut from grain leather at established piece rates. In a changeover to pigskin, new rates were established and resulted in a union grievance that current earnings were below the average for cutting grain leather. The arbitrator concluded that the union had failed to sustain this allegation, referring to five time studies of the job which indicated previous earnings were possible by the exertion of normal effort. The arbitrator was particularly impressed that the youngest and least experienced of the cutters made out on the job.

A major technological change [24] resulted in a rate change and a radically increased incentive quota (more than 80-percent increase). It also resulted in a reduction in crew size. Upon a review of the circumstances, including remarkably uniform production results, the arbitrator concluded that employees were controlling production and that they could produce to the prior earnings level with time to spare. Consequently, there was no abrogation of the contract's maintenance-of-earnings clause. The arbitrator also observed there were no data with which to make a judgment on whether or not the skill-effort relationship of the old job had been changed.

In another situation [25] there had also been technological changes, a major feature of which was the addition of a second furnace. These resulted in a rather marked reduction in crew size. The union argument, under an earnings-potential-maintenance contract requirement, was that the potential had been

---

[22] 28 LA 259.
[23] 15 LA 195.
[24] 39 LA 102.
[25] 33 LA 29.

lessened because employees had to produce 33 tons of marble to earn 25 percent above standard, whereas 22 tons had yielded the same earnings under the previous incentive. Also, it was argued that the new incentive required greater effort from the smaller crew. The arbitrator noted that the incentive was expressed in terms of standard hours per ton and was in no way dependent upon the number of man-hours utilized. He also concluded, and demonstrated, that there had been no real change in the incentive offered the employees.

The cases indicate a rather widespread practice of quantifying the contractual commitment on earnings opportunity. When it is not explicitly stated as a percentage-earnings relationship, a variety of qualitative terms are used; they add up, in substance, to maintenance of previous earnings relationships. The cases make it clear that contract provisions on earnings opportunity do not add up to a guarantee, so that mere failure to maintain previous earnings does not, in and of itself, mean the new rate is improper. Rather, the cases clearly show that skill-effort relationships—before and after—will be adjudged in determining company compliance with its contractual commitment. In some cases, arbitrators attempt to measure skill-effort relationships directly, while in others they judge them on other bases, including such extrinsic factors as workload and crew size.

2. EARNINGS GUARANTEES

Probably the most common circumstances where a guarantee comes into play are those involving nonstandard operating conditions. Thus, weavers found that faulty stock from which a certain style was woven reduced output per loom more than 30 percent.[26] The union supported a claim for average earnings. However, the only guarantee in the contract was a guaranteed minimum rate of 80 percent of average earnings.

It was pointed out that the company had on past occasions made allowances to average earnings. The company conceded this had been done in connection with certain experimental work but denied the generality of the practice. The arbitrator

---

[26] 7 LA 585.

concluded he had no power to grant the union grievance, but recommended that the company pay the average earnings, as requested, on the basis of past practice.

Another case [27] involved a welding operation performed under off-standard conditions. Certain braces to be welded to bar shafts were too short to be formed so as to provide the weld called for in the standard. The result was "excessive gap" calling for extra welding. Upon a grievance requesting average earnings, it developed there was no directly applicable contract clause. However, there was a provision in the contract requiring payment of average earnings to an operator taken from his regular incentive work to perform rework on another employee's defective work, the employee performing the defective work not being available to do the rework. This provision did not fit the facts of this case, however, so the arbitrator denied the grievance. He pointed out that the ruling required by the contract did not satisfy the equities of this case.

In a contrasting situation [28] a contract clause provided for payment of "average piecework earnings" (A.P.E.) for specified occurrences. The problem arose over employees permanently transferred to different jobs. The company thought this average should not apply, because it was based on the employees' performance on their previous jobs. The arbitrator pointed out that, unlike occupational rates which attached to classification or operation, A.P.E. was a personal rate and attached to the individual employee. Therefore, until a new A.P.E. had been established, through operation of applicable contract provisions, the old A.P.E. was to be paid when circumstances were appropriate for A.P.E. payment.

Soon after World War II, a company [29] changed automatic-screw-machine assignments from one machine to two machines. (It appears that dual-machine operations had been the pre-war practice.) The union asked for a wage increase, and the company offered one which was considerably below the union request. While this matter was being discussed, the company proposed an incentive system and proceeded to install it.

[27] 25 LA 394.
[28] 14 LA 815.
[29] 7 LA 943.

Apparently, employees did well on the incentive system. The union, however, thought the plan should be discontinued, and the matter came before an arbitrator. He first concluded that equity required a wage increase, larger than the company offer but less than the union request. He also concluded that the company had the right to change to the incentive system. He noted that it was relatively common to give employees assurances of the desirability of a change to incentive through some form of guarantee, and he thought there was need for a guarantee "at least until the novelty of the present type of operation has worn off." He thereupon awarded a guarantee of 15 cents above the former straight-time hourly rate for a period of six months.

Maintenance of Earnings

A company [30] corrected an error in a piecework price. It developed that the erroneous rate had been paid for a period of about six months. The union claimed that the rate had become the existing rate and that it would be improper for the company to change it. While in some circumstances an erroneous piecework rate might become established as the permanent rate, said the arbitrator, such circumstances were not present in this case. As soon as the erroneous rate was discovered, the company changed it and therefore avoided the possibility of its becoming an established practice. Where the contract [31] provided for maintenance of earnings, and the company had instituted a replacement incentive as a result of certain changes, the arbitrator ruled that the maintenance-of-earnings clause required that certain time values in the replacement incentive be increased.

A reduction in crew size from four to three was followed by a drop in the crew's earnings.[32] The crew members argued that the contractually provided incentive factor should somehow be differently applied so as to permit them to maintain their earnings. The arbitrator, however, concluded that the reduction in earnings was caused more by production scheduling than by application of the incentive allowance.

---

[30] 45 LA 1015.
[31] 46 LA 660.
[32] 47 LA 1089.

Somewhat similar was a situation[33] in which the real thrust of the union grievance was that the incentive earnings of a group on indirect incentive had not increased proportionately with the earnings of employees on direct incentive doing the same type of work. The earnings of similarly situated employees under other indirect incentive plans had increased by roughly the same percentage as production-operation earnings. The grievance asked that a different incentive be utilized, one which the union believed would yield the desired results. The arbitrator concluded that the established incentive was within the requirements of the contract and that the arbitration board was without power to order a change in type of incentive.

Whenever his machine broke down, an operator would call in maintenance for prompt repair of the machine.[34] During the down-time period, the operator was paid an average departmental incentive rate. On the day in question, the maintenance department was not able to repair the machine immediately, so the operator was asssigned by his foreman to laboring work. This lasted for over four hours, and the operator was paid at the day rate for such laboring work. When he claimed he should be paid the average departmental incentive rate, the company replied that its established practice was to pay the day rate to operators doing laboring jobs. The arbitrator concluded that, while there may have been such a practice, the operator nevertheless was entitled under the contract to the average incentive rate.

The parties had negotiated and signed a memorandum of agreement that a pressman would receive past average hourly earnings for any "wait time" which he might have between operating cycles.[35] The pressmen took advantage of this system by hurrying through cycles to increase the wait time for which they would be compensated in addition to their regular piecework earnings. The company refused to make the wait-time payments under these hurried circumstances, and a grievance resulted. The arbitrator pointed out that the memorandum of agreement committed the company to make the wait-time payments only when operators, working at regular speed, skill, and effort, were

[33] 44 LA 774.
[34] 43 LA 722.
[35] 47 LA 170.

unable to earn $26 per day. What the operators were doing was outside the scope of this guarantee and, consequently, the grievance was denied.

A contract [36] provided for personal and fatigue time allowances. It also provided in the same paragraph for "contingency" allowances to be included in production standards when the job so required. In the situation brought to the arbitrator, a welder was moved from one welding booth to another in the same area, then back to the first booth when work was available on it. The distance from one end of the welding department to the other was about 100 feet. The grievance sought a down-time allowance under the contingency clause for moving from one welding booth to another—the theory being that incentive opportunity was impeded by the assignments. The arbitrator concluded that there was nothing in the job requiring a contingency allowance. In his view the personal and fatigue allowances, together with a "miscellaneous" allowance, were sufficient. If, in fact, there was any adverse effect upon earnings opportunity, it had to be *de minimis.*

A company's longstanding practice [37] was to pay union stewards at the day rate for time spent in grievance meetings. The contract, however, specifically provided for payment of "average earnings" to stewards in such circumstances. An arbitrator held that the company was bound by the contract despite the longstanding practice of paying the lower day rate. Involved in this situation was a zipper clause, whereby the parties undertake, through contract language, to eliminate previous understandings and past practice.

The cases indicate both the relative persistence of the guarantee concept and the relatively narrow construction accorded to it, in contrast to the generality of the earnings-opportunity concept. The earnings guarantee is most generally applicable to nonstandard occurrences affecting employees on incentive—and is, therefore, a type of supplement to the structure providing earnings opportunity. Sometimes the guarantee appears as a rate personal to an employee.

---

[36] 46 LA 557.
[37] 48 LA 691.

3. PLANS AND THEIR UTILIZATION

In addition to time study, a number of other measurement systems are used in establishing performance standards and, in some cases, incentives. Representative are MTM [38] (methods-time-motion measurement), MTA [39] (motion-time analysis), MSD [40] (Master Standard Data), Work Factor,[41] and the Bedeaux System.[42] The two-step procedure for instituting a new incentive commonly used in the steel industry appeared in some cases.[43] The arbitrator in one case [44] noted that the company was replacing a "money piecerate" plan with a new incentive based on time.

A "standard minute" plan [45] provided that operators would be paid earnings above base rate in direct proportion to increased production above the standard set by the company. The contract also provided for the use of standard data on as many elements of operation as possible; time studies were to be used where standard data were not available. (This case is also of interest for the number of specific standards and incentive provisions spelled out.)

Another contract [46] provided that the company should establish wage incentives for productive classifications, that it might establish incentives for classifications other than productive, that the establishment and administration of such incentives should be the "sole responsibility of the Company," but, finally, that the company should not change permanent time values of any incentive job absent change in method, product, tools, material, design, qualitative requirements, work assignments, or other production or job conditions. Instead of sole administration,[47] provisions were made in the contract for the company to set up new or revised incentives, as conditions warranted, after which they would be instituted on a trial basis. But if the parties did not agree through the trial that the rates were

---

[38] 38 LA 1208, 39 LA 102, 41 LA 1147.
[39] 40 LA 33.
[40] 41 LA 953.
[41] 18 LA 459.
[42] 12 LA 603.
[43] *E.g.*, 29 LA 784.
[44] 31 LA 20.
[45] 51 LA 682.
[46] 47 LA 382.
[47] 47 LA 1157.

equitable, the new incentives could be presented for decision through the arbitration procedure.

A contract [48] provided: "The present bonus rate will be in effect until such time as a more effective, updated incentive plan can be inaugurated by management with the consent of the union." On the basis of this language, an arbitrator concluded that the company's action in unilaterally changing from the existing three-operator incentive plan to the previously utilized two-operator incentive plan was in error.

A somewhat unusual contract provision [49] provided:

"In addition to basic hourly rates, wage incentives will be paid in certain departments *on the same basis* as heretofore subject to being removed on sixty (60) days' written notice to the Company and subject to a majority of the employees involved and their Shop Steward, if such steward is employed in unit involved, voting in a closed ballot to remove same at the end of said period. Subsequent votes may be held in like manner on like notice to remove same. Only those employees who have been working in the Shop at least thirty (30) calendar days prior to the election shall be eligible to vote." (Emphasis added by arbitrator.)

A grievance involving this provision posed a question of the company's right to change existing standards and the basis thereof. The company argued that the issue was not arbitrable, but the arbitrator thought it was. While the issue involved in arbitration [50] is not of particular relevance, quotations concerning the company's incentive plan are:

"All incentive standards will be established in accordance with generally accepted industrial engineering practice, using timestudies by stopwatch, standard data and data developed from other sources and will include the three basic elements that comprise all *R.F.I.* time standards:
(a) Average leveled time.
(b) Allowance for personal needs, fatigue and unavoidable delays.
(c) A 10% addition to the sum of 1 and 2 above, to enable the employees to begin to earn bonus when they produce at 91% normal."

Changes Requiring Justification

A contractual requirement [51] was that incentive standards would not be changed, once established, unless there were

---

[48] 50 LA 804.
[49] 47 LA 541.
[50] 48 LA 893.
[51] 44 LA 1006.

changes in various conditions (material, design, or equipment), or unless an error was discovered. Also of interest is a contract provision,[52] as follows: "The Company agrees that any standard task once issued shall not be adjusted downward or upward unless the entire operation has been changed by an accumulation of changes equal to 5%, or unless an error in the computation of the applicable standard task is discovered. . . ."

A contract [53] gave the company the right to make changes in methods of production or equipment and to make changes in the rate of production in accordance therewith, after reasonable prior notice to and consultation with the union. Despite this contractual right, an arbitrator concluded that the company was not privileged to increase unilaterally the speed of a certain packaging machine. Involved in the arbitrator's decision was the fact that the company had, during contract negotiations, introduced a discussion on this matter and sought union approval for the change, but had later removed the issue from negotiations. In addition, the arbitrator concluded that the contractual requirements of notice and consultation had not been fulfilled.

The reasoning in two cases is particularly noteworthy. In one case [54] the issue was discharge for failure to maintain production standards. One of the arguments advanced was that the standards had been unilaterally established, using a measured-day work system. Since the standards did not affect wages or hours but were merely objective measures of performance, and in the arbitrator's view were realistic and reasonable, the fact of unilateral initiation was not considered fatal. In coming to this conclusion, the arbitrator pointed out that, absent an objective system of measurement, the employer would make a subjective determination, through supervision, as to whether or not the employee was working at proper efficiency. Had such a determination resulted in discharge, it would have been sustained if the employer's judgment were found reasonable under the circumstances. Therefore, the arbitrator reasoned, the presence of an objective system of measurement was a more effective and fair means of evaluating efficiency.

---

[52] 49 LA 912.
[53] 47 LA 986.
[54] 36 LA 1442.

Plans as Yardsticks

The other case [55] explains and emphasizes that any particular measuring system is just that and no more. A standard is developed from the application of the measuring system (yardstick), but the system is not the standard—and, more particularly, not the monetary consequence which is called incentive. In this case, one issue concerned the company's unilateral use of MTA instead of time study; the arbitrator commented:

> "It must be clearly understood that MTA is primarily a yardstick and not a standard per se. It is a yardstick just as MTM, DMT, Work Factor, etc., are yardsticks. It happens to be an integral requirement of all these yardsticks that the cycle being measured be standardized. This requirement usually calls for changes in elemental line-ups and, in general, a critical review of all of the elements which enter into the cycle as well as the specific positions they occupy. This requirement frequently results in the elimination of useless work, the rearrangements of useful work to eliminate idle time and other efficiency considerations. All this, however, is also peculiar to the orthodox time study approach even though it is only infrequently carried out. In this instance, the application of the new yardstick no doubt resulted in rearrangements and quite probably, in a reduction in some of the established job time-standards. Nevertheless, this change in time-standards is still not a peculiarity of the yardstick; no change would have been needed if the jobs had been finalized in the 'best cycle' sense when they were studied originally."

The use of one yardstick as a means of checking the results of another measuring system frequently occurs. In one case,[56] in which a buffing operation had originally required eight passes, employee-initiated improvements reduced this to five passes. A new rate was established by time study. However, primarily to establish the fact of methods change, work factor analyses were made disclosing 58 motions required in the eight-pass method as compared to 37 motions in the five-pass method.

One arbitrator [57] reviewed a company's master standard data sheets and found them to represent standard MTM values. Consequently, since the parties had agreed to them in specific contract language, these plus any properly computed derivative values were not open to contest in arbitration. The arbitrator

---

[55] 40 LA 33.
[56] 18 LA 459.
[57] 38 LA 1208.

also reviewed and found competent the company's technical analysis of fundamental motions in the manual part of the job in question—although he found possibilities for error in the analysis of the process part of the job (largely on the basis of his perception of a possible technological problem in the welding). It is interesting to note that the issue here was stipulated as: "Is the standard for anode welding properly set?"

In another MTM application,[58] the arbitrator reviewed the company's analysis and found it proper except for the possibility that it might not have accounted for all possible delays encountered by operators. He also noted that a company witness had testified that the rate set had been influenced by a need to yield a certain result (maintenance of earnings). Consequently, it was observed that MTM, while yielding correct absolute values, did not fit the work-wage relationship in the plant. In another case [59] the parties agreed to the use of MSD to establish standards, with the company having the right to monitor these standards by any system it chose; one monitoring yardstick was MTM.

Workload Yardsticks

These yardsticks are often used in workload determinations. When a plant was operating at full capacity, the union felt that the two men in a particular occupation were overloaded, and filed a grievance to that effect.[60] An MTM analysis indicated that the full-capacity manpower requirement in this occupation was 1.96590 men; hence, the two-man assignment was proper manning. The single issue in another workload case [61] was whether the established production quotas on certain jobs were reasonable. The quotas had been established by time study. The arbitrator reviewed the time studies involved, found them to have been procedurally quite inadequate, concluded the company had thereby failed to establish reasonableness of the quotas, and upheld the grievance.

Because incentive operators had been earning substantially (up to 400 percent) more than the day-rate employees, a company proposed and the union agreed to eliminate such inequities by

---

[58] 39 LA 102.
[59] 41 LA 953.
[60] 41 LA 1147.
[61] 14 LA 638.

removal of the incentive plan and institution, by the company, of a measured-day rate system.[62] The system provided that the standard would be such that a qualified and properly trained employee, working at normal pace, could produce 100 percent of the standard. It also provided that a standard, once established, would not be changed except for changes of 5 percent or more. There were other provisions, but the salient one stated: "In no event are employees expected to make less than 95% of Standard under normal conditions." The grievance arose because incentive employees had developed the habit under the previous system of working fast, making quota, and then sitting around, or visiting, or doing other nonwork activities until it was time to go home. The system was, the arbitrator observed, so ingrained in the employees that they looked upon the 95-percent provision as their operating production standard. Whether employees could quit under the measured-day work system, when they reached 95 percent of standard was the issue posed in arbitration, and the arbitrator concluded that 100 percent was standard. He pointed out that the measured-day rate system was not piecework but was, rather, an hourly-rated plan with standards affixed to the job.

Other Measurements

Finally, some other contractual arrangements should be considered. One contract [63] provided that employees performing nonincentive work, in a department functioning on an incentive basis, should participate in the incentive plan on the basis of average incentive earned by the group "when said employees are required to feed materials directly to production workers." A master agreement [64] covering dairies in the particular area contained a schedule of wage rates for milkers; there was also a production standard whereby an individual milker was to milk 90 cows per day. In the arbitrator's words, "For cows milked in excess of ninety per day, the Agreement provides that employees will receive wages at the rate of cow and one-half for such excess cows milked."

A company [65] had a system of grading employees from A to D for the quality of the work they produced. In addition, it had a

---

[62] 46 LA 193.
[63] 45 LA 955.
[64] 45 LA 964.
[65] 43 LA 1208.

bonus system whereby employees with A-quality work received a 6-percent premium in wages and those with B-quality received a 3-percent premium. When the disciplinary layoff of each of certain employees who had received a third D within a month's time was challenged by the union, the company threatened to discontinue the system of grading quality and the bonus. The contract contained a provision that existing incentive rates would remain in effect for the duration of the agreement. The arbitrator concluded that the company was not privileged to remove the quality-bonus system; it was, in his opinion, an incentive system.

A fundamental consideration in the performance of work is that the performance will be measured. Measurement can be subjective, observational, or impressionistic, or it can be done by objective methods. The various plans for measurement, including time study, some of which are noted herein, all have objectivity as their purpose. Equally fundamental is that measurement is just that, and no more. Various allowances and allied considerations go into the transposition of measurement into a standard. The interrelating of standard with wage payment is the quantification of the equities discussed in Chapter III and provides the basis for incentive systems.

The cases reflect the need for understanding of the measurement and standards-development processes, their meaning and application, and their administration. Various contractual provisions relative to standards and incentive systems appear in the cases.

In particular, a general rule emerges from the cases that standards, once established, are to continue in effect and not be changed except in response to various conditions usually identified, in summary form, as methods changes.

4. SOME APPLICATIONS

The two-step, trial-period process for introducing new incentives that is often found in steel contracts is involved in some of these cases. One union argued that the incentive on a particular line should have been based on time values already established on certain other lines in the plant, rather than on studies made by the company directly on the line in question.[66] The arbitrator pointed out that the union's view confused the question of equitable earnings relationships among incentive employees on similar jobs with the question of the time standards on the basis of which incentive earnings were determined. Since the lines were clearly different, in the arbitrator's view, there was no basis for the union's claim.

Another case [67] called for a decision relative to two separate incentive provisions in the contract. One clause empowered the company to establish, or not to establish, incentives for new jobs. The other clause required that existing incentives be modified or replaced by new incentives when operating conditions changed. The question posed to an arbitration board was which clause governed when new, automated primary mills were built; the board held that this was a matter for the company to decide on a case-by-case basis. Criteria for the decision in this case were: first, the new mills were an entirely new operation; second, they were in new buildings at a substantial distance from old mills; third, they required new skills which necessitated a training program; fourth, the mills could not be manned without a special understanding on seniority and training; fifth, many employees were on other incentives, many of which continued in effect; and sixth, manning arrangements were so different as to render irrelevant employees' experience under previous incentives.

Two cases [68] are concerned with the question whether an existing incentive should be modified "to preserve its integrity" or replaced with a new incentive. In both, the arbitrator concluded that the changes involved were not such as to require replacement incentives, as the companies had urged, but rather could be accommodated by modification of the existing incentives. The second of these two cases was marked by the considerable vigor with which the company pursued its view—including a challenge to a previous ruling by the same arbitrator, a ruling which the arbitrator specifically endorsed.

The adjustment of an incentive based on tonnage led to trouble in one case.[69] A large quantity of "pickled and limed

---

[66] 29 LA 784.
[67] 39 LA 4.
[68] 28 LA 144, 42 LA 1327.
[69] 6 LA 579.

rods" were flowing through the shipping department and, being heavy, they distorted the regular tonnage mix in the department. The contract provided for rate adjustments whenever there was a change in any "factor which would affect operations." The arbitrator found there had been a fairly constant mix of light, medium, and heavy packages and that these rods did, in fact, affect the mix and, therefore, were a factor affecting operations.

The final case [70] of these steel types presented a situation wherein one party argued that the progress of negotiations and changing contract language over the years had brought about a contract situation under which adjustments to preserve the integrity of existing incentives were no longer provided for. The arbitrator handled this argument with dispatch, pointing out that there had been a regular practice of such adjustments over the years.

Arbitral Review of Changes

An arbitrator's review of a revised standard expressed in standard hours provides an instance of application.[71] He weighed the considerable number of studies made by the company, considered the arguments of the union, which included an allegation that allowances were inadequate, and concluded the standard was fair and correct. In another case,[72] after reviewing evidence and concluding there had been a substantial method change, the arbitrator refused to rule as to appropriateness of the new rate. He took this position both because there had not been sufficient evidence presented at the hearing and because there had been no showing the parties could not resolve this issue in negotiations. He did indicate a willingness to hold the matter open and to schedule a new hearing on the issue should the parties fail of agreement. (This was before a tripartite board, the union-appointed member of which agreed on the first issue but objected to holding the second issue open; he thought the board should proceed to determine the proper rate.)

---

[70] 26 LA 812.
[71] 42 LA 661.
[72] 21 LA 387.

In an interesting situation,[73] the company had discretion by contract as to the establishment of new incentives. However, it had committed itself in negotiations to put inspection on incentive. The arbitrator upheld the union claim that the company had been dilatory, stating that the discretion of the general contract clause was replaced by the commitment with respect to the inspection function. He set the date of grievance as the retroactive date for installation of the inspection incentive by the company.

A rather novel argument was advanced in one case.[74] The contract provided that the company would not reduce the rate of a job by removing, from the time study, time which had been saved "entirely by the operator's effort." The company made extensive changes which mechanized a considerable part of the coremaker's job, thereby reducing the skill requirements. The argument advanced was that the changes rendered useless the efficiency coremakers had built up, and that this was violative of the "operator's effort" provision. The arbitrator did not concur.

Sufficiency of Measurement

A recurring problem in standards application is the sufficiency of the measurement. The comments of one arbitrator [75] are informative:

"Possible errors (up or down) in these time-allowances which are necessarily based on judgment, can be reduced by increasing the number of cycles being observed and by scattering the observed cycles over more operators and over a greater period of time. However, the economics of the situation normally does not permit extending the study beyond a certain point, that is, once the number of cycles studied will yield a result which represents, in the probability sense, a rational measurement."

Later on, in the same case, the arbitrator stated these conclusions:

"The new standard (1.04) is technically correct provided the sample studied (22 typewriters) is sufficiently large to account for all delays, complications, etc. for which allowances must be provided. An analysis of the studies and of the check studies (in-

---

[73] 37 LA 279.
[74] 4 LA 189.
[75] 45 LA 996.

cluding the Union's check study) coupled with the generally accepted tolerance-variation in rating, coupled further with the history of the old rate, leads your arbitrator to conclude that the proper task for the performance of the work in question here is 0.980 units per hour."

Just as employees desire that standards be permanent except for specified changes, management would like limitations on when standards may be attacked through grievance. Contractual provisions on the latter were quoted in one case: [76]

" 'Time Study standards are factual and not subject to negotiations. Should a complaint arise it will be handled as a grievance in the usual manner.

"However, (1) grievance shall not be filed until after a permanent standard has been in effect for a period of sixty (60) calendar days, or production thereunder has exceeded 40 hours at standard, whichever is longer. (2) In no event shall a permanent standard be subject to the grievance procedure after it has been in effect for a period of one (1) year unless a change in method or conditions is claimed to have occurred.' "

5. CHANGEOVERS

The cases presented some interesting issues which are summed up here as changeovers. This term is used to represent situations in which one of the following takes place:

—a change from day-work organization (which usually means lack of work regularization) to a plan providing work standards, with or without incentives;

—a change from incentive to straight day work or some form of measured-day work; or

—a change from one plan to another.

Day Work to Standards

The right to change from day work to work standards, sometimes including incentive, was explicitly stated in some contracts.[77] In one,[78] the contract also permitted the company at its discretion to change to an incentive basis of payment, with the proviso that the incentive "produce at least the hourly rate from which changed." The contract in another case [79] stated that,

---

[76] 48 LA 974.
[77] 21 LA 550, 26 LA 3, 37 LA 279, 42 LA 1127.
[78] 21 LA 550.
[79] 26 LA 3.

wherever practicable, operations should be performed on an incentive basis. This, said the arbitrator, supported unilateral action in changing certain jobs to incentive. Earnings, however, had to be 15 percent above day rate as the contract provided; otherwise, the matter was subject to negotiation.

The arbitrator observed in another situation [80] that the union allegations were not over discipline for failure to meet standards nor even that the new standards were unduly stringent. Rather, he considered the union's position to be a general attack on the company's power to establish production standards. The "unambiguous" language of the contract gave the company such power. The arbitrator further commented that any contention that the company's exercise of its power was "discriminatory or unreasonable" would be the subject of another arbitration.

The unilateral establishment of work standards was upheld by an arbitrator where it was not arbitrary (the company had advised the union during negotiations that it no longer would permit employees to set their own work standards), burdensome, or unreasonable.[81] In fact, a result of standards setting had been crew reduction, considered appropriate in the circumstances.

The contract in another case [82] stated that "no incentive, task, bonus, or piece rate system will be established," except upon mutual agreement. The arbitrator ruled that this provision did not preclude unilateral establishment of production standards. In particular, he determined that standards did not amount to a task system since employees were not privileged to quit and go home upon completion of a fixed quota of work. His own study of the concept had convinced the arbitrator that this was an essential characteristic of a task system.

Incentive to Day Work

One company [83] changed from piecework to day rate on certain operations, primarily because assembly jobs customarily had been day rated. The contract provided that piecework prices were to remain unchanged except when "a change in

---

[80] 42 LA 1127.
[81] 41 LA 1038.
[82] 37 LA 758.
[83] 27 LA 758.

process occurs," which was understood to mean a change to an-other piecework rate. The company attempted to establish that the changes related to "methods" and not "process," but the arbitrator upheld the union grievance.

A contract [84] provided for cancellation of piecework prices when certain changes occurred. However, such cancellation was to be interim in nature, until new rates could be established. The arbitrator ruled, in sustaining a union grievance, that ab-solute cancellation of piecework prices was not permissible un-der the contract. In another case,[85] the company argued that no specific section of the contract had been violated when it changed piece rates to day rates on certain jobs. The arbitrator pointed out that the wage section carefully distinguished be-tween rates for pieceworkers and those for hourly-paid workers. This, plus details on handling the two systems of wage pay-ments, convinced the arbitrator of the merit of the union griev-ance, and in his award he directed the company to negotiate with the union about the desired change in payment method on the jobs involved.

Largely because of the parties' common understanding, it was determined that the company [86] could unilaterally change a job from an incentive to an hourly basis of payment. The contract provided that wages were fixed for the contract period in ac-cordance with the wage plan. In this wage plan was a descrip-tion of the incentive system. The parties both testified to an understanding that the general structure of the incentive system was fixed, but that this did not contemplate freezing of indi-vidual jobs under the incentive system. Similarly, because instal-lation was progressing so slowly, the parties in another case [87] had expressly agreed to delete incentive programs from the con-tract. The arbitrator decided that it would be appropriate to in-corporate the measurements made for incentive installations into work standards.

With respect to changes from one type of plan to another, the change from money piece rate to a time incentive has already been noted.[88] A change from a one-man operation to a two-

---

[84] 21 LA 124.
[85] 23 LA 490.
[86] 20 LA 639.
[87] 40 LA 875.
[88] *Supra* note 44.

man operation was thought appropriate under the contract.[89] However, in this case another provision, under which temporary rates became permanent after being in effect for six months, precluded company action. The idea of a change to two-man rates was generalized [90] to endorse a change from individual operation to group incentive on an assembly line. (In fact, the main issue in the case devolved around allowances for interferences rather than the right of the company to make the change.) The reverse occurred in another case,[91] where, pursuant to negotiations, the change was from a general performance bonus to individual incentive.

The parties [92] agreed in negotiations to change their old incentive system to a new standard-hour incentive plan based upon MTM. Negotiations were not present, however, in two other cases.[93] And, finally, the situation [94] of a company "buy-out" is of interest. This concerned a lump-sum payment to adversely affected employees in a change from one incentive plan to another. (The grievance was concerned with whether the buy out should be included in gross earnings for vacation pay computation; the arbitrator held that it should.)

The cases involved in this section stand for some straightforward propositions. When the change is from an hourly or day-work basis to some form of work standards, arbitrators uphold the action. This is so whether or not the contract or negotiations expressly allow such action or are silent (no cases were found in which the action was specifically forbidden) and whether or not the change is solely to work standards or to work standards coupled with an incentive system. As might be expected, the resulting structure must be reasonable and equitable, and consistent with other contract provisions.

When the change is from incentive to day work or from full incentive application to work standards only, arbitrators generally do not permit the action unless it is grounded in contract

---

[89] 2 LA 469.
[90] 10 LA 480.
[91] 43 LA 33.
[92] 38 LA 1208.
[93] 40 LA 33, 40 LA 866.
[94] 49 LA 841.

or negotiations. However, when change is from one plan or program to another—as, for example, from one type of incentive to another—arbitrators again support the action, with or without negotiations (in none of the cases did the contract language or negotiations prohibit a change from one plan to another).

6. PRINCIPLES AND PROCEDURES

One contract [95] provided that the incentive system would be extended to other groups whenever possible. The union requested that the small-motor-assembly-reoperations department (a rework group) be placed on incentive. This group previously had been on an incentive derived from the incentive in the small-motor-assembly department, but the company had discontinued it as inequitable. The company view was that no two motors required the same amount of rework, so that the tie-in to original assembly was improper; also, the company did not consider that an incentive on its own merits could be applied to rework. The arbitrator concluded that the rework was so closely related to the regular assembly department that incentive payments could be based upon average efficiency in regular assembly, and he so ordered.

A similar pattern was present in a case [96] in which an employee classified as a burner performed all burning for five different operations. The grievance contended that the burner incentive provided inadequate yield. The arbitrator took note of the fact that the burner's actual work time was only 22.5 percent of total shift time. He further found that the company had taken this fact into account in determining that an 8-percent incentive yield was appropriate. That is, the company's rationale was that earnings of x percent above classification rate were equitable for employees with workload of y percent.

The arbitrator, stating that there was no basis for this assumption by the company, held that actual yield over time was the best test of incentive earnings. Since adequate data were not available, he proceeded to an examination of the actual standards. With this information—plus the company's tacit admission that weighting of time was proper—the arbitrator

---

[95] 7 LA 21.
[96] 28 LA 126.

made calculations of actual work time in relation to the incentive yields of each of the five operations and concluded that a 14.5-percent yield was equitable for the burner.

Problems and Principles

In another case,[97] the union requested an upward adjustment of one of the several rates on jobs under a group incentive. The arbitrator decided that, under the contract, the matter was not arbitrable. He went on to observe, however, that adjusting one rate without adjusting all other out-of-line rates in the group rate structure would not be proper. (The company here admitted the one job was underrated, but refused to adjust it without adjusting others within the group which were over-rated.)

Machining of the bores on two rings was performed in the prescribed manner, using a boring head on a vertical boring drill.[98] When completed, it was found that a taper had developed and that additional material would have to be removed because of the hardness of the steel. The company rigged a grinding head on the boring drill and the operators salvaged the parts. Paid day rates, they filed grievances demanding average incentive earnings. The company had stated that no incentive was possible because this particular grinding work was not measurable.

A main argument of the union was that the grinding constituted a change of method, and applicable contract language required the average incentive earnings in certain cases. The arbitrator found that the regularly prescribed method had been followed for the job. The trouble was that, when completed, the rings were not to specifications. The added operation of grinding thus was necessary, and there was no contract support for the payment requested.

An unusual aspect of one of the cases[99] in the preceding section was that a change was made in an incentive without there having been an initiating change in method. In a contrasting case,[100] specific contract language provided that changes

---

[97] 3 LA 353.
[98] 30 LA 316.
[99] *Supra* note 86.
[100] 42 LA 661.

in standards were to be made only upon methods change and, even then, were to be limited to those parts of the job affected by the change.

A grievance requesting that a new incentive plan be adjusted to yield the earnings opportunity provided for in the contract was rejected by the company on the ground that employees were not following prescribed working procedures,[101] thus causing delays and preventing full equipment utilization. The union argued that the operators felt it unsafe to follow prescribed procedures. The arbitrator denied the grievance since the union had not availed itself of the contractual procedures on safety matters. However, he held the case open for 60 days, directing the employees to follow operational procedures and the company to make sufficient time studies to assure compliance with the earnings opportunity commitment.

Standard Data

One case [102] is especially interesting in that the controversy developed out of what can be considered a working model of how standard data is developed and applied. (The case is also important in terms of criteria on delay allowances, discussed in Chapter X.) Company engineers made initial observations of the job in question over six complete shifts, recording and timing the elements of work performed as well as interferences with work. These studies, in accordance with the going procedure, were used to simplify and remethodize the job. Then, again following practice, the actual rate for the remethodized job was made up by selection and reconstruction of data from the original time studies; that is, the original studies were the source for standard elemental time values. (This process is often referred to as constructing the rate from standard data.)

The union claimed that the rearrangement of job elements, the simplification and remethodizing subsequent to original time studies, resulted in a situation in which interferences with work performances were not reflected in the constructed rate; consequently, a check study was requested. The arbitrator supported the request for a check study, and made these observations: "In the checking of detailed sequence and component elements

---

[101] 21 LA 755.
[102] 19 LA 856.

of a job it should not be too difficult where the job is definite and repetitive. This would be the case in most operating details in a rate set by application of 'standard data.' Determining the allowance, however, is a very different matter." The allowance mentioned would include time allowed because of interferences, as the check study would help to determine.

An issue concerning standard data came up in another case.[103] The union thought it improper to import standards from other departments. Again a quotation from the opinion is pertinent. "Such standard data must be presumed to have been based upon an accumulation of individual time studies taken upon *identical* elements in jobs throughout the factory; the controlling factor is not the type or location of the jobs upon which the standard data is based, but rather the identity of the particular *elements* of the instant jobs with those upon which the standard data was accumulated."

One contract [104] required that standard times be established by such methods as time study. The union argued that time studies necessarily involved the use of a stopwatch. The company, on the other hand, argued that it could use formulas derived from standard data where applicable. The arbitrator supported the company position, stating that the use of formulas developed from previously accumulated standards or standard-time elements, or synthesis from many previous studies, was but a variation of basic time-study procedure.

Union Right to Data

Then there is the all important question of unions' right to examine the data involved in the setting of standards. It was reported to one arbitrator [105] that the company was reluctant to have outsiders, international union staff personnel, examine data and/or make studies. Such a position was "untenable," in the opinion of the arbitrator. The fact that the parties had agreed to the institution of an incentive system forced the company to open all pertinent records to the union, he said, and automatically gave the union the right to check the validity of all standards.

[103] 29 LA 828.
[104] 9 LA 659.
[105] 37 LA 279.

Under a contract [106] granting access to an international representative of the union, when accompanied by a company industrial engineer, to investigate a time-study grievance, an issue arose over the local union president's leaving his job to accompany these people during the investigation. The arbitrator decided the contract permitted such action. Implementation of the right to time-study data was involved in another case.[107]

A board of arbitration [108] was asked by a union to direct the company to keep records so that grievances could be filed when the records indicated the company was withholding incentive pay from certain employees. The board replied that it lacked jurisdiction to issue such an order. The filing of such grievances, it said, did not have be conditioned upon the availability of company records.

A number of grievances about time-study procedures were arbitrated in the same case.[109] It was alleged that some rates had been established by studying members of supervision and others on the basis of allegedly correct times established in a laboratory. Rates so established were not a true application of time study, it was claimed, since they reflected ideal conditions rather than regular operators working under normal operating conditions. All such rates were to be disregarded, said the arbitrator. Other grievances alleged that individual time studies were made without rating the observees for speed, skill, and effort. Here, too, the arbitrator ordered such rates disregarded; rating of the operator, he said, was an "absolutely necessary concommitant of the standard."

The use of check studies to resolve disputes over standards has already been seen. It is so general a practice to restudy operations that are questioned that few controversies over the use and application of check studies are likely to reach arbitration. However, that some do reach arbitration can be illustrated,[110] including a case discussed above.[111]

[106] 48 LA 524.
[107] 49 LA 922.
[108] 47 LA 1150.
[109] 32 LA 640.
[110] 21 LA 755, 38 LA 1208.
[111] *Supra* note 102.

A case [112] in which the company cited performance of a pick-up crew as evidence that new standards provided the contract target earnings opportunity of 20 percent is of interest. One of the issues in that case developed from the company's refusal to permit staff experts of the international union to observe the jobs on which the standards were questioned and to make stopwatch check studies thereof. The pick-up crew's performance was cited as proof that such check studies were not needed.

However, the contract gave the union explicit right to bring in "any" union representative, including a nonemployee, to investigate grievances. The fact that the union had not previously done so in no way diminished the right, and the argument that a union representative would disrupt work and jeopardize trade secrets was without merit. Such was the reasoning of the arbitrator in sustaining the union position on the grievance. On the last point, he also observed that union industrial engineers would be no more disruptive than would outside consultant industrial engineers brought in by the company.

Errors

A final area for consideration concerns the problems involved when errors are found in standards. A contract clause [113] dealing with this subject provided that incentive rates should not be changed unless there had been "obvious typographical or arithmetical" errors in computation or changes in equipment or methods of production. In another situation [114] certain grinders had been allowed double setup time. They performed two different tasks, each requiring setup time when performed separately. However, because of clerical error they also had been allowed double setup time when performing both tasks simultaneously, and the company sought to discontinue this practice. The arbitrator examined the standard data upon which the rates were based and supported the company's position, holding that the clerical errors were not binding upon the company.

A standards-setting clerk, under supervision, would review applicable drawings and then apply the rate structure to the

---

[112] 41 LA 1053.
[113] 4 LA 189.
[114] 38 LA 1068.

job involved.[115] When improper applications were discovered, the company sought to correct them, and a grievance ensued. The arbitrator stated that arithmetical errors and misapplication of existing data were "clerical errors" and correctable. However, misjudgment or mistakes made by this clerk in carrying out his duties were not clerical errors which could be corrected unilaterally. The same result was reached in a situation [116] wherein the company, subsequent to a standards audit, sought to correct leveling in certain rates and a dwell-time allowance in another. Neither constituted "an error in computation," concluded the arbitrator.

Because the original incentive rates on certain operations were "too tight," the industrial engineer constructed synthetic rates and made a notation that the rates were "for Order No. 4166 only." [117] When a second order for the same products came in, the employees performed the operations believing that the synthetic rates were applicable. The arbitrator concluded that in the circumstances they were, even though the company could, if it wished, have established permanent, time-studied rates on the operations.

Error Correction

Permanent incentive standards were to remain in effect for the duration of the contract unless "conditions on the job are changed" by reason of changes in methods or the like.[118] In that case, new standards were to be established. In negotiations, the company had proposed a review of all rates but the union did not agree, although it did agree to an overall reduction in standards allowances.

It appeared that two years earlier the company had made methods changes in certain operations. It did not undertake to revise the standards, however, until after the current contract had been negotiated. The union grievance, in effect, alleged that the company could not change the standards because the original rates prevailed when the contract became effective and the union had a right to rely on them. The arbitrator con-

---

[115] 43 LA 33.
[116] 49 LA 912.
[117] 47 LA 1157.
[118] 23 LA 522.

cluded that the word "are" used in the above quotation had a different effect by itself than if it had been modified by restrictive wording (as, for example, "are hereafter"). He thereupon concluded that the company could establish new rates for the operations affected.

Under a procedure of marking rates permanent or temporary, as appropriate, the arbitrator concluded it was a correctable error when a rate had erroneously been labeled permanent.[119]

However, while recognizing that errors are generally correctable, the arbitrator in another case [120] concluded that the use of erroneous rates for some six years—except for a few instances where the correct rates were applied—coupled with evidence that supervision had clearly understood that it was applying the wrong rates operated to prevent rate correction by the company.

Incentive standards, once issued, became permanent unless revised by the company within 30 days or unless unusual cases of "gross inequities" developed within one year of initial use of the standard.[121] The rate in question was issued originally as 0.850 hours. The job was discontinued the following year, and was then reinstated three years later but at an erroneous rate of 1.328 hours. This erroneous rate continued for over two years, and it had become well known to all parties.

A grievance arose because the company corrected the error when it revised the rate to account for a minor cycle change. The arbitrator found that the clear language supported the union view that the erroneous rate could not be changed because it had become permanent. It should be noted that major changes in methods or operations were cause for revision of standards under the parties' contract, but a minor cycle change was not such a methods change as to permit complete revision of the rate in question.

A contract stated that incentive standards became permanent after 30 days and were not changeable thereafter except for methods changes or the like, "or unless an error is discovered." [122]

---

[119] 51 LA 682.
[120] 7 LA 575.
[121] 9 LA 66.
[122] 44 LA 1006.

This meant, the arbitrator stated, that errors were correctable at any time, as soon as discovered. Moreover error correction was not blocked by a new contract negotiated after the error occurred. The arbitrator's comments are of interest:

> "Perpetuation of error is not defensible on any basis. There should be no double standard regarding the correction of discovered error. There *is* a double standard built into the contract in terms of the adequacy or inadequacy of a standard.   On the latter point, it is crystal clear that the Company has only 30 days in which to effectuate a decrease in a standard resulting from a change in material, design or equipment.   It is equally clear that there is no time constraint of a similar nature on the Union or the employee for alleging the inadequacy or insufficiency of a changed standard."

Correction of errors as soon as they are discovered seems to have general support of arbitrators.[123]

A rather unusual case [124] involved a company decision to grind less stock from mill rollers, thereby extending their useful life. In conjunction with this decision, incentive standards on grinding operations were adjusted. In support of its grievance alleging failure to maintain the integrity of incentive standards, the union argued that there had been no actual reduction in the amount of stock removed and that the data from one study showed there had been an increase in work time per roll rather than a decrease.

The arbitrator accepted, as conclusive, company evidence from the standards that there should have been a discernible decrease in the amount of stock removed in grinding and, therefore, there should have been a reduction in work time per roll. Consequently, either it was not true that no actual change had taken place, or less stock was being removed prior to the change than had been reported. If the latter were the case, said the arbitrator, the aggrieved employees were not entitled to inflated earnings because of a contract provision which permitted the correction of errors in rate applications.

The cases in this section reflect a wide variety of ideas about standards and incentives. The first cases presented indicate that

---

[123] 50 LA 293, 50 LA 1086.
[124] 39 LA 9.

when the incentive concept is accepted, both the parties and arbitrators find it relatively easy to extend. The reasoning of the arbitrator in the rework case reflects this, since he considered (as had the parties at an earlier date) that incentive averages from a related department represented an equitable basis for providing incentive to rework operators. No doubt, there is an opposing view which says that this action is antithetical to incentive principles. The relational idea was accepted by both parties and the arbitrator in the burner incentive problem; it apparently required the perception of the arbitrator to determine an appropriate formula for satisfying both parties. There was, finally, the concept that group incentives require group attention in adjustment, since it is inequitable to adjust one component rate without adjusting others which are also out of line.

An important aspect of incentive administration is presented in the boring case, namely, that provision need be made for operations *added* beyond those specified in the standard. This particular situation called for payment of day rate, although the case indicated there were other circumstances which required payment at average incentive earnings. (Actually, there are added-operations situations in which actual, temporary, or some form of interim rates are applicable.)

In consonance with the above ideas is the requirement the employees follow prescribed operational procedures before claiming that rates are not equitable. Inherent in all standards and explicit in some is the specification that the work performed shall be of required quality.

A very general principle in concepts of standards and incentives is that the standards remain constant and cannot be changed except upon bona fide changes in methods or operations. Also indicated is a rather general view that standards become permanent immediately or after a stated period of time, to permit adjustments and accommodations during initial installations. Standards are standards, so to speak, so that their basis need not be restricted to data developed through time study. Standard data may be used, and its origination and meaning are discussed in the cases. (All of the copyrighted, predetermination systems utilize standard data, variously generated.) The clear right of the union to have access to and examine the data used in constructing standards is noted.

A fundamental rule in setting standards is that they are to be established by studying regular operators doing their assigned jobs at their assigned work place under normal working conditions. Rates set by observing supervisors or under ideal laboratory conditions are not proper rates. If time study is to be used, the observed operator must be effort rated at the time the study is made. Also, the general procedure is to initiate and/or permit check studies whenever a particular standard is questioned. Such check studies are useful in resolving controversy; and even if they are not, many practitioners use them as a means of satisfying employees as to the fairness of the standards.

Finally, the question of errors is considered. Generally, clerical errors are correctable when discovered. However, this may not be true of longstanding errors which should have been corrected earlier—the implication of laches. As to substantive errors, they are generally not so readily correctable as clerical errors. In fact, if the circumstances indicate that an attempted correction is truly substantive and not clearly an innocent error, arbitrators are unlikely to permit correction. The cases suggest that arbitrators will "do equity," considering all the circumstnces, when the situations permit them discretion.

CHAPTER VI

PRACTICE

The first and primary reference used by arbitrators in the resolution of grievance disputes is the collective bargaining agreement. If the facts of the dispute point clearly to one or more express provisions in the contract, the facts are interpreted against such provisions, and the matter is settled. Where search for the parties' meaning with respect to an issue in dispute is needed—whether to dispel ambiguity, fill in omissions, or otherwise—then the practice of the partes can become significant for decision (occasionally even despite clear and unambiguous contract language).

Comments by the arbitrator in one of the cases studied are pertinent: [1]

"Collective labor agreements are not negotiated in a vacuum but in a setting of past practices and prior agreements. Such an agreement has the effect of eliminating prior practices which are in conflict with the terms of the agreement but, unless the agreement specifically provides otherwise, practices consistent with the agreement remain in effect. The written words of the contract may express the entire agreement as is provided here, but practices are not necessarily matters of agreement. Practices arise from custom, usage or continued toleration by one party of action by another which is not in violation of the contract."

Reference to another report [2] indicates the effect of the so-called zipper clause on practice. Quoted therein was language from the parties' agreement stating that it (the agreement) ". . . constitutes the sole, entire, and existing agreement between the parties hereto, and supersedes all prior agreements and understandings, oral or written, express or implied, or *practices* . . ." (emphasis supplied by the arbitrator).

---

[1] 16 LA 115.
[2] 48 LA 691.

159

It should be noted that practices held by arbitrators to be binding on the parties to a contract are most often referred to as past practices, and will be so termed in the following materials because it is convenient shorthand, commonly understood. In point of accuracy, however, the practice salient to arbitral decisions is *current* practice—currently binding on the parties—which has its genesis in the past relationships of the parties.

1. DEFINITION, FUNCTION, AND INTERPRETATION

There are a number of informative references on this subject [3] and extensive comments in some of the arbitration cases, all seeking to define, describe, and delimit past practice as well as to outline and discuss applications. The consensus is that a behavior pattern is binding on the contracting parties if it is clear and unequivocal, uniform and repetitive, has existed over a reasonably long period of time, and gives evidence of mutual acceptability. It was noted [4] that uniformity need not be completely so; what is required is a "predominant pattern" of behavior so that, in fact, the dimension of predictability is introduced. Mutual acceptance is inferred from the behavior of the parties since explicit mutual acceptance would be recorded within the contract.

This last idea has had particular emphasis. While it is often overlooked in thinking about past practices, no union or group of employees can by itself establish a practice.[5] There must be, at least, knowledge and acquiescence by management. It has been stated, alternately, that "supervisory origination" [6] is not required for a work practice to become established. Hence, it is possible for management to sleep on its rights, with adverse ef-

---

[3] Aaron, *The Uses of the Past in Arbitration*, ARBITRATION TODAY 1 (1955); Mittenthal, *Past Practice and the Administration of Collective Bargaining Agreements*, ARBITRATION AND PUBLIC POLICY 30 (1961); Block, *Customs and Usages as Factors in Arbitration Decisions*, NEW YORK UNIVERSITY FIFTEENTH ANNUAL CONFERENCE ON LABOR 311 (1962); Wallen, *The Silent Contract vs. Express Provisions: The Arbitration of Local Working Conditions*, COLLECTIVE BARGAINING AND THE ARBITRATOR'S ROLE 117 (1962); McLaughlin, *Custom and Past Practice in Labor Arbitration*, 18 ARB. J. 205 (1963).

[4] Block, *Customs and Usages as Factors in Arbitration Decisions*, NEW YORK UNIVERSITY FIFTEENTH ANNUAL CONFERENCE ON LABOR 311 (1962).

[5] Steiber, *Work Rules Issue in the Basic Steel Industry*, 85 MONTHLY LAB. REV. 267 (1962).

[6] Davis, *Arbitration of Work Rules Disputes*, 16 ARB. J. 51 (1961).

fects—thereby sugesting a possible analogy to the real property concept in law, known as adverse possession.

This idea of a developing behavior pattern has been stated expressively:[7]

"From time immemorial and in practically all spheres of activity, it has been common understanding that the natural, spontaneous evolutions of habit determine not merely the bounds of reasonableness but our choice of paths when a choice is available."

In fact, this general concept of an evolving pattern (and a suggestion in another reference [8]) leads to a definitional approach which is simple, direct, and integrative with contractual terms. This takes the form of the question: Given a fact situation, what is the usual, normal, proper method of the parties for handling it? A possible utilization of this approach will be suggested shortly.

Functional Uses of Practice

Another area of general comments about past practices, variously expressed, is that the use and application of past practice is one important way by which an arbitrator responds to the will of the parties. The point appears in this commentary: [9]

"Whether the past has been peaceful or stormy, whether its disputes have been resolved informally or through grievance and arbitration machinery, the experience of the past is a factor in any present dispute involving the meaning or application of general terms. It is available to the parties and if they cannot or will not resolve their dispute, it is available to the arbitrator who has the curious role of revealing their intentions to the parties themselves."

The areas for functional use of past practices, once established, have been identified [10] as: when contract language is ambiguous; when contract language is general; when the contract is silent; [11] when contract language has been given specific meaning; and when contract language is clear and unambiguous.[12] This last function of practice is not universally accepted

[7] Platt, *The Silent Contract vs. Express Provisions: The Arbitration of Local Working Conditions,* COLLECTIVE BARGAINING AND THE ARBITRATOR'S ROLE 141 (1962).
[8] McLaughlin, *Custom and Past Practice in Labor Arbitration,* 18 ARB. J. 205 (1963).
[9] Block, *supra* note 4.
[10] McLaughlin, *supra* note 8.
[11] Wallen, *The Silent Contract vs. Express Provisions: The Arbitration of Local Working Conditions,* COLLECTIVE BARGAINING AND THE ARBITRATOR'S ROLE 117 (1962).
[12] Aaron, *The Uses of the Past in Arbitration,* ARBITRATION TODAY 1 (1955).

by arbitrators, the opposing view [13] being that clear and unambiguous language is just that, and it should govern all pertinent fact situations.

It is this last functional aspect of practice which suggests a use of the simplified definition: Given a pattern of facts, what is the usual, normal, and proper method of the parties for handling it? If the contract prescribes one procedure but the parties have consistently followed another, then the contract procedure is not usual, normal, and proper for the parties.

The contract in such an event has been, in fact, amended (and it really does not matter whether this is explained by a doctrine of legal reformation,[14] a living-document theory,[15] or otherwise). Thus, a practice is a practice—whether based on contract or otherwise.

There remains the distinction [16] between the two types of practice (indicated in the frequently cited 19 LA 237). This is the distinction between practice which is or becomes bilateral in effect and practice which is and remains unilateral in nature. Whether a particular action (or inaction) is one or the other can be judged by the circumstances. It will be practice binding on both parties to a contract (the sense of the term as used herein) if it represents the usual, normal, and proper method of the parties (not one party) for the particular action.

The probative value of the absence of past practice has functional interest. In an arbitration [17] of a grievance challenging assignment of a supervisor to work certain weekend graveyard shifts, the chairman of a tripartite board stated:

> "The Chairman, however, wishes to make it explicit and clear that his determination that the action violated the collective bargaining agreement is based upon his conclusion that there was no past practice permitting the assignment of supervisory employees to regular shifts, as opposed to the performance of work upon an emergency basis caused by equipment breakdown or failure of scheduled employees to report for work."

The dissenting arbitrator held a contrary view on this point, as follows:

---

[13] 42 LA 1025, for example.
[14] Wallen, *supra* note 11.
[15] McLaughlin, *supra* note 8.
[16] 48 LA 1192.
[17] 51 LA 1221.

"In other words, while past practice does not *control* the case, in favor of the employer, the absence of an identical practice, in no sense controls the case in favor of the union" (emphasis added by the arbitrator).

Practice in Technical Cases

An "impression" has been reported [18] that past practice is cited least frequently in cases involving incentives, job evaluation, and related matters. Possible verification exists in the relatively small number of the cases studied relevant to this chapter. However, it should be noted that only cases in which past practice is the sole or a major factor in decision appear herein, and that practice is cited or alleged in an additional number of the cases studied.

Frequency may be greater, depending upon one's interpretation of reported decisions and opinions. This is aptly illustrated by one of the cases studied,[19] in which past practice may or may not be classified as the principal issue. This case has been cited a number of times in past-practices discussions.

The issue arose over combination of two of three technician positions, by integrating equipment and combining duties, in a television station control room. There was, apparently, a single classification under which all incumbents could perform most or all of the duties within the control room. There were also, as the arbitrator found, three actual jobs or positions identifiable in the pattern of work performance. The arbitrator stated expressly that the "point of departure" for decision was the principle that "an employer has the right to decide how many men he needs to perform the work unless he is restricted by law or by collective bargaining contract." He found neither to be restrictive in this case.

The union arguments were; that there had been three contracts under which three men had manned the control room; that there had been no discussion or other indication of company intent to make the changes; that the union had taken for granted there would be no changes; and that the changes allegedly were a matter for negotiations. As the arbitrator put it, these arguments assumed the very point at issue.

---

[18] Davis, *The Uses of the Past in Arbitration,* ARBITRATION TODAY 12 (1955).
[19] 33 LA 421.

Clearly, the issue was one of management rights, so identified by the arbitrator. In accord with that analysis, the case is classified (among several categories) with those contained in Chapter II, Section 6; however, discussion of the rights aspect of the case was deferred to this point.

It can be argued that, in keeping with the first quotation in this chapter, those practices consistent with the agreement which continue, as well as (or including) the "custom, usage, or continued toleration" practices must be considered in addition to the contract. In such perspective, it can be reasoned that management, in the circumstances, had not slept on its rights and, therefore, a practice adverse to management had not been allowed to develop. This somewhat indirect, though not illogical, process places the case within past practices rulings. However, it is thought to be better classified as a decision on management rights.

The above digression into the analysis procedures used herein will also serve to illustrate the close interrelationship of past practice and the rights issue.

2. CLASSIFICATION AND ASSIGNMENT PRACTICES

Note should first be taken of an interesting observation [20] that the "content of various jobs really amounts to the set of past practices." Disputes develop when changes occur, in methods, equipment, materials, and the like.

If contractual language exists and is found by an arbitrator to be applicable, it will govern any dispute which may arise. Thus, a contract [21] provided for the continuance of past practices in the shipping and delivery departments and, as a consequence, a union grievance alleging that supervisors were improperly performing bargaining-unit work was denied by the arbitrator; such work was within the practices in the departments.

There was an established practice [22] whereby the company would slot new equipment and machinery into existing wage-rate classifications. Nevertheless, when the union challenged the slotting practice, the arbitrator concluded that a contract

<hr />

[20] Bailer, *The Uses of the Past in Arbitration*, ARBITRATION TODAY 18 (1955).
[21] 47 LA 748.
[22] 48 LA 518.

provision—establishing a duty to negotiate on wage rates when a new job was established—was controlling. In another case,[23] the contract provided that the company would make assignments to employees when regular classifications work ran out. Such assigning, said the arbitrator when a grievance challenging job elimination occurred, was not a binding practice extending the contract terms. The union argument was that the job duty still existed because of these more-or-less regular assignments which took place when a higher skilled job was completed (the higher skilled job not requiring 40 hours per week). Finally, note [24] should again be made of the so-called zipper clause, which, by its language, was an explicit rejection of past practice.

Meaning of Classification Practice

The allegation of past practice, of course, occurs most usually when the contract is not specific on a particular point. It is in situations of this type that an arbitrator is called upon to make decisions relative to a claimed practice and its binding effect.

There was an established practice [25] of having two sample clerks go aboard a ship when it arrived at the company's warehousing and storage facilities outside regular working hours. They would take initial samples of the ship's cargo and carry them back to the laboratory, where higher classification personnel would analyze the samples. This was done as a matter of quality assurance before the shipment was piped into storage facilities. Once these samples were taken, the sample clerks were idle until they took what were known as in-line samples during the course of the unloading of the ship. Since all of this involved overtime costs, the company initiated what it called a new "tanker-callout" procedure for handling the overtime situations. The revised procedure called for only one sample clerk, plus the higher classification personnel used before; it also provided that one of the higher classification personnel would assist in the initial sample taking, in order to reduce the previous idle time of sample clerks.

It is interesting to note that the grievance filed in this case

---

[23] 43 LA 353.
[24] *Supra* note 2.
[25] 44 LA 1219.

was not initiated by the sample clerk classification but by one of the higher classification personnel, seeking punitive damages. (It is interesting, also, that this was the first arbitration between the parties in 15 years). The arbitrator dealt with the claim of punitive damages, which is not important to the present circumstances. On the issue of past practice, the arbitrator ruled that this did not govern. His comments relative to this issue are interesting, in that they reflect the two kinds of practices which were discussed in Section 1:

> "It is not the age or length of time or the way it was done which necessarily controls the right (or the restriction) of management to effect changes in methods and the assignment of work but rather the managerial freedom (or lack thereof) with respect thereto.

> "The basic and primary function of management is to operate on the most efficient basis attainable, to see that unnecessary costs are eliminated and that the labor force is efficiently and productively utilized. Unless restricted by the labor agreement or by oral understandings, interpretations and/or mutual commitments of the parties which have grown up over the course of time so as to form an implied term of the contract, management cannot and should not be put in a straight jacket preventing it from exercising its basic responsibility and legitimate function to control methods of operation and to direct the work force."

In another case [26] the union had sought, in negotiations, to develop a bilateral pattern relative to changing the duties of job classifications. While this was not accomplished, it was agreed in the negotiations, that the company would not disregard past practice in changing and modifying jobs. The company made some changes in certain job classifications, unilaterally, and the grievance which followed challenged company action on the basis that it was contrary to past practice. The evidence on past practice related to a document which the company had sent to the union several years earlier, which detailed staffing arrangements on the jobs in question. The arbitrator found that this constituted the basis of agreement between the parties since it had been followed, in various contract changes and in job postings, up to the time of the grievance. He held that the document and the actions thereunder amounted to past practice, and upheld the grievance of the union.

---

[26] 44 LA 1230.

Time Considerations

One of the intriguing questions about the past-practice issue is that of time; how much time does it take before the practice has matured into something which is binding upon the parties? The answer, of course, is that there is no set time which automatically makes a past practice binding. However, the time aspect appeared in several of the cases and it is interesting to note the variety.

It proved to be 20 years in one case.[27] Finding itself overstaffed in firemen, the company eliminated one of three fireman classifications, redistributed duties, and reduced this activity by the number of firemen in the abolished classification. The arbitrator upheld the union's grievance challenging the action, pointing to the fact that the company had operated for 20 years on the basis there was a full day's work for the three classifications on each of three shifts on round-the-clock boiler-room operations. He pointed out: that during the 20 years the company had not questioned the abolished classification and had regularly filled vacancies when they occurred; that existence of the classification raised a presumption that it would be filled, although he pointed out that this classification existence was not a guarantee of work; and, finally, that there had been no change in operations or equipment.

As essential element in the decision of another arbitrator was that the company had failed to revise the description of the job at issue or reclassify the job for a period of at least three years and, possibly, for an additional five years.[28] This was in response to a grievance challenging reclassification of production schedulers to a clerical classification. There had been a gradual centralization and automation of the company's production scheduling system so that the higher classification skills were, in fact, no longer required. This case does reflect the idea of management sleeping on its rights, thereby setting up conditions for the equitable estoppel analogy.

In contrast are the views of an arbitrator that three men operating two kilns—"for approximately eight or nine years"—neither established a contractual precedent nor proved that

[27] 38 LA 799.
[28] 42 LA 1123.

three men was the proper manning.[29] The arbitrator also felt that three men working two kilns did not necessarily establish that they had been fully occupied over the years.

In a case [30] involving a special rate for small workers, it developed that five years was significant with respect to the establishment of past practice. During this five years, the company could have, because of manufacturing changes, reduced this particular small-man premium, but did not. Consequently, the arbitrator concluded that the practice had become established and it would be inappropriate to discontinue it unilaterally. For a period of 12 years, another company [31] had been following a practice of having warehouse employees move railroad cars within the warehouse area, and this was held to constitute a binding past practice when the union filed a grievance challenging the activity.

Twenty years seems to be a popular time period within the arbitration cases analyzed. In one case [32] the classification working foremen had been in contracts between the parties over a period of 20 years and, in fact, was a part of the negotiations for and included in the most recent contract between the parties. Under these circumstances, the arbitrator ruled that the company had negotiated away its management right to unilaterally eliminate this classification and was bound by the practice of the several years. Similarly, 20 years of having union employees disconnect electric meters was a well-established practice, and the arbitrator upheld the union's grievance against the company's unilateral decision to have bill collectors, not union employees, disconnect these meters.[33] On the other hand, a 20-year custom of having members of a cooperative read their own meters was a sufficiently well-established practice to have an arbitrator deny a grievance that union members were not doing this particular work.[34]

Effect of Established Job Content

Failure to revise the job description was involved in an arbi-

---

[29] 42 LA 125.
[30] 49 LA 294.
[31] 50 LA 361.
[32] 51 LA 303.
[33] 48 LA 1192.
[34] 50 LA 194.

tral decision discussed earlier.[35] Problems of practice also are involved when there are no job descriptions. For example, in upholding the union challenge to the company's unilateral changing of certain job titles, an arbitrator concluded that job titles were an integral part of the past.[36] The particular job titles involved had existed for about 15 years.

Protesting a transfer of duties from one classification to another, the union in another case argued that the absence of job descriptions meant that job classifications and the duties incidental thereto should be considered as custom or past practice.[37] Developed further the argument was that since practice was controlling, the company was not privileged to make changes. In denying the union grievance, the arbitrator made this statement:

> "Past practice in relation to any matter which normally would lie within the exclusive right of control or change by either the union on one hand or the company on the other does not become binding upon them unless the past practice is expressly fortified by agreement that it shall not be subsequently changed without mutual bargaining and agreement."

For comparison,[38] an arbitrator decided against company action of requiring personnel in a helper classification to perform what was higher classification work prior to technological changes. While there had been a considerable practice of such assignments, the arbitrator pointed out that the union had not acquiesced in the practice and had both filed grievances and protested such assignments. The company argument had been based on the fact that the issue had not been discussed during contract negotiations. Along the same line was a case [39] wherein the company had unilaterally hired a finisher trainee, relying upon past practice for the action. The arbitrator felt that such a practice needed to be clearly spelled out in order to be effective. That is, this was not the kind of practice which became binding between the parties, especially since it had to include, to be binding, union waiver of a contractual requirement to bargain about pay rates. The arbitrator commented:

---

[35] *Supra* note 28.
[36] 45 LA 923.
[37] 45 LA 557.
[38] 43 LA 651.
[39] 46 LA 1208.

"A waiver of a clause of such importance cannot be predicated upon inaction, especially since multiple reasons may exist to explain failures to grieve. No affirmative action by the Union was shown recognizing the Company's unilateral authority to set the rates of pay for a Finisher Trainee classification. Any inference to that effect is not in keeping with the history of collective bargaining."

History of Operations

A history of numerous changes in jobs, over a two-year period, with no questions raised by the union save those relating to the negotiation of wage rates, was determining in one case.[40] The arbitrator concluded that the wages section of the contract was considered by the parties to refer to negotiations about the wage rates to be paid for work in the various classifications, but not to encompass the changing of duties within the classifications. This was in response to a grievance challenging the company's right to unilaterally combine classifications and eliminate jobs during the term of the contract.

History of operations figured in another, somewhat unusual case.[41] The general structure in the plant was that higher classification jobs were on piecework, whereas the rest of the jobs known as assembly jobs, were on day work. The contract provided that piecework prices were not to be changed absent change in process. There were changes in a particular job, but the arbitrator upheld the union grievance against reclassifying it as assembly, on the basis the changes were not sufficient in the circumstances to justify the classification change. By the same token, the general plant custom did not override the specific contract requirements.

A requirement that machine operators break in new employees figured in one case.[42] The practice had been in effect for many years, so the parties by their conduct recognized this as an appropriate duty of operators. In a second case,[43] it had become "accepted practice" for toolsetters to produce parts during and after testing of the setup, until a piecework operator could be profitably assigned to the job.

---

[40] 34 LA 209.
[41] 27 LA 758.
[42] 26 LA 172.
[43] 20 LA 586.

In another situation,[44] it had been operating procedure for the supervisor to make oven heat and speed adjustments in the baking process, although oven men made the majority of adjustments. Pursuant to methods changes introducing considerable automatic equipment, one of the two oven men was removed from this work. The grievance concerned the continuation of adjustments by the supervisor. The arbitrator concluded the previous practice supported continued supervisory adjustments, noting that adjustments under the new system were limited and would require no more than a maximum of about 30 minutes per day of supervisory time.

Skilled Trades Assignments

In Chapter IV, Section 4, it was indicated that an arbitrator[45] viewed practices as particularly significant in dealing with cases involving overlapping capabilities among skilled trades. An expansion of the arbitrator's comments is appropriate:

". . . [C]learly established practices of job assignment which are based on agreement or mutual understanding, or which are characterized by acquiesence for a long enough time to justify the inference that the parties agreed to the practices and for their continuance, and practices based on accepted standards in the trades generally are entitled to great weight in a determination as to the propriety of an assignment in the skilled trades. If a clear line of demarcation is thus shown to exist between trades, it must be observed until changed by mutual consent; if a line of demarcation is not thus shown to exist, then work which falls within the scope of two or more trades may be assigned to any of the trades within whose normal and proper scope it falls."

Incidentally, a general company challenge to prior arbitration awards about assignment of skilled tradesmen was involved in this same case. The arbitrator upheld prior awards that a skilled tradesman could not be required to do work wholly different from and unrelated to the central skill of his trade and, if the company attempted such an assignment, the tradesman could refuse it and take a layoff instead. This was different from established practice with respect to unskilled employees. However, the arbitrator also ruled that, in emergencies, assignments across established trade lines could be made—an

---

[44] 32 LA 836.
[45] 30 LA 46.

emergency to be determined by the circumstances prevailing at the time of such assignment.

While the contract in another situation [46] required that consideration be given to past practice in the assignment of skilled work, the arbitrator found there had been no violation of such practice when welders were assigned to clean weld, inasmuch as the work was something done by both welders and chippers, and both were in the same craft jurisdiction. He also noted that this particular work was something welders had been doing for some time.

For a period of 25 years in a different situation painters had been allowed 10 minutes of overtime known as brush time; this was used for cleanup and putting away brushes and other equipment.[47] The practice had been instituted because there had been so much congestion, and even accidents, due to painters leaving at the same time and from the same place as other crafts. The company established field shops, near the work locations, at which painters could turn in the equipment which was issued daily to them, thereby eliminating the basis on which the practice had been established. As a consequence, the arbitrator held the unilateral discontinuance of the 25-year-old practice was appropriate.

Diverse Assignment Situations

In an overlapping-of-duties situation,[48] the arbitrator concluded that the company's removal of certain duties was consistent with its established pattern of behavior. He therefore denied the union grievance challenging removal, from bargaining-unit personnel, of the duties of witnessing and signing off certain operational tests on nuclear power plants. In another case,[49] the arbitrator found a long standing practice of assigning jobs on pipe still units without regard to the operators' classification on the basis that there was physical interchange of employees between work locations and the work classifications. As a consequence, a claim for higher rate by a lower classification employee, both classifications being in the same job family and

---

[46] 50 LA 1001.
[47] 48 LA 1239.
[48] 43 LA 364.
[49] 49 LA 445.

requiring substantially the same kind of work, was denied by the arbitrator.

Somewhat different from the rest of the cases herein, was a situation [50] in which "for years" the company had permitted various contractors to haul away its scrap products. The company discovered that the sale of waste papers could generate some income, so it set up a procedure for segregating the waste papers from other kinds of trash, installed baling machines, and proceeded to produce bales of saleable waste. The company subcontracted the work, which led to the grievance. The contract provided that, in the event that any new products were brought into the company, there would be negotiations on the jobs resulting therefrom. The company argued that its well-established practice had been to have subcontractors haul away its trash. In fact, subcontractors continued to haul away trash other than this waste paper, which was being handled by the specific subcontractor who was baling and selling it. In addition to the argument on past practice, which failed, there was considerable discussion in the case about subcontracting.

For comparison, a union challenged the company's discontinuance of a particular business activity—that of pulling wires for electrical power from company poles or from company manholes to customer terminal boxes.[51] It developed that this was something which the company had been doing for customers, on a per charge basis, for many years. The union relied mainly on past practice, claiming that, having done this activity in the past, the company was required to continue it. The arbitrator concluded that there was nothing in the contract that required continuance, and, since the company had acted in good faith and the decision had had little impact upon the bargaining unit in terms of loss of work, the company's action was appropriate. As the arbitrator stated: ". . . [A] past practice of engaging in particular activity of itself provides no contractual assurance that such activity will be continued."

The general rule that governing contract provisions take precedence over past practice in arbitral decisions receives substan-

---

[50] 49 LA 544.
[51] 43 LA 193.

tial reinforcement in several of the cases in this section. Where the contract does not clearly cover a specific dispute, arbitrators look to practice—but distinguish nonexercise of essentially unilateral rights from mutually accepted practice, which is binding on the parties. Arbitrators determine mutuality from the circumstances between the parties, interpreting whatever explicit evidence is available. Parties to a contract may or may not have slept on or waived their rights in favor of binding practice, according to arbitral judgment of the circumstances. The seemingly ubiquitous factor of time—within which a practice can be said to have matured to mutuality——is a factor in arbitrator decisions. However, the varying durations, from two to 25 years, offer no basis for generalization.

3. INTERUNIT PRACTICES

Most of the cases in this section could have been grouped with classification and assignment practices in Section 2, but are separated because they concern interunit practices.

The first case,[52] involving an arbitrability issue, was on industry and area practice. The arbitrator based his decision of nonarbitrability on the wages section of the contract and on an apparently successful presentation of past practice urged by the company. This practice was that "never before has there been an attempt made by this Union or any other to change wage rates by arbitration" in the paper industry in the northeast area. This industry practice, regionally extended, was held to be binding upon the union, and its grievance seeking wage adjustments for two classifications affected by methods changes was dismissed as nonarbitable.

Interplant Practice

A job of quantometer operator was transferred from another plant.[53] Despite the company argument that the job, having been salaried at the other plant, should be salaried at the new location, the arbitrator agreed with the union that the circumstances at the new location, including the contract, required that the job be placed within the bargaining unit. However, in a different case [54] one of the union arguments against a transfer

---

[52] 41 LA 1169.
[53] 46 LA 978.
[54] 50 LA 1165.

of work to non-bargaining-unit employees at another warehouse location (within the same city) was a contract clause proscribing the performance of bargaining unit work by "supervisory and other salaried employees. . . ." The arbitrator noted the clause had been in the contract for 18 years and never before used as a basis for such a claim. He thought this history of non-utilization was persuasive of intent, even though it was not conclusive.

The contract in another case [55] provided for changes in incentive rates (using the Bedeaux wage system) when an existing operation was substantially changed—this in the processing of cattle hides into sole leather. In considering the question of substantiality presented to him, in connection with the element of a relatively short-time transfer, the arbitrator commented that, undoubtedly, industry practice should be applied to such a question. However, since none was presented in evidence, he made a determination—special for this case—that two seconds per skin was the break point for substantiality.

A company [56] had been capping bearings on a punch press. An entirely new operation, involving a drill press equipped with a spinning head, was introduced. The dispute involved the appropriate base rate for this new operation. The arbitrator found an historical pattern of transfer of such rates from the company's Philadelphia plant and he held this practice governed the particular operation (while expressing an opinion that this rate seemed low). It is interesting to note that the parties' contract contained an explicit procedure for rate determination when a new method was introduced into the plant. Also interesting is the union's statement that it was not bound by the Philadelphia plant operations and that it did not represent the employees there.

The same pattern of practice was held to apply between plants of another company.[57] Here the union submitted a list of jobs transferred without retiming, most of which the company challenged. However the company conceded that one or more jobs had been transferred without retiming. Such concession, said the arbitrator, was inconsistent with company argu-

---

[55] 12 LA 603.
[56] 4 LA 415.
[57] 7 LA 718.

ments of job methods being different on transfer and the un-
familiarity of personnel with the work. Balancing the equities,
as he saw them, the arbitrator ruled that a binding practice
of transfer without retiming existed. (He also agreed with the
company suggestion that final disposition of the problem
should come through negotiations.)

Interdepartmental Practice

There was an argument presented by the union in a different
case [58] that work assignments had always been by function
within departments and that the company's combination of jobs
from different departments violated well-established practice.
The arbitrator agreed that this practice argument was very relevant since there had never previously been a cross-department
combination. However, the decision went against the union because of a contract clause stating that, in effect, past practice
could not be prohibitive of action taken to improve inefficient
or uneconomic operations, and the company's actions were intended for and accomplished such improvement.

Unusual Claims of Practice

A grievance [59] challenged company lease of one of its studios
to a broadcasting company which would use its own technicians. One of the bases for the arbitrator's decision against
the union was the fact that the company had previously leased
equipment and facilities to other companies.

Another union opposed company adoption of a new marketing
system having an impact on the bargaining unit.[60] Among the
the arguments advanced was a prior grievance, the settlement
terms of which were quoted in the report: " 'The company will
not call in outside workmen nor contract out work that can be
done by its own employees in the bargaining unit, except to the
extent that it is not equipped to do the work.' " The arbitrator
discussed the claim based on the grievance settlement and his
conclusions thereon.

"In the excessive liberality of an arbitration proceeding the
Arbitrator admitted an alleged mutual agreement against contracting out said to have resulted from a prior grievance settle-

[58] **42 LA 643**
[59] 51 LA 600.
[60] 51 LA 660.

ment. (Union Exhibit No. 4). The surrounding evidence was
vague and the document was unsigned. Under these circumstances the Arbitrator cannot accord any great degree of probative value to this so-called agreement which has not been written
into the labor contract. Conceding *arguendo* that such an understanding may have been reached at one time, I do not feel
that the so-called agreement could possibly have been intended
to cover the kind of situation before your present Arbitrator.
It is much more reasonable to conclude that the type of rearrangement of marketing practices here involved would not be proscribed by any such agreement even if reached under circumstances
as to which we cannot even speculate. I rule that Union Exhibit
No. 4 cannot control in the disposition of this grievance."

In general, the analysis of Secton 2 has applicability here.
However, it will be noticed that the cases hereunder do not
seem to be as solid, generally, as those in the previous section.
In particular, it is difficult to describe the practice of transferring jobs between plants without retiming as binding past practice by any of the usual standards—a fact which the arbitrator
himself recognized in designating his decision as an interim
ruling, pending negotiations by the parties.

The relationship of express contract language to interunit
practice is neatly illustrated, both ways. In the Philadelphia reference case, practice prevailed over express language, whereas
very explicit contract language prevailed over a clear practice
against interdepartmental job combination.

Contract language and prior grievance settlement will not
become the basis for binding practice when the arbitrator considers the allegations thereof to strain the usual meaning and
application beyond what the parties apparently intended. However, it should be observed that grievance settlements are frequently the genesis of binding practice.

4. WORKLOAD AND METHODS PRACTICES

The first case [61] hereunder is interesting in that contract
language and practice are mutually reinforcing. The grievance
arose because the company changed workloads and job assignments, giving notice to the union as required, and then unilaterally revised piece rates (no doubt an aggravating circum-

---

[61] 14 LA 802.

stance was a five-week delay in issuing revised rates). The union argument was that the company should negotiate on the rate changes.

The parties' contract spelled out in detail procedures on job changes and wages. The arbitrator concluded, however, that the language on wage changes accompanying workload changes was permissive and not mandatory. He found as past practice that the company had always introduced workload changes together with unilaterally initiated piece-rate changes.

Changes in Workload or Methods

The agreed-upon past practice in another situation [62] was that the rates could be adjusted up or down upon substantial change in method. However, the arbitrator found no support for a claim by the company that it could unilaterally reduce piece rates so long as it maintained the contractually guaranteed minimum. In reviewing the facts in the case before him, the arbitrator found there was no change in method and therefore concluded no reduction in rates was justified.

With the idea of saving the costs of setting standards on new products with limited sales, a company applied the standards from related products [63]. Later, when the new products exceeded the related products in sales (and production), the company set standards on all of the new products although there was little by way of methods changes. One company argument in support of this action was the past practice of rerating jobs even though methods changes were not involved. The arbitrator reviewed the evidence and concluded it did not support the company position.

Prior to World War II, tire builders themselves had trucked defective tires back to their workplace.[64] Then, to increase production during the War, a utility man had been assigned to this trucking. Upon discontinuance after the War, a grievance was filed protesting this change in practice. The arbitrator found no binding practice. He considered this to be a de minimus situation involving no more than 30 minutes work per week and no loss of earnings (and he also noted tire builders

---

[62] 12 LA 1084.
[63] 50 LA 882.
[64] 2 LA 217.

had ample time for the trucking since they habitually stopped work 15 to 45 minutes early each day).

A contract provided that, when the labor of employees was materially increased, the company would either increase wages or provide additional labor.[65] The grievance asked for increased wages due to increased workload, occasioned at least potentially by a high absentee rate (7 percent). However, a clear practice of assigning employees from other departments, when available, was established—at least two thirds of the absenteeism was covered in this manner. In view of this, the arbitrator decided against the wage increase, but only so long as the company continued its practice of assigning substitutes from other departments when available. For the company to do otherwise would be a change in operations increasing the labor of employees, thereby making applicable the contract provision mentioned above.

Employee Improvements

An interesting, well-established practice [66] dealt with employee-initiated improvements. The practice, it should be noted, stemmed from a previous arbitration in which a ruling contrary to a contract provision was specifically endorsed and was to hold until the termination of the contract. The precise ruling was that operator-introduced or -developed technical improvements could not be recaptured by the company until expiration of the agreement during which the company became aware of the improvements, unless the employee were compensated for the idea through the suggestion system.

Work Breaks

Of interest are two cases [67] involving the same parties but before different arbitrators (cases which have been noted previously). A number of actions were taken with respect to the departments concerned—remethodizing, workload and work-standards quantification, crew reduction, and regularization of lunch and rest periods. While the union resisted company actions generally, it was soon apparent that a principal attack was on the break-periods changes in terms of established practice.

---

[65] 8 LA 503.
[66] 40 LA 1106.
[67] 41 LA 1038, 42 LA 1127.

The union position also appeared in two other grievances.[68] The practice the union sought to uphold (it was not) concerned employee determination of lunch and rest periods, both as to frequency and duration. This resulted in some interesting observations and comments by the arbitrators: "It is inherent in any practice that it is not to be abused." [69] A company can remedy a practice which it has found to be abused (referring to work breaks).[70] Also: "The right to make discretionary changes in informal and imprecise practices is too basic, too vital to the survival of a plant, to be limited inferentially." [71] If the right is to be limited, then: "A unique principle should be set forth in writing in clear and unmistakeable terms." [72]

These additional comments about discretionary practices are of interest: "There are many practices which are vague, ambiguous or inconsistently applied. There are others which are the result of chance or choices of Management in its exercise of its managerial discretion as to convenience or expedient methods of operation. Discretionary practices are not ordinarily considered to be prescribed and unchanging." [73] "The significant fact is the managerial freedom to exercise its discretion in such basic matters as directing the working force so as to reduce costs and increase efficiency and enable a plant to survive in a competitive economy." [74]

Also to be noted, with respect to the formalizing of rest periods, was the caution that the ruling should not have broader application than intended.[75] That is, the company was not to establish rest periods "of unreasonably short duration," considering the welfare of employees and the nature of the work. There was no showing that this was the situation but, as the arbitrator implied, it behooved management not to let it become so.

Work Standards

Finally, should be noted a statement with respect to work

---

[68] 39 LA 1265, 51 LA 549.
[69] 41 LA 1038.
[70] 39 LA 1265, 41 LA 1038, 51 LA 549.
[71] *Supra* note 69.
[72] *Id.*
[73] *Id.*
[74] *Id.*
[75] 42 LA 1127.

standards:[76] "The failure of the Company to formalize work standards in the past is not significant as a failure of a Company or a Union to exercise a right does not destroy or waive such right." In fact, noted the arbitrator, a prohibition against such waiver was contained in specific contractual language.

The cases indicate that practice can have an effect upon workload changes initiated by management. However, concurrent methods changes are a key to arbitrator evaluation of such practice. Generally, practice does not substantially modify the general rule that management may initiate workload changes when there are methods changes.

Not all methods changes, however, result in workload changes. Employee-initiated improvements may be vouchsafed to them, for a contract period, by practice applying thereto. On the other hand, an arbitrator may deny practice despite an automatic, but small, increase in workload due to change. The several arbitral comments reflect practical views about practice related to ongoing working conditions, particularly rest periods.

5. WORK STANDARDS AND INCENTIVE PRACTICES

In the last section it was noted that failure of management to exercise its right to establish work standards did not constitute waiver of the right. Although in the context of a specific case, this was stated as a general principle. The contract in another case [77] provided that operations would be performed on an incentive basis, whenever reasonably practical. The company unilaterally changed an operation from hourly to incentive. Grieving, the union included in its arguments allegations of past practice. This was based on such criteria as previous discussions and a letter from the union to the company. The arbitrator concluded the evidence was conflicting and that there was no clear and unequivocal past practice such as to modify the explicit language of the contract.

One interesting situation,[78] mentioned in the last chapter, involved a union claim that the past practice of setting rates was by time study, so that standard data should not be used on the

---

[76] *Supra* note 69.
[77] 26 LA 3.
[78] 29 LA 828.

particular rate in question. The arbitrator said that, since there was nothing on the point in the contract, the company had the exclusive right to determine rate-setting procedure unless existence of a practice were established. However, any such past practice would no longer be binding if the basis had changed so that the practice was no longer necessary. He then reasoned that the basis—i.e., absence of standard data—had changed, eliminating the need to follow the practice of rate setting by time study.

Output Requirements

Two standards practices were found in a situation where assemblers were being required to produce more units than previously but for the same take-home pay.[79] One was an established practice that the company could expect an individual employee on incentive to produce at a rate of 125 percent. Beyond that, however, it was strictly bilateral. The other practice concerned accepted procedure that standards issued by the time-study department were either permanent or temporary. Estimated standards were always temporary, by practice, and could be converted by time study to permanent rates at any time, again as a matter of established practice.

In another case [80] the arbitrator found that the parties' practice on normal production, under a contractual definition thereof, amounted to a slow pace—in comparison with other plants. As the arbitrator stated: "I do not think we can ignore what the parties themselves have done over a period of decades."

As a result of negotiations in a different case [81] the company agreed to convert a half-automatic, half-merit rate range into a fully automatic range. The company insisted that employees achieve the same progress toward the previously established production standards as they had achieved, through time, in progress up the rate range. Essentially, the union argued that such measurement (of production) ceased with the change to automatic rate progression. Since the standards had been applied for years, said the arbitrator, their abandonment required much

---

[79] 17 LA 293.
[80] 33 LA 725.
[81] 50 LA 136.

more explicit evidence than the negotiated change in wage administration.

Perhaps the circumstances of an arbitral ruling that a company had improperly disciplined an employee should be compared.[82] The arbitrator found the employee had reached 85 percent of standard after 10 weeks, compared with the 40 weeks' experience of the employees who made the standards. He also found a record of several years of effective progress with the company. The practice here, of course, is personal—the several years of successful service. (This was not directly part of the arbitrator's reasoning in the case.)

Formula Requirements

There were two cases in which standards were expressed in charts. In one,[83] a chart showing the operating speed of specified slotting machines had been posted for a period of eight years. Employees were not to operate at lower speeds without permission; apparently none of the machines had been operated above chart speeds during the period. Management ordered above-chart speeds for certain machines and a grievance followed. The arbitrator concluded the chart had become standard, on the basis of long-established practice.

The other chart involved grinding.[84] Some time previously, a change had been made from three- to five-machine assignments. Time studies were made for the five-machine operations and a chart prepared showing rates at various speeds, including 110 feet per minute, to yield 130 percent earnings. At the time of the change, speeds were set at 94 feet per minute and the machines ran at this speed continuously for an extended period. More than six years and two contracts later, management ordered speeds increased to 110 feet per minute. A grievance was filed asking for a new rate—which the company said was already on the chart. On the company argument, the arbitrator said the chart did not preclude the grievance; this was the first time speeds had been set at 110 feet per minute and therefore the first opportunity the union had had to challenge the rate at this speed. Clearly, this chart was not a standard for the higher speed.

[82] 51 LA 1280.
[83] 13 LA 220.
[84] 28 LA 259.

The foundry scrap plan case,[85] discussed at the beginning of this chapter, involved a union argument that the plan, unmentioned in the last contract, was automatically eliminated because of a statement that the contract expressed "the entire agreement between the parties." Not so, said the arbitrator, whose reasoning, stressing the importance of past practice, is quoted above. He considered a contract requirement of quality work (which endorses the scrap plan idea) and the absence of any contract provision precluding the plan or any evidence that the plan was onerous, then denied the grievance challenging the application of the plan.

A contract [86] provided incentive participation for those hourly rated employees working in incentive departments who fed materials "directly" to incentive employees. The reasoning was that the work of such employees had a definite bearing on the performance of incentive workers. The issue in arbitration concerned the meaning and application of "directly"; the arbitrator's decision was based specifically on the prior practice of the parties as worked out through a number of grievances.

Rate Applications

In the mid-1930s, a piece-rate differential allowance was established because of difficulties in sewing furniture upholstering materials with rubberized backing.[87] This differential continued until a general rate audit in 1950, although the difficulty had been removed several years earlier by the introduction of a new sewing machine. In arguing the grievance, the union claimed practice had developed from the company's having slept on its rights for a number of years. The arbitrator disagreed, saying that the basis for the differential having ceased to exist, the company could cancel it—and he thought it was not material whether done immediately or later on. If this were not appropriate, it was suggested that erroneous rates detrimental to employees could mature into practice through absence of timely challenge.

In a claim [88] that downtime was not being paid properly—at average earned rate—the arbitrator said the union position was

---

[85] *Supra* note 1.
[86] 45 LA 955.
[87] 17 LA 391.
[88] 33 LA 29.

essentially one of past practice. For such to be determinative, its existence had to be proven and it had to be established that both parties were aware of and lived with the practice—"thereby giving their tacit blessing to it." Since these conditions were not fulfilled, the claim had to be decided according to contract standards.

In comparison with the two preceding cases is a situation [89] wherein certain rates were applied erroneously for five or six years; management was aware of the misapplications and permitted them to continue. In such circumstances, clear practice had developed—so that the arbitrator thought the erroneous rates had become "an unquestioned part of the actual wage structure in effect."

Revised past practices with respect to incentive compensation were to continue for the agreement's duration—such was the contract provision brought to bear in a case where the company added an operation to a new machine and retimed it.[90] The arbitrator ruled that the language did not preclude the improvements nor the setting of a new rate. It did, however, require that the effort-earnings relationship from the old job be the same for this job, and the arbitrator outlined a computational plan for accomplishing this.

The final case [91] to be considered was concerned with a new Air Arc process of welding. Employees on this job during the two-and-a-half-year experimental period were paid average past earnings. The company decided the job had progressed sufficiently to become a regular production item, and established a regular incentive for it. The union protested, on the grounds that average earnings had been paid for so long that a protected past practice had evolved.

The arbitrator reviewed the subject of past practice in considerable detail, with references to cases and other source materials. He found the two-and-a-half-year experimental period had not resulted in the establishment of a practice, concluding his analysis of the case as follows:

"It is clear that the parties contemplated the trying out of

---

[89] 7 LA 575.
[90] 22 LA 450.
[91] 42 LA 965.

new processes and experimentation. Likewise, the inherent prob-
abilities of the situation negate any agreement by the Company
that in situations like the present, the mere passing of a period
of time would of itself be sufficient to establish a protected past
practice."

This section illustrates the broad generalization that arbitrators do differentiate, at least in standards and incentive cases, between management-oriented situations involving the efficiency
of the business and employee-oriented situations involving employee welfare (with respect to standards and incentives).

Thus, the cases on changing to incentives, use of standard data
in standards, the automatic rate range-production standards
equivalency issue, the foundry scrap plan, and the Air Arc cases
reflect, in their conclusions, the efficiency concerns of management. The long-term differential sewing allowance may be considered of the same nature; however, it appears likely that the
long delay changes the perspective to one of employee interest.

In other words, this differential allowance case could well have
lined up with: the erroneously applied rates which grew into
the regular rate structure; past practice governing incentive coverage for support personnel; the effort-earnings relationship situation; and the two chart cases to reflect the well-being of
employees.

Atypical illustrations are to be expected, examples being the
two standards practices found in one case and the normalized
slow-pace situation.

CHAPTER VII

METHODS AND PROCESSES

When the manner in which a product (or a component thereof) is produced undergoes revision, the revision is usually referred to as a change in method. Another frequently used term is change in process.

To be accurate a component material itself may undergo change, thereby bringing on the kind of revision commonly referred to as a methods change; the same is true when the end product is redesigned. In fact, the manner of production may be completely the same, but faster (as with increased machine feed, for example). Whether the resultant qualifies as methods change is the opinion of the parties to a contract and/or an arbitrator.

This roundabout description emphasizes the fact that there is some imprecision in the designation of methods—at least in contracts and/or by arbitrators. This is due partly to a tendency by the parties (and industrial engineers as well) to use terms interchangeably, particularly methods, processes, and operations. More importantly, it is also attributable to the desires of the parties to a contract to either broaden or narrow the construction of methods, changes in which might meaningfully affect their relationships.

Some terms from the cases which are used to designate bases for effective action under the contracts are good examples. References appear to changes in methods, conditions, equipment, process, operations, duties, requirements, design, materials, machines, tools, mechanical improvements. This is not necessarily an exhaustive list, since the cases are to be reviewed in this chapter.

In one case [1] the union urged that the governing contract language be restricted to "major" changes or only to "changes in equipment or machinery." In response to this, the arbitrator commented:

> "The term 'changes in operations' is by hypothesis a broader and more flexible term than 'changes in equipment' and/or 'changes in machinery'. It must be held to include these but need not be limited to them. In the absence of a restrictive qualification, I see no reason why a change in operation cannot embrace what has been done here, namely a reshuffling of duties in the interest of a more efficient operation. Nor is there any basis for writing the qualifying word 'major' into the contract."

The circumstances in another case evoked these comments: [2]

> "The Arbitrator sees no valid basis here for upholding the Union's contention that the Welder's job, and the three jobs in the Flow-Coat Building, are new jobs *simply because the work done by the employees in these instances is not exactly like the work done prior to changed production methods, or like the work done elsewhere in the plant under the same job classification and title.* Though it is obvious that each of the jobs has changed somewhat, all are substantially like the originals in general duties and responsibilities. Although moving the workman into a new building in which revised production methods are used, separating him physically from other employees in the same classification, may raise the presumption that sufficient change has taken place to establish a new job, *such does not follow automatically.* Likewise, when a new machine is installed and an employee is assigned to its somewhat more complicated or more responsible operation, *it does not follow automatically that a new job has been created."* (Emphasis added by the arbitrator).

One report may possibly reflect the ultimate effort by a company to establish a prescribed method, so that deviations could be identified.[3] The report indicated arbitration of two issues, in both of which the company exhibited an operation analysis. The operation analysis (which is good engineering procedure) documented the sequential steps in the method for manufacture of the item involved and, in one of the issues at least, contained a detailed diagram of the method to be followed. This latter document also carried a legend: "No deviations from this method unless new time study is made."

---

[1] 40 LA 700.
[2] 31 LA 111.
[3] 18 LA 459.

Significance of Methods Changes

It is important to realize that while the question of methods change can be and sometimes is the principal issue in an arbitration, it is not merely this question which is involved. Except for individual reaction and resistance to change simply because of the fact of change, method change of itself would probably cause no labor relations problems. However, problems derivative from methods changes are common—in wages, classifications, workloads, crew size, and incentive requirements.

In the most usual arrangement, these various factors in the work relationship are considered stabilized within the explicit terms of the contract. That is, they are not to be changed except upon or pursuant to changes in method (as this phenomenon is variously described). Thus, methods changes are conditions precedent to the effectuation of changes in the vital wages and wage-related aspects of the collective-bargaining agreement.

The proposition, as stated above, that there will be no changes in wages (individual rates rather than the general level of wages) or in the areas closely related to wages except for and pursuant to changes in methods is the general rule in labor-management relations. Like all rules, it has its exceptions. However, this general rule is the practical embodiment of the balancing of interests, the need for which is reflected in Chapters II and III. In seeking to strike such balance when methods changes are involved, arbitrators look to contractual provisions and practices of the parties—plus other appropriate criteria.

It is the natural, logical presumption that management initiates changes in methods for reasons of efficiency, cost reduction, "a fair day's work," and so forth. This general idea of improvement seems to be borne out in the cases (again logically so, since methods changes involve capital investments and/or expense outlays).

However, one of the arguments advanced in opposition to a company-initiated change [4]—which involved replacing female operators with male operators—was that the male operators were actually less efficient. This was a fact, but management be-

---

[4] 7 LA 691.

lieved greater efficiency would result in time. In sustaining management's right to make the change, the arbitrator stated:

> "It is an exclusive prerogative of management to devise new methods and employ different techniques in the operation of the plant and while it, of course, hopes that greater efficiency and lower unit costs will result, the company is under no obligation to insure or guarantee that this result will follow, nor is it under any obligation necessary to revert to the previous work practice, although it is free to do so if it so elects."

The different sections hereunder reflect some of the variety of activities within industrial engineering relating to the generalized question of methods changes. The section titles were suggested by the discussion of stages of industrial engineering set forth in *Methods Engineering*,[5] although the particular listings used do not appear in such form in the reference. The title of Processes, for Section 6, has the particularized meaning of continuous-flow operations generally represented by the cases in that section.

1. EQUIPMENT

Was the old drive shaft suspended from the ceiling, disconnected and unused, machinery or scrap? [6] That was the essential question posed to an arbitrator in a grievance over which of two local unions—the one representing machine workers or the one representing millwrights—should have the job of removing the shaft. The parent lodge for both of the locals insisted this was a work-assignment dispute, requiring internal-disputes procedures, not a jurisdictional dispute. An interesting facet of the case (the shaft was not machinery) was the rather extensive review of legal opinions and some arbitration reports to determine what machinery is.

In another case [7] the contract provided that rates were not to be changed "except for a change of equipment or a process." The company had made broad changes in its product lines, necessitating the introduction of new machines, combinations of machines, and similar moves. Based on the changes the company felt that the prior system of allowances based on actual downtime had to be replaced by predetermined downtime al-

[5] E. KRICK, METHODS ENGINEERING (1962).
[6] 47 LA 414.
[7] 41 LA 721.

lowance based on calculation of average experience. The arbitrator stated that the company was confusing changes affecting operations, which could be accomplished under contract provisions thereon, and changes in the administration of the wage system. The contract provisions on methods changes did not extend to the wage system.

Combination of Machines

The result of a change in layout was a two-machine assignment to one employee, whereas the prior assignment had been one man to one machine. [8] One argument on the grievance was there had been no change in the physical structure of the machine nor in the manner in which it operated. The arbitrator thought the governing clause was not restricted to changes in machines, ". . . and I take the fair meaning of the term 'changes in equipment' to include changes in layout, location or tempo as well as changes in the physical structure of machines."

Unilateral assignment of one tool grinder to simultaneous operation of two grinding machines was endorsed by an arbitrator as an application of the management-rights clause of the contract.[9] It was determined that safety devices were on the machines, no additional safety hazard arose through the combination assignment, and the extra machine did not create an undue workload for the operator.

A methods change involved relocating a machine close by another, placing a conveyor between them, and assigning both machines (performing successive operations) to one operator.[10]

The issue here was the combination of two jobs, which the arbitrator viewed as the exemplification of a fundamental change. He went on, however, to point out that the right to make combinations was not unrestricted. The union could challenge combinations involving widely diverse skills or imposing undue physical burdens, and slotting of the combined job if unfair. Summarizing, he thought combinations could be attacked as unfair in themselves or as being attended by unfair

---

[8] 18 LA 612.
[9] 49 LA 487.
[10] 10 LA 94.

conditions or unfair pay; however, the power of the company to effect fair combinations could not be denied.

Another case [11] involved the elimination of the operator. Such occurred with respect to the operators of certain threader machines subsequent to the installation of automatic controls. The arbitrator upheld the company action under the circumstances.

Major and Minor Equipment Changes

Under steel-type provisions, incentives are either to be revised (replaced) or adjusted, depending upon circumstances. Under a contract with these provisions the arbitrator concluded that charging operations, though simplified and made more efficient, were not so changed by the addition of a new third crane as to require revision; this was the sort of change which would only require adjustment.[12] In another grievance in the same arbitration, the change involved physical enlargement yielding a greater heat capacity for an open hearth. The arbitrator concluded the change here was unmistakably of such nature as to require overall revision of the incentive.

Another of the steel types [13] presents an interesting aspect of methods change. The job at issue was known as "No. 4 Drawbench," and was a two-man operation for stretching alloy tubes to produce uniform wall thickness and inside diameter. In this operation a bar is inserted into a tube; the unit is then drawn through a die. Afterwards, the two men lift the tube with bar to another bench where a reeler loosens the bar and it is removed.

The original reeler was replaced by a new one which operated much faster, decreasing the reeling time. The company made studies and presented a revised incentive to the union— to initiate the trial period thereon. Since the union did not respond, the company initiated a grievance which came to arbitration. The union argued there had been no change in method to justify a change in the incentive plan; all duties previously performed were still being performed.

The arbitrator recited the contract specification for incentive changes as being changes in "job duties or requirements," not-

---

[11] 49 LA 874.
[12] 26 LA 812.
[13] 28 LA 129.

ing the apparent union view that the two were synonymous. The arbitrator stated "requirement" had a broader meaning, referring to a dictionary meaning of "an essential condition." He thought the essential condition of the job had changed even though job duties had not.

The somewhat unusual circumstances [14] of the removal of a long-existing allowance were discussed in the last chapter. The allowance originally had been established because of difficulties in sewing materials with rubberized backing on chain-stitch machines. A substantial reason for the arbitrator's decision was the fact that these machines had been replaced by lock-stitch machines which eliminated the difficulties in sewing rubberized fabrics.

Finally, the methodizing in another case [15] should be noted. The company undertook a major re-engineering of the manufacture of box springs, involving: a motorized conveyor line; air-powered stapling equipment; breaking down large-group operations into a series of two-man stations; and use of a single line to produce all types of springs. Despite the extent of the methods changes they were not disputed nor, interestingly enough, were the extensive time studies which were taken; the real issue was pace, which is discussed in Chapter X.

Major rearrangements, particularly when major equipment changes are also present, present few difficulties to the parties, as the case above illustrates, or to an arbitrator, as demonstrated by the case of the open-hearth rebuilding. Plant rearrangements not involving new equipment may be questioned by unions, but arbitrators endorse such layout "methods changes" if not prohibited by the contract. Other equipment changes described above indicate that the impact on relationships is the critical feature, not the change itself. Company misunderstanding of impact is seen in the attempt to extend methods changes into wage administration. Finally, it is worth recalling the reeler situation, since it represents the knotty problem of replacing equipment with improved equipment performing the same

---

[14] 17 LA 391.
[15] 33 LA 725.

function. The question raised, about this being a change in method, will be seen again.

2. ASSEMBLY

Concern over low production or high production costs, or both, usually stimulate management interest in changes for improvement. It was so for an assembly line manufacturing power lawnmowers.[16] After time studies and line balance, and communication with employees, the new and balanced assembly procedures were initiated with 15 men on this line instead of the previous 19. The issue of disciplining employees for not meeting the new standards went to arbitration, and the company's actions were supported as consistent with the contract.

Fiber shipping drums were built on another assembly-line operation, involving 20 men paid on group incentive.[17] The company had introduced four machines, which performed two operations previously done on the line, to replace the one machine formerly used. The crew was increased to 28 men and production potential increased substantially. Since the contract provided for changes in method, the only argument was that the new rates were too tight. The contract, with a union agreement to cooperate fully in methods improvements, called for rates in line with others in the plant. The arbitrator, following assessments by technical experts (of U. S. Conciliation Service), concluded employees could meet the rates "with normal effort."

Changes in Assembly Operations

In another situation [18] the company changed the assembly of small ventilating units from floor and bench type to line assembly. The action followed product design changes which permitted standardization of parts and, therefore, station-by-station operations along the line. Again it was not the changes which were at issue, but rather the proper evaluation of the line-assembler job under the negotiated evaluation plan. Challenged were factors of education and experience. After testimony and inspection of the line and comparable assembly lines in the plant, the arbitrator upheld the original evaluation.

---

[16] 50 LA 888.
[17] 6 LA 218.
[18] 30 LA 423.

With the introduction of a new starter, a company changed from continuous assembly with one combination classification to what were described as production "islands," at each of which the component jobs of assembly, testing, and packing were performed.[19] The union protested the change, primarily because the tester rate was lower than the other two. In the circumstances, company action was upheld.

In another case [20] there had been a stationary work station where welders burned an opening for a side door and installed a tube brace—from which the unit went on to the assembly line. Manufacturing procedures were changed so that this activity was integrated into the moving production line. Grievance alleged retiming of the job was contrary to the contract. The arbitrator upheld the change on the basis that jobs could be retimed when there were changes in methods of manufacture. He also pointed to minor changes in the door-burning and tube-bracer functions.

A case [21] to be compared with the reeler case of Section 1 involved the assembly/manufacture of voice coils for radios, record players, and television. Considerable skill was required to wind these coils, develop a "feel" for correct tension on the windings, and, generally, finish operations with usable voice coil assemblies. Not all employees could be trained for the job. The company was finally able to automate this activity, which considerably reduced skill requirements and increased production eightfold. When the company established a labor grade for the automated job, the union grievance was that this was not a new job.

Changes in Assembly Jobs

The arbitrator noted that the company had a right to establish new production methods under the contract. He also observed that the contract had an established classification for this work and a negotiated rate. The same product was being produced as before; this product had continued to be produced by the same classification; the grievance was sustained.

At the end of the line, in food-canning operations, there was a job of labeller operator and stack-off man, with a combina-

---

[19] 46 LA 39.
[20] 4 LA 399.
[21] 35 LA 662.

tion of duties.[22] As a result of changes in the food processing, the cans could be cooled much faster (before coming to this last position). The company sought greater efficiency by removing duties of marking and stacking cartons from this particular job, and assigning them to another classification. The reevaluation of the resulting labeller-operator job led to a grievance.

The contract provided there would be no change in a job classification unless the operation were changed or new equipment were installed. The arbitrator concluded the removed duties, although comprising the lesser functions (in terms of skill and other evaluation factors) of the previous combination job, did constitute a change in operations.

The use in another case of small assembly parts by assemblers of a Bockel portable electric oven for in-process drying was challenged as being a part of heater-treater work.[23] The arbitrator denied the union claim.

A change in the job known as packaging two-fender assemblies, from a two- to a one-man operation, constituted a change in method under the contract provision restricting piece-rate changes to those resulting from methods change.[24] However, the arbitrator concluded the previously established temporary rate had become permanent under a contract provision thereon.

The practice [25] (in a case discussed in Chapter VI, Section 2) was to have higher classification jobs on piecework, all the rest of the jobs in the plant being assembly on a day-work basis. The job in question was the handling of leads within electric motors. These leads had been taped, on a piecework basis; however, a redesign of the motor permitted the use of fiber clips to fasten these leads and this, in the company view, was in the historic category of assembly.

The interesting aspect of this case was the contract provision that piecework prices would not be changed except upon "change in process," and if so, to a revised piece rate. The com-

---

[22] 33 LA 296.
[23] 50 LA 1048.
[24] 2 LA 469.
[25] 27 LA 758.

pany attempted, unsuccessfully, to demonstrate that the lead-fastening change was a change in method subject to managerial prerogative rather than a change in process.

These cases on assembly-type operations indicate that, generally, clearly recognizable changes in methods are not challenged, although the impact of such may lead to dispute over incentive rates or over evaluated base rates. That is not universally so, however, as is seen in the door-burning case, where it was claimed no methods change had occurred. The last case illustrates the relative interchangeability of terminology—the company distinction between "change in process" and "change in method" did not receive arbitral approval.

3. METAL FORMING

The craneman in a cast house raised and lowered crucibles of molten metal into position for pouring.[26] He was helped by another man using a long handle to guide and tip crucibles in pouring. A second hoist was attached which permitted the craneman to pour unaided. The company conceded there had been some change, but not sufficient to justify a classification change. The arbitrator ruled that there had been a major change in the job, affecting skill and responsibility.

In view of this conclusion, a second issue in the same arbitration is particularly interesting. This concerned a group job of "pot ramming," the hot and dirty work of spreading a carbon paint lining on the inside of pots to reduce molten metal stickage. The company built a large rammer on a frame large enough to fit over a pot, which substantially reduced but did not eliminate hand ramming. The union grievance asked for a new classification; the company argued (as had the union in the reeler case, Section 1) that it had merely replaced one tool by another. The arbitrator ruled that the union could not ask for a new classification under the contract, since decision in such matters was in the company, and dismissed the grievance. The union's recourse was to challenge the rate on the job, which could be accomplished by a grievance to that effect.

---

[26] 33 LA 385.

Crew Changes

The issue in another case [27] arose from substantial changes in the manufacture of iron castings. As a result, the crew was reduced and new incentives installed. The challenge was on the basis that only modification of existing incentives, as opposed to new incentives, was appropriate. The arbitrator concluded that whether the job were changed or new depended upon how the contract term "job" was interpreted. He found "job" to have two meanings under the contract—work performed at a work station and work performed by an individual operator. He concluded the second meaning applicable to the methods changes here, and decided that the previous incentive should have been modified only, not completely replaced.

Crew reduction was also the issue when the job of cleaning ingot moulds, by mould-dipping laborers, underwent methods change.[28] The arbitrator reviewed the changes and concluded they justified the crew reduction.

Job Changes

When, in rolling mill operations, the installation of new master controls eliminated a motor tender classification, a grievance ensued.[29] The arbitrator ruled that neither the classification system nor the contract provisions prevented realignment of jobs based upon genuine changes in operating conditions. For comparison was an arbitral decision against splitting an existing job of setup and operate (die-cast machine) into two component jobs of setup and operate.[30]

> "It seems clear that it never was intended that mere rearrangement of duties to accommodate shift or trainee problems was contemplated by the parties, and of course, mere labels on jobs would have no significance. The intention was not to fetter the Company when it comes to technological and production improvements, but that test is not met by the facts here, because the older men affected are functioning virtually the same as heretofore and their duties are not materially altered, nor have there been significant technological or production changes."

The right of a company to establish production quotas and

---

[27] 28 LA 144.
[28] 46 LA 733.
[29] 30 LA 1014.
[30] 24 LA 713.

piece rates was conceded by the union in another case.[31] Therefore, the only question in arbitration was one of reasonableness. The arbitrator concluded that the increased quotas set
were unreasonable, since there had been no methods changes
over the preceding two years which had not been reflected in
revised standards.

The company in a different case added 19 more driers to
core making (sand cores for castings), claimed this was a job
change, since it facilitated drying, and reduced the piece rate
by estimation.[32] In the course of discussing the resulting grievance, the company made a time study which resulted in further
reduction of the piece rate. There being no directly governing
contract clause, the arbitrator found the prevailing practice allowed rate changes only pursuant to methods changes. Concluding there were no methods changes, he decided the reduction
of rates was unwarranted. His opinion was that the only as-
certainable advantage of the additional driers was in making
possible longer runs, but there was no assurance of such longer
runs; also, it had not been proven that rates were set to vary
with size of the run. (An earlier grievance concerning the addition of 5 core driers, plus a change from wooden to aluminum
core boxes, for which rates had changed, had been introduced
as pertinent to the case. The arbitrator said there was no evidence of how much this particular rate change was influenced
by the aluminum boxes.)

Impact of Changes

Two aspects of another case [33] are worth noting. One is the
contract provision that standards had to be increased or decreased when accumulated changes in work content amounted
to 10 percent or more. The other is the quotation from the
opinion:

> "A plant wage incentive system cannot be administered in a purely
> mechanical manner. The Company and the Union both must give
> consideration to the employee's attitudes and feelings involved. The
> way people *feel* about their jobs, work loads, and pay is just as im-
> portant as the objective conditions of work determined by a system
> of engineering logics."

---

[31] 14 LA 638.
[32] 12 LA 1084.
[33] 42 LA 661.

Also noteworthy are the circumstances in which the number of operators was reduced and a new helper classification initiated (there were methods changes and a relocation to another plant).[34] The company conceded the helper was working 50 percent of his time on babbitting, work previously done by the eliminated crew member. The union alleged the helper was spending 75 to 80 percent of his time on babbitting. Conclusion of the arbitrator was that a savings of one quarter to one half of a job was substantial.

Finally, there is a case [35] in which it was decided that a rate could be changed even though there had been no substantial change in method. The rates in question were "bargained" before time study became practice in the plant. The company changed rates on certain of these jobs. The union argued that rates should not be changed except when the jobs actually changed. The arbitrator noted the requirement that rates were to be set by "sound time study methods." Finding nothing in the contract to prohibit it, the company action was upheld. (No doubt, a grievance testing whether or not such rates had been set by sound time-study methods would be appropriate, as would be allegations of erroneous applications thereof.)

The cases in this section indicate again that it is often not the methods change itself, but its impact which is important. The reeler-type problem reappears. (It is interesting to compare the interpretation of contract language, to "do equity," in the reeler case (Section 1) with the interpretation of language here.)

Finally, it will be seen that a number of the cases hereunder go directly to the meaning and substantiality of the alleged change in method. The change attempted in the die cast job was not within the meaning of methods change; the setting of quotas was not based upon methods changes (except those already reflected in standards changes); and more driers for core making did not represent methods change. To the contrary, the motor-tender case was based upon methods change;

---

[34] 34 LA 365.
[35] 14 LA 490.

savings of one quarter to one half of a job were substantial; and 10 percent or more change in work content required rate changes.

4. METAL WORKING

In Chapter V, Section 6, reference was made to a case [36] involving the boring of rings which, after the operations had been completed, were not to specifications. A taper had developed during the machining due to the hardness of the steel. The argument there was whether or not the required added operation constituted a methods change; the arbitrator thought not.

In another materials case,[37] the contract provided that standards were to remain unchanged unless there were a change in "operation, methods, materials, equipment, quality." Under this language, the arbitrator held that a change from hard steel to leaded, free machining steel would constitute methods change, as to both material and quality. The fact that machining would be accelerated was undisputed, said the arbitrator, the sole question thus was how such acceleration was to be computed in revising standards.

Changes in Machining Operations

A change in the method of machining a wheel, involving a change to a new turret lathe, was a change in method permitting retiming.[38] Here, however, as was discussed in Chapter VI, past practices on incentive compensation required that the new rate be modified so as to maintain the same effort-earnings relationship as existed previously.

There were three component operations, with set piece rates, in an established job known as "drill and ream bolt holes." [39] The rates included estimated time for tool changes, which often proved inadequate, and additional tool time had to be allowed. This was unsatisfactory to the company, so it divided the single job into three jobs—the exact components of the single job—and established piece rates for tool changing for each of the three jobs. Under a contract allowing changes in rates only upon substantial change (e.g., in method or tools),

---

[36] 30 LA 316.
[37] 32 LA 640.
[38] 22 LA 450.
[39] 13 LA 414.

the arbitrator upheld the union grievance on the basis the company action was merely a paper transaction.

The contract in a different case permitted no rate changes unless there were a "major change in the operation of the job . . ." [40] The union reasoned that removal of the work of straightening (58 percent of cycle time) was not a change in the established job of bending and straightening. The arbitrator thought it was.

In another case the union claimed that a crossbar added to the die on a foot-operated press was a safety measure, and therefore the rate on the machine was not susceptible to restudy under the contract clause on methods change.[41] The company said its function was that of a tripper head, which made the job easier and faster because stock could be more readily freed by the operator. The arbitration board upheld the company position. The "most persuasive factor" was production figures indicating an immediate increase of more than 20 percent in hourly production, and increasing.

An interesting case [42] illustrates a practical problem with tool wear over time. Involved was the replacement of a low-pressure injection die—for which the product inspection standard had increased (more allowed time) by more than 100 percent from the original standard. With the new die, a new standard, a little more than 60 percent of the former, was set on inspection. The arbitrator concluded that "newness" and "probable improvements in . . . design" of the replacement die, requiring less inspection of parts produced by it, constituted methods change in this instance.

In another situation a certain color-removal operation in ring polishing was no longer required.[43] The arbitrator commented that removal from the rates of the time for this operation was proper. However, the company had completely revised rates, which was not proper under the contract.

Product Design Change

Another company had had field complaints about an idler with a forged steel hub having rim and side disks welded to

---

[40] 9 LA 659.
[41] 11 LA 432.
[42] 9 LA 66.
[43] 50 LA 882.

it, so it was redesigned in a single piece of cast steel.[44] The particular duties of the grievant—who performed operations of drill, countersink, and tap on six holes in the hub—were unchanged by the changeover to a new product design. However, the rate was changed by the company (apparently there was a reduction) which resulted in the grievance.

Under the contract, rates were not to be changed except for substantial change in method, machine, "or design of an operation." The union argued the change here was in product design, not operation design, and therefore the rate was not to be changed. The arbitrator said the quoted language referred to a change in operation on a part, not to changes in the part itself. There was a new part here, said the arbitrator, so that the methods clause was not applicable. "The grievant is performing the identical job on a new part." The grievance was denied. (Not discussed in the case was the possible effect on the grievant's job of the change from forged to cast steel.)

Changes in Job Requirements

A contract provided for rate changes pursuant to methods changes.[45] It also provided: "Increasing the speed and feed gears alone to increase the output" will not be a basis for rate changes except with prior notice to the union. The argument was that this required bilateral determination, throughout the whole procedure of rate setting, when speed and/or feed changes were involved. The arbitrator ruled that a joint meeting was necessary only for the purpose of deciding upon a rerate.

Another contract provided that, if new classifications were necessary or the work in a classification had changed materially, the rate of pay was to be negotiated.[46] Based on this, an arbitrator upheld the company's unilateral change of engine lathe and borematics from single- to dual-machine assignments.

"Contract provision specifically contemplates changes in job classification, and does not limit employer's right to make either qualitative changes in job content or changes in quantity of work performed where, as here, change is not made arbitrarily or capriciously, but is

---

[44] 16 LA 331.
[45] 16 LA 770.
[46] 34 LA 827.

reasonable and made for sufficient cause, and change does not result in excessive workload."

Employee-Initiated Changes

There is a series of cases in this section dealing with employee-initiated changes in method. One of them [47] (discussed in Chapter VI) held, on the basis of past practice, that the benefits of employee-initiated changes were vouchsafed to them for the duration of the contract unless "purchased" through the suggestion system. The same arbitrator, in a situation where there was not the element of practice present,[48] ruled that employees were to be credited for their own improvements. If the company wished to use them, it had to purchase them from the employees. Payment was subject to the parties' agreement, and could take such forms as suggestion awards or percentages of savings.

Another case,[49] noted in Chapter V, dealt with a company commitment not to change standards when an employee operated certain equipment at higher speeds or feeds with company approval. The arbitrator concluded that the commitment extended to new machines of the same type as listed in the contract clause. Also to be noted, in a different case there was a supplemental agreement wherein a company agreed not to take, from time-study standards, any time saved entirely by the operator's effort.[50]

There was a reference to and a brief quotation from the next case in the introduction to this chapter.[51] In a grievance involving a buffing operation, employees initiated a five-pass method which yielded acceptable parts, although the company-prescribed method called for an eight-pass operation. The arbitrator specifically ruled that the reduction in the number of passes was a change in method. He held immaterial whether the change was company or employee initiated; the rate could be changed in either case. This was based, no doubt, on the existence of operation analysis cards specifying the method, from which the employees had no right to deviate.

---

[47] 40 LA 1106.
[48] 5 LA 231.
[49] 27 LA 389.
[50] 4 LA 189.
[51] 18 LA 459.

The final case [52] involved a company decision to install a larger piston bore drill and to eliminate a roughing operation. The union claimed this operation had already been eliminated by the operator seven years earlier, and, therefore, there was no change in method to justify a rate change. However, it appears that each time the job was time studied, the operator performed the unnecessary operation in order to avoid a rate reduction; he never notified supervision of the improvement. Since the company had been unaware of the employee improvement, said the arbitrator, it could not have taken advantage of it.

It can thus be seen that contract, practice, or the equities support the proposition that an employee-initiated change in method be credited to the employee, either by permitting him the work benefits or by appropriate purchase of his ideas. The common requirement is that the improvement be made known to the employer. If there is a carefully prescribed procedure the employee has been instructed to follow, if the employee fails to disclose his improvement to management, or if the claim of improvement is not substantiated by the facts in the case, then management may make methods changes which possibly incorporate employee-initiated improvements.

Otherwise, the cases in this section represent a considerable variety of methods changes, with a clear indication of the requirement for substantiality. Comment should be made on the possible unreliability of using production figures as a guide to the efficacy of a change in method.

Methods changes were sustantiated in cases involving: new materials; removal of a substantial part of a job; modification of a die by a stripper head; the number of passes of the machine in buffing; dual machine assignments; and changes in speeds and feeds. A new product design may be said to be a change in method, although the arbitrator, not illogically, held the new product to be outside contract provisions on methods change.

Also held to be a change in method was the change in ma-

---

[52] 32 LA 383.

chining operations on a wheel, however, the effect thereof was limited by a past-practices proviso. An added operation was not a change in method—as compared with the removal of an operation (in the bending and straightening case). Both should be compared to a change which failed to qualify as a methods change—the paper transaction of breaking a job into its three component jobs (which usually can be done, but not with accompanying rate reductions for the component jobs). Special note should be made of the case in which a new die replaced a worn die, because of the practical nature of the problem there represented. This case, too, is to be compared with the reeler case of Section 1.

5. GENERAL MANUFACTURING

During World War II a simpler method of folding shirts was devised for shirt pressing operations, primarily to conserve metal by using five pins instead of nine.[53] Rates, however, were not reduced. The company, after the war, returned to the fancier, nine-pin folding method—without increasing rates. The arbitrator upheld the union grievance for an increase, on the basis the contract presumably had been negotiated to cover the folding method then being used. Similarly, company action in reducing a printing press crew—printing a beer company's identification on cartons—from three to two men was upheld under the contract.[54] The company had changed its method of requiring 100-percent inspection of the printing on the boxes and the inspection had been the principal part of the third man's job. There was no question in another case of management's right to adopt new packaging, for better marketing, and to make a minor adjustment in rates to reflect the change.[55] However, employees retaliated with a deliberate slowdown, despite the fact that production standards had been met, without issue, during a previous production run.

Bulk Handling Problems

In a case involving newspaper operations,[56] the old system for color sections involved considerable manual handling subsequent to the tying of the sections into bundles of 30. A new

---

[53] 4 LA 482.
[54] 29 LA 687.
[55] 49 LA 581.
[56] 45 LA 860—also appears at 46 LA 151.

system was adopted whereby, after being tied, the bundles were palletized and 80 bundles metal banded to the pallet. The pallets were moved by a power dolly, via freight elevator, for direct loading onto trucks at the loading dock. A small power dolly and power tailgate were used to remove the bundles at established receiving points for various customers.

Five drivers were displaced by the new system; two were laid off, one resigned, and two were promoted to managerial positions. The union grievance alleged failure of the company to notify the union "6 months prior to the introduction of such technological changes or improvements." In holding that the changes involved only machinery and equipment already widely in use, the arbitrator said:

> "It is apparent from the language of the provision that it is not any kind of change or improvement that displaces employees which is covered by this provision. The crucial modifying adjective is 'technological'—only 'technological' changes or improvements are covered by this provision.

> "Technological is a word whose meaning cannot be broadened to include any kind of change or improvement without destroying the meaning of the whole phrase. As the word has come to be used, it has reference to the application of scientific research to the problems and processes of industry. Putting machines of common use and existence and machines which are already in wide use in the plant— machines which are not particularly unique or special—to uses which are fairly within their intendment, but simply have not been availed of before, does not fall within the meaning of 'technological' improvements as I understand that term."

A very similar kind of bulk delivery system was involved in another case.[57] Here the contract stated that when any mailing was to be done by mechanical means, "the manner of operating the machines and the number of men" needed for the work would be determined by a joint committee. At a brief meeting the employer requested the new system be given a trial. The arbitrator held that this did not meet the contract's requirement of joint determination of the new system's operations and of manning questions (with arbitration if joint determination failed).

Inspection

Troubled with rejects of chain, a company took inspection

---

[57] 50 LA 186.

away from incentive workers and assigned it to hourly paid in-spectors.[58] The arbitrator concluded there had been no change in the procedure for inspecting except for the assignment of the work to hourly paid employees; there was not, as claimed by company, removal or change of any physical elements of the job, hence, no methods change. In contrast is a situation[59] wherein the course of collective bargaining made it clear to the arbitrator that pay was integrally related to classification. Consequently, the arbitrator upheld the company's action in putting an hourly paid job on an incentive basis (there was evidence this had been done before). He reasoned that a change in the method of payment was, effectively, a change in method under the governing contract provision, in view of the developed understanding of the parties.

Substantiality

A particular stringing element in an operation had been dis-continued for five years.[60] It was then reintroduced, but with the use of coarser emery requiring fewer strokes for necessary quality. The arbitrator concluded that the coarseness of the emery was a change in "method" or "quality." Likewise, a change from 00 to 000 sandpaper, in belt sanding, was a change in method.[61] There was a suggestion in both cases that the im-pact might be de minimis. In this connection, and also related to the following case, is an arbitral opinion that a 3-percent wage adjustment had a bearing on the substantiality of the methods change.[62]

There was an interesting case concerning a safety-appliance attendant whose duties, it was claimed by the union, had in-creased over the years.[63] The arbitrator pointed out that the mere accumulation of a variety of duties in a single job, or the total duties being required of a single person, was not of itself a basis for concluding the individual was working at a higher classification. However, it was determined that specific, higher grade work had been added—which the company conceded but thought was not the substantial change required by the contract.

[58] 23 LA 490.
[59] 15 LA 945.
[60] 29 LA 828.
[61] 12 LA 273.
[62] 41 LA 1038.
[63] 11 LA 490.

(Company estimate was that these duties required about 1/120 of the employee's work week.) The arbitrator reasoned that the test was not necessarily volume nor percentage of time spent on the duties in question, ". . . but whether the services are essential to the job rather than merely sporadic, occasional or isolated." He sustained the grievance.

Much the same reasoning led to the same conclusion where a company, as a result of a change in the method of splicing wires in vaults and manholes, required lineman helpers to splice wires as done by the higher rated splicers.[64] Under the former method—tight wire splicing—helpers spliced wires only under direction of splicers (only one man could work at a time). The new, slack-wire method permitted wires to be pulled out so that more men could work simultaneously. (The two methods and the duties of the two classifications are given in the report, in considerable detail).

Job Requirements

There was no significant technological change necessitating job changes, said an arbitrator, in ruling against company establishment of two new skilled classifications.[65] The duties of the proposed new classifications were within an already existing classification. Practically the same language appeared in another case [66] where the union grievance was sustained. The company had created a new, common laborer classification, at a lower rate, to do some of the work which was within the established operator classification—no change in rate for operators had been proposed.

The problem in another case [67] developed because the company planned to eliminate a job by automation and to receive and utilize the automatically generated information in a non-bargaining-unit, production-scheduling department. Involved were weighmasters, who weighed pans of produced nuts and bolts and computed the number produced from the weight. Automation of the work was not challenged, but removal from the unit was, successfully.

---

[64] 43 LA 651.
[65] 27 LA 81.
[66] 42 LA 697.
[67] 46 LA 730.

In another case [68] there were members of two different bargaining units in the company classified as production planners, who planned the manufacturing processes for electrical and electronic products. The arbitrator found a distinction in the job descriptions for each group based on the dimensional character of the item to be produced. One group would perform the work if the item were fully dimensioned—the other if not. The dispute was settled on this basis. (The second union did not participate in the arbitration).

The cases herein reinforce the findings in other sections that actual methods changes must exist before management may take actions based on such, and that rate changes are the normal and expectable result of methods changes requiring substantially more from employees. However, the results are different if the methods changes tend toward de minimis or the impact of the changes on employees is not material.

Of particular interest is the idea that substantial change relates to essentiality, rather than volume, percent of time involved, or the like. The relationship of this idea to cases in Section 3 (a saving of one quarter to one half of a job, for instance) should be noted.

An interesting variety of methods changes is illustrated, ranging from bulk delivery methods which are not technological improvements to nine pins instead of five.

6. PROCESSES

A new deionization unit was installed in the glycerin department of a chemical plant which, admittedly, did bring about changes in the operator's job.[69] The question posed in arbitration was whether or not this was the same job, although altered, or a new job, requiring negotiations on description and rate, as well as posting for bid. The decision was that this was not a new job, even though the equipment had materially changed the nature of the operator's duties. The arbitrator commented: "The job continues to involve the same object, namely, the production of glycerin."

---

[68] 51 LA 902.
[69] 39 LA 801.

The contract in another case required that, to make changes, the company first notify the union and, if requested, confer with the union representatives about the matter.[70] If disagreement were to ensue, the company could proceed with the methods change and the union could test its views through grievance arbitration. The particular issue involved loom assignments in textile manufacturing. Testimony indicated that the company had instituted a number of improvements over the years (which related to workload) without conferring with the union. The company position was that these were all known to the union at the time of the grievance. The arbitrator ruled that such "derivative" knowledge did not satisfy the contract requirement.

Job Duties or Requirements

In the case now identified as the reeler case, discussed in Section 1, a meaning for the term "requirements" in the contract was set forth.[71] Two cases hereunder are concerned with the same term; they involve the same arbitrator and same union (although the locals are different).

In one,[72] the methods change involved considerable and substantial modifications in continuous pickling lines in some of the company's sheet and tin mills. In the other [73] the company rebuilt its patenting furnace, for greater heat capacity and the processing of more rods at higher speeds. For both cases, the requirements for instituting new incentives were methods change and change in "job duties or requirements." In both cases, the arbitrator found there had been methods change, within the contractual provisions, but there had not been significant change in job duties.

The term "job requirements" in incentive applications, said the arbitrator, represents

". . . the amount of standard work effort required in performance of job duties under existing rates. . . . [T]he job requirements are constituted by the amount of standard work effort required per unit of incentive production. If the ratio between incentive effort and incentive production remains constant there will be no change in job

---

[70] 15 LA 314.
[71] 28 LA 129.
[72] 5 LA 712.
[73] 8 LA 846.

requirements. If the ratio between incentive effort and incentive production changes, a change in job requirements would occur automatically."[74]

The arbitrator then concluded that this ratio had changed in the pickling operation. "Such a significant increase in productivity brings out convincingly the substantial importance of the change in 'job requirements' in the form of operating the lines at higher speeds."[75] He therefore decided a new incentive was appropriate.

He found in the patenting furnace case[76] that there had been no change in the effort/production ratio. That is, work effort increased *pari passu* with the increase in tonnage resulting from greater speed and increased amount of product being heat-treated. Hence, a new incentive was not appropriate in this situation.

Other Process Changes

To reduce costs a company changed its rotary furnaces for incinerating certain caustic materials used in papermaking from coal firing to gas firing.[77] The arbitrator decided that the substitution of gas for coal "unquestionably provided a change in equipment and method." He awarded to helpers the same five-cent increase which the company had granted to firemen.

In the continuous forming department of another company continuous filaments of fiberglass were formed by a bushing and then wound on tubes by winding machines.[78] In a dispute over revised incentive standards, the arbitrator found there had been methods change—both machine and engineering—such as to satisfy the contract requirement. He noted changes in the bushings (increase in number and size of holes), in wall thickness, in temperature, and in points of heat contact. The variety of the methods changes was noted because of the union charge that the company had merely increased the speed of equipment which, it was alleged, was a violation of contract. The arbitrator concluded there had been substantial changes, a result of which was increased flow of glass and faster winding, that such con-

---

[74] *Id.*
[75] *Supra* note 72.
[76] *Supra* note 73.
[77] 15 LA 754.
[78] 31 LA 662.

stituted methods change within the contract, and that revision of incentive standards was proper in the circumstances. (It is interesting to note that the reeler case [79] was a reference citation in this arbitration.)

The cases in this section indicate that substantial methods changes are usually recognized by the parties but, if not, they will be recognized by the arbitrator (as in the fiberglass case). However, arbitrators will insist on compliance with notice and other contract procedural requirements (the loom-assignment case). Finally, these cases reinforce the view already developed, that the impact of methods change is of particular concern. The usefulness of the "job duties or requirements" criteria, appearing in many contracts in the steel industry, for arbitral judgment about such impact is neatly demonsrtated above.

7. EFFECT ON OTHER OPERATIONS

The first case [80] to be considered has previously been reviewed, in Chapter V, Section 4, and criteria for decision as to when a new incentive program was proper noted. The situation arose from the building of completely new primary rolling facilities. Based on some prior arbitration decisions, the union thought existing incentives from other rolling mills, modified as might have been necessary, should have been instituted. The basic question, then, was if the building of a new mill were such a methods change as to justify installation of new incentives. The arbitrator said yes for this case, and suggested the criteria for judgment.

Another case involved shearing to resquare stainless steel sheets following cold rolling.[81] This was done by a group of five shears, the operators of which were paid on a pooled incentive computed from the weight of material handled. Sheet size varied but the differences in weight going over the various shears was balanced through the group incentive.

The company undertook an extensive modernization program, which resulted in capacity to cold roll substantially heavier

---

[79] *Supra* note 71.
[80] 39 LA 4.
[81] 20 LA 455.

sheets. In the rearrangements one of the shears was moved closer to the mill. The job of running the separate shear was offered to the men in the group, but refused by them. When moved this shear was taken off incentive, but the company had said it would be put on an incentive basis shortly.

The union grievance challenged management's actions generally. But the arbitrator said the essential question was whether or not there had been a methods change. He found that the new cold rolling permitted wider and thicker sheets and, therefore, heavier sheets. Thus, the average weight of sheets sheared at the new location was three to four times the average sheared at the previous location. Consequently, ". . . while there has been no change in the material in one sense, i.e., it is still stainless steel of the same composition, there has been a very material change in another sense, i.e., in size and weight on the average."

Similar was a situation [82] in which the union claimed that the standards for a particular slitting and welding line should be based upon standards already in effect for certain other slitting and welding lines in the plant. The arbitrator thought this unsound because it overlooked differences—in available horsepower, width of coil processed, loading devices, and in the take-up reels—among the lines. He also thought the union view confused equitable earnings relationships among employees with the standards on which incentive earnings were determined (as noted in Chapter V).

Prior to changes,[83] the largest slabs which would normally be handled in a company's mill were just under 50 inches in width. (Slabs up to 62 inches in width could be handled by cross rolling, but this was inefficient use of capacity.) An extensive modernization program enlarged capacity permitting the normal rolling of $62\frac{1}{2}$-inch slabs; this involved larger ingot molds, a new soaking pit and, of course, enlargement of the mill.

Arbitration resulted because the company thereafter changed the incentive on what was known as the "B" line pickler, a subsequent operation. The previous incentive plan had expressly

---

[82] 29 LA 784.
[83] 21 LA 84.

referred to coil widths up to 78½-inches and all coil weights—even though the wider and heavier coils would never have been available. The company specifically claimed the right to change this pickler incentive because of the changes in preceding operations. The arbitrator denied this, suggesting that such a view meant that any change any place could have an effect, however indirect, on a particular unit covered by an incentive plan. He further determined there had been no direct methods change on the pickler operation; he felt this opinion was reinforced by the provision for wider coils in the old incentive.

In another case [84] the arbitrator commented about the possible impact on employees of increases in prior operations and stated: "To deny redress just because the increased production is not literally due to a physical change in equipment, process or material is hardly equitable." The fact pattern here was essentially that a bar mill was changed to permit processing of longer and heavier bars, while the grievants operated shears in a subsequent operation. The arbitrator compared tonnage figures before and after and concluded actual tonnage handled, after the increased production in the bar mill, was somewhat less than before. (The actual facts showed progressive events and were more involved; however, they did follow the simplified outline.) The grievance was denied.

Logic suggests, and the cases tend to substantiate, that methods changes in certain operations might have a substantial impact on other operations; this might also hold for completely new facilities. However, whether or not there is a substantial impact is a matter for factual determination by the arbitrator.

---

[84] 7 LA 718.

CHAPTER VIII

THE IMPACT OF CHANGE ON JOBS

Dynamic change, the basic characteristic of the American economy, was briefly discussed in Chapter I as the underlying cause of most of the disputes which come before arbitrators. Organizations must, over time, respond to this feature of our system or cease to exist.

Response means change, which is primarily incumbent upon management in its initiatory role, and adaptation. Management actions are very likely to impinge upon union policies and objectives. When conflicts result one viable means of resolution is arbitration.

The preceding chapters not only highlight the basic problem, but reflect the numerous methods used by the parties to regularize and control change as it affects their relationships. They also focus upon the many tools used by arbitrators in resolving consequent disputes.

In this and the two succeeding chapters the emphasis is on the scope and variety of problems caused by change. Categories, however, cannot be sharply exclusive; and a problem is often difficult to identify without reference to its governing contract clause (s) .

The regulatory aspects of Job Structuring, such as contracts and their administration, were discussed in Chapter IV. In this chapter, specific problems relating to Job Structuring are considered. Since all Job Structuring cases of the study are involved, the presentation must be particularly representative. Certain situations are highlighted because of their interesting or informational qualities.

The problems discussed hereunder all develop from change—methods changes, as discussed in the last chapter, and/or changes due to management belief that efficiency can be improved. All of the job (including classification) effects of change which can occur are presented in the cases: new jobs, abolished jobs, combined jobs, and split or subdivided jobs. Also presented are changes which only partially affect jobs, when duties are either added or taken away. Often the problems arise from claims of either error classification or pay in dealing with the job structure. Finally, there are allegations of erroneous assignments, based on belief that the job structure was not properly applied.

Some of these types of changes have been discussed in the literature and will be noted; most of them appear, although with different designations, in the detailed study of one company's experience.[1]

1. ESTABLISHING NEW JOBS OR CLASSIFICATIONS

The categorization of cases in this and succeeding sections is based upon efforts to identify a single, predominant issue. But the fact patterns did not necessarily conform to any particular system; there was, inevitably, overlapping between and among categories. These interrelationships are ignored for the purposes of this analysis.

There were 24 cases in which the main issue involved the company action of establishing new jobs or classifications. Of these, company action was upheld in 20 cases;[2] however, there were lesser remaining problems with some of them, such as erroneous classification or evaluation, a need to negotiate on pay rate, or to raise an assigned rate held too low. In a total of five cases, decision was that the company action in attempting a new classification was incorrect.[3] It will be noted that one case[4] appears on both sides of the issue; there were two grievances involved, with opposite results.

---

[1] H. SHERMAN, ARBITRATION OF THE STEEL WAGE STRUCTURE (1961).
[2] 4 LA 716, 5 LA 290, 7 LA 368, 7 LA 691, 11 LA 544, 11 LA 822, 12 LA 676, 30 LA 290, 30 LA 423, 32 LA 115, 34 LA 365, 35 LA 856, 40 LA 879, 46 LA 39, 46 LA 295, 47 LA 716, 48 LA 518, 49 LA 202, 50 LA 823, 50 LA 997.
[3] 11 LA 822, 21 LA 784, 27 LA 81, 35 LA 662, 39 LA 1058.
[4] 11 LA 822.

There were 10 cases [5] in which the union initiated action for new jobs or classifications; the arbitrators upheld these requests in five instances, denied them in five.

Company Initiative

Among the company-initiated new job cases, five will be considered in some detail. In one,[6] the company advised the union that it planned to install a reperforator switching-center system, to handle certain incoming messages and to transmit them to branch offices, and that it planned a new classification of Plan 38 operator. (Plan 38 was the new system.) Since this system would take over much of the work of existing classifications of automatic and teleprinter operators and city route clerks, the union resisted the proposal and the company initiated arbitral process. (Those employees who would be displaced were to be trained as Plan 38 operators, if they desired training.)

The principal argument of the union was that the proposed Plan 38 amounted to a transfer of work, not a new classification, and therefore the action violated seniority provisions. The arbitrator concluded there was seniority protection for the soon-to-be-displaced employees and decided the company was properly within the scope and procedure of a clause on "New Job Classifications." In commenting as to when new job classifications became established under the clause, he stated:

> "This occurs when work is required which is entirely new and different from that which is presently being performed. So too will it occur when, though the same end-product or service is involved, the equipment, method or process and the working procedures for obtaining the same is different from that which presently obtains. In each of such situations, the existing job classifications will not suffice. And so, the establishment of a new job classification becomes necessary."

A second case [7] had a contract provision giving the company the right to establish new job grades for new or changed "tours of duty," revising existing job grades upward or downward in accordance therewith. This was, of course, subject to the right of the union to file grievances and to arbitration. The com-

---

[5] 5 LA 241, 13 LA 223, 13 LA 763, 31 LA 111, 32 LA 216, 34 LA 278, 39 LA 801, 46 LA 870, 46 LA 978, 49 LA 544.
[6] 35 LA 856.
[7] 40 LA 879.

pany established a new job of expediter which, effectively, combined some existing classifications. Since the resulting tour of duty was not illogical, was not arbitrary or capricious, and was for efficiency of operations, the arbitrator upheld it.

Limitations on Company Initiative

There were three welder classifications in a third case,[8] the top of which—called combination welder—had historically performed any required work of cutting up scrap with a hand torch; this was so at the time the contract was signed. Parties agreed the volume of such work had greatly increased. An employee, classified as combination welder, was essentially full time on this duty, but he was paid at the rate of the lowest of the three classifications for the work. A grievance was filed, and the company conceded error since the lowest classification covered cutting scrap by machine, rather than by hand torch. Simultaneously, the company introduced a new classification, which specifically covered this hand-torch method of cutting scrap.

An employee bumped the grievant in the above situation. The new man was told he would receive combination-welder wages when on maintenance assignments, but the newly established rate when cutting scrap. The company advised him that this was a dual-rate situation, one rate for each of the jobs involved. This man filed a grievance, which came on to arbitration. The union position—that the hand cutting of scrap had always been a part of the combination welder's job—was sustained by the arbitrator. The work was combination-welder work at the signing of the contract, and no other description in effect at that date covered the work. He also pointed out that work done by the employee here was "virtually identical" to that done by the employee whose grievance had been settled, the sole difference being the newly established—and improper—job description.

In another case [9] the contract permitted the company to establish new classifications, discontinue classifications, and reassign duties among classifications, but required it to notify the union about any such changes and to negotiate a wage rate

---

[8] 21 LA 784.
[9] 47 LA 716.

when appropriate. There was also provision in the contract for "Job Family" seniority, primarily for reductions in force.

The company acquired some new machines and assigned the operations thereon to job family 3, which encompassed repair classifications, rather than to job family 1, covering machining classifications. This action was challenged by the grievance. The arbitrator decided the company had violated the contract. He felt that a rule of reason dictated interpretation of the company rights in conjunction with the job-family provisions and that company action was thereby limited to assignments to "congruous" and not "incompatible" classifications.

For comparison is a situation [10] wherein the arbitral reasoning appeared to be that a company right to post new jobs implied a parallel right to set the rates for such new jobs. It is to be noted that the job in question represented substantial changes—from manual to automatic operation—from the pre-existing job.

Union Initiative

Among the union-initiated actions for new jobs or classifications, seven will be noted. One [11] concerned new equipment installed in an acid plant, which resulted in additional duties for an operator. The grievance asked for a helper, because of both additional duties and safety hazards. Before concluding that the new installation was simpler than the old and therefore no helper was required, the arbitrator visited the plant, talked to company and union representatives, talked to representatives of the company which had installed the equipment, and made reference checks on the process involved.

With respect to practices in acid plants, he was referred to a magazine entitled *Industrial and Engineering Chemistry,* in which the acid-making process—contact sulfuric acid from sulfur—was described. This source stated that, regarding the type of equipment installed, instrumentation was particularly important. The centralized control room contained all instruments necessary for a single operator to check performance throughout the plant.

[10] 49 LA 202.
[11] 13 LA 223.

Three grievances dealt with multiple-machine operations. The basic issue in the first [12] concerned the aluminum shop of the company. The union felt the rate should be higher than in the babbitting shop, where smaller Kingsbury machines were already in use. The arbitrator found the new machines did not demand a higher skill level than the earlier, smaller machines. In an arbitration [13] involving a change to two-machine assignments, the decision under the evaluation plan was that the job classification had not been changed by doubling up machines. In discussing the responsibility factor, the arbitrator pointed out that it was the ". . . level or degree of responsibility, not the volume of product or number of machines which is the primary factor . . . ."

Union Requests Supported

Prior to change, the operations in another plant were performed on two different machines—boring and facing on one machine, recessing on another.[14] The change in equipment resulted in all of the operations being done on one machine. Also the operators under the prior arrangement had done their own setup; a setup man did this on the new equipment. The union urged labor grade 5 for the new job, the company valued it at labor grade 9, while the arbitrator assessed it at labor grade 8—and ordered that a new description be prepared.

A company [15] introduced new welding equipment and assigned the work thereon to employees in the Weldor's bargaining unit. The arbitrator, in his ruling, upheld the IAM union's allegations that the work was covered by a clause in its contract calling for preparation of an appropriate job description by the company to cover a new job or position resulting from introduction of new work comparable to that covered by existing job descriptions. The company, in the new products case,[16] discussed in Chapter VI Section 2, had not considered this a new job until the arbitration results indicated that the new product, salvageable waste, functioned to invoke a contract clause governing jobs created as a result of new products.

[12] 32 LA 216.
[13] 34 LA 278.
[14] 5 LA 241.
[15] 46 LA 870.
[16] 49 LA 544.

In the final case hereunder the company moved the job of operating a quantometer from one plant to the laboratory at another, where the grievance arose.[17] The arbitrator ruled that this constituted a new job, and he decided it belonged within the bargaining unit.

In a discussion of arbitral disputes on job evaluation,[18] it was stated that to determine whether or not a new job had in fact, been created, the arbitrator should look to both the nature and magntiude of the changes involved, and then compare skills needed before and after such changes. Generalized to include disputes where job evaluation is not involved, this aptly sums up the cases in this section.

2. JOB ELIMINATION

It is a general rule, truly reflective of the change-adaptation force at work, that management has the right (and the duty) to eliminate jobs not necessary to the enterprise, in the absence of contractual limitations and if done in good faith (and not in derogation of the bargaining unit).[19] An alternate view generally rests on the belief that the wage structure, including classifications, having been negotiated, should remain inviolate for the contract term (unless change provisions are included in the contract).

Incidentally, the first reference above[20] provides interesting comparisons for some of the topics covered in this book, including this section, because the cases contained therein are from the files of the American Arbitration Association.

While there are conceivable circumstances under which a union would initiate a grievance to have a job eliminated, this is not a likely course of action—and none of the cases hereunder are so classified. The most frequently appearing bases for job elimination are methods and process changes, plant moderniza-

---

[17] 46 LA 978.

[18] Sherman, *Arbitrator's Analysis of Job Evaluation Disputes,* 43 PERSONNEL J. 365 (1964).

[19] M. STONE, MANAGERIAL FREEDOM AND JOB SECURITY (1964); F. ELKOURI & E. ELKOURI, HOW ARBITRATION WORKS, 2nd ed., (1960).

[20] M. STONE, MANAGERIAL FREEDOM AND JOB SECURITY (1964).

tion, mechanization, and automation. There were 17 cases [21] in which management actions to eliminate jobs for these reasons were upheld by arbitrators. Sometimes the secondary question involving any duties remaining after job elimination—at times so important that it becomes controlling—is nonexistent because the job is completely eliminated.[22] More typically, the cases reflect arbitral opinion [23] that the few remaining duties may appropriately be redistributed within the bargaining unit. Such residual duties, if de minimis in nature, could even be assigned outside the bargaining unit.[24]

Job Abolishment

In some cases such as the following,[25] the allegation of job elimination is not construed as such because of circumstances. A second bottling line was installed, close to an existing line. The company decided that the sealing machine operator and stacker could handle both lines, whereas they had handled but one line previously. The union grievance was that such action by the company amounted to job abolishment. The arbitrator ruled that abolishment was not properly descriptive of the action here. The result of the action, he found, was to equalize the work of the grievants, who bottled half-pints, with the amount of work performed by similarly classified employees on lines bottling fifths.

A bakery [26] undertook a major modernization of its facilities, so that bread was fed into the ovens by conveyor and was automatically unloaded. Both duties had previously been performed by a classification known as oven men. In addition, heat and speed controls were set and then automatically maintained, thus requiring little adjustment. In the grievance challenging the elimination of one of two oven men previously employed, a principal argument was that supervision was performing work formerly done by the second operator. The arbitrator found that supervision had, before automation, made heat and speed adjustments along with the oven men. He concluded that such

[21] 4 LA 136, 10 LA 812, 12 LA 865, 21 LA 586, 30 LA 1014, 32 LA 836, 35 LA 72, 35 LA 113, 42 LA 945, 43 LA 353, 44 LA 359, 46 LA 4, 46 LA 572, 48 LA 72, 48 LA 746, 49 LA 874, 51 LA 296.
[22] 46 LA 4.
[23] 48 LA 72, for example.
[24] 48 LA 746.
[25] 10 LA 812.
[26] 32 LA 836.

activities were minimal under the new system. Otherwise, as the arbitrator pointed out, there was no work for a second oven man—the work had disappeared because of automation.

In another case [27] the introduction of self-service procedures in a storeroom eliminated the need for the *primary* duties performed by the storeroom attendant. Arbitral endorsement of the company's elimination of the job was facilitated by the reduced demands on the storeroom because of a reduction in the work force. The arbitrator found nothing in the contract to preclude elimination of an unnecessary job and distribution of the few remaining duties to other employees.

Insufficient Work in Classification

Five cases [28] reflected in various degrees a category wherein arbitrators upheld job elimination because there was insufficient work for the classification (this was also involved in some of the first cases discussed) or the work could otherwise be accomplished. Thus, a company abolition of an oiler's job was upheld because his duties required only about two-and-a-half hours per day, and could be conveniently handled by a helper classification.[29] Similarly, the job of a fireman, in a boiler-room operation, was eliminated when study indicated that fireman duties could be absorbed by the engineer classification without overburdening this second job (and without violating city and state safety regulations).[30] In a somewhat unique situation the abolition of a bargaining-unit job was upheld due to an overlap of responsibilities with both supervision and an outside contractor.[31] (Since the job was not posted after the incumbent retired, it was eliminated by attrition.)

In addition to the foregoing cases, note should be made of a case [32] wherein the arbitrator upheld the abolition of a carpenter classification (subsequent to several years of reduction in the work for the classification) and merger of the duties into a general maintenance mechanic classification. There was substantial precedent for this action, since classifications such as

---

[27] 44 LA 359.
[28] 16 LA 252, 48 LA 24, 48 LA 901, 50 LA 752, 51 LA 1269.
[29] 16 LA 252.
[30] 48 LA 24.
[31] 51 LA 1269.
[32] 44 LA 33.

blacksmith, tinsmith, welder, and millwright had previously been combined into the general classification. In a different situation a company's elimination of a classification was appropriate under the contract, but violated the concomitant requirement to "advise and discuss" the elimination with the union.[33]

The situations in which arbitrators decided against company elimination of jobs generally involved conclusions that the *primary* function of the eliminated job remained or significant duties had been transferred from the eliminated job to other classifications within the bargaining unit. Five cases [34] are so categorized. In three other cases [35] it appears that any duties remaining subsequent to job elimination (except in de minimis situations), were transferred or assigned outside the bargaining unit. In these situations, the grievances were denied.

Primary Function Continuing

To illustrate the first proposition above, a company [36] introduced an automatic sampler and abolished the classification of sample boy. In supporting the union grievance protesting the elimination, the arbitrator concluded that, although the duties of sample boy had been substantially reduced, the primary function of the classification remained. It may be noted that this same case has previously been cited;[37] two issues were involved in the one arbitration. In another case,[38] the elimination of a job and the distribution of a major portion of its duties was improper. Similarly, a company [39] eliminated the job of inspector and combined its duties with those of a lower rated job of journeyman. Such action was held improper when it developed that journeymen spent at least 50 percent of their time on inspection duties.

Elimination [40] of a timekeeper job was found to be a violation of contractual relationships where some timekeeper duties remained and were being performed outside the bargaining unit. The arbitrator ordered reinstatement of the timekeeper

---

[33] 50 LA 344.
[34] 22 LA 785, 41 LA 120, 46 LA 396, 47 LA 396, 48 LA 901.
[35] 10 LA 143, 33 LA 188, 44 LA 840.
[36] 48 LA 901.
[37] *Supra* note 28.
[38] 47 LA 396.
[39] 41 LA 120.
[40] 10 LA 143.

job, to the extent of the duties which were not, in fact, abolished. He also suggested the parties negotiate for equitable disposition of these remaining duties or, if the parties chose to continue the job, the company could add duties to make it a full-time job. While another company [41] could, under its contract, redistribute duties within the bargaining unit, it was a violation of that contract, after elimination of a bargaining-unit job, to transfer its duties outside the bargaining unit.

Somewhat special are three other cases. Elimination of a job where justification is questionable (helper classification abolished on two shifts but continued on first shift) will not receive arbitral approval.[42] This case was complicated by the existence of a special progression system in the department, different from that in the rest of the plant. In a second case subcontracting of work still needed within a department, and elimination of jobs associated therewith, was held inappropriate.[43] The subcontracting of the same type of work in other departments within the company lent credence to the arbitrator's analysis that management did not come to this issue with "clean hands."

Finally, there was a case [44] wherein the arbitrator decided against the company's unilateral elimination of a working-foreman classification. What might have been, at one time, a unilateral right had become circumscribed to a bilateral matter as a result of 20 years of bargaining about the classification.

The main principles deducible from these cases do not require further summarization. There is an informative reference [45] dealing with various aspects of job elimination as reflected in arbitration cases.

3. COMBINING OR SPLITTING JOBS

Of 24 cases having job combination as a principal issue, man-

---

[41] 44 LA 840.
[42] 41 LA 268.
[43] 51 LA 842.
[44] 51 LA 303.
[45] Teple, *Contract Provisions Affecting Job Elimination,* 17 WESTERN RESERVE L. REV. 1253 (1966).

agements' actions were sustained by arbitrators in 20 [46] while in four cases [47] the action was held to be improper. Decision in one of the cases,[48] in which job combination was appropriate, was based on a contractual requirement that the job resulting from combination of duties normally performed within the bargaining unit with duties performed outside unit should be a unit job. The arbitrator ruled that this provision governed the facts in arbitration.

The Wage Issue

It happens not infrequently that a combination may be satisfactory but a major issue arises over wages. The wage issue in one case [49] was particularly interesting. Two jobs existed under a general category of providing raw mix to the conveyor, one known as stone feeder, the other as shale feeder. These two jobs carried more responsibility than other conveyor jobs and therefore had a higher pay rate. Over the years, apparently, changes in equipment and material handling had lessened the responsibility aspect of these two jobs. This seems not to have been seriously contested.

The company instituted changes, resulting in a combination job wherein one employee did both stone and shale feeding. The union filed a grievance when the rate for the combination job was set at the amount paid only one employee prior to change. The company conceded the combination job contained more than the individual jobs just prior to the change, but contended that the jobs had become easier from the time they were originally set up and, therefore, the changes over time had to be considered in the slotting of the combination job.

The arbitrator ruled that the proper comparison was with the two jobs as they were at the time the combination job came into being, noted "somewhat greater" duties and responsibilities, and returned the matter to the parties to negotiate the proper rate.

For comparison, there was a combination warehouseman-

---

[46] 10 LA 94, 18 LA 166, 24 LA 665, 27 LA 689, 33 LA 300, 33 LA 421, 34 LA 226, 34 LA 827, 35 LA 434, 37 LA 711, 38 LA 584, 41 LA 1076, 41 LA 1150, 42 LA 643, 45 LA 778, 46 LA 36, 46 LA 730, 47 LA 282, 50 LA 287, 51 LA 1051.
[47] 41 LA 285, 41 LA 997, 41 LA 1161, 43 LA 1048.
[48] 46 LA 730.
[49] 18 LA 166.

truck driver job [50] initiated for warehouses having insufficient work for both jobs; the two separate jobs continued where sufficient work existed. The union felt this combination job, under a formal evaluation plan, should receive a higher classification—on volume of work and on judgment. The arbitrator thought the company evaluation correct, because this was not a combination which required performing both jobs simultaneously but rather required performing these jobs alternately. His opinion was that neither factor exceeded that of the component jobs in such circumstances. In another case [51] the company stated that it would not have entered into a special agreement (combining two departments into one) had it expected that the resulting combination job would justify a higher rate. The arbitrator here said that the wage rate was a matter of evaluation, not of company expectations.

An arbitrator upheld a combination of jobs, even though the combination took in jobs from two departments having separate seniority.[52] By contrast is a specific ruling [53] that the combining of two jobs into one, for legitimate reasons, was appropriate so long as duties were not transferred across seniority lines. The latter case involved company action to combine certain jobs, in consonance with an overall program of operational improvements. Since the union was resisting the changes, the company initiated a grievance which came to arbitration—with the result noted above.

About as unusual as the company-initiated grievance, above, was a union grievance [54] requesting that a new classification be established to cover what it considered to be a combination job. Actually, this was the union's tactic for seeking a wage increase when the company required an employee who had previously operated only one grinder to operate two. In fact, a new classification was, apparently, the only possibility for such a wage increase in the circumstances. However, these tactics were not fruitful since the arbitrator found that the contract provided for company initiative in establishing new classifications.

[50] 27 LA 689.
[51] 38 LA 584.
[52] 42 LA 643.
[53] 37 LA 711.
[54] 24 LA 665.

One case [55] involved a number of machine combinations—a vertical and a horizontal milling machine, a horizontal milling machine and a drill press, and a light drill press with two automatic turret lathes—each to be set up and operated by the same employee. The arbitrator concluded that such combinations warranted a higher labor grade. The essence of his decision was the setup requirements. While the purposes of the machines so grouped in each case might be quite similar, there were, clearly, different skill requirements, particularly for setups.

The governing contract provisions reported in one arbitration [56] are of interest since they permitted the company discretion to combine jobs in response to changes in production requirements. The combination of jobs in another case [57] was permitted under the contract. However, the arbitrator found the company remiss in its contractual obligations to advise and discuss with the union and to consider union recommendations.

Finally, on nonendorsement of management action, is a case [58] in which the company combined three jobs, with common title of conveyor tender, into one new job. This was done after substantial changes in equipment and controls, which eliminated much of the work done on the three jobs. Arbitrator decided that the duties had not substantially changed, at least not enough to warrant a position that they no longer existed. The arbitrator stated that the $12,000 capital investment to diminish duties of the original jobs was not, of itself, determinative. In another case,[59] the arbitrator ruled that three jobs, which the company had combined into one, were not sufficiently changed to warrant the combination.

Splitting Jobs

There were only three cases in which job splitting was identified as a principal issue, and no pattern is clear on this particular aspect of Job Structuring. One case [60] reflected approval of the split (it actually was agreed upon by parties, after discussions). The arbitrator sustained management in another

[55] 41 LA 1076.
[56] 50 LA 287.
[57] 46 LA 36.
[58] 41 LA 1161.
[59] 41 LA 997.
[60] 30 LA 194.

case,[61] but held its action on wages erroneous. The arbitrator disagreed with management actions in attempting job splitting in the third case.[62]

Of these three, the last [63] is of interest since it is the reverse of the machine-combination case noted above. Here the standard classification for automatic screw machine operators was setup and operate. When this department was enlarged by addition of a new machine, the company established a production worker classification, the incumbent to operate only, with setups to be performed by the regular operator classification. The arbitrator said the company could establish a new job, under a contract provision thereon, but was required to get union concurrence on an action which concerned the use of less skilled employees. Since concurrence was not had, company action was incorrect.

It has been observed [64] that, unless restricted by agreement, the right to combine jobs when technological changes occur or where there is insufficient work in the jobs being combined is vested in management. The cases herein endorse this view, as a general proposition. Disapproval of management action normally is based on belief that the duties of previous jobs are not sufficiently diminished to justify the combination. Also, the appropriate wages to be paid to employees on jobs resulting from combinations of other jobs is of particular moment.

The effects of splitting a job have been noted:[65] it could result in increased work for employees in other classifications; it could have significant consequences on skill, status, and compensation, and it could have the effect of lessening crew size or manning schedules. The author reported a majority of arbitration awards holding that management could make such changes, absent contractual limitations, and that the impact of the changes on wage rates was a major concern. The minority view, against such changes, usually occurred in situations where

[61] 33 LA 296.
[62] 41 LA 1140.
[63] Id.
[64] F. ELKOURI & E. ELKOURI, HOW ARBITRATION WORKS (2nd ed., 1960).
[65] Rubin, *The Right of Management to Split Jobs and Assign Work to Other Jobs,* 16 INDUS. & LAB. REL. REV. 205 (1963).

the contract contained a list of job classifications and job descriptions.

4. ADDING OR REMOVING DUTIES

The less drastic action of adding duties to or removing them from a job is expected to occur with jobs, as a result of changes in product and processes over time. The idea of gradual changes and adaptations in jobs over time appeared, in various ways, in a substantial number of the cases; one of the cases in the last section illustrates.[66] Also, a principal concern is the proper wages to be paid when a job is so changed.

Added Duties

There were 26 cases in which a principal issue was concerned with duties added to an existing job. Of these, eight were primarily concerned with issues other than the wage rate resulting from duties added. One [67] involved what the arbitrator determined to be an unreasonable and unduly burdensome addition to a cleaning job of unloading dust cars. A particular element was the requirement of hurrying up several flights of stairs when an emergency occurred (this case was discussed in Chapter IV). In another [68] the job of oiling equipment was assigned to certain operators, and protested. The arbitrator held that the addition was appropriate, but that the company was required to negotiate any change in the wage rate necessary to reflect the additional duties.

Similar to the last case was a situation [69] wherein the addition of boiler-operator duties to the job of process operator, in a highly automated titanium tetrachloride plant, was upheld as reasonable in the circumstances. Two other cases [70] were similar. And then there was a case,[71] from which a quotation appears in Chapter I, wherein the protest was that major rearrangements of duties, coupled with methods changes, had resulted in the performance of a female job by a male, contrary to the contract. The arbitrator ruled that the rearrangements, and this resultant, were appropriate and not in violation of the contract provision.

---

[66] 18 LA 166.
[67] 18 LA 827.
[68] 39 LA 1065.
[69] 33 LA 758.
[70] 46 LA 1027, 48 LA 24.
[71] 35 LA 63.

In another case,[72] the contract stated specifically that the assignment of routemen to other than route work was a matter for "discussion between the Company and Union committee." Accordingly, the company was in error in assigning the duties of inserting and removing tachograph charts from tachographs installed in their vehicles—and the minimal time involved was not a countervailing factor, in the arbitrator's judgment.

Another case,[73] while diverging somewhat from the main theme, presents an interesting factual situation. Employees from the maintenance division performed temporary and vacation relief work (T&VR) in operating departments, and held regular T&VR designations, though not seniority, in the operating units. The company created single additional positions in the bottom classifications in the operating units involved, allowing all employees to bid for these jobs (including T&VR people, some of whom received permanent operating jobs). While the action did not eliminate T&VR work, it was greatly curtailed by the additional positions, resulting in a grievance. The arbitrator decided there was nothing to prevent such action by the company.

Money Issue in Added-Duties Situations

The other 18 cases are concerned primarily with the money issue, either directly or through changes in application of an evaluation plan. Arbitrator conclusions were: upward adjustments were justified in six [74] of the cases, adjustments were denied in six,[75] while negotiations were directed in four.[76] The wage issues, and other aspects, of two cases [77] were precluded from consideration by decisions of nonarbitrability.

While ruling against a wage increase under all the circumstances,[78] an arbitrator made these interesting statements (in commenting on a company argument that the absence of methods changes precluded wage adjustments even though duties had expanded) :

---

[72] 47 LA 547.
[73] 42 LA 647.
[74] 2 LA 572, 19 LA 358, 21 LA 609, 27 LA 906, 31 LA 121, 43 LA 318.
[75] 23 LA 340, 27 LA 324, 28 LA 530, 29 LA 123, 41 LA 1169, 51 LA 1194.
[76] 6 LA 24, 23 LA 829, 47 LA 601, 49 LA 874.
[77] 41 LA 1169, 46 LA 1189.
[78] 27 LA 324.

"To hold that there can be no relief because the substantially increased amount of work required is not in a literal sense the result of physical changes, but is due rather to certain psychological changes in the way men work, does not seem to violate the intention and spirit of the provisions . . . ."

Money Issue in Removal-of-Duties Cases

In view of the significance of the wage question in added-duties cases, it is interesting that this issue arises directly in only two of the 17 cases involving withdrawal or removal of duties. In this group, retention of the duties themselves is most important—indirectly reflecting concern about earnings. Of 17 cases, opposite decisions were reached in the two directly related to wages, while the arbitrator supported removal of duties in 13 other cases.

In one of the cases where wages were at issue, the fitting of a punch to a die for a stencil-cutting machine required considerable skill.[79] Involved were staking, shearing, swedging, and filing as a combination hand operation on a special punch-fitting machine. A complete redesign of the machine resulted in elimination of the punch fitting. The arbitrator sustained the company action in downgrading the jobs involved on the basis that skill requirements were substantially less. In the other wages case,[80] the arbitrator overruled a company action establishing a rate for special door-frame assemblers lower than that paid to the regular, wooden-door makers. (Actually, the arbitrator's ruling appeared to be in the nature of a penalty for failure to notify the union of the action in advance, as required by the contract.)

Removal of Duties

Circumstances vary in situations where arbitrators support removal of duties. In one case the withdrawal of duties (adjusting and changing creel tension posts and discs on yarn-winding machines) from the textile engineering department, and the assignment of such duties to production workers, was upheld.[81] In another case [82] the union attack on the problem was indirect. It alleged that any job for which any duties remained (75 per-

---

[79] 33 LA 1.
[80] 17 LA 361.
[81] 30 LA 705.
[82] 36 LA 1097.

cent of the duties had been withdrawn or eliminated) had to be manned—but the arbitrator disagreed. Discontinuance of the page palming operation in a composing room [83] and withdrawal of the opportunity for bargaining-unit employees to do guard duty [84] were approved by arbitrators. An arbitrator-imposed removal of duties [85] developed in a situation where the arbitrator concluded that male vocational nurses should not attend female patients.

Complete jobs may have been involved in a different type of case.[86] The company informed one union that window cleaning, previously done by members of that union, was being assigned to employees who were members of another union. This resulted in an "interpleader" situation, in which the union not a party to the contract voluntarily joined the arbitration proceedings.

Complete removal of duties from the bargaining unit was sustained as logical and/or not in violation of the contract in several cases. Involved were: a relatively small amount of clerical work in connection with a computer installation;[87] the witnessing and signing off of operational tests;[88] the withdrawal of secondary supervisory duties;[89] and two cases of transferring duties into newly created supervisory positions.[90]

Where a removal [91] of duties from millwrights accompanied introduction of new tools eliminating the previous skill content, the arbitrator upheld the action. However, removal [92] of a specific type of welding from a higher classification and its assignment to a lower classification was an improper management action, which, observed the arbitrator, could vitiate the agreement between the parties.

Contrary decisions were reached in two similar cases. In each the company separated a combined setup-and-operate job into

---

[83] 51 LA 1174.
[84] 49 LA 471.
[85] 48 LA 1138.
[86] 50 LA 1186.
[87] 50 LA 322.
[88] 43 LA 364.
[89] 33 LA 557.
[90] 50 LA 107, 51 LA 293.
[91] 48 LA 1000.
[92] 46 LA 62.

two classifications of setup and operate. The arbitrator ruled against such a separation in the earlier case;[93] it was upheld in the later.[94]

It is generally accepted, by parties to contracts and by arbitrators, that job changes through addition of duties represent the normal course of events, whether the changes are accretive or managment initiated. The cases show this view prevails even when management action is challenged. Management is restricted by requirements that the action be reasonable and not unduly burdensome. An implied prerequisite is that the action not be in derogation of the bargaining unit; this requirement pervades labor relations. Clearly, the principal concern in added-duties situations is appropriate adjustment of the wage rate.

These generalities are substantiated in the literature.[95] The article by Bailer is particularly interesting in its identification of five categories of "permanent assignments," some of which would be classified as added-duties situations herein.

Finally, it will be observed that arbitrators generally support the removal of duties, applying the same qualifications as for the addition of duties—that is, it must be for good business reasons (but, apparently, that requirement is not so stringent as with job creation or elimination), reasonable, not unduly burdensome, and (again only implicit) not in derogation of the bargaining unit.

5. CLAIMS OF CLASSIFICATION ERRORS

There are 26 cases (and more grievances) in this category, so defined because the cases generally proceed from an allegation that a particular job or classification is improperly slotted within the job structure utilized by the parties. The union objective in all cases is higher wages. However, there is some variety in the cases which lends itself to interesting subgrouping.

---

[93] 24 LA 713.

[94] 48 LA 339.

[95] Supra note 19; Handsaker, Classification Problems, MANAGEMENT RIGHTS AND THE ARBITRATION PROCESS 54 (1956); Bailer, The Right to Assign Employees in One Job Classification to Jobs in Another Classification, 16 INDUS. & LAB. REL. REV. 200 (1963).

The only case [96] hereunder which can be designated pure error involved improper addition of the points for a job, under the company evaluation plan. When the error was discovered and corrected, a grievance was filed—based primarily on estoppel. The arbitrator did not think the theory applied to this case.

Three grievances [97] involved situations in which the company used skilled or experienced workers, paying their high earned rates during the development of new manufacturing methods. When these methods were refined to the point that regular production could proceed, the company assigned lesser skilled production workers to the work. Grievances in each case requested continuation of the higher rates paid during the development period. The arbitrator in each case said no.

Requests for Higher Classification

Claim of classification error was the major issue in 12 cases. Of these, the request for higher classification was approved in two [98] denied in eight of the cases.[99] In two cases grievances arose despite straightforward applications of the formal job evaluation plans utilized by the parties. The arbitrator upgraded one job and denied upgrading of a second in one case.[100] In the other,[101] the arbitrator upgraded one job and denied upgrading of four others.

A grievance [102] asked that the classification of hood assembly be changed to the higher grouping containing the door line-up job, but the change at issue was not enough to justify classification change. In the absence of bench lathes in another situation,[103] operators were performing bench-lathe work on engine lathes and claimed a higher classification on the basis of the machines used. The arbitrator thought that the particular labelling on a machine should not determine classification. Similar was the case [104] where salvage yard helpers requested higher classification. They felt because the machine-operator

---

[96] 6 LA 236.
[97] 6 LA 200, 6 LA 575, 21 LA 424.
[98] 5 LA 540, 18 LA 352.
[99] 2 LA 214, 3 LA 454, 5 LA 278, 6 LA 366, 9 LA 735, 20 LA 463, 23 LA 804, 37 LA 155.
[100] 11 LA 703.
[101] 51 LA 1194.
[102] 6 LA 366.
[103] 2 LA 214.
[104] 3 LA 454.

classification had been established in the yard, their job should be equivalent to the helper job in mechanical departments. In denying the request, the arbitrator pointed out that the mechanical department helpers had to have skill and knowledge relative to machinery not required of the salvage yard helper.

Two of the cases make interesting comparison. In one,[105] there had been a junior and senior coater, both operating the same machine, with the senior, essentially, directing the work efforts of the junior. Later, a new machine was brought in, with the senior coater being responsible for the work on it. From that time, it was pointed out, the junior coater operated the original machine and was entirely responsible for its output. The arbitrator supported the request that the junior coater be given the same classification as the senior. In comparison is the case [106] of a small machine shop with considerable intermix of the work of A, B, and C machinists. Claiming he had performed many jobs done by A machinists, the B-grade grievant requested upgrading. It developed that most of his comparison situations involved B- or C-level work, whereas the employee could point to only one or two small jobs he had done which could have qualified as A work. Grievance was denied.

Pay for Setup

The next case is particularly interesting.[107] As the arbitrator put it, he was being asked to establish criteria for judging "routine repetitive setup," important to the parties because other-than repetitive setups meant additional wages. He did establish such criteria for milling machines, automatic screw machines, and punch presses. The criteria for each type of machine are instructive, as may be illustrated by these given for the punch press operator. The punch press operator A was considered by the arbitrator to be working within his job description and classification on routine and repetitive setups unless:

"1. He is taken off an active run to set up another press while his run is continued by some other operator.
"2. The setup is an experimental one or involves a new die never before used in this plant or involves any multi-stage die."

---

[105] 18 LA 352.
[106] 9 LA 735.
[107] 39 LA 173.

Claims for Higher Rates

Of the remaining nine cases [108] in this category either the claimed error was that wage rates should be higher, and/or there were multiple issues essentially directed at this point. There were 15 grievances involved in the nine cases; the request for a higher rate was sustained in nine and denied in six. Judgments are based on the discrete facts of each case; no pattern is apparent. Three will be discussed briefly.

After reviewing the component operations in one situation,[109] the arbitrator found that women were, in fact, performing all duties which the similarly classified men performed and, therefore, should receive the higher male production worker's rate. There was no question in a different case [110] that a job had changed, so that the company action in reducing employees' rates was seemingly appropriate. Nevertheless, the arbitrator worked out a personal-rate application as a basis for restoring the cut in wages. What had happened, he said, was that the job had changed, but the operators had not and, consequently, the rates paid to them should continue.

Finally, the opening comments of the arbitrator in his analysis of the case [111] before him are of interest. It seems the company paid a five-cent differential for warehousemen on generalized assignments, without stock replenishment responsibilities, and who usually did not operate an electric truck full time. The union felt that those whose primary occupation was operation of the electric truck should also receive the premium. In concluding the five cents should apply to this type of warehouseman, the arbitrator stated: "Aside from any academic discussion of the degree of skill required to operate the electric hand pallet trucks as compared to the non-electric trucks, the company, by its willingness to pay 5¢ more to those who are assigned to operate the electric trucks full time must have recognized some difference in the operation."

Clearly, the cases in this section highlight wages as the most

---

[108] 2 LA 223, 3 LA 855, 6 LA 156, 6 LA 304, 7 LA 467, 8 LA 572, 18 LA 513, 26 LA 564, 42 LA 638.
[109] 42 LA 638.
[110] 2 LA 223.
[111] 18 LA 513.

basic issue —which is consistent with the title for the section and with the facts of industrial life. Normally, only the conviction that his wages and/or his classification are low for the work he is doing or has done, or in comparison with the work of others, would impel an employee to file a grievance alleging classification error. Equally clear from the cases is that arbitral decisions are based on the factual circumstances presented, and claims of classification error are generally supported or denied on the basis of how the developed facts apply to the job structure existing between the parties.

There were some specifics brought out in the cases. An error in arithmetic or computation in summing up an evaluation is correctible—and this is believed to be the general rule even though represented by only one case herein. Rates paid to employees during experimental development are not precedent for rates to be paid regular production workers once the experimentation has been completed. Finally, explicit criteria for distinguishing routine setup from that necessitating wage adjustment were illustrated.

CHAPTER IX

WORKLOAD AND CREW SIZE

There are two aspects of work assignment, the assignment of men to jobs and the assignment of tasks to men.[1] The first area is concerned with questions like seniority, layoff, and overtime (not of major interest herein). The other area deals with questions of workload and crew size, that is, with how much work is assigned.

A somewhat different expression of this idea of "how much" appeared in a discussion on work rules.[2] There it was suggested that the implicit assumption was: Management is entitled to that volume of work produced by full exertion just short of physiological and psychological limits. The author commented that unions never openly rebelled against the concept, but rather couched arguments against it in terms of health and safety. Expressions somewhat similar to the full-exertion expectation were noted in another reference.[3]

How much assigned work—in terms of workload and crew size—is the subject matter of this chapter. The relationship of this area to Job Structuring will be pointed out. Also, some aspects of the topic of working conditions related to this subject will be discussed. Exclusive compartmentalization is no more possible here than elsewhere.

1. THE NATURE OF WORKLOADS

As stated, the concern is about how much work is assigned. In the first instance, and as seems implicit in the comments

---

[1] Wallen, *The Arbitration of Work Assignment Disputes*, 16 IND. & LAB. REL. REV. 193 (1963).

[2] Gomberg, *The Work Rule Problem and Property Rights in the Job*, 84 MONTHLY LAB. REV. 595 (1961).

[3] Hutchinson, *Managing a Fair Day's Work*, U. OF MICH., BUR. OF INDUS. REL., REP. 15 (1963).

above,[4] it is a function of management to determine workload. Such determination, however, will be subject to contractual limitations, if any, and to a rule of reason. The following sums this up:

> "The dominant line of decisions is to the effect that management, in the absence of specific limiting contractual language, retains the right unilaterally to determine work loads or crew sizes. But most of the decisions state or imply that such determinations are subject to review on the basis of their reasonableness—that is, to determine if they impose a workload that exceeds the concept of a fair day's work. Hence the right to assign work is limited as to amount by the concept of a fair day's work, and the grievance procedure is available to protest excessive work loads. . . ."[5]

The Performance Component (Quantity)

An issue in one case [6] was the workload resulting from removing male employees and adding bag stacking in deep boxes to female employees, subsequent to methods changes facilitating this activity. The report headnote contained these statements:

> "Employer had right to replace male with female employees to stack bags into deep cartons, where work does not involve any immediate or serious health hazard, and women employees have performed work without any apparent damage to their health. Composition of work crews and how work shall be done are within unilateral powers and discretion of employer and arbitrator is without authority to limit these management rights; moreover, employer had previously discussed change with union and adjusted female employees' pay rate."

Disputes over workloads usually occur when changes are instituted, although other circumstances will be noted. When an increase in workload does occur, the reaction may be resistance. If it appears that the increased workload cannot be successfully resisted, a request for increased wages will certainly result. That such compensatory adjustment does not necessarily follow was the comment of one arbitrator:

> "It does not follow that, simply because work has been added to a job, there must necessarily be an increase in pay, though presumptively there should be. Whether there should or should not be depends upon whether the workload was too light and the increase does not make it too heavy or whether the workload was proper and the increase is material and makes it too heavy." [7]

[4] Gomberg, *supra* note 2.
[5] Wallen, *supra* note 1.
[6] 50 LA 871.
[7] 6 LA 924.

The question of quantification is often significant. In one case,[8] a standard was defined in terms of the amount of work that 75 percent of the employees within a classification could reasonably be expected to do. This standard was expressed in the contract. Chapter III is relevant here, particularly the third section.

The case just cited is interesting in that the workload—on a bag-sewing machine—had been in effect since the first contract but never previously questioned. Employees transferred to this machine from another machine thought the workload required extra effort; the arbitrator disagreed. This points up what is observable in the cases; it is often employee perception of the workload which gives rise to grievances, rather than workload in relation to a quantitative standard.

In the arbitration [9] from which one of the above quotations was taken, the arbitrator sustained that portion of the grievance which requested a reevaluation of the job. This highlights the classification or job-content aspect of certain workload questions, which sometimes is important.

The Effort Component (Quality)

Two components of workload were identified in Chapter I. The performance component is what has so far been discussed— in fact, it is the feature of workload which is usually under consideration in arbitration cases. It is truly "how much," sometimes quantified. The effort component is more concerned with what may be designated the quality of the workload. To illustrate, the major factor of effort, in job evaluation plans, is broken down into subfactors designed to measure various qualities of the effort. Is it physical or mental, or both? Is the effort sustained or intermittent? Is physical effort light or heavy, or in between? Is the employee constantly required to range over a large area, or is his work localized? Is mental effort continuous, or not? Is mental effort characterized by tension (caused by a need to complete it according to a fast-moving schedule), or by lack of pressure?

It is unlikely that the questions as posed will be specified in formal evaluation plans. Nonetheless, they are reliable rep-

---

[8] 13 LA 227.
[9] *Supra* note 7.

resentations of the quality aspect of workload. Explicit subfactors in various evaluation plans, can, of course, be illustrated.[10]

Some of the cases reflect this evaluation aspect of workload, at least in part. Thus,[11] in bakery-products manufacture, there was a molder operation in which one employee fed empty pans into the machine, another removed loaded pans and put them on racks, while a third loaded racks into the proof box. The company rearranged facilities into a horseshoe pattern so that the loader and the unloader worked side by side. The third man was laid off. Some of his duties were assigned to the other two, with the remainder distributed to other classifications.

The arbitrator's first inquiry was if the new layout eliminated duties; he found that it did not. Therefore, since it was conceded the men were doing a satisfactory day's work prior to the changes, he had to conclude that extra effort was required by the addition of duties to the two jobs of loading and unloading. He also observed that the increased pace required after the changes reinforced the finding that workload had been unreasonably increased.

In a closely related pattern of facts,[12] essentially the same result was reached when the arbitrator ordered negotiations as to the impact of the added duties. He also observed that a consideration in negotiations should be the improvements in the equipment used, brought about by the company changes.

The arbitrator in another case [13] held that an unquestioned workload increase was not such as to warrant increased wage rates for the two classifications involved (there was also job elimination here). The arbitrator in this case, as in the earlier quotation, stated that work added to a job did not necessitate an increase in pay. It was essential to consider how much of the operator's time had been occupied prior to the additional work. He also observed:

> "It is quite possible that an employee whose time may be only 50% occupied could have work added that takes only a few minutes more, but would require some special higher skill than used previously.

---

[10] C. LYTLE, JOB EVALUATION METHODS (2nd ed., 1954).
[11] 23 LA 188.
[12] 12 LA 631.
[13] 35 LA 113.

This could raise the rate in this Arbitrator's opinion before adding 50% more of the exact kind of work that he had been doing."

Another case [14] is particularly interesting in that the arbitrator applied industry-wide standards, rather than intraplan comparisons, in judging effort (which is also performance in this case). Certain warp doffers requested a wage increase because they lifted from 33,000 to 35,000 bobbins per 40 hours, whereas other doffers averaged 31,600. The company conceded this disparity, but alleged both types of doffers were underloaded in comparison with the industry norm of 40,000 bobbins per 40 hours. As the arbitrator viewed it:

"The issue before the board boils down to a matter of judgment as to whether when two jobs exist in a plant, both materially underloaded when compared to the industry generally, the one should be awarded a wage differential over the other simply because it comes somewhat closer to industry practice than the other. We are not persuaded that in such circumstances a wage increase is in order."

The arbitrator also stated:

"Simply because with two underloaded jobs one is somewhat heavier loaded than the other is, in our judgment, no basis for ordering a wage increase for the one. If the heavier one of the two was so overloaded that it exceeded the corresponding jobs in the competitive plants in the industry, then we might have a somewhat different situation."

And he added:

"As a matter of fact we feel that such a decision might well be better for the union, as well as for the company, in the long view."

Also, there was a case [15] involving the effort factor and crew size. The arbitrator concluded that crew size did not have to be retained at the previous level when only 25 percent of one job remained and a substantial part of another job had been eliminated. If the company had the right to combine parts of existing jobs to create a new job, as it did in this situation, then the arbitrator believed the company also had the right to reduce crew size to man the remaining jobs.

It is, therefore, apparent that workload is a multiple-dimensioned concept, and its meaning for a given situation is to be

---

[14] 9 LA 83.
[15] 36 LA 1097.

judged in context. Of practical importance is the idea of relative workload, most frequently occurring in the absence of measurement (standards).

2. WORKLOAD PROBLEMS

In 30 cases, including four noted in the preceding section, workload was considered a principal issue. The company action in increasing workload was upheld in 18 cases,[16] representing considerable variety in work patterns.

In five of the cases,[17] the arbitrator did not disturb the workload increase but concluded that wage negotiations were appropriate in four cases, and directed a wage increase in one somewhat special case, the circumstances of which will be noted. The arbitrator in one case [18] noted that the matter had already been discussed with the union and a wage adjustment made (see quotation last section). In another case, [19] the arbitrator indicated he lacked jurisdiction to order negotiations but recommended to the company appropriate action on wages.

The decisions in four cases [20] were that the workload increases were improper, with negotiations directed in one of them.[21] Changes in machinery leading to elimination of personnel and increased workloads figured in two of the above-noted cases,[22] while unreasonable production quotas highlighted a third. [23] The final case [24] involved management rights under particular circumstances, as will be noted.

Processing Issues

While the increased workload in bakery operations was improper in the bakery case discussed in the last section, an increased workload was upheld in another baking case.[25] A slight decrease in the prebaking weight of dough for bread resulted in workers handling 888 loaves per bake compared to 870 per

---

[16] 5 LA 30, 6 LA 774, 7 LA 27, 8 LA 88, 8 LA 503, 9 LA 83, 11 LA 108, 17 LA 268, 18 LA 612, 20 LA 309, 33 LA 537, 34 LA 278, 35 LA 113, 41 LA 1147, 42 LA 125, 42 LA 661, 49 LA 487, 49 LA 669.
[17] 5 LA 247, 16 LA 76, 23 LA 782, 44 LA 992, 49 LA 874.
[18] 50 LA 871.
[19] 47 LA 577.
[20] 12 LA 631, 14 LA 638, 15 LA 314, 23 LA 188.
[21] 12 LA 631.
[22] 12 LA 631, 15 LA 314.
[23] 14 LA 638.
[24] 20 LA 890.
[25] 20 LA 309.

bake before the change, and this resulted in a grievance. The arbitrator ruled that an increase in workload without a change in the type of duties performed, was not a classification modification such as would require negotiations, pursuant to contract requirements. He also stated that any unilaterally imposed workload increase in such context must not be unreasonable or unduly burdensome.

The situation [26] in another case involved addition of a fifth foods-packaging line, but no addition of personnel. The arbitrator found from the evidence that workload was not unduly increased, since the company never operated all five lines simultaneously. Also, an arbitrator found, in another situation,[27] that workload subsequent to changes was actually less than before.

A stipulated issue [28] was whether or not the company's changes in the tacking operations (cloth manufacture) resulted in excessive workload—which terminology, incidentally, was not contractual. Actual workload increase was not in dispute, and the arbitrator found it not to be excessive. He thought the substantial question, also stipulated, was if the four-cent increase in wages were an appropriate measure of the increase; he concluded it was. Machine speedup figured in another case,[29] with somewhat less than 10 percent more pieces handled per hour, but with some decrease in overall poundage of material handled. On balance, the arbitrator concluded, the workload increase was slight and not material; the contract provided for a rate increase when workload was materially increased.

Similar in pattern were the following decisions. Six steel rolls per employee, in candy manufacture, was an appropriate workload [30] (as opposed to four as contended by the union, in a situation where the new rolls substantially increased productivity). The mechanical improvements in kiln operations for ceramics did not result in an unreasonable workload even though productivity increased from three men/two kilns/three-plus cars per shift to three men/two kilns/five and one-half cars per shift. [31] The assignment [32] of additional duties to operators on a crude

[26] 41 LA 1147.
[27] 42 LA 661.
[28] 8 LA 88.
[29] 11 LA 108.
[30] 17 LA 268.
[31] 42 LA 125.
[32] 6 LA 774.

oil unit, using some but not all of their idle time (some 12 percent unscheduled time remained after the addition of duties) did not result in an excessive workload. The testimony of four supervisors figured prominently in this last case.

Chief operators, who were supervisors, were removed from crews functioning in crude oil cracking and gas plant operations.[33] The grievance alleged increased workload for the seven-operator crew, now without the eighth man. The arbitrator concluded that some quasi-supervisory duties devolved on number one operators and ordered negotiations on a rate to reflect the additional duties. However, he rejected what amounted a kind of "domino theory" that the addition of duties to number one operators meant, as a consequence, more duties for number two operators, and so on.

The real complaint,[34] when job changes were made in tube curing, was that workload had been increased. Finding that average working time was about 50 percent and that 392 tubes were cured four years earlier in comparison with 214 tubes involved in the dispute, the arbitrator observed that workload, "far from being too heavy, is still entirely too light . . ." This arbitrator also observed that a slight increase in workload should no more require a rate change than should a slight decrease (to be compared with the last case in this section). In connection with a Voelker rotary-press operation, in fabric finishing,[35] the arbitrator felt there should be no wage increase following a workload increase, where "the change results in raising an abnormally slow job rate to a still slow rate, with pay that is not inequitable in terms of comparable rates in this plant or in other plants and leaves the part-time nature of the operation unchanged."

Machining Issues

There were a number of cases dealing with workload problems arising from multiple-machine assignments. (Compare the discussion of multiple-machine assignments affected by methods changes in Chapter VII, Section 1). Two machines were

---

[33] 44 LA 992.
[34] 5 LA 30.
[35] 7 LA 27.

thought by arbitrators not to be an excessive workload, in the circumstances, in five cases.[36]

In one situation the automatic grooving machines in a department were increased from 33 to 38, but three were used only part time.[37] Since three men had also been added to the department rolls, the arbitrator found that average workload had actually decreased.

Seamers, in can manufacture,[38] were relocated so that one girl could now attend two machines instead of one. Evidence showed that this reduced waiting time from 72 to 41 percent. The contract required that, when the labor of an employee was materially increased by changes in operations, "consideration shall be given" to a rate adjustment. While the workload change was thought appropriate, the arbitrator also thought the commitment required "serious, honest, and good-faith consideration" and that an increase—perhaps "of relatively small amount"—should be given. He also stated that a factor in this consideration would properly be the relatively light workload. Much to the same effect was a case involving wire-winding operators,[39] except that specific negotiations on the rate question were directed.

Also to be noted are the circumstances of the removal of threader operators when newly automated threaders requiring no operators were put into use.[40] The arbitrator found that the foreman had assumed some duties, as had the machine setters. He ordered correction on the foreman and negotiation of a new rate for machine setters. The contract involved provided for procedures (negotiations) relative to "new and improved machines." It also stated: "There shall be no increase in the work load of the individual during the life of this Agreement." While the report is not explicit about the assessment of the second clause, it is clear that the two provisions were accommodated in the decision.

Other Manufacturing Issues

In addition to two cases discussed in the last section, there

[36] 18 LA 612, 33 LA 537, 34 LA 278, 47 LA 577, 49 LA 487.
[37] 8 LA 503.
[38] 5 LA 247.
[39] 23 LA 782.
[40] 49 LA 874.

were two cases in which the workload increase was found to be improper. In one,[41] an attempted workload increase from 60 to 70 looms (in textile manufacture) was held to be a violation of the company's obligation to notify the union of and, if requested, to discuss proposed changes. Evidence of the long-standing 60-loom assignment came, in part at least, from testimony establishing supervisory communication of this as the assignment. A special award of $40 per affected employee was ordered, as the most equitable redress in the circumstances.

The arbitrator in a second situation[42] concluded that the increased production quota (20 percent)—for welding hanging brackets on transformer tanks—was not reasonable because the company's time studies, on which the quota was based, were procedurally (and seriously) defective. Total elapsed time was not identified; no delay times were recorded; elements varied among the studies; and other inconsistencies were noted. The arbitrator also commented that the proposed quota was "obviously prejudiced" by undue weight given to the work of the best three operators studied.

However, where production standards were properly established, an arbitrator upheld demotion of certain female employees who were producing at only 40 percent of the standards six months after promotion to the jobs.[43]

Indirect Effects

A somewhat different case[44] evolved from workload increases to production workers, accompanied by three-cent-per-hour wage increases. Service (indirect) employees sought wage increases on the basis that their workloads were derivatively increased; the company agreed to one-and-a-half-cent-per-hour increases for service employees closely associated with production. However, the company balked at generalizing the increase on the basis the contract permitted utilization of employees' working time most productively. The arbitrator ruled that all service employees' workloads had increased to some degree, and he awarded the smaller increase to all.

---

[41] 15 LA 314.
[42] 14 LA 638.
[43] 49 LA 669.
[44] 16 LA 76.

In another situation [45] there was a man stationed at the head of the glass furnace building who, on signal from the floor man, would close an electric circuit causing a hoist to move a car of materials into position for discharge into the furnace. Switches were relocated, eliminating this particular man's job and permitting direct control of the moving by the floor man. A grievance was filed that the company violated a contract requirement that various kinds of changes could be effectuated only upon mutual agreement. The arbitrator stated, with respect to the changes clause, that it "must be taken not to mean the minor omission or increase of extremely non-onerous details of job duties of one or two men, but rather the important major changes."

These cases make it clear that the relativity factor is important in workload cases. Otherwise stated, judgments are made on the basis of the workloads before changes are made, together with the impact on workload of the changes. Arbitrators generally will support workload changes when the workload before change is less than a fair day's work and is not more than a fair day's work subsequent to changes. However, when the starting point is a fair or a full day's work, or the company by its conduct indicates an acceptance (60-looms case) of the workload as fair or full, arbitrators oppose workload increases.

When the relativity range is from below-normal to a higher but still below-normal workload, or from below-normal to a full workload, arbitrators will generally support the increase without an accompanying wage increase. A minority view is that the wage increase should accompany the workload increase, regardless of the relative before-and-after positions with respect to a full workload. Normal workload, here, means reasonable and not unduly burdensome in arbitral judgment.

Finally, it is noted that minor shifts in workload will be supported by arbitrators, regardless of the status of workload regulation in the parties' contract (*i.e.*, whether or not mutual agreement on workload increases is required) .

---

[45] 20 LA 890.

3. PROBLEMS OF CREW SIZE

The basic question of how much work concerns both work-load and crew size.[46] Crew size is closely related to workload, for the work of members of a crew is increased (or decreased) if crew size is reduced (or enlarged) while the work require-ments remain unchanged. Reduction in crew, the work remain-ing unchanged, increases workload as effectively as additional output requirements through workload increases to individual employees. Given this relationship, all of the comments about workload apply equally to crew size.

Twenty-five cases were identified as having crew size as a principal issue. In 14 [47] of the cases, the arbitrator supported company action in reducing crew size. In one,[48] the arbitrator apparently supported the reduction, but ordered a wage in-crease; another arbitrator thought the facts called for a trial, pursuant to contract, of a reduced crew [49]; and a third arbitrator concluded he was not dealing with a crew, as such.[50] Of the eight decisions against crew reductions, four [51] were based directly on contractual proscriptions, two [52] on implications from contract provisions, and two [53] on equitable grounds.

Two of the cases [54] are on precisely the same point, namely, that the crew used during break-in or shakedown of operations does not set the standard for the proper crew size when opera-tions are running on a regular basis. In each case, the arbitrator (who decided both cases) supported a reduction by one of the break-in crew. These cases compare directly with the cases, dis-cussed in the last chapter, which held that rates paid during the developmental period were not determinative of regular production workers' rates.

Newspaper Operations

Six cases are closely related in that they involve operational aspects of the publications business, of newspapers in particu-

---

[46] Wallen, *supra* note 1.
[47] 12 LA 865, 28 LA 651, 30 LA 115, 33 LA 29, 33 LA 421, 37 LA 915, 40 LA 70, 40 LA 487, 42 LA 294, 46 LA 70, 46 LA 140, 46 LA 733, 50 LA 458, 50 LA 752.
[48] 5 LA 115.
[49] 36 LA 86.
[50] 40 LA 67.
[51] 43 LA 1048, 49 LA 1018, 50 LA 186, 50 LA 804
[52] 46 LA 503, 49 LA 521.
[53] 38 LA 799, 39 LA 432.
[54] 12 LA 865, 30 LA 115.

lar. In one,[55] crew sizes for mailers (and other classifications) were negotiated. The contract also provided that if either party claimed the agreed-upon manning schedule was "unsatisfactory in operation," the matter could be brought to arbitration if not adjusted between the parties. The arbitrator pointed out that the company's initiation of such procedure would be grounded on the operating economics of the business, thought there was good faith in the company position, and ordered a trial of the proposed reduced crew size. In another case,[56] the arbitrator thought the economics of the business should not be the controlling factor in manning determinations, suggested criteria he thought appropriate, and upheld the company in its proposed crew size reduction. The contract,[57] in another situation involving mailers, specified negotiations on manning when mailing was to be done by mechanical means. Such negotiations were not restricted to the introduction of new equipment, but applied also after the mechanical equipment was installed.

The contract in another case [58] provided that the parties negotiate any reduction in manning which was the economic result of installing laborsaving or automated equipment. The company was allowed to operate the new equipment with various crew sizes for the first 45 days (interim manning) to determine what it considered efficient manning. The arbitrator ruled that the reference point for such manning consideration was the negotiated manning prior to the automation, and that engineering studies which indicated that smaller crews were efficient were not relevant—only the manpower savings over the reference manning was to be considered. In the case, the installation of digital posters had, essentially, no effect on manning. By implication in a case where the contractual provisions resembled the above, interim manning was not to be established in such a way as to prejudice the position of either party in the negotiation on permanent manning.[59]

In the sixth case [60] of this type the contractual requirements

[55] 36 LA 86.
[56] 37 LA 915.
[57] 50 LA 186.
[58] 49 LA 1018.
[59] 49 LA 521.
[60] 46 LA 70.

were not present and the arbitrator upheld the company reduction of a lithograph press crew from five to four—primarily
on the grounds the five-man operation was needed during a
period of high turnover, when one man was always in training—
a condition no longer existing.

Expanding or Changing Operations

A problem developed in another situation [61] when a second
furnace was added in the company's marble department. The
crew on the single furnace consisted of one furnace tender, two
machine tenders and one bagger. For the second furnace, only
one machine tender was included. This, effectively, was crew
reduction and brought on the grievance. The arbitrator found
that there had been, essentially, an inequity in production pace
of machine tenders, compared with the other two classsifica-
tions, and the move by the company tended to correct this
inequity. In these circumstances, the arbitrator decided the crew
adjustment was appropriate.

Essentially similar were company actions [62] in expanding open
hearth operations, first adding four furnaces to the existing six,
then an eleventh. Studies were made of various jobs, duties real-
located, and personnel added as needed. Since personnel increases did not maintain the previous crew size, a grievance was
filed alleging failure to provide an adequate work force—on
health/safety grounds, to which the arbitrator's jurisdiction was
limited. The arbitrator reviewed the operations in detail and
concluded health and safety were not endangered by the lack
of more personnel.

Issues related to the maintenance of local working conditions
appeared in some of the cases. The customary crew size under
shut-down conditions in a hot mill was one craneman.[63] Hence,
a reduction to one craneman was upheld. In a second case [64] the
elimination of a stillman's job, reassigning his remaining duties
to a pumpman after discontinuing operation of two coke-byprod-
ucts columns, represented the kind of change in operating conditions which negated the maintenance-clause protection and per-

---

[61] 33 LA 29.
[62] 28 LA 651.
[63] 40 LA 487.
[64] 40 LA 70.

mitted crew-size reduction. Circumstances [65] also validated the reduction of the number of mould dipping laborers in a crew. However, conditions [66] had not changed sufficiently—only one minor change over a 21-year period—to justify elimination of one of a two-man crew.

Under a similar type of requirement [67]—that the company maintain the number of men for the "then existing operations" —the company made extensive changes in boiler-house operations, including automatic equipment, and eliminated a helper job. In support of its grievance, the union argued that just as much raw water was being treated as before, so that the existing-operations requirement precluded this crew reduction. The arbitrator decided this was not the sole criterion, that process and method should also be considered. He thereupon concluded that the contract did not rule out the reduction, and that the elimination of the helper did not unduly burden the remaining crew.

What Constitutes a Crew

The boiler house of a company [68] also figured in one of the special cases noted at the beginning of this section. Here the company made changes, which resulted in reduction of the number of repairmen and helpers on the third shift. On the local-working-conditions argument, the arbitrator said no job classifications had been created or eliminated, there had been equipment changes, and the reduction had not placed undue burden on the remaining employees.

In particular, the arbitrator held these repairmen and helpers did not constitute a crew. To constitute a crew, he thought most arbitrators would agree, it was necessary that

> "the employees making up the work force have a relationship that is interdependent to each other. This would mean that, when one member is removed or absent, the remaining workers are required to assume an increased amount of work, or there is a significant change in the type of work they are required to perform. In other words, there must be a relationship between the repetitive nature of the work and the interdependence of the workers to each other."

The next case [69] is particularly interesting, in view of the

---

[65] 46 LA 733.
[66] 43 LA 1048.
[67] 42 LA 294.
[68] 40 LA 67.
[69] 33 LA 421.

foregoing, because it has been cited on the crew-size issue. There were three technicians in a television station control room. They were all under one classification but, apparently, assignment practices had resulted in three more or less differentiable positions. The issue was whether or not the station could combine two of these positions or, alternatively, eliminate one man from the control room; there was a process of equipment integration coupled with the company's action. The arbitrator concluded there was nothing in the contract or the relations of the parties to preclude the elimination and combination which took place.

Impediments to Crew Reductions

Various equipment changes, mechanical changes, and methods improvements in another situation [70] resulted in a starch department crew reduction from five to four and a reduction from four to three in the "washer tenders and sour washer tenders" group (in textile manufacture). There seems to have been no argument on the reductions, but only about wage increases for those remaining in the crews. The company thought there might have been some increased workload but not sufficient to warrant upward rate adjustments.

The arbitrator suggested and parties agreed to have the Bureau of Labor Statistics survey the industry for rates and workloads. Apparently, the report favored the company position. The arbitrator stated, effectively, that the BLS report was not a substantial guide for decision, that the remaining workers were surely "required to do some amount of work which is more than they were required to do formerly," and awarded a 5-percent increase in the base rates.

In another case,[71] elimination of a sack catcher from crews sacking and handling salt was held improper by an arbitrator, even though there had been installation of new conveyor equipment. During negotiations, the company had insisted on discontinuance of a piecework system. Remaining in the contract, however, were statements of piece-rate factors (two-cents per ton bonus) for the crews here involved—and the crews were identified by jobs and size. The arbitrator held that the union reasonably could believe these special provisions embodied a promise

---

[70] 5 LA 115.
[71] 46 LA 503.

that these crew sizes would not be unilaterally reduced. A more specific contract stated that the present incentive system would prevail until a new one was mutually agreed upon.[72] Thus, a three-woman shirt pressing crew could not be reduced to the predecessor two-woman crew. But, in a different case,[73] where the contract stated the company should maintain "adequate manpower," eliminating a second can filler was upheld when new equipment removed most of the duties previously necessitating two can fillers.

In a case [74] for comparison with the first pair of cases discussed in this section, the arbitrator ruled that a period in excess of three years—"without any hint from the Company that it contemplated any reductions"—was too long a "shakedown" period to justify a crew reduction on the basis that fewer workers were required for regular operations. Involved here were changes in a patenting furnace. The arbitrator examined the changes made by the company and found they were primarily aimed at getting more efficiency from the furnace, and that reduction in crew size was not warranted by the technological changes.

Another case [75] involved the long-established shift crew in a company's power division, consisting of head fireman, second fireman, and third fireman (four crews). Pursuant to studies by an outside industrial engineering firm, the company reduced the crews by eliminating the four third firemen, stating (from the studies) that the reduced crews still had 5.87 hours of unused time per shift. As noted in Chapter VI, the arbitrator ruled that the company had accepted, for a period of 20 years, the idea that regular manning was the three-man crews. While it was a fact that methods changes, under the contract, would likely have permitted the crew changes, all that occurred here was a study which revealed idle work time for all firemen. Such, in the arbitrator's opinion, was not a plausible basis for crew reduction, considering that all duties remained and were being performed, and that three-man crews had existed for a 20-year period.

[72] 50 LA 804.
[73] 50 LA 458.
[74] 39 LA 432.
[75] 38 LA 799.

Effects of Cumulative Changes

Finally, there were two cases involving the same company and union, whose contract provided that full crews, as determined by the company, were to be maintained. In one,[76] the arbitrator upheld the company's reduction of the refineries operator classification by one man per shift, concluding there was no unreasonable increase in workload resulting from this redetermination of crew size. The issue was complicated by allegations that no specific technological improvement justified the reduction. The arbitrator said:

> "While the force reduction in this unit was not related to any particular technological change, the Arbitrator believes and finds that there was an accumulation of improvements and smoothing out of operations over a period of time all of which combined to make the Company's action a reasonable exercise of managerial discretion keyed to 'operational needs'. . . ."

Additional comments by the arbitrator are of interest:

> "On general balance it is the Arbitrator's view that improvements over a long period of time tended to cancel out any increased workload resulting from the new equipment. The Company was not compelled to act in reducing the crew at the exact time of the changes in equipment to produce stability of operation. To so rule would, in my opinion, adversely affect the interests of the work force. It was convincingly shown that the Company policy has generally been to reduce the force by attrition rather than by eliminating jobs at the exact time a situation of over-staffing may have been believed actually to be present."

The second case [77] indicated the company had advised the union of force reduction through attrition. Here, a paint foreman was promoted but the company did not fill the vacancy, and the grievance ensued. No violation of the full crews provision was found.

Not unexpectedly, these cases indicate that arbitral opinions on crew size fall into essentially the same pattern as workload cases. Hence, the summary statements in the preceding section also apply here. In particular, the above cases emphasize that arbitrators will insist on substantial changes as a condition prece-

---

[76] 46 LA 140.
[77] 50 LA 752.

dent to crew-size reduction (or workload increase). While the relativity aspect was not as pronounced in these crew-size cases, it was certainly inherent.

The cases herein do reflect, more than the workload cases, the fact that explicit contract language can, sometimes drastically, modify the general rule that arbitrators support substantial, economically based, noncapricious changes by management in these areas.

One particular feature herein should be emphasized—the quality of interdependence which characterizes the crews discussed. If this quality were not present, then reduction of personnel would present problems of classification, seniority and layoffs, rather than appropriateness of crew size.

4. WORKING CONDITIONS

Reference was made to the maintenance of established working conditions in the last section. By reason of express contract language or for other reasons, arbitrators will normally refuse to disturb the established pattern of working behavior, unless there are specific grounds (usually methods changes) for disturbing such behavior. The noncontractual basis for maintaining conditions is practice, the subject of Chapter VI.

Problems of working-conditions maintenance, of course, extend far beyond the scope of this study. The subject is briefly examined here only in terms of its relationship to workload and crew size. In such context, there is a significant paper [78] which reported that standards of arbitral decisions differ on crew-size problems under the silent contract (no working-conditions clause) from those under specific provisions on working conditions. (For matters such as washup, lunch period, and subcontracting, the standards for decision were found to be about the same.) The report suggested that arbitrators were generally not prone to uphold crew sizes which adversely affected efficiency (within the limits suggested in this chapter), although crew size tended to be protected, to a considerable degree under 2B-type contracts.

Steel Industry

This last refers to the most widely known "local working con-

---

[78] Wallen, *The Silent Contract vs. Express Provisions: The Arbitration of Local Working Conditions*, Collective Bargaining and the Arbitrator's Role 117 (1962).

ditions' " clause, that associated with the steel industry and identified as Section 2B of the contract with the Steelworkers. Whether this clause was adopted by bleary-eyed bargainers at 4:00 a.m. one April morning in 1947 with no expectations as to what it would become,[79] or whether what it has become is confusing because of variations among companies and among plants of a company,[80] it has, in fact, been an impediment to crew size changes as stated.[81] Section-2B-type clauses typically provide that change is appropriate when the underlying basis for the protected working condition no longer exists; changes in equipment or methods accomplish this.[82]

The comments about the working-conditions clauses of the steel industry are included because some of the cases in this chapter—and, more generally, in this study—are disputes involving various steel companies and the Steelworkers. Dispute settlements involving Section 2B and all other aspects of the industry's contractual labor relations are well reported.[83]

The restrictions on management action of these working-conditions clauses cease when the conditions themselves change and, therefore, no longer support the previous relationships. For example, the construction of a new mill, changing relative location and sequence of work, changed the basis for the local working condition claimed to prevent a combination of two jobs.[84] Similarly, changed conditions[85] supported removal of a helper who had worked with a ram-truck operator.

Other Industries

Two cases[86] held that elimination of a fourth man from train crews engaged in private haulage of ore from plant to harbor was appropriate. A number of technological improvements, including a redesigned caboose which permitted simultaneous observation by one person of both sides of the right

---

[79] *Steel; 2B or not 2B,* 60 FORTUNE 174 (1959).
[80] *What Work Rules?,* 60 FORTUNE 215 (1959).
[81] Wallen, *supra* note 78.
[82] Steiber, *Work Rules Issue in the Basic Steel Industry,* 85 MONTHLY LAB. REV. 267 (1962).
[83] THE STEEL ARBITRATION DIGEST (Pike & Fischer Inc.) (2 vols., 1946-1962 and 1963-date) ; THE STEELWORKERS HANDBOOK ON ARBITRATION DECISIONS (United Steelworkers) (1960).
[84] 45 LA 778.
[85] 43 LA 770.
[86] 38 LA 228, 39 LA 341.

of way, removed the basis for the previously existing four-man crew. The basis for the local working condition in another case [87] had also been eliminated or changed when the company closed down one mill served by narrow gauge trains, since all other operations were served by standard gauge trains. Hence, elimination of narrow-gauge-train crews was upheld.

On the other hand,[88] economic circumstances were not sufficient justification for eliminating a deckhand. The contract provided that any custom or practice observed on a fleet-wide basis for at least two years was to be maintained unless the basis therefor were changed or removed. Since the deckhand position had existed for more than two years, it had become a protected working condition.

A contract [89] stated that one "intent and purpose" was to set forth "other conditions of employment." Such language did not, said the arbitrator, establish a local working condition which would prevent management from unilaterally reducing a three-man drilling crew to two. The action was held not arbitrary or capricious; it was to meet competitive conditions, and was accompanied by technological improvements. However, in a different case [90] management's handling of maintenance crews over the years was such that the crew had become, in the arbitrator's opinion, a protected working condition. It is interesting that the circumstances in one case, discussed *infra*,[91] seemed clearly to have the requisite interdependence therefor but the case was not handled in terms of crew relationships.

Bases for Protected Work Conditions

To conclude that the underlying basis for a local working condition no longer was applicable, it was not necessary that all of the work done previously be removed.[92] It was sufficient, said the arbitrator, if enough of the work had been eliminated so that there was no longer "any real basis" for the claimed working condition. Tools and dies tended to warp in heat treating, requiring prior grinding to "fit up" these tools. For this

[87] 41 LA 884.
[88] 40 LA 73.
[89] 33 LA 442.
[90] 45 LA 104.
[91] 15 LA 603.
[92] 36 LA 162.

reason and because of their general knowledge of tool locations (there being no crib at the time), die setters were, in effect, also tool crib attendants. A tool crib was established, with an attendant classification, and tooling methods changed so that little or no grinding was required, and such as was required occurred after heat treating. Thus, die setters were needed only occasionally. The change from continual to occasional need was held to remove the basis for the local working condition.

A new cutting-up line [93] was installed, in hot mill finishing, and the company required the inspector thereon to direct and assist the piler in removing rejected sheets and keeping certain production records. The union alleged that these two duties were not required of inspectors on other cutting-up lines, so practice or custom prohibited the requirement on the new line. The arbitrator supported company action, on the basis that there were particularized job descriptions for inspectors on each of the other lines and, therefore, the circumstances (equipment, procedures and so forth) on this line should be the basis for its inspector's description.

Under a contract [94] requiring maintenance of local working conditions, an arbitrator ruled that the job description and classification of storeroom attendant did not constitute a local working condition such as to prevent the company's elimination of the classification, as a result of operational changes. Similarly,[95] the fact that employees regularly worked less than 40 hours per week in classification and filled in with various assignments did not constitute a binding pattern that prevented company elimination of one such classification.

In the processing of hogs,[96] in meat packing, the carcasses came down a gravity-operated inclined conveyor which made an approximate U-turn. At the "U" was a man, classified as "Feed Chain," who spaced hogs, turned them, stopped them from swaying, and engaged hooks which carried them on to two "Head Droppers" who worked side by side. A mechanical spacer was installed which spaced and hooked the carcasses, but did not turn them or stop the swaying. Head droppers objected

---

[93] 11 LA 544.
[94] 44 LA 359.
[95] 43 LA 353.
[96] 15 LA 603.

to doing these functions in close quarters where cutting operations were taking place. The arbitrator agreed that this presented a real safety hazard and ruled that the company must negotiate with the union about the impact of the changes.

A company reduced a two-man pumping station crew to one, by eliminating a helper.[97] The basis for a local-working-condition claim was removed because of installation of new automatic equipment. The arbitrator upheld the company action; he also decided that requiring the one man to work alone at the station, two miles from the main plant, was not a violation of the contract's safety provisions. Similarly, where large shovel operators complained of unsafe conditions because they were required to operate "alone in an isolated area," [98] the arbitrator found that, with improved safety arrangement, conditions were at least as safe as before (in fact, safer).

In another case [99] operation of the furnace was not sufficiently safe, despite technological improvements, to justify not scheduling operators whenever the furnace was "alive." The arbitrator commented:

> "It is not surprising if occasionally a temptation exists for employees to fight for the retention of a job after technological improvements have eliminated all, or most, of the required work duties. We have carefully considered this possibility in our evaluation of the present fact situation, but find as a fact that the evidence proves that a genuine safety hazard exists which will be substantially reduced by the presence of an Operator on all turns when the furnace is 'alive'."

Perhaps this temptation was at work [100] when the local-working-conditions clause was invoked against the company's change in food service, from food trucks to coin-operated vending machines. The arbitrator concluded the condition, if established, required only the provision of reasonable food service to employees, not its provision in any specific way.

Maintaining Beneficial Conditions

A contract clause [101] required the maintenance of working conditions "beneficial" to employees. This, said an arbitrator,

---

[97] 41 LA 300.
[98] 43 LA 427.
[99] 43 LA 583.
[100] 48 LA 55.
[101] 44 LA 563.

operated to prevent a company's unilateral installation of a closed-circuit television system on the production floor. Working without such surveillance was a condition beneficial to employees. In a similar case [102] the arbitrator considered such an installation to be an alternate method of supervision, and upheld the company action. This case was distinguished from the earlier case in that no beneficial-working-conditions clause existed.

The statement made in the last section—that arbitrators look for substantial change as a condition precedent to crew-size reduction—receives reinforcement and further emphasis when the element of working-conditions maintenance is considered. Only where changes in equipment or operations justify the overruling of the local-working-conditions restraints will arbitrators endorse crew-size reductions despite established work behavior patterns. This is so no matter how logical from a workload perspective. Economic considerations are not enough. Also, disposition of safety problems is requisite.

Otherwise, the cases in this section give a good indication of how far-reaching are the efforts to apply the local custom/practice concept. Prime examples include the attempted maintenance of narrow-gauge-train crews when narrow gauge trains no longer functioned in company operations, and the food service problem. The cases also indicate that changes which remove the basis for maintenance of established working conditions can be expected to offset such restraints. Very likely, as has been suggested,[103] the long-run effect of these restraints is favorable, since they spur management to be vigilant in preventing loose practices from becoming established and they inspire innovative efforts to avoid established practices which contribute to inefficiency.

---

[102] 46 LA 335.
[103] Wallen, *supra* note 78.

CHAPTER X

STANDARDS PROBLEMS

Every employment contract can be thought of as embodying two bargains,[1] one called the wage-rate bargain (per time or output) while the other is designated the effort bargain. This dichotomy of bargains is another and useful way of expressing "a fair day's work for a fair day's pay."

In particular, the concept of the effort bargain is useful for determining the relevance of industrial engineering principles and practices to the problems which come before arbitrators. While there may have been no explicit bargaining over effort, there is no question but that a bargain has been struck each time a contract is negotiated. This has been summed up as follows:

> "Time study and its derivatives, standard data and predetermined times, provide the management of a company with a rational system for translating the company's *de facto* work pace, or general work tempo, into individual production standards or output requirements for particular jobs."[2]

This quotation highlights one of the standards problems, work pace, which will be discussed herein. Before that, however, it is desirable to summarize the interrelationships of standards problems.

Range of Standards Problems

Four broad areas of such problems may be identified. These four are contained within the report of a National Academy of

---

[1] Behrend, *The Effort Bargain*, 10 INDUS. & LAB. REL. REV. 503 (1957).
[2] Kilbridge, *Effort Bargaining in Industrial Society*, XXXIII J. OF BUS. 10 (1960).

Arbitrators workshop,[3] but not identified in the same fashion. The first area of standards is designated policy—what initiatives has management in this area, what restrictions, what general commitments? Standards policy, then, is a function of contract and/or management rights (Chapters II and V). Secondly, industrial engineering problems often turn on whether or not there have been changes in methods. If methods change has not occurred, policy limitations may, and usually do, preclude management action—for new evaluation, new standard, new workload or crew size. Interpretations and applications of methods is this second area (Chapter VII).

The third area in standards problems is knowledge of the details and administration of the plan or plans used in setting standards (Chapter V and this chapter). Understanding this third area (and the fourth, as well) is especially important to the parties and to the arbitrator and widely emphasized.[4] In the last reference, it was stated as "absolutely essential that the arbitrator make no final decision until he is satisfied that he knows how a particular time study system works and how it has been applied."[5]

This idea of application—use of the details by which a standard has been developed for determining effort required or wage incentives [6]—is the last area. The present chapter is particularly concerned with this area of standards problems.

It should be observed that, whether or not the standards battles ahead are "stiffer"[7] or are characterized by more understanding,[8] motivation,[9] and/or participation,[10] those which come before arbitrators will involve all four of the areas outlined, no doubt with varying emphasis.

---

[3] Davis, *Incentive Problems*, MANAGEMENT RIGHTS AND THE ARBITRATION PROCESS 50 (1956).

[4] *Id.*; McCulloch, *The Arbitration Issue in NLRB Decisions*, 19 ARB. J. 65 (1964); Myers, *Arbitrating Industrial Efficiency*, XXXI HARV. BUS. REV. 60 (1953); Haughton, *Arbitration of Disputes Involving Incentive Problems*, CRITICAL ISSUES IN LABOR ARBITRATION 94 (1957).

[5] Haughton, *Arbitration of Disputes Involving Incentive Problems*, CRITICAL ISSUES IN LABOR ARBITRATION 94 (1957).

[6] O'Connor, *Wage Incentives*, XIV J. OF INDUS. ENG'R 41 (1963).

[7] Hutchison, *Stiffer Battles Ahead over Work Standards?*, 40 PERSONNEL 47 (1963).

[8] Myers, *Arbitrating Industrial Efficiency*, XXXI HARV. BUS. REV. 60 (1953).

[9] Foley, *How not to Handle Productivity Disputes*, XXXVII HARV. BUS. REV. 68 (1959).

[10] Torbert, *Making Incentives Work*, XXXVII HARV. BUS. REV. 81 (1959).

In the cases considered hereunder one or more of the following specific problems were stressed: temporary standards, work cycle, machine speeds and feeds, pace, and allowances. As before, mutually exclusive categorization was not possible.

1. TEMPORARY STANDARDS

Employees in an incentive shop do not usually perform very efficiently on unrated jobs, since earnings are less. Primarily because of this, estimated or temporary standards are frequently put on jobs until such time as they can be regularized as to method and a regular or permanent standard set. When this procedure becomes a matter of commitment, arbitral problems are likely to result.

A contract [11] provided that incentive standards became permanent unless revised by the company within 30 days after issuance. It also provided for correction of "gross inequities" within one year, under carefully circumscribed conditions. Several grievances were considered in the arbitration, involving "temporary" or "unrevised permanent" rates, by which terms, apparently, the company sought to avoid application of the 30-day rule so as to revise these standards. (One had been in effect for 11 years.) The arbitrator ruled that the contract provision applied to any issued standard, regardless of the label affixed to it by the company.

Because of the 30-day restriction in this case, the parties had developed through practice what may be termed as an interim rate procedure, designating such interim rate as a "half rate." Such a rate came into being when a temporary or initial rate was assigned to a new job and it developed that the time study people could not retime the job within the 30-day period. In such a situation, the custom was to assign the half rate when both parties were aware of this; the half rate was just one half of the temporary rate established.

A particular job was on temporary rate. When the job had not become regular production at the end of the 30-day period, it was placed on half rate with the understanding it would be properly rated when next the job ran and the company had an opportunity to study it. The union was notified of this half

---

[11] 9 LA 66.

rate but no operator was, since the job was not then running. When next the job ran, through foreman error, the temporary rate was assigned; however, this was quickly caught and corrected in the payroll department.

The grievance alleged that the 30-day period had passed and since operators were not notified of the half rate but were, instead, led to believe the full rate applied, the temporary rate had become permanent under the contract. The arbitrator decided the half rate applied since that decision had been made before the 30 days were up and the union was advised. The use of the full rate was considered merely a clerical blunder. The arbitrator thought the situation would have been different if the rate-fixing unit of the company had been responsible for the error.

Various Time Limits

Somewhat similar was a situation [12] in which the established piecework rates for setting sleeve linings in ladies garments was four cents per unit for open sleeves and five cents per unit for closed sleeves. Through error, both types of sleeves were paid for at the five-cent rate until, six months later, the error was detected and immediately corrected. The union claimed the five-cent rate had become permanent for open sleeves, but the arbitrator considered the company action proper.

There was a six-months provision, in another contract,[13] after which a rate became permanent. The argument here involved a two-man rate for a two-man job, the company alleging both that the rate was estimated and that the method was an alternative for a one-man operation. The evidence on this was not conclusive, and the company's allegations of methods changes were held inapplicable to material changes in methods. Consequently, said the arbitrator, the six-months rule applied and the two-man rate was held to have become permanent.

In another case [14] a company simply applied existing rates to similar new products, advised the union of the application, but did not suggest to the union that the application was either temporary or preliminary until studies could be made. The ar-

---

[12] 45 LA 1015.
[13] 2 LA 469.
[14] 50 LA 882.

bitrator ruled it improper for the company, a year later, to attempt to set such rates by established standards-setting procedures. The applied rates had become permanent.

In a case [15] for comparison, the arbitrator interpreted the contract language and its applications to mean that standards were either temporary or permanent, "estimated" standards were always temporary, and that temporary rates were always so and could be converted into permanent rates at any time, even years later. The arbitrator found that the practice of the parties supported these conclusions (the case was noted in Chapter VI).

Company-Initiated Grievances

In a situation [16] where an association initiated a grievance against the union, because of employee resistance to an improved toe lasting machine and in which the association was upheld on the main issue, the arbitrator ruled against a retroactivity claim by the association. He pointed out that there existed a specific procedure in the contract whereby, when the parties were unable to agree on a rate, the company was empowered to institute a temporary rate which would remain in effect until the regular rate was settled through the grievance-arbitration route. Since the company had failed to take advantage of this self-help procedure, they were not entitled to retroactivity.

The company in another case [17] changed from wheelbarrow to lift-truck operations in its burnt brick department and, according to procedure, instituted a rather substantial hourly rate as a temporary rate until new piece rates could be established. However, the employees seemed quite content with the temporary rate, and productivity was so low that company felt it could not establish satisfactory piece rates to reflect the change. It initiated a grievance, which resulted in arbitration.

Apparently, there was recognition of a company-initiated grievance here, but the union felt that no violation of the contract was alleged in this particular grievance. The arbitrator concurred, and commented, as in the above case, that the company had failed to utilize self-help available to it—in this case the exercise of normal managerial prerogatives to institute a

---

[15] 17 LA 293.
[16] 10 LA 535.
[17] 28 LA 132.

rate (by broad leveling, if necessary), and leaving the union to file a grievance if it thought such a rate was inequitable.

Correction of Error

A contract [18] provided that, for new operations where standard data were not available, the letter "T" would be stamped on rates to indicate their temporary nature. The contract further stated:

> "1. Upon completion of time studies of that part of a job where a temporary rate exists, the applied results of that study will make that rate permanent herein. In the event the temporary rate is lower than the permanent back pay rate, the individual shall be compensated for the difference in time on that operation completed before the permanent rate was placed on the coupon."

The problem for arbitration concerned the rate established for upholstery of furniture involving a different attachment than the one for which standard data existed. After some months under the rate, classified as permanent, the lack of standard data was discovered and the company time studied the particular attachment being used. The actual dispute was not in the changing of a designated permanent rate but, rather, over retroactivity. The arbitrator ordered retroactivity in accordance with contract language quoted.

It can be seen, from these cases, that temporary rates are both a help and an annoyance to management in its efforts to establish and maintain a program of standards. Time limitations on temporary rates are, clearly, of value to both management and the union—since the objective is to have standards which are equitable applications of the rate system in use. However, but for the one case where practice developed otherwise, true equity requires that regular rates be established on a reasonably prompt basis. That a 30-day period is probably not reasonable in all circumstances may be deduced from the development of the unusual half-rate procedure.

The two cases of company-initiated grievances give further illustration of the use of a temporary rate—for the specific purpose of enabling the parties to set an agreeable regular rate.

---

[18] 51 LA 682.

These two cases are also valuable in reemphasizing that management's job of managing includes taking initiatory actions which will, eventually, bring about agreement on permanent rates.

2. WORK-CYCLE PROBLEMS

One of the most basic aspects of a good standards program is a clear organization of the processes involved. This is accomplished through application of layout, flow-analysis, and work-simplification principles to achieve what is termed standardization of the work cycle. Only by such work organization and standardization does the company realize the productivity it seeks and gain employee confidence in its standards. This is graphically illustrated in the following quotation: [19]

"This brings us to our third factor: variation in work per cycle. It was painfully obvious during our visit to the different sections of the plant that the employees were anything but assured of the validity of any standard in relationship to any other standard. They pointed out a large number of variables which they 'felt' had not been taken into account when the particular standard was constructed. To mention a few, illustrative of the major categories, the employees felt that the standards were not adjusted for:

"a. Variable distances to the (unfortunately located) tool room. b. Some awkwardly placed pipe-elevating devices. c. The lack of rapid traverse on some mills. d. Variation in raw material standard (pipe-thickness). e. The entire handling problem of pipe sizes.

"These represent an example each of the five major categories of objections raised by the employees, who, it must be stated, indicated a remarkable sense of analysis of the work elements which go to make-up a time-standard."

The procedural guide [20] in one case stated that the entire work day should be considered as comprising three kinds of activity, one of which would be "Producing time" (the others, two types of delays). Producing time would include all cyclic work normally performed on the operations, as well as elements which could logically be determined on a frequency basis. The arbitrator, in another case,[21] noted that the company had determined that a particular work cycle, set up some years earlier, was wasteful and that a shorter work cycle could be determined through rearrangement of work elements, changes in some of

---

[19] 37 LA 279.
[20] 51 LA 101.
[21] 45 LA 996.

the elements, addition of new elements, and elimination of some of the old elements. In a third case [22] inspection of 32 of 1000 cores was the inspection output standard in one case, the frequency being determined by averaging the output of all inspectors over a time interval.

Changes in Work Cycle

Along with establishing work cycles are the problems of change related thereto. The problem in one case [23] arose because the company was able to increase steam pressure, which reduced cycle time on the presses producing molded goods. The specific issue in another case [24] was the removal of the time, from piecework rates, associated with an element eliminated from the cycle. The arbitrator held that the same contractual provision calling for the adding of time for added elements applied equally to removal.

A particularly instructive case [25] posed the question: "Is the standard for anode welding properly set?" The arbitrator concluded that it had been, except for two possibilities—and he directed the parties to make check studies to determine possible impact on the final rate.

The nickel anodes, used in plating, were flats and sheared to approximately three-foot lengths; however, they varied as to length, thickness, and weight. Two sets of two strips were butt welded together, and these assemblies were tack welded on both sides. A used (i.e., partially dissolved) strip was tack welded to this assembly, as well as a half-inch diameter hook (used to suspend it into the plating tank); a wide rubber band was placed over the center butt welds, to protect them from dissolving; the entire assembly was put into two cloth bags, one inside the other, and laid on a skid ready for use.

The arbitrator commented that the cycle was quite closely controlled by the process and the work-place layout, but not entirely so. This meant there were certain features of the cycle variable among the three operators; for example, one operator carried one anode between skid and welding table while another carried two.

---

[22] 51 LA 1280.
[23] 47 LA 170.
[24] 43 LA 1028.
[25] 38 LA 1208.

The final cycle, on which the rate was set, was synthetic, based upon selection of the best of the various elements from the studies made. To this cycle, the MTM system was applied in establishing the rate. This whole process, including the rate setting, was in accordance with established practice.

However, it appears that the company had published this cycle only to the union, not to the employees involved. The arbitrator emphasized the need to generally publish the cycle since it was the reference by which disagreements over rates would usually be settled.

In particular, the arbitrator thought the controversy before him could be traced to the company's failure to generally publish the standard work cycle. He stated:

"[I]t is basic to all predetermined time applications, whether MTM, Work Factor, BMT, or any other System, that the time values be applied to a rigidly defined set of elements, hence cycle. Furthermore, it is also basic that such an analysis must include all work-elements that go to make up the task with proper credit for frequency. Thus, if an operator is performing a work-element which, in the opinion of management, is not needed, he should be so informed."

Idle Time in Work Cycle

In another case,[26] in which there had been substantial methods changes in the forming and hemming of toys made of steel, the company claimed the hem operators could perform the remaining material handling duties of an eliminated helper classification. To resolve the dispute on this point, the arbitrator examined the time studies subsequent to the changes. He found that the forming operations controlled the work cycle, by so much that there was ample time for the hemmers to perform the material handling and still leave time in the hemmers' rate to accommodate the variations and delays argued in support of the grievance.

Utilization of operator time while his machine was in cycle was the specific issue in another case.[27] The assignments were various manual tasks to be performed "during machine cycles only when time permits." The arbitrator supported the company when grievances were filed against such assignments.

[26] 39 LA 102.
[27] 43 LA 1006.

Loose Rates

A rather unusual case [28] represents a somewhat different aspect of the rate question. A certain incentive operator worked on a variety of incentive jobs. However, he was paid day rate rather than incentive on certain "cripples"—jobs on which the rates were loose. As partial compensation therefor, the company had not cut his other incentive rates at a time when there had been a general cut in incentive rates in the plant. The company pointed to this last fact, in arguing against the grievance. The arbitrator's position was that two wrongs did not add up to a right; since others were paid incentive on the cripples so, too, should the grievant be—to do otherwise would be discriminatory. He did, however, refuse to grant retroactivity, on the basis of the company's effort to "do equity."

Loose rates figured in another situation.[29] One of the arguments made against a new incentive plan was that, for particular jobs, which were pointed out, earnings opportunity under the new rates were less than under the old rates. While he found the new plan wanting in other respects, the arbitrator did not concur on this particular argument which the union had thought was significant. His comments were:

> "Quite aside from the fact that they are based on hypothetical assumptions as to welding times, delay time, etc., they represent an effort to test an entire incentive plan upon the basis of a few selected rates. The substitution of a new incentive plan for an old one frequently involves the 'tightening' of rates which are too 'loose' and the 'loosening' of rates which are too 'tight'. It would obviously be unfair to the Union to base a comparison of the two plans on the basis of the 'loosened' rates alone. And it would be no less unfair to the Company to base such a comparison on the 'tightened' rates alone."

Assembly Line Problems

Two cases [30] bring out scheduling and line balancing problems, more complicated aspects of the work cycle because of progressive stations in assembly operations. First, both cases emphasize that scheduling, for assembly operations (or others, for that matter) is a management right—one more significant than

[28] 12 LA 273.
[29] 31 LA 20.
[30] 12 LA 949, 17 LA 293.

the right to set standards in a case [31] where employees could, on notice, strike over production standards. That such right to schedule does have limits is seen in both cases.

In the second case,[32] the arbitrator pointed out that no overall standard for the assembly line could exist. The company could adjust individual cycles, the number of employees on a line, and line speed—all for various total rates of production. However, he stated that the standards for individual suboperations were fixed (*i.e.*, permanent) and could not be changed except for methods changes. On the charge the company was changing such standards, the arbitrator found that only estimated standards had been changed (which the company could do).

Since the assembly line positions were on incentive, the arbitrator found the clear understanding to be that the company could make unilateral schedule changes and within line adjustments up to the 125 percent incentive. Above that, however, changes could be made only on a bilateral basis. As the arbitrator put it:

> "The individual cycles can vary as to difficulty of performance; the order in which the elements occur can have a bearing upon the total time; one combination of elements may be easily obtainable within the allowed time whereas another combination can be attained within this time only after lengthy practice, if at all; and all of this is further affected by the incentive pace set by the line, by individual differences, etc. All of which indicates that this matter of scheduling at rates above 125% is not an open-and-shut proposition of simple arithmetic, but involves careful analysis of individual work tasks as well as bilateral cooperation."

The arbitrator in the other case [33] reached essentially this same conclusion relative to scheduling above 100 percent (in a nonincentive situation)—under a different contract and a somewhat different logic.

Incidentally, one arbitrator [34] stated—in response to a union argument thereon—that the rearrangement of elements on an assembly line "can, and frequently does, result in an increase in output without an increase in take-home pay." This view is not antithetical to the arbitral views in the earlier case.[35]

In another case,[36] time studies indicated the employees were

---

[31] 12 LA 949.
[32] 17 LA 293.
[33] *Supra* note 31.
[34] *Supra* note 32.
[35] *Supra* note 31.
[36] 50 LA 888.

away from the assembly line 45 percent of the time. Based on the studies, management rearranged duties and balanced out the line to 14 assemblers plus an inspector, a reduction of five employees. The grievance arose because of company discipline of employees for failure to meet the standards set after the assembly line was balanced out for the smaller group.

These cases bring out the vital necessity of management action to assure that the best work cycle—for the layout, equipment, and tools available—is carefully established and used in rate setting. The payoffs for so doing are efficient production and equitable treatment of employees (or, at least, regularized treatment of employees). That this extends even further is shown by the cases on loose rates.

The problems of the work cycle increase exponentially when the scheduling and line balancing of progressive assembly lines is considered. That the same sort of approach to the organization of the work is required, and that management is empowered to so organize the work, is shown in the cases. That management's right has its limitation in this regard, as in other aspects of management, is also demonstrated.

3. MACHINE SPEEDS AND FEEDS

One aspect of establishing the best work cycle relates to the speed and/or the feed of the machine or equipment used. Obviously, where there is a long operating cycle, so that the operator can readily accomplish all or most of his required manual work while the machine is cycling, there is not much employee concern as to how fast the machine runs—at least within a broad tolerance. Equally obvious is the fact that a majority of production jobs involving machinery are man-machine interrelationships, with manual effort in some intimate functional relationship with machine speeds and feeds.

Consequently, employees are concerned with the speeds and feeds at which machines operate—both in terms of the work cycle on which the standard is set and in terms of changes therein. In fact, a major issue is management's right to increase machine speeds and feeds.

Mention should first be made of two cases [37] discussed in the

---

[37] *Supra* note 30.

preceding section. They both indicate arbitral approval of the proposition that management is privileged to determine the speed of an assembly line—up to the limits noted. In particular, the report in one of these cases [38] explained that the question of pace (the subject of the next section) had come to arbitration because the parties chose that route instead of a negotiated determination following a strike on production standards. In the strike settlement agreement, while the company's right to determine assembly line speed was recognized, the company nevertheless committed itself to keep line speed constant and units evenly spaced.

Right to Specify Speed

Operating speed of a "No. 2 Wheelabrator Line" was involved in an incentive dispute.[39] The parties' contentions about incentives and the effects of line speed are contained in this excerpt from the report:

> "The Union attempts to show that there is a reduction of 55% in the standards of the 1964 incentive plan over the standards in the 1953 incentive plan. But the Company points out that the calculations in the Union exhibit are based on an invalid premise. They assume an operating speed of 100 feet per minute, which is not possible. The operating speed of the Line is 40 to 60 feet per minute. If it is assumed that 50 feet per minute is the prescribed speed, the values in the Union's calculations for the 1964 incentive plan would have to be doubled under the following formula (set forth in the 1964 and 1967 incentive plans); 'To adjust to proper standard minutes per 1000# based on specified operating speed, multiply the above standard by the factor, 100 ÷ specified speed.' "

The arbitrator concluded that the company had prescribed speed, and had issued standing instructions thereon. Hence, employees were not to operate at a faster speed despite a claim that this penalized them in their earnings.

An early case [40] disposed of the question of whether or not rates could be changed when newer and faster machines were installed. The arbitrator said they could; he even cited War Labor Board orders to that effect. It seems unlikely that this bare question would again come before an arbitrator. (How the employees are to receive their share of the "fruits of progress" is a different matter, of course.)

---

[38] *Supra* note 31.
[39] 50 LA 930.
[40] 3 LA 677.

The particular requirements [41] for prior notice to the union on increasing speed and feed gears "alone" as a basis for increased output, and grievance arbitration if no agreement were reached, were discussed in Chapter VII.

Management's right to increase machine speed is highlighted in another case.[42] Weatherproof polishers, machines used to apply a finish coat of asphalt and mica to the outer surface of a weatherproof wire, had operated for about 10 years without change. The company increased machine speed from 210 feet per minute to 250 feet per minute, and set new, lowered incentive rates. The arbitrator stated that there was no question but that the company could do this, and pointed out that this change was not one made pursuant to methods changes but was simply and directly the speeding up of the machines. He went on to determinations of increased workload and increased earnings for the operators.

Right to Specify Feed

In the bag-sewing case,[43] noted in the last chapter, transferred employees objected to rates which had been proved, accepted, and worked under by other employees without dispute. The problem arose this way. The complaining employees had worked on a machine identified as 1800 (model number, it is believed). Upon transferring to 51100 machines, they argued that they were sewing 37 percent more stitches per inch—which was approximately true. However, this was misleading so far as a workload was concerned, in the arbitrator's opinion.

As he pointed out, rates on both types of machines were set at about the same time, using the same principles and procedures.

"The fact that the '51100' machine sews more stitches per minute is irrelevant since the lineal speed of that machine is in fact slightly slower than the lineal speed of the '1800' machine. What happens is that the needle on the '51100' machine moves up and down at a faster rate, sewing 5.5 stitches per inch, as compared with 4 stitches per inch on the '1800' machine."

Thus, the case indicates, rather graphically, that increased feed is appropriate management action.

---

[41] 16 LA 770.
[42] 10 LA 20.
[43] 13 LA 227.

Effects of Increases

Two cases between the same parties but before different arbitrators concerned increased machine speed. In one,[44] there was an increase in the speed setting for automatic machines used in cut-pointer operations in screw manufacture. The argument here was not the increased speed but if rates should be adjusted to reflect the speedup; the arbitrator thought not. The other case,[45] in the company's slotting machine department, also involved machine speedup. Here, the arbitrator thought wage adjustments were in order.

The last case was paired with another [46] as "chart" cases in Chapter VI. There was a specific increase in the speed of grinders, from 94 feet per minute to 110 feet per minute. Again, the fact of increase was not a major issue. The arbitrator finally concluded that employees could operate at the higher speed, with not too much more scrap, and still have an opportunity to earn the target 130 percent without a change in rate.

In another case a larger gear [47] was installed on a Voelker rotary press, in fabric manufacturing. This increased the speed of the press—the speedup increasing output about 7.5 percent. Again the argument centered on a rate increase, which the arbitrator denied.

One case [48] presents an interesting comparison to the case [49] of the worn injection die (discussed in Chapter VII). One of the operations in wall-tile manufacture is that of pressing "dust" into the tiles. The equipment had operated at speeds of 11 to 13 impressions per minute; however, after reconditioning, the presses operated uniformly at a speed of 14 impressions per minute. The arbitrator upheld the company argument that all that had happened was a return of the presses to former operating efficiency. He therefore concluded this was not a speedup such as would require negotiations (although he did direct negotiations on the impact of the elimination of a classification).

Limitations on Change

A case [50] concerned with operator ingenuity revolved around

---

[44] 11 LA 108.
[45] 13 LA 220.
[46] 28 LA 259.
[47] 7 LA 27.
[48] 12 LA 631.
[49] 9 LA 66.
[50] 27 LA 389.

a contract provision: "When there is an approved change in feeds and speeds on existing turret lathes, milling machines, drill presses, Do All saws, and power hack saws and there is no change in tooling, design, material, methods or machines there will be no change in the standard applicable to machine times." The actual dispute was over the meaning of "existing," the company contending it meant only machines "in house" at the time of the contract. The arbitrator disagreed, pointing out that such an interpretation could effectively destroy the very incentive the contract clause sought to offer.

Contract language in one situation [51] was found to limit management's control over speed. The arbitrator made this specific statement: "Speed or rate of production is not a 'process or method' within the meaning of (the applicable section)." In another case [52] management's actions resulted in a negative decision on a unilateral increase in the speed of a packaging machine (bagging potato chips).

The contract in this last case [53] specified that management could make changes in methods and change production rates accordingly, with prior notice to and consultation with the union. However, management's whole pattern of conduct with respect to the speed increase was such that the arbitrator upheld the union grievance protesting the change.

The cases uniformly, but for one, indicate that arbitrators endorse management's right to increase speed and feed of machines. This right clearly extends to discussions affecting the speed of assembly lines. However, the consequence of restoring equipment to its rated performance, by overhaul and reconditioning, will not be considered machine speedup.

Implicit in some cases and specific in others, however, is a requirement that such increases be reasonable and not unduly burdensome on employees. Management must also consider operator ingenuity when the contract so directs, and deal with the union in good faith when adjusting machine speed.

Increased machine speeds and feeds, will, generally, affect

---

[51] 21 LA 84.
[52] 47 LA 986.
[53] *Id.*

the work cycle and therefore have an impact on standards. Wage increases to accompany machine-speed increases are sometimes judged appropriate by arbitrators, but the cases highlight the fact that such a result does not automatically follow a speed increase; the attending circumstances—for example, a below-normal workload—govern decisions on wage increases.

4. PACE

In an article [54] quoted in part at the beginning of this chapter, the author divided the effort bargain into two components. The one which he identified as task-level bargain represents the general effort level of the plant (and may be management-imposed, union-dominated, or somewhere in between these two extremes). This is what is commonly referred to as "pace," "normal" effort, or some similar term. It is integrated into a particular work performance standard by such processes as "leveling" and "rating," which refer to the methods used by industrial engineers to translate the general task level into individual standards.

In fact, the concept of pace is more often thought of in terms of individual performance standards—particularly in arbitral disputes—than in terms of the general task level, although this second is the general referent. This point was recognized in the same article [55] where the following statements were made about the output bargain:

> "When a company's general task level has been fixed, either overtly or tacitly, subsequent production standards are based on it. The output bargain, or agreement on production standards for individual jobs, thus assumes a prior task-level bargain. Using as its measuring stick an abstract concept of 'normal pace' derived from its accepted task level, management establishes individual production standards. That is, management translates the plant task level into individual output requirements for each job. This process of work measurement is extremely difficult to carry out in such a way as to apply the normal pace concept uniformly throughout the company. It is a continuous job, since product and processes change, and is usually performed by a number of time-study men."

Definition

Later in the same article [56] appeared this definition: "A 'cor-

---

[54] Kilbridge, *supra* note 2.
[55] *Id.*
[56] *Id.*

rect' production standard can be defined, for the output bargain, as one which, in the views of management and labor, accurately translates the company's normal task level into an acceptable output requirement for a particular job."

In view of the output-bargain quotation, the following from one of the cases [57] is of interest:

"Work-pace is a function of agreement: it varies radically from industry to industry and from plant to plant in any given industry. Normalcy for this factor is one concept in the Building Trades Industry and quite another in the Textile Industry, still another in Glass, in Steel, and so on. The normal work-pace for hourly rated personnel is frequently arrived at without negotiations, but such a norm exists, nevertheless. It exists in this plant; lacking more specific documentation, it represents the general pace that was current at (or around) the general period of the signing of the Agreement. If, at that time, neither party objected to the generally practiced pace level established over the years, then there was 'agreement' reached as to pace. If, on the other hand, either side challenged the status quo and agreement was reached to change such status quo, then the work-pace is subject to revisions during the life of the Agreement."

Progressing from the abstract concept of normal to its application in a particular job is, as already noted, the process of leveling or rating. Why such a process should be necessary has been neatly summed up:[58]

"From our observations and experiences we know there are wide differences in capacities and abilities of individuals in every walk of life. Although this variation in performance may be caused by many different things, they all affect the two main factors that govern the output of the operator. These are his skill and his productive effort or effective speed. Thus, of two people exerting the same productive effort, one may accomplish more in a given time because he possesses greater skill than the other. One has only to compare the clumsy way an apprentice handles his work with the smooth, easy manner of the experienced operator to see extremes in skill. In a like manner of two people possessing the same skill, one might do more work in a given time because of his greater physical exertion. More work is accomplished by moving at a faster pace."

The Normalizing Process

The above article [59] proceeded to comment on the only way to relate the observed level of skill and effort to the abstract. To do this, the time-study analyst must reduce or increase, to

---

[57] 40 LA 33.
[58] *Rating Factor, or Leveling the Study,* 49 BUTCHER WORKMAN No. 6, 24 (1963).
[59] *Id.*

normal time, the times he has observed for each element of the study.

That the normalizing process must be undertaken, because of skill/effort differences, is substantiated by the remarks of an arbitrator in one of the cases [60] in the study:

"Rating the operator is an inherent and absolutely necessary concomitant of the standard. The data obtained by stop watch studies merely discloses the actual time taken by an operator to perform a cycle of work. This data cannot disclose the speed, skill, output and effort applied while the study was being made. It is an absolute requirement to determine the extent of the operator's skill and effort in order that a proper standard may be fixed to permit the *average* operator to do the same work in the time set. Even when the cycle may be machine paced, speed, skill and effort must be rated, for though machine pacing tends to bring the performance of operators to a much more uniform level, there is still considerable variation in output per unit of time."

It is interesting to note that this arbitrator also pointed out that standard data (which is the basis of the various indirect systems of measurement) consists of innumerable individual time studies, each of which was rated when taken. That is, the normalizing process has been built into standard data.

Two other general comments seem useful. It has been observed in some of the references [61] and, generally, that trained, experienced time-study observers will level the performance of workers within a range of plus-or-minus five percent of the norm. A variety of useful efforts have been made to quantify this norm; however, the application of an explicit model to an observed worker is subjective, so that this range of accuracy makes the art of leveling very useful. (Despite the variety of statistical processes which have developed in this field, it must be remembered that probable error is an integral part of probability theory, on which statistical sampling plans are based.)

The other comment concerns the necessity for arbitrators to inform themselves of the parties' underlying premises as to pace [62] or of the history of the pace tradition under similar circumstances in the plant and, if possible, in the industry.[63]

---

[60] 32 LA 640.

[61] *Supra* note 58; Fairweather, *Arbitration of Disputes Involving Incentive Problems: An Industry View*, CRITICAL ISSUES IN LABOR ARBITRATION 61 (1957).

[62] Waite, *Problems in the Arbitration of Wage Incentives*, ARBITRATION TODAY 25 (1955).

[63] *Supra* note 3.

Effect of Practice on Pace

The question posed in a particularly interesting case [64] was if the company had established new production standards in the box-springs department, consistent with the production attained "by a normal, proficient operator working at a normal pace and accurate within the usual variances determined by Time Study Engineers," and, if not, what remedy should apply?

There had been a major re-engineering in this department, after which production operations were organized along a single line using a series of two-man stations. The arbitrator was "expected to avail himself of technical assistance" and an industrial engineer on the engineering faculty of the University of California was retained. This man spent several days at the plant, and made a confidential report to the arbitrator.

The company officials, who had had assistance from their corporate industrial engineering staff, alleged the rates, which the union thought were too tight, had been based upon a general or universal concept of normal effort, equivalent to rather widely used standards of "walking three miles per hour or turning 52 cards in half a minute." The union emphasized past practice at the particular plant, which was thought to indicate a slower pace than that used by the company.

The arbitrator concluded both positions were correct, specifically stating that the new standards were well within the concept of normal "as generally conceived by industrial engineers." They would have been, he said, appropriate for a new plant. However, he ruled that the practice of decades could not be ignored, since during that period the same definition of normal continued, numerous standards had been established, and many grievances settled. "In the process a certain pace of work has become 'normal'. Seen by an outsider, this pace appears slow. Nevertheless it cannot be stripped of contractual significance." He later stated: "I do not think I am entitled to discard their concept of 'normal' in a dispute of this kind." One of the arbitrator's concluding remarks is also of interest:

"Finally, I am not suggesting that the concept of 'normal' effort in a given plant is unchangeable, nor that a leisurely pace award

---
[64] 33 LA 725.

must be maintained perpetually where the result is inefficient production and economic difficulties. The proper approach is to consider the problem as a whole, however, rather than establish new standards in one department that are out of line with the remainder of the plant."

Time studies which had been leveled, at the time the studies were made, presumably would have been properly and accurately adjusted for the task-level bargain, if not challenged when issued. The arbitrator concluded this had to be the appropriate position in a case where the company attempted to "correct" some established rates on the basis that there had been errors in leveling. [65]

Contract Provisions

Contractual provisions sometimes define pace. In one case,[66] it was specified that

"the performance of the operator in question will be rated upon the basis that the performance of an average operator working with average skill and effort under average conditions is equal to 100%, not 120% as it has been assumed and applied in the past. The Union also understands that the incentive standards reestablished or initially set after the date hereof will require an experienced and competent employee to work at an incentive pace and to fully utilize the time, throughout the shift, to earn twenty-five (25) per cent in excess of the base rate for the operation."

In another report [67] standard time, reflecting an interesting procedure guide, was defined:

"The standard time in the *Timken practice,* is the time required for performing the operation at a normal pace or "day work" pace and *includes adequate time for rest and personal needs. An average operator, qualified for an operation can usually produce approximately 30% more than the standard calls for without undue hard work.*" (Emphasis added by arbitrator).

The arbitrator in a different case [68] discussed the concept of pace as it related to pressmen operating molded-goods presses. He stated:

" 'Regular speed, skill and effort' means the usual or normal speed, skill and effort of individual pressmen. This is not necessarily a speed identical to the allowed cycle time on a particular combination of molds. Individual pressmen may be able to beat the cycle

[65] 49 LA 912.
[66] 49 LA 320.
[67] 51 LA 101.
[68] 47 LA 170.

time by working at their regular speed. By the existence of the Memorandum, however, both the Company and the Union concur that 'regular' speed does not mean a pace that is clearly excessive or abnormal. . . .''

Another arbitrator ruled [69] that a contract provision required that the effort-earnings relationship which existed before had to be maintained after a new machine was installed, and he adjusted the new rate to reflect this requirement.

Effort-Earnings Relationships

One of the allegations in another situation [70] was of improper leveling (that the company had decided upon an output and then rigged the study to show such output). On this the arbitrator stated:

> "The issue cannot be decided on the basis of the 'levelling' arguments; they are based upon judgment and vary from person to person and place to place. There was, however, no indication in any of the material submitted that the time-studies were levelled in reverse as claimed by the Union. In other words, we could find no evidence to the effect that the studies were made without levelling and then levelled to result in the 'pre-determined' 1719-set value. There is, in fact, very little that can be done about the entire levelling problem; even if an independent study were to be made, it would represent the independent's evaluation of pace rather than what is normal to this plant. We must therefore fall back on direct evidence, upon direct observations, and upon direct testimony."

This effort-earnings relationship was described in two cases [71] (discussed in Chapter VII), where the arbitrator interpreted job requirements in the contract as reflecting the ratio of incentive effort to incentive production. That is, if this pace-results ratio had changed, job requirements, under the contract, had changed.

In one case [72] the company's standard was 191 pieces per hour, whereas a standard developed from a union time study worked out to 180 pieces per hour, a difference of about 6 percent. Such a difference was thought to be within expected differences from two studies made by the same person at different times; hence, the rate was set in between, at 185 pieces per hour. In the opinion were these comments:

---

[69] 22 LA 450.
[70] 39 LA 102.
[71] 5 LA 712, 8 LA 846.
[72] 10 LA 480.

"An examination of the time study records of both the company and the union reveal that difference between the company and the union suggested standards is largely, if not entirely, attributable to the rating factor. Inasmuch as the efficiency ratings of the operators involved is a result of the exercise of subjective judgment, it is difficult, if not impossible, for the arbitration board to judge the validity of the respective ratings."

Incidentally, at least one writer [73] has warned against splitting the difference, as ruinous of the equities and the incentive system.

Interpretation of Required Pace

The particular issue in the assembly line case [74] referred to in Sections 2 and 3 above, was: Could the company require an employee to perform his work on any unit in less time than the company's time study showed for his assignment, provided he were assigned no more than 480 minutes of work—as measured by time study—in an eight-hour shift? The question was answered in the negative. As stated in Section 3, this arbitration was part of a strike settlement. It is interesting that the case was heard by a tripartite board, whose chairman was the permanent umpire under the contract.

The report on the case [75] is extensive, as well as informative. The gist of the two positions relative to pace is important for understanding the ruling. The union argued that what has been described herein as the output bargain was the standard per unit of the output, that the standard was expressed in terms of allowed time (including allowances) per unit, and, therefore, an employee could not be required to work at a pace exceeding this pace. The work involved was, as noted, line-controlled, non-incentive assembly work.

The company argument was, essentially, that the production standard was the work to be performed within a day as "480 standard minutes" of work, that cycle-balancing problems on the production line sometimes made it imperative that employees at particular stations work as a pace greater than the allowed time per unit, but that this would not exceed the 480 minutes of the shift.

---

[73] Fairweather, *Arbitration of Disputes Involving Incentive Problems: An Industry View*, CRITICAL ISSUES IN LABOR ARBITRATION 61 (1957).
[74] 12 LA 949.
[75] *Id.*

The majority opinion was that the contract did not spell out either of these conceptions of the meaning of production standard. Employees are no more hired by the eight-hour shift than by the week or by the hour. Employees on the line who work on every unit have the same production schedule, said the arbitrator, but their production standards differ because of the per unit measure of their work; this latter is the same, regardless of whether the employee works four hours, eight hours, or one hour of overtime.

The report goes on:

> "The requirement that the employee meet his standard of production, as actually and necessarily enforced by the company, is not a requirement that he merely finish an eight hour shift with a given quantity of work. It is rather a requirement that he meet the standard fairly consistently throughout the day from unit to unit. This is particularly true of line operations where an employee's failure to meet the per unit standards may interfere with the performance of the whole line.
>
> "In the absence of convincing evidence, which is here lacking, that the parties used the phrase 'standards of production' in some esoteric way, it should be given its normal meaning as just stated."

There was a vigorous dissent [76] by the employer-appointed arbitrator (which cannot be reported in full, any more than can the majority opinion). One major point was that, since the contract was silent as to the meaning of production standard, the practice of the parties of treating all-day production as the standard and/or management discretion should prevail.

> ". . . [I]t is common knowledge that production standards in the automotive industry as well as others frequently are established in terms of the number of pieces to be produced for a stated period of time.
>
> "In the absence of any claim or proof to the contrary produced by the Union, the panel is not warranted in characterizing such use of the term 'standards of production' as 'esoteric'."

Pace and Performance

In another situation [77] there were six two-man crews, known as bias cutters, in tire manufacturing. For undetermined reasons, their production fell off from what they had done previously. The company concluded they were engaged in a slowdown, and issued written warnings to them (there were some, not illogical,

---

[76] *Id.*
[77] 42 LA 1162.

deviations) for failing to maintain their "established level of production."

The arbitrator first noted that such a standard (*i.e.,* what a crew had been doing) was not in the contract. Consequently, no particular significance could be attached to this "established level of production," as would be the case if the crews were found to be performing at below-normal piecework pace or failing of satisfactory piecework production.

However, considering a usual measure of satisfactory production—average classification earnings—their productivity was satisfactory. Therefore, although the individual crew's production was down when compared to earlier production, the reduced yield was still above an acceptable average. Since there was no substantiating evidence of a slowdown, the arbitrator thought there was no actual dispute under the contract to be decided.

The arbitrator did comment, however, that the company's attempt to set individual crew standards—the crew's "own proven capacity"—was an error. The company, it was held, can set a standard of production only for a job.

Required Performance

There was a situation[78] involving discharge for a number of rules infractions, one of which was willful limitation and control of output under an incentive system. The arbitrator commented that a decision by an employee as to how much he would produce under an incentive system was inherent in such a system. Its basic purpose was to encourage additional output for additional compensation, which meant the employee had to make a choice (which would be, the company hoped, the maximum of which he were capable). Therefore it was an error to discipline an employee for making a choice, so long as he produced the minimum output required by company rules.

On the point of the man who deliberately controlled his production to certain performance percentages, the arbitrator stated: "The fact of control is, to repeat, in itself a neutral matter." Here, again, was the proviso that the employee produce at or above required minimum output.

For comparison is another disciplinary situation [79] (where the

---

[78] 8 LA 234.
[79] 42 LA 298.

arbitrator found the action improper), of interest because of some comments in the opinion. An unusual question was posed: Is the pace at which pieceworkers who have already "made their rate" their own affair, or is it also a legitimate concern of management? The arbitrator stated that standards are established for "a steady and sustained level of effort," and that the employee who races along so he can be idle later is no friend of management nor of fellow employees. "He distorts the entire time study picture, and his erratic pace is a burden to his fellow workers and his supervisor."

The arbitrator then indicated what is generally known: that employees often make some formal or informal determination of output. This led him to consider whether it was to be deduced that output on piecework was entirely up to the worker. The answer was, clearly, that such a view ignored manufacturing costs and particularly the relationship of overhead costs to the number of units produced. Continuing work pace, even on piecework, was thought to be a legitimate concern of management.

Finally, there was a case [80] in which the arbitrator upheld a company requirement that employees make equivalent progress toward 100 percent of the production standard as they progressed along the automatic wage progression range. By the same reasoning,[81] another arbitrator held a company to be unreasonable in demotion of an employee who had progressed to 85 percent of standard in 10 weeks whereas fully competent employees had 40 weeks or more of experience.

The issue of pace or normal effort is undoubtedly the most important aspect of a standards program—because of employee lack of understanding about the normalizing function in standards and because of the judgment content in such normalizing. It is very easy to appreciate how an employee might accept without comment a time study observer's measurement of his work patterns, but still emotionally react to the same observer's judgment that his pace was below normal. No doubt others, including arbitrators, experience similar reactions to pace judgments.

---

[80] 50 LA 136.
[81] 51 LA 1280.

The most basic consideration in pace is the realization that there is a general output norm for an industry, for a geographical area, for an individual plant. All plants of a particular area or a particular industry will not have the same norm, but can be generally categorized as high- or low-paced plants. The important point here is that the general norm exists; it may or may not have been negotiated, but it is there. Incidentally, this general norm can and does vary with time, usually on a long-cycle basis.

This general norm is the basis on which an individual standard is brought into equitable relationship with other standards in the plant. The processes of leveling or rating, seeking to translate observed effort to equivalence with the general norm (by adjusting time measurements), are essentially equitable since they make uniform the effort required for standard performance.

These are the factors which make it exceedingly important that arbitrators thoroughly inform themselves about the history and premises concerning pace in handling disputes involving effort rating. As it was put in one of the cases, this means observation, evidence, and testimony. The importance of this was illustrated in the box-spring case where the pace of the plant in question was found to have existed for years at a level below the industry norm, and the plant practice was held to govern standards in that plant.

An example which appears to illustrate how not to resolve a pace issue was the split-the-difference situation. However, this case does bring out, as did others, that effort is intimately related to earnings. In fact, some form of effort-earnings relationship is the way generally used by labor and management to mutually fix or stabilize pace in the contract.

The interpretive problems facing an arbitrator when the contract is not clear or is silent on this aspect of relationships are especially well illustrated in the assembly case. It is believed that this case, including the dissent, is of considerable value because it highlights the importance of standards practices in pace decisions.

In addition, this assembly case, and subsequent ones, demonstrate a general rule about management's ability to secure more productivity under a standards program, particularly when coupled with an incentive feature. Once the standard is set (including allowances), an employee is expected and may be required to (on penalty of discipline or discharge) produce to the standard—that is, maintain the agreed-upon pace.

However, management cannot require performance at an above-standard (or faster pace) basis, unless the particular relationship has developed otherwise (the 125-percent incentive case). Above-standard performance is, by the general rule, held by arbitrators to be a matter of unilateral decision by the employee. And the employee is not bound by a decision to produce over standard; that is, his established level of production does not become the performance level which management can hold him to, so long as he performs at or above standard. That this general rule is not the best from a costs-rationalization viewpoint was noted.

5. ALLOWANCES

When a job has been thoroughly methodized and the best work cycle established, this work cycle is measured—by time study, or by one of the various indirect, standard-data types of systems. The computed time resulting from measurement is usually referred to as standard time—per piece, per cycle, per time unit, and so forth. But this is not the production standard since no provisions are made in the time for worker comfort and/or for interferences with direct accomplishment of the work cycle; these are collectively called allowances. When allowances are added to standard time, the resultant is usually called allowed time—per piece, per cycle, per time unit. This allowed time is the production standard.

Types of Allowances

Since in most plants, more than 10 percent of the workman's total day (exclusive of personal time) is involved in allowable factors, stewards and operators were cautioned to give careful study to allowances.[82] Allowances are significant in production standards and, for this reason, often become a matter for arbitral decision.

In one case,[83] an arbitrator observed that an average of

[82] *Allowances*, 49 Butcher Workman No. 7, 24 (1963).
[83] 6 LA 774.

12 percent of unscheduled time came close to a reasonable minimum allowance (of nonproductive time). In another case [84] it was reported that 18 percent allowances—here including personal time—were a part of the production standards.

A contract [85] provided that allowances would be made for personal time, wash-up time, necessary paper work, and fatigue of not less than 25 minutes per day. It also provided allowances for delays and excessive fatigue as "determined by the requirements of the operation." Another contract [86] had somewhat similar provisions, plus a 20-percent incentive factor which became 33 percent on machine-controlled elements or jobs.

In the case [87] involving the procedure guide, quoted in Section 4 and noted in Section 2 (producing time), both avoidable delays and unavoidable delays for which allowances were appropriate were identified, as were classifications of allowance:

"2—*Avoidable Delay*—This time includes elements of delay that would be considered avoidable and not allowed in the standard.
"3—*Unavoidable Delay*—This time includes elements of delay that are either necessary to the operation or random occurrences that interfere with production and that cannot be entirely eliminated. This type of delay is provided for in the time standard by means of allowances as follows:

GROUP I

Fatigue
Miscellaneous Variable Delay
Interference

GROUP II

Major Machine Repair

GROUP III

Personal
Shift Constant Delay
Lunch

GROUP IV

Scrap and Repair Allowance."

---

[84] 50 LA 888.
[85] 49 LA 320.
[86] 47 LA 1089.
[87] 51 LA 101.

Determination and Interpretation

One general comment may be appropriate at this point. Quite often in time-study practice a particular standard is considered incorrect because of interferences and delays (noted in the cases below) which are not accounted for in the study. In such situations, the solution is usually to make all-day production studies, so-called because the time-study observations continue for eight hours, 24 hours, and even longer.

Reference is made to the assembly-line case,[88] previously considered. That issue arose, apparently, from a company practice of speeding up the assembly line at various times to accomplish scheduled production—which was not being achieved due to various occurrences which resulted in line stoppages. It was uncontroverted that line stoppages did occur during the workday.

Because of this fact, the company urged and the dissenter argued that such delays should be offset against the rest (fatigue) allowance in the standards. The majority opinion was that such offset could be possible except that no equivalence was demonstrable. This was because of the company practice of overall leveling (and the inclusion of percentage allowance) by time-study observers. To demonstrate equivalence, said the arbitrator, fatigue and available rest time had to be separately appraised in determining offset since, otherwise, "equivalence would be only accidental." (The minority view would construe this overall leveling as evidentiary of the company view.)

Personal Allowance Usage

Two cases,[89] discussed in Chapter VI, indicated that a company could move to correct loose practices on lunch periods and rest periods, and that excessive rest breaks did not become a practice binding upon the company. However, another case[90] held that a company could not unilaterally reduce established 15-minute washup periods to five minutes.

In another case,[91] a company installed a new (tire) tube-making unit which it desired to run as a continuous operation. Accordingly, it successfully negotiated with the union on allow-

---

[88] 12 LA 949.
[89] 41 LA 1038, 42 LA 1127.
[90] 51 LA 549.
[91] 6 LA 681.

ance to be applied to piece rates in lieu of a 20-minute washup period in existence for noncontinuous operations. Later, when other machines were changed to continuous operations and washup time converted to the piece-rate allowance, the arbitrator held that further negotiations were not required since the principle was already a matter of agreement.

An agreement [92] specified 10-percent personal allowance in the standards (MSD developed). The question was if this covered all allowances, as the company contended, or not, as the union claimed. It was a fact that the contract was silent on other allowances. The arbitrator apparently did considerable research on the subject, since he cited a number of useful references, including the MSD manual, to find that normal allowances usually considered applicable to standards were personal, fatigue, and unavoidable delays. Therefore, since agreement thereon was missing, he suggested that provisions be made for the last two. He also suggested that the liberality of the personal allowance should be considered in determining the other allowances. (Included in the report are some guidelines on the usual magnitude of the various allowances.)

In a case like that of the excessive work breaks, a company changed plant rules to control and restrain such breaks.[93] The union argued that employees could take 12 minutes (20-percent allowances in the standards) of each hour for coffee breaks, if they so desired. The arbitrator's reaction was summed up in the report headnote: "Fact that production standards for incentive workers contained 20 percent allowance for personal relief, fatigue, unavoidable delays, etc., does not entitle employees to 12-minute work break every hour. Purpose of allowance is to permit inclusion in standard of variables that affect productivity but are virtually impossible to measure by time study."

Fatigue Allowance

The issue in a grievance on a certain rate narrowed to an interpretation of a new contract clause stating that the fatigue allowance would range from 7 percent to 30 percent with factors

---

[92] 41 LA 953.
[93] 39 LA 1265.

stated for appraisal.[94] The union contended the language meant that the least fatiguing job would be assigned 7 percent with the remainder raised proportionally higher. The company view was that the commitment called for raising lower rated jobs to the 7-percent minimum, but that the higher percentages applied only when the appraisal factors so indicated. The arbitrator thought that either interpretation was appropriate under the contract language. However, he found that the company had been setting standards under its interpretation of the language for more than a year, without challenge on the point.

Delays and Interferences

In Chapter V, Section 6, there was a quotation [95] with a comment implying that determination of an interference and delay allowance could be a difficult matter, despite various ratio-delay (a frequency sampling procedure) studies. Why the arbitrator believed this, and ordered the recheck study asked by the union, was indicated in his comments. He noted that:

". . . [W]here an integrated 'universe' of activity—such as an operating department—consisting of complementary productive jobs, ancillary activities, indirect jobs and extraneous interruptions, is importantly revised with eliminations and revisions, the new pattern of interrelated activities defies prediction by any device of logic."

This arbitrator also pointed to the judgment area relative to inclusion or exclusion of various activities in allowance computation. He stated the considerations in these terms:

"Some things are clearly in the discretion of the worker, not essential (at least in an excessive degree) to the work, readily preventable; therefore, charged to him as avoidable. Other items, 'beyond his control,' not predictable, pure interruptions, may be handled separately, as items of obvious import and rather infrequent occurrence to be segregated and paid to the worker only to protect his earnings."

Sometimes, depending upon the nature of the work, delays can be equitably accounted for by an average delay allowance in the standard. In one situation [96] such an allowance was challenged by the union, alleging that it impeded production and was unfair. It should be noted that the average delay allowance applied only to delays of less than 15 minutes duration; longer delays were separately accounted for, in the manner indicated in the preceding case.

---

[94] 11 LA 633.
[95] 19 LA 856.
[96] 31 LA 20.

The arbitrator's analysis is of interest.

"Delay allowances are sometimes suspect—for delays can vary so widely in cause, nature and length, that setting a realistic average may often approach in difficulty the timing of an immeasurable job. It is clear, nevertheless, that if a time allowance for delays is realistic and fair, delays which exceed the allowance should in the long run be offset by delays which fall short of it. And if this is true, there is obviously no basis for the claim that the failure to pay separately for delays discourages production."

Interpretation of Interferences

A company [97] ran check studies of several operations and found—and corrected—a 35-percent add-on allowance for machine dwell time. The restudy on this job indicated there was no machine limitation in the operation. The rate in question had been in effect for a considerable period of time, and the arbitrator upheld the union grievance. The claimed error was judgmental and not computational, for which a correction would have been permissible. (It would have to be assumed that the observer who originally set the rate either observed machine interference at that time or goofed—neither alternative being a proper basis for correction after the rate became permanent.)

An incentive plan [98] provided percentage allowances for certain electrical and mechanical delays. When such delays occurred during a shift, all agreed the incentive allowance applied. However, the grievance was that, when one of those delays prevented start of actual work at the scheduled start for a shift, the time should be separately paid and not considered to be within the allowances; it was argued that the incentive plan, with allowances, was not in effect when such conditions obtained. The arbitrator thought the plan was in effect.

The contract in another case [99] provided for the payment of down time, at a straight hourly rate, for such situations as machine failure, faulty material, or waiting time. Employees on the line—oiler filter production—claimed 240 minutes of down time for faulty material, irregularity of the tubes used in the filters. The union claimed the 10-percent delay allowance in the time standards did not apply to this situation, and the arbitrator

---

[97] 49 LA 912.
[98] 31 LA 447.
[99] 35 LA 859.

agreed. However, he found the material was to specifications and disallowed the claim. Another claim [100] in the same case was for 240 minutes of down time because of reworking faulty filters, on the same basis of irregularities in the materials used. On this claim, the arbitrator again found the material satisfactory and pointed out that the incentive was paid for correct filters.

In still a third claim,[101] the employees had worked only a few minutes when it was discovered that the wrong paper was being used. A spool of proper quality paper was found and production resumed. The foreman allowed employees some 290 minutes of down time. Later, employees claimed another 300 minutes of down time because of loss of incentive earnings due to the incorrect paper. The arbitrator ruled that the hourly rate for down time was to compensate for loss of incentive, and was the only compensation so provided. To allow down time for unavoidable delay and then allow more down time for loss of incentive would be a pyramiding of earnings not provided for in the contract.

Allowance Claims

The union in a different case [102] requested that down time—in excess of that provided for in the incentive standards—be compensated at the averaged earned incentive rate. The arbitrator denied the request on the basis of the established practice of day-rate payments for down time. On the other hand, where the contractual arrangements indicated that average earnings should be paid to machine operators for down time,[103] an arbitrator so ordered despite the company's argument that day rate had always been paid for down time. In a third situation,[104] where average earnings were paid for wait time—for presses to cycle—employees could not hurry through cycles to increase the amount of wait time compensation in addition to incentive earnings. This particular wait time allowance was phrased carefully to provide a specified earnings opportunity, but was not an earnings guarantee.

In one [105] of two similar cases a company unilaterally changed

[100] *Id.*
[101] *Id.*
[102] 10 LA 480.
[103] 43 LA 722.
[104] 47 LA 170.
[105] 41 LA 721.

from actual down-time allowance to a system of predetermined, average allowances. The arbitrator ruled that the company could not unilaterally make this change under the contractual relationships between the parties. The other case,[106] involving a tool-changing allowance, was similarly decided.

A 3.7-percent fatigue allowance in another situation [107] was challenged by the union. The arbitrator found it to be consistent with the established, plant-wide procedure for setting fatigue allowance. Time studies on certain group piece rates were questioned in a different case.[108] It was alleged that the company had not made proper allowances for interferences and burdensome tasks. This attack on the validity and fairness of the established allowance schedule was, in the opinion of the arbitrator, a matter for collective bargaining.

Finally,[109] there was the situation in which a welder requested a 3-percent allowance because he had to move from one welding booth to another as work was available (within a department having a maximum of 100 feet from one end to the other). The arbitrator ruled that various allowances in his rate should cover such moves but, otherwise, any actual impact on earnings opportunity would be de minimis.

The cases show that allowances are a matter of agreement or understanding between the parties. Where they are not specifically negotiated, they have become agreement through use. This latter situation frequently occurs when an incentive program is installed (sometimes before union organization) and the system, including allowances, becomes the accepted way of standards setting. In these cases the allowances are as much agreement as if they had been negotiated.

To be expected from the above, the cases hold that allowances, once established, may be changed only through negotiations. There can be no question but that they are conditions of employment in relationships where standards are utilized. It does not matter whether a change in allowances is sought through managerial initiative or through union grievance; arbitrators

---

[106] 13 LA 414.
[107] 38 LA 1208.
[108] 10 LA 480.
[109] 46 LA 557.

will not rule on attempted changes but rather will refer such attempts to collective bargaining.

The foregoing seems clearly to apply to personal time allowances, which are always stated in terms of percentages and/or specific time (as in rest periods). Application is equally clear to fatigue allowances which also are usually expressed in percentages and/or specific time, although elaborate systems for fatigue allowances have been set up; one case indicates this. The point is that these two types of allowances are relatively explicit, at least in applications, and therefore create few problems of interpretation.

Such is not completely the situation with the third category of allowances—variously called delays, interferences, or some special term such as tool-change allowances. (As a matter of fact, tool-change allowances can be stated explicitly in many situations.) These delay allowances are unpredictable, for neither observer nor the employees involved can tell whether the delays experienced during time study will be truly representative of the employees' actual delays over time.

This has been rationalized, in part, by separating long-time delays and interference from what are termed minor delays (less than 15 minutes, in one case). Given a representative study, such minor delays can be allowed for on a standardized basis (often as a percentage of time), so that the minor delays encountered will not overbalance the total of the allowance- and delay-free experience. However, as one arbitrator pointed out, good (and equitable) practice is to include only delays beyond the control of the operator. Classification of delays on this condition can be a problem, of course; the start-of-shift case is an unusual illustration thereof.

Delays and interferences of longer duration cannot be provided for by allowance, on any rational basis. In fact, delays of long and uncertain duration prevent operations under any standard. Hence, usual practice follows the logical course of suspending the standard during such delays. When a standard is suspended, an operator is said to be on down time, a term which refers to being off the standard and to being paid an hourly rate designated for such conditions. The oil filter case illustrates the variety of such circumstances and problems which can arise therefrom.

CHAPTER XI

ARBITRATOR QUALIFICATIONS

It is the purpose of this chapter to consider the qualifications needed by arbitrators for knowledgeable resolution of industrial engineering disputes. This discussion, however, is limited to the specific qualifications required for handling such disputes. Other characteristics—such as knowledge of labor relations, impartiality, and the attributes set forth in Chapter I—are assumed to be present. That is, given all such characteristics, what else is required for the arbitral handling of industrial engineering cases?

As the initial consideration in response to this question, the nature of industrial engineering disputes is reexamined in the light of the cases reviewed. Thereafter, the qualifications of the arbitrators who decided the cases herein are reviewed, in a collective way, in connection with judgments about the technical content of the cases. Commentators' views about technical competence in the arbitration of industrial engineering disputes are considered. Finally, a succinct statement is made about when technical knowledge is required in such disputes.

1. A CRITIQUE OF INDUSTRIAL ENGINEERING DISPUTES

The main thrust of industrial engineering cases is, clearly, their technical or engineering content. This essential engineering nature of the disputes coming to arbitration can be seen, in better perspective, at three levels of application and meaning.

First are those aspects of industrial engineering cases which represent the parties' commitments to each other. These are most often found in the contract, supplemental agreements, and written plans and procedures. They are also found in the established practices, understanding, and behavior of the parties. It may accurately be said that other features of the collective relationship have the same explicit commitments. However, arbitrators must, in most instances, interpret the cases of the type covered in this study in terms of and with reference to the technical matters involved.

To illustrate, consider a fairly common contract clause to the effect that earnings will be maintained, in a standards program, if effort is sustained. Fair disposition of a grievance under such a clause is not achieved by examining earnings records, finding a reduction of earnings, and concluding there is a violation of the clause. Obviously, there must be an investigation of the effort side of the equation. Such investigation not only would seek evidence relating to employee effort, but would also be concerned with aspects of the technology (including the standards program) interfering, or tending to interfere, with performance.

This may come into sharper focus by comparing a contract provision on, say, departmental rotation of overtime. A look at the record, within whatever factual pattern has developed, gives a conclusive answer; there are no engineering technical areas to probe and assess.

Second Level

The second level of application and meaning is concerned with the applications and administration of the various plans, programs, and procedures by which industrial engineering principles are carried into action. This level refers, for example, to the details of rate-setting practices in a standards program: How is the work cycle described? Is it uniformly followed in measurements (time study or otherwise)? Is the effort-rating a problem? And what about strike-outs—are the allowances properly computed?

Or, to take an illustration from job evaluation, the concern may well be the intent of the parties in their specifications for the responsibility factor. If such specifications are in writing, there would seem to be no question about this particular factor; what is written is there for all persons to read and to understand. However, experienced engineers and arbitrators are very likely to ask for "key" job illustrations, to find out what meaning for this responsibility factor has, in fact, become institutionalized by the parties. The identical language in specifications for the responsibility factor can and does have different meanings for different contracting parties, even though they may have adopted the same formal evaluation plan.

This second level, then, is concerned with the "special idiosyncrasies of the establishment," [1] and the myriad details of the application plans and procedures used to implement engineering principles and practices. These first and second levels, so designated, are not mutually exclusive categories; they are, rather, interdependent, together providing the bases for arbitral decisions—along with the third level.

It is believed that the cases herein rather extensively illustrate the first two levels just described. In point of fact, most of the industrial engineering cases appear in one or both of these contexts.

Third Level

The third level of application and meaning also appears in most of the cases, although it is not always so readily recognizable. It was emphasized in Chapter VII. This level refers to the basic engineering involved in the integration of men, materials, plant, equipment, tools, methods, and procedure—the whole complex from which the cases herein arose—which can be collectively designated as manufacturing engineering. Such an array of functions includes design activities, as well as the applications engineering which is readily apparent. (A reasonably concise and not overtechnical description of these functions is set forth as a chapter, entitled "Manufacturing Engineering," in one of the references.[2])

This third level is particularly important to a fundamental understanding of industrial engineering disputes. If we again consider the first example—the earnings-effort problem—it will be seen that a thorough understanding of the meaning and application of the contractual commitments rests upon understanding of the meaning and application of the standards program involved — and, especially, the effort-measurement aspects thereof. However, this second-level understanding rests in turn

---

[1] Unterberger, *Arbitration of Job Evaluation Cases,* 17 ARB. J. 219 (1962).
[2] R. VAUGHN, INTRODUCTION TO INDUSTRIAL ENGINEERING (1967).

upon an understanding and comprehension of the manufacturing methods employed, the equipment being used, the utility of transfer equipment installed, the applied usefulness of tools, jigs, and fixtures, and so on.

In other words, for the understanding needed to arbitrate industrial engineering disputes equitably, it is fundamentally important that the arbitrator know and appreciate both aspects of the man-machine relationships which make up the industrial engineering disputes which come to arbitration. It is in this perspective that the A.I.I.E. definition of the profession, given in Chapter I, is significant—because it emphasizes knowledge, at the minimum by inescapable inference, of the principles by which equipment operates and materials function, as well as knowledge of human behavior.

2. THE ARBITRATORS WHO DECIDED THE CASES

There were 207 arbitrators who decided the 502 cases contained in this report. Not every arbitrator, of course, had an average case load; many are represented by only a single case. Appearing most frequently was an engineer, who decided 26 of the cases herein. The next two most frequently appearing arbitrators were lawyers, with 16 and 11 cases respectively. Fourth in frequency of appearance, with 10 cases each, were an economist and a lawyer. These statistics, while interesting, are of no particular significance since, as explained in the Preface, the cases were selected by content and not by arbitrator.

Various volumes of *Labor Arbitration Reports,* from which the cases in this study were drawn, contained relatively standardized biographical data about the arbitrators. From these, it was possible to develop a useful, though inexact, combination education-experience classification system for the arbitrators involved. Insufficient data were available for 20 of the arbitrators, who decided 29 of the cases, and they were unclassified for this analysis. All other arbitrators were identified, primarily, as lawyers, economists, businessmen, engineers, and social scientists.

From such a classification pattern, it was found that 57 percent of the arbitrators were lawyers, with various experience backgrounds, who heard and decided 61 percent of the cases. If the assumption is made that the social science category and the lawyers are least likely, by virtue of their training, to have an understanding of industrial engineering problems, then the statistics indicate that 63 percent of the arbitrators were within this category and they heard and decided 64 percent of the cases.

It is assumed that an arbitrator whose background was engineering or business would have knowledge of the problems involved in the cases. Sixteen percent of the arbitrators were so classified, and they heard and decided 19 percent of the cases. If we add to the engineers and businessmen the one arbitrator classified as an economist but who was identified in *LA* as an "incentive and job evaluation" arbitrator, the statistics show that 17 percent of these arbitrators heard and decided 20 percent of the cases.

The economists, excluding the one above, represented 10 percent of the arbitrators and heard and decided 10 percent of the cases. It seemed that this group of arbitrators were in-between with respect to knowledge of the subject areas herein, based upon the individuals' particularized education and experience. Consequently, these arbitrators and their cases can be, for this analysis, divided between the two collective categories established above.

By such reasoning and without further considerations, then, 69 percent of the cases were decided by arbitrators who could be deficient in terms of industrial-engineering knowledge, with 25 percent of the cases decided by qualified arbitrators, and 6 percent of the cases unclassified.

For further analysis, the above 69 percent of the cases were segregated between those decided *ad hoc* and those with some other condition of arbitration, such as a permanent arbitratorship or multimembered boards, either *ad hoc* or permanent in nature. Clearly, the permanent arbitrators—umpires or chairmen—will tend to learn about the special idiosyncrasies indicative of the second level of awareness discussed in the preceding section, and also to acquire considerable knowledge about the manufacturing engineering problems of the establishment. Also, it seems logical to assume that multimembered boards, which are tripartite in nature, offer opportunities for introducing industrial engineering know-how into the arbitral process.

The segregation of cases, as described, indicated that *ad hoc* cases accounted for 48 percent of the total—a figure to compare with the 69 percent above.

Finally, from careful study of the biographical materials—for judgments about arbitrator qualifications in industrial engineering areas—a conclusion was reached that approximately one in four did not fully reflect such qualifications. Obviously, this determination has to be qualified, since it is based upon the compressed biographies in *LA* and, in some cases, estimates about the relevance of some of the items reported.

Since the percentages of arbitrators and cases are of the same general magnitude, this statistic can be applied to the 48-percent figure above—to indicate the possibility that insufficient industrial engineering knowledge was brought to bear on some 12 percent of the cases reported herein.

Such pyramiding of assumptions is, of course, not scientific and the end result is speculation rather than fact. Particularly, it must be noted, judging by study of the cases, that arbitrators whose backgrounds seem unrelated to the technical aspects of the study have, in fact, acquired substantial knowledge and understanding of industrial engineering as it appears in arbitral disputes. For example, one of the most knowledgeable arbitrators is a man whose educational background is in sociology.

The utility of this assumptions-on-assumptions analysis is that is does seem to relate to a judgment reached from studying the cases. That is, a careful reading of the 502 cases indicated that at least 12 percent appeared to reflect some deficiency in terms of arbitral understanding of the industrial engineering content of the issues being considered. This was most often inferred in terms of the third level of understanding discussed in Section 1.

3. THE NEED FOR TECHNICAL QUALIFICATIONS

The opinions expressed on this subject all reflect the need for understanding of the processes involved or suggest procedures for exclusive or cooperative handling of industrial engineering cases by qualified technical personnel—except for one line of opinion which will be examined. Most of the commentators herein are arbitrators, the balance representing parties interested in the arbitral process. The overall impression is that specific utilization of the technically qualified arbitrator is supported.

The need to view a job in dispute receives particular emphasis. As was said: "Testimony is an aid to resolution of the difficulty but is no substitute for an informed personal observation of actual performance of the job." [3]

In discussing preparation for an arbitration case, a regular practice [4] was recommended

"of actively studying, in the shop itself, the operational problems and processes which give rise to the particular dispute. Only by actually seeing, hearing, touching and thus understanding what are sometimes complex machines or operations can the representative of the arbitrating party later present his facts and arguments to the arbitrator with sufficient clarity."

These ideas of viewing the work area of a job in dispute are part of a more general idea of understanding. The problems hereunder are technical, and it takes more than ordinary effort to understand them—and, as one author said, ". . . [M]ost arbitrators are limited in their capacity to cope with the more complex cases." [5]

Arbitral Understanding of Technical Issues

The observations of one commentator [6] relative to understanding lend substantial support to the analysis in the first section of this chapter. In a discussion under "Machine Tools" he stated:

"In several cases I have been able to bring the parties to a mutually satisfactory settlement without any formal award. One such case involved a keyway-cutter which left a shaky edge; another, a thread-milling machine which did not produce a thread acceptable to the workshop inspector; some cases dealt with leakage of oil, noisy gears, defective slides, and so on. These were all technical matters requiring expert technical knowledge to understand their relative importance and propose satisfactory solutions."

Later in the same paper, under the heading "Process Plant," this commentator stated:

---

[3] Waite, *Problems in the Arbitration of Wage Incentives*, ARBITRATION TODAY 25 (1955).

[4] Livingston, *Arbitration: Evaluation of its Role in Labor Relations*, NEW YORK UNIVERSITY TWELFTH ANNUAL CONFERENCE ON LABOR 109 (1959).

[5] Simkin, *The Arbitration of Technical Disputes*, NEW YORK UNIVERSITY SIXTH ANNUAL CONFERENCE ON LABOR 181 (1953).

[6] Bentham, *Experiences of an Arbitrator in Engineering Disputes*, 5 ARB. J. 296 (1950).

"Another type of case which required high technical knowledge involved process results from a series of machines or operations: e.g., a wire rope plant which from a number of machines did not give the combined result required, a galvanizing plant including a complete process, and equipment for manufacturing cloth caps."[7]

Also, some of the comments relative to understanding give support to some of the thinking in the preceding section. Thus: "There are lawyers who understand job evaluation, engineers who know the principles of contract interpretation, and teachers and clergymen who enjoy an outstanding reputation as labor arbitrators."[8] In discussing presentation of job evaluation cases, it was stated: "Well, here the company's engineer, or an outside consulting engineer, might make a better presentation than a lawyer."[9] In this discussion, note was also taken of the difficulty in obtaining engineers as arbitrators, which has been a matter of frequent comment.

Of interest with respect to the concept of understanding was a series of articles in *Butcher Workman,* two of which have been cited.[10] The objective of these articles was to explain time study to the union's members. Cautions and precautions to union members were contained in another reference.[11]

More generally, there is the very logical approach[12] of offering to union officers and representatives a series of Institutes on various aspects of industrial engineering.

Finally, there are articles by two arbitrators who are also industrial engineers[13] urging industrial engineers to become more involved in the labor-management relationships affecting their profession—collective bargaining, the grievance procedure, arbitration, and, even, serving on arbitration boards.

---

[7] *Id.*

[8] *Six Cues to Better Arbitration,* 114 FACTORY 108 (1956).

[9] *Experts Give You Practical Answers on Arbitration Grievances,* 27 FOOD ENG'R No. 12, at 63 (1955).

[10] *Rating Factor, or Leveling the Study,* 49 BUTCHER WORKMAN No. 6, 24 (1963); *Allowances,* 49 BUTCHER WORKMAN No. 7, 24, at 40 (1963).

[11] Gottlieb, *Time Study and Union Safeguards,* 72 THE AM. FEDERATIONIST No. 11, at 15 (1965).

[12] Tibbetts & Gottlieb, *Protecting the Worker on Job 'Standards,'* 73 THE AM. FEDERATIONIST No. 5, at 9 (1966).

[13] Presgrave, *Grievance Arbitration and the Industrial Engineer,* XVIII J. OF INDUS. ENG'R 605 (1967); Lehoczky, *Industrial Engineering and Collective Bargaining,* 17 LAB. L.J. 393 (1966).

Excluding Technical Matters From Arbitration

A completely opposite tack has also been noted.[14] This view seems to rest on the theory that arbitrators cannot be expected to reach proper decisions in industrial engineering cases or, alternatively, that too much is involved to permit third-party decision. Thus, technical problems should be excluded from arbitration.

The above view, as well as other opinions on how to handle arbitration of industrial engineering cases, was reflected in some of the cases. The others to which it pertained are noted in Chapter XII.

In the opinion of one observer,[15] incentive standards do not need to be heard before an arbitrator knowledgeable in industrial engineering matters:

"If management believes that it cannot convince an Impartial Arbitrator who is not an industrial engineer of the fairness of an incentive standard, it is admitting that it cannot convince just an ordinary fair-minded person that an incentive standard it has established is fair. If that is true, how can it convince one of its employees, or the union leader, none of whom are trained industrial engineers, that a standard it has established is fair?"

How Much Technical Knowledge

In a discussion of the above paper [16] and the "not-so-mysterious art of industrial engineering," these comments were made:

"Because of the foregoing facts, I suggest that management not include in their arbitration clauses the frequently encountered provision requiring that the arbitrator of incentive grievances be a 'qualified industrial engineer.' Avoid the resultant search that leads round and round to nowhere.

"Instead provide that the incentive arbitrator be one familiar with incentive systems and incentive methods—or words to that effect. The consequences will be more expeditious and fruitful. Such per-

---

[14] Simkin, *The Arbitration of Technical Disputes*, NEW YORK UNIVERSITY SIXTH ANNUAL CONFERENCE ON LABOR 181 (1953); Davey, *The John Deere-UAW Permanent Arbitration System*, CRITICAL ISSUES IN LABOR ARBITRATION 161 (1957); Murphy, *Arbitration: Evaluation of its Role in Labor Relations*, NEW YORK UNIVERSITY TWELFTH ANNUAL CONFERENCE ON LABOR 281 (1959); McManus, *Right-to-manage is Caught up in Arbitration Crosswind*, 192 IRON AGE No. 21, at 41 (1963).
[15] Fairweather, *Arbitration of Disputes Involving Incentive Problems: An Industry View*, CRITICAL ISSUES IN LABOR ARBITRATION 61 (1957).
[16] *Id.*

sons can now be found and will, I hope, be available in increasing numbers in the future."

Another reference [17] adopted the same view about technical arbitrations, stating the first of the above-quoted paragraphs in a footnote (but not the second). Another author [18] quoted the original article,[19] but he also recommended that an industrial engineer be involved in the arbitration of technical matters. Reflecting essentially the same viewpoint is the statement [20] that "there is no particular magic about industrial engineering any more than there is any special mystique about arbitration."

Finally, these statements appear in a discussion of one of the references:[21]

"Our goal should be to promote the workability and acceptance of incentive systems wherever they exist. While he should be judicial, the measure of the arbitrator's success will be his capacity to bring to the parties a better understanding of the system which they themselves have created, so that they may sense its possibilities and limitations as an instrument for enabling them to live together productively and harmoniously.

"I think we arbitrators can do much to take the mystery and pseudo-science out of wage-incentive arbitration. Common sense is still the foremost requirement for an arbitrator, and if he possesses an optimum amount of this quality he need not fear to step in, regardless of technical shortcomings. Common sense should also tell him when he is over his head, and when to go for help if he needs it."

Providing Technical Knowledge

There remains consideration of two approaches to providing technical knowledge for arbitration. One of these may be termed the indirect method of supplying this knowledge, using one of two procedures. One procedure is to have engineers act as technical assistants or advisors to the arbitrator.[22] The other is the

---

[17] C. UPDEGRAFF, ARBITRATION OF LABOR DISPUTES (2nd ed. 1961)).

[18] Werner, *Industrial Engineers, Incentive Systems, and the Contract,* XI J. OF INDUS. ENG'R 231 (1960).

[19] Fairweather, *supra* note 15.

[20] Davey, *The Arbitrator Views the Industrial Engineer,* VII CALIF. MGMT. REV. 23 (1964).

[21] Waite, *supra* note 3.

[22] Simkin, *The Arbitration of Technical Disputes,* NEW YORK UNIVERSITY SIXTH ANNUAL CONFERENCE ON LABOR 181 (1953); Gomberg, *Arbitration of Disputes Involving Incentive Problems: A Labor View,* CRITICAL ISSUES IN LABOR ARBITRATION 85 (1957); Unterberger, *Technicians as Arbitrators of Wage Disputes,* 4 LAB. L.J. 433 (1953).

use of a professional as a fact-finder,[23] with his findings considered with other testimony and evidence presented in a case.

The second approach to supplying the needed technical knowledge is the direct approach—have technically qualified arbitrators hear and determine technical cases. In discussing the advantages of various conditions of arbitration, it was stated: [24] "Use of an *ad hoc,* or one-time, arbitrator is helpful if a case requires some highly specialized knowledge, such as that of an industrial or other engineer." In the same article were the comments that ". . . what the arbitrator needs most—in addition to judicial temperament—is a knowledge of shop practice he almost never has . . . ."

A preference for industrial engineers in job analysis and incentive rate cases was expressed in comments responding to a survey questionnaire.[25] What was suggested as a new approach consisted of segregating industrial engineering cases for handling by industrial engineers.[26] (Actually, this system is somewhat at variance with customary arbitration procedures.) Interestingly, the company involved in this new approach was a tannery; a tannery was also involved in the elimination of "the meaningless gesture" of referrals and direct utilization of industrial engineers in standards issues.[27]

The idea of having technically qualified arbitrators hear and decide industrial engineering cases has been expressed a number of other times.[28] In a previously cited article,[29] there are also these statements:

"From the above, it is clear that the arbitration of job evaluation cases is a specialized area which has more than the usual share of

---

[23] Haughton, *Arbitration of Disputes Involving Incentive Problems,* CRITICAL ISSUES IN LABOR ARBITRATION 94 (1957); Unterberger, *Technicians as Arbitrators of Wage Disputes,* 4 LAB. L.J. 433 (1953).

[24] Seward, *Man in the Middle Talks Shop,* 15 MODERN INDUS. 67 (1948).

[25] Warren & Bernstein, *A Profile of Labor Arbitration,* 4 INDUS. & LAB. REL. REV. 200 (1951).

[26] McCrensky, *Settling Work-Standards Disputes: A New Approach,* 38 PERSONNEL 68 (1961).

[27] S. SLICHTER, J. HEALY & E. LIVERNASH, THE IMPACT OF COLLECTIVE BARGAINING ON MANAGEMENT (1960).

[28] Simkin, *The Arbitration of Technical Disputes,* NEW YORK UNIVERSITY SIXTH ANNUAL CONFERENCE ON LABOR 181 (1953); Sherman, *Arbitrator's Analysis of Job Evaluation Disputes,* 43 PERSONNEL J. 365 (1964); Werner, *Industrial Engineers, Incentive Systems, and the Contract,* XI J. OF INDUS. ENG'R 231 (1960); Deloff, *Incentive Clauses: The Costly Clinkers,* 36 PERSONNEL 52 (1959); Rubin, *The Right of Management to Split Jobs and Assign Work to Other Jobs,* 16 INDUS & LAB. REL. REV. 205 (1963).

[29] Unterberger, *supra* note 1.

technical concepts and vocabulary. For this reason, the ideal qualifications for a job evaluation arbitrator would probably include long
and responsible experience both as an industrial engineer in the
field of the installation and administration of job evaluation programs and as a labor-management arbitrator. There are not too
many persons available who possess this particular combination of
qualifications."

The same author has commented about the arbitration of
wage incentive cases, including the qualifications of arbitrators
for such cases—indicating as an ideal a combination of industrial
engineering and arbitration experience.[30]

Need for Understanding

It is therefore clear that most of the commentators are of
the opinion that the content of industrial engineering cases is
such that industrial engineering know-how should be available
in the arbitral process. The extreme view holds that the risks
of arbitration are so grave that the process should be avoided,
regardless of arbitrator qualifications.

With respect to the divergent line of opinion, which appears
to be a minority view, these comments seem apropos. If one
thinks about the art and science of industrial engineering, as
the field is officially defined (Chapter I), it must be accepted
as a profession. It hardly seems plausible to expect a professional so to simplify his profession that he handcuffs himself,
so to speak, each time an issue comes before a lay arbitrator.
This is expected of no other profession, including the legal
profession.

Also, unions are not uninformed in technical matters. Some
of the real advances in industrial engineering have come from
union-oriented industrial engineers. In addition, employees are
not novices with respect to industrial engineering applications
which touch their jobs.

As for the arbitrator, what is important is that he have the
knowledge and understanding for handling the technical issues.
Industrial engineering training and experience is the best way
to acquire such knowledge and understanding; certainly it is
not the only way.

From the cases, the critique, and the commentaries, two ma-

---

[30] Unterberger, *The Arbitration of Wage Incentive Cases*, 23 ARB. J. 236 (1968).

jor concepts emerge. One is the need for understanding of industrial-engineering kinds of problems in arbitration and, particularly, the idea of actually promoting such understanding. The other concept points to having industrial engineers, as such, as arbitrators.

4. WHEN IS TECHNICAL KNOWLEDGE REQUIRED?

There remains the single question of what aspects of grievance disputes should be handled by arbitrators knowledgeable in the field. It was suggested [31] that general interpretation of contract terms did not pose technical issues; this relates, generally, to the first level suggested in Section 1.

Such a differentiation seems logical, with one caveat. When the interpretation does, or could, affect meaning or application at the second or third level, then technical knowledge should be involved in the decision.

Otherwise, it is believed that the problems identified at the second and third levels are the ones requiring industrial-engineering knowledge and understanding for proper arbitral judgments.

---

[31] Davis, *Incentive Problems*, MANAGEMENT RIGHTS AND THE ARBITRATION PROCESS 50 (1956).

CHAPTER XII

SUMMARY AND CONCLUSIONS

Disputes reaching arbitration which are industrial engineering in nature have much in common with other arbitral issues. They commence with disagreement arising from a labor-management relationship, they involve interpretation of the nature of that relationship, explicit and/or implicit, and they seek resolution through the informed, impartial judgment of an arbitrator (as opposed to other solutions, such as strike or lockout).

The similarities go beyond this, of course. Problems of procedure, evidence, and a whole gamut of related questions, not excluding arbitrability, appear in all types of arbitration cases, including the industrial engineering type.

On the other hand, it has been demonstrated that the principal feature of industrial engineering cases in arbitration—which distinguishes the 20 percent or more cases so classified—is their engineering content. This engineering content is different from other aspects of arbitration problems because it is often not the principal focus of the arbitration—which proceeds on contractual terms and practices—and yet is of vital importance in interpreting and applying such terms and practices.

The similarities to other types of cases are apparent when the results of the various parts of the study are considered in summary form. Distinguishing characteristics are also seen in this summary, with reemphasis upon underlying industrial engineering aspects of the cases.

1. GENERAL CONSIDERATIONS

All of the cases demonstrate that the problems which come on to arbitration arise from change, in one form or another,

315

which is an inevitable process in industry. The arbitrator's job is, therefore, broadly speaking, to determine and apply the rules which the parties have generated for handling change— not excluding ideas of management rights and implied limitations.

There was clear evidence, sometimes by explicit identification, of the two major philosophical concepts of the arbitrator's role in the arbitral process, the "quasi-judicial" and the "harmony-promotion" perspectives. As was pointed out in the analysis on this point, the differences are not so large as would seem at first glance. Nonetheless, differences do exist and do influence arbitrators' decisions.

A similar difference in viewpoint exists with respect to the approach to interpretation of the parties' contract, literal as opposed to equitable interpretations thereof. Here, too, analysis indicates the differences should be minimal in view of the fundamental principle of arbitrator responsiveness to the parties' desires.

Restrictions and Limitations

A number of restrictions and limitations were present in the cases. Since they have not been included in the analysis, representative case citations are noted. Arbitration was restricted by the impact of government administrative agencies, particularly the NLRB.[1] The effect of prior arbitral awards, involving the same as well as different parties, was considered a number of times; general rejection of *stare decisis* in arbitration was verified. The cases also showed how the parties may, sometimes inadvertently, limit themselves by stipulations and by grievance definition; however, grievance definitions may also prove, in arbitration, to be broader than the parties intended.[2]

The general rule that wages, generally, are not subject to arbitration is seen in the cases, being equally applicable to a wage reopener. This generalizes even further, with indications that arbitrators quite consistently refuse to proceed in arbitration on a matter which should be negotiated. It was found that production standards and incentives were sometimes excluded

---

[1] 39 LA 483, 42 LA 1056, 46 LA 499, 46 LA 746, 46 LA 750, 46 LA 865.
[2] 7 LA 467, 21 LA 550, 31 LA 659, 46 LA 517, 47 LA 601, 49 LA 355, 49 LA 744, 49 LA 922, 49 LA 981.

from arbitration, although the distinction of standards from wages *per se* was often made.[3] Also, in appropriate circumstances, arbitrators do decide about specific applications of incentives as distinct from wages generally; if standards and/or incentives may not come to arbitration directly, they do receive consideration under health and safety provisions.[4]

A number of cases indicated either a preference for an arbitrator who is an industrial engineer or has equivalent background and experience, or else a contractual specification of such qualifications.[5] Explicit prohibitions against arbitration of specified types of industrial engineering problems were found in other cases.[6]

The issue of nonarbitrability often appeared in the cases, based on claims that the subject areas involved were wages, management rights, or methods changes (or lack thereof). While there were situations where nonarbitrability was upheld, it developed that arbitration would ensue if the status of employee working conditions was or seemed to be affected.[7] The present trend—both in parties' views and under recent Supreme Court decisions—is away from nonarbitrability as an issue of substance, except under clear and unequivocal language stating the area of nonarbitrability.

Broad Principles

Two broad principles frequently were referred to in the cases—management rights and "a fair day's work." A number of cases were decided in interpretations of management rights (or, conversely, union rights under the implied limitations perspective). They showed clearly that exercises of management rights which negatively affect the bargaining unit will not be supported by arbitrators; the few exceptions are not very significant. However, the cases also showed that arbitrators quite universally support changes for efficiency purposes, when not precluded by the contract between the parties and when management's acts are in good faith and not arbitrary, capricious, or in derogation of the bargaining unit. Rate changes, negoti-

---

[3] 10 LA 480, 12 LA 1055, 13 LA 217, 24 LA 665, 46 LA 1189.
[4] 28 LA 651, 41 LA 997, 43 LA 1181.
[5] 15 LA 314, 30 LA 194, 33 LA 296, 37 LA 756, 42 LA 661.
[6] 3 LA 353, 16 LA 115, 44 LA 774.
[7] 20 LA 463, 23 LA 228, 44 LA 469, 46 LA 890, 46 LA 1018, 47 LA 425, 48 LA 339, 49 LA 515.

ated or otherwise, may or may not be required as a result of the changes, depending upon circumstances. These generalizations applied to management-rights issues in changes in classifications, workload, crew sizes, production standards, methods, and incentives.

The other broad principle, a fair day's work, appeared both as contractual or stipulated requirements and as arbitral shorthand for productivity problems. The slogan appears in the cases in terms of qualitative judgments about productivity and in relation to another generalized principle enunciating "equal pay for equal work." A quantitative approach to the same principle was also found in the cases, pointing toward performance levels under established production standards. It is in this sense that a fair day's work is kin to the subject of pace. The impact of this principle upon employees is noted, along with the need for explanation and understanding.

2. PRINCIPAL BASES FOR ARBITRAL DECISIONS

The two broad principles previously referred to—the arbitrator's personal orientation and views of the contract's status— and the various limitations, restrictions, and exclusions, all figure in arbitral decisions; one or more of these may be conclusive.

However, the main or primary basis for arbitral judgments is the parties' pattern of behavior as demonstrated in writing or by practice. Three chapters highlight contractual commitments, various industrial engineering plans and their administration, and practice.

The general rule of contractual content with respect to Job Structuring states that management may change job descriptions and classifications for good business reasons, either because of changes in operations or for efficiency. A minority view is that jobs are frozen for the duration of the contract unless mutually changed. Such changes, by the general rule, will be reflected in wages through operation of the wage administration program or by negotiations. The principal contractual problem in Work Performance (Measurement) was found to be concerned with language dealing with maintenance of an employee's earnings opportunity (with a few cases dealing with earnings guarantees). Earnings opportunity is usually related to effort, and the arbitral problem of balancing the earnings-effort relationship is indicated.

A variety of job evaluation plans appeared in the cases and were noted in the report, together with such evaluation principles as history of rates, evaluation by location, attempted evaluation by commodity, and discussions about applying evaluation to the job and not the man and how "red circle" rates are not generally considered applicable to successor employees. In approaching problems in classifications and evaluation, the arbitrator has need to understand fully and apply the parties' system, and a rule of reason governs various fact situations which arise under plans' administration.

Problems of work measurement and/or incentive applications appear to be more complicated because of dual and multiple provisions applying thereto. The cases do indicate a number of plans which have been used, ranging from time study to a variety of predetermined, standard-data types—including use of one plan or system to check another. A condition precedent to changes in specific applications is most usually some form of methods change; however, arbitrators generally oppose management's taking advantage of employee-initiated changes. Once the various requirements are fulfilled, the same rule of reason seems to be the underlying guide for arbitral decision. Management changes from day work to work standards—with or without incentives—and changes from one system to another find arbitral support; changes from incentives to work standards only, or to day work, usually will not be supported. Generally, clerical-type errors in work standards are correctable; other errors are generally not correctable, except that correction within specified periods often is permitted.

Together with express contract language and the details of plans or programs in question, arbitrators look to the practice of the parties for resolution of disputes presented to them. Practice is particularly important when at variance with the parties' written commitments. This is an important reason why arbitrators are urged to seek out the "special idiosyncrasies of the establishment" in their search for understanding of the problem in arbitration and the points of reference for decision.

Practice in industrial engineering cases seems quite consistent with general applications of the idea—that is, the practice must be clear, consistent, essentially uniform and repetitive, in existence a reasonably long time, and giving evidence of mutuality in some form. The cases indicated a differentiation between management's interest in efficiency of the business and employees' interest in their own welfare, with decisions going both ways depending upon the circumstances. Thus a management will be supported against past-practices claims if the change sought to be initiated outweighs its impact upon employees, and vice versa.

3. APPLICATIONS

These various bases for arbitral decisions were present in a large number of cases involving job changes, workload and crew size, and standards problems. Another important basis for decision, methods change, was also present in the cases and is included in this applications summary.

The cases show clear support by arbitrators of management actions in combining jobs, splitting jobs, creating new jobs, or eliminating unneeded jobs, in the absence of contract language proscribing such actions. Such actions, however, must be for good business reasons, reasonable, nonarbitrary, and not in derogation of the bargaining unit. The results of such actions must be consistent with the established modes for accommodating job changes by proper slottings within the established classification/evaluation system(s). The less drastic actions of adding or subtracting duties were also upheld by arbitrators.

A principal concern of unions and employees was with the appropriate wages to be paid for new or changed jobs, assuming the general handling was consistent with established patterns. This was indicated by several claims of error in job slotting, either within an evaluation plan or a more general classification system.

The same general viewpoint was found with respect to workload and crew-size problems. A substantial majority of the cases reflect arbitral support of managerial changes in workload and crew size. The significant feature on workload was the relative impact of the managerial action as judged against full workload—in which the subjective standard of a fair day's work finds application. Hence, additions to a full workload, variously measured, including practice of the parties, will not be supported; additions to less-than-full workload generally will be supported.

The particularly significant aspect of crew-size problems was the degree of interdependence within the crew. If there is little interdependence, the problem is simply an individual employee's workload—of particular importance under local-working-conditions clauses.

An existing maintenance-of-local-working-conditions clause has a specific deterrent effect upon workload or crew-size problems; substantial changes in methods or processes are necessary before an arbitrator will find that the basis for the local custom or practice has been removed. The same type of restraint was found not be as effective in the absence of an explicit contract clause, although the allegation of protected practice is often made in such circumstances.

Standards and Incentives

The usual arrangements in standards applications provide for continuance of such standards without change except when there have been changes in operations, methods, equipment, machinery, and the like. Hence, the first and primary test is whether or not one such condition precedent exists to justify the change. Arbitrators—and the parties, for that matter—generally do not have a problem with major, easily comprehended changes; opinions vary when the changes appear to be minimal, such as in a simple change in equipment layout.

Beyond this basic problem of methods change in support of standards change, a number of practical operating problems arise from standards and/or incentives. One particular problem concerns the use of temporary rates pending establishment of permanent rates. The cases show that arbitrators uphold indicated duration limits on temporary rates, on the logical reasoning that temporary rates are not full exemplification of equity between the parties. However, if contract or practice does not limit the duration of temporary rates, management apparently enjoys more latitude.

The work-cycle cases emphasize the vital importance for management to have work processes rationalized in the best cycle sense, considering the equipment and technology involved.

Failure to do so means arbitral support for continued application of so-called loose rates. The particularly complex problems of scheduling and balancing progressive assembly operations emphasized the need for work-cycle control.

Closely associated with line-balancing problems were the cases on machine speeds and feeds, wherein were found arbitral support of management actions to increase them, when reasonable in the circumstances. The cases hereunder generally reflected the same arbitral views as in the workload cases (as might be expected), including views about accompanying wage changes. The particular action of restoring worn equipment to previous operating efficiency with application of the full-efficiency rate had the support of arbitrators.

The most important problem in standards applications was found to be the question of pace, in terms of the general plant norm (task-level bargain) and its applications to individual rates (output bargain). Understanding of the concept of norm for a plant (or industry or region) was found to be particularly important, together with understanding of the processes by which this norm is applied in individual situations. This pointed up the necessity for arbitrators to acquaint themselves fully with the ongoing concepts of pace and pace applications which the parties have developed through contract and practice. This was seen as especially important when, as frequently occurred, administrative procedures and practice were not fully spelled out. The cases showed that arbitrators supported management actions to increase standards, when appropriate under governing circumstances, up to full, normal productivity, but not efforts to secure above-normal productivity.

Important component aspects of standards—allowances—were also discussed in the cases, with emphasis on the fact that allowances are primarily a matter for negotiation (or practice) and, once established, are changeable only through negotiation. Generally, it was found that personal and fatigue allowances do not usually give rise to significant arbitral problems because they are customarily established as percentages of cycle time. The substantial problems occur with respect to allowances for delays and interferences because of their relative unpredictability. The cases reflect the well-established practice of separating minor delays, with allowances provided therefor, from major delays for which standards are suspended and employees paid at established down-time rates. Arbitral problems are usually concerned with questions of when and what rates and/or allowances apply; they are usually resolved in terms of arbitrator interpretations of the parties' expressed purposes and ongoing practices.

4. UNIQUENESS

Contract provisions and other written documentation of parties' agreements about industrial engineering matters are unique because of the subjects covered therein. More important and more significant, for arbitral understanding of industrial engineering cases, are the various industrial engineering plans and programs and their applications, procedures, and administration.

Most important and most significant for arbitral understanding is the underlying engineering and technical content of manufacturing engineering in industrial engineering disputes. Throughout the book (and specifically in Chapter VII), an effort was made to reflect—in the abbreviated case synopses—the technological content of the cases involved. The aim was to emphasize the basic importance of understanding the equipment, tools, layout, methods, and procedures of manufacture in order properly to perform the arbitral function in industrial engineering cases.

An especially significant aspect of the manufacturing-engineering content of industrial engineering cases is that this underlying technology is present in all such cases, although it may be called to the forefront of consideration only if there is a methods-change proviso for interpretation, and then, perhaps, only in gross application. The fact is, however, as analysis of the cases verifies, such technological content is often involved in explicit language interpretations, is always involved and interrelated with the various industrial engineering plans and programs, and, as stated, undergirds the whole structure of the parties' relationships from which industrial engineering disputes arose.

It is from such considerations that the three-level analysis presented in Chapter XI evolved. It is also basic to the conclusions that knowledge and understanding of industrial engineering was deemed essential for capable handling of industrial engineering cases at levels two and three, and sometimes at level one.

A review of the literature revealed that a substantial consensus of commentators believed that technical know-how was necessary for handling technical cases (although these views were not expressed in terms of the three-level analysis). A special analysis of the arbitrators handling the cases in the report verified this viewpoint.

BIBLIOGRAPHY

Aaron, B., *The Uses of the Past in Arbitration*, ARBITRATION TODAY (Washington: The Bureau of National Affairs, 1955).

American Bar Association's Section of Labor Law, *Report on Developments in Labor Arbitration*, LABOR RELATIONS YEARBOOK—1967 (Washington: The Bureau of National Affairs, 1968).

American Bar Association, Section of Labor Relations Law, Committee on Improvement of Administration of Union-Employer Contracts, *Arbitrability*, 6 ARB. J. 200 (1951).

Bailer, L. H. *The Right to Assign Employees in One Job Classification to Jobs in Another Classification*, 16 IND. & LAB. REL. REV. 200 (1963).

Bailer, L. H., *The Silent Contract vs. Express Provisions: The Arbitration of Local Working Conditions*, COLLECTIVE BARGAINING AND THE ARBITRATOR'S ROLE (Washington: The Bureau of National Affairs, 1962.)

Bailer, L. H. *The Uses of the Past in Arbitration*, ARBITRATION TODAY (Washington: The Bureau of National Affairs, 1955).

Behrend, H., *The Effort Bargain*, 10 IND. & LAB. REL. REV. 503 (1957).

Benewitz, M. C. and Rosenberg, M., *The Arbitration Reporters as a Reflection of Arbitration Issues*, 18 ARB. J. 162 (1963).

Bentham, C., *Experiences of an Arbitrator in Engineering Disputes*, 5 ARB. J. 296 (1950).

Block, S. L., *Customs and Usages as Factors in Arbitration Decisions*, NEW YORK UNIVERSITY FIFTEENTH ANNUAL CONFERENCE ON LABOR (New York: Matthew Bender, 1962).

Braden, J. N. *The Function of the Arbitrator in Labor-Management Disputes*, 4 ARB. J. 35 (1949).

Brooks, G. W. *Unions and Technological Change*, 5 CONF. BD. REC. 46 (1968).

Burstein, H., *Labor Arbitration—A New Theology*, 10 VILL. L. REV. 287 (1965).

Chamberlain, N. W., *Job Security, Management Rights and Arbitration*, WORK ASSIGNMENTS AND INDUSTRIAL CHANGE (Washington: The Bureau of National Affairs, 1964).

Chamberlain, N. W., *Management's Reserved Rights*, MANAGEMENT RIGHTS AND THE ARBITRATION PROCESS (Washington: The Bureau of National Affairs, 1956).

Chamberlain, N.W., *The Union Challenge to Management Control*, 16 IND & LAB. REL. REV. 184 (1963).

Davey, H. W., *The Arbitrator Views the Industrial Engineer,* VII CALIF. MGMT. REV. 23 (1964).

Davey, H. W., *The John Deere-UAW Permanent Arbitration System,* CRITICAL ISSUES IN LABOR ARBITRATION (Washington: The Bureau of National Affairs, 1957).

Davey, H. W., *The Supreme Court and Arbitration: The Musings of an Arbitrator,* XXXVI NOTRE DAME LAW. 138 (1961).

Davis, P., *Arbitration of Work Rules Disputes,* 16 ARB. J. 51 (1961).

Davis, P., *Incentive Problems,* MANAGEMENT RIGHTS AND THE ARBITRATION PROCFSS (Washington, The Bureau of National Affairs, 1956).

Davis, P., *The Uses of the Past in Arbitration,* ARBITRATION TODAY (Washington: The Bureau of National Affairs, 1955).

Deloff, I. A., *Incentive Clauses: The Costly Clinkers,* 36 PERSONNEL 52 (1959).

Elkouri, F., & Elkouri, E. A., HOW ARBITRATION WORKS, 2nd ed. (Washington: The Bureau of National Affairs, 1960).

Emerson, H. P., *The New Outlook,* VII J. OF INDUS. ENG'R 139 (1956).

Fairweather, O., *Arbitration of Disputes Involving Incentive Problems: An Industry View,* CRITICAL ISSUES IN LABOR ARBITRATION (Washington: The Bureau of National Affairs, 1957).

Feinberg, I. R., *The Arbitrator's Responsibility Under the Taft-Hartley Act,* 18 ARB. J. 77 (1963).

Feinsinger, N. P., *Collective Bargaining and the Arbitrator,* COLLECTIVE BARGAINING AND THE ARBITRATOR'S ROLE (Washington: The Bureau of National Affairs, 1962).

Fleming, R. W., *Arbitrators and Arbitrability,* 1963 WASH. U.L.Q. 200 (1963).

Foegen, J. H., *Synthesis: Evolution of Industrial Power,* 33 ADVANCED MGMT. J. 75 (1968).

Foley, J. J., *How not to Handle Productivity Disputes,* XXXVII HARV. BUS. REV. 68 (1959).

Fuller, L. L., *Collective Bargaining and the Arbitrator,* COLLECTIVE BARGAINING AND THE ARBITRATOR'S ROLE (Washington: The Bureau of National Affairs, 1962).

Garrett, S., *The Role of Lawyers in Arbitration,* ARBITRATION AND PUBLIC POLICY (Washington: The Bureau of National Affairs, 1961).

Ginzberg, E., & Berg, I. E., DEMOCRATIC VALUES AND THE RIGHTS OF MANAGEMENT (New York: Columbia U. Press, 1963).

Goldberg, A. J., *Management's Reserved Rights: A Labor View,* MANAGEMENT RIGHTS AND THE ARBITRATION PROCESS (Washington: The Bureau of National Affairs, 1956).

Gomberg W., *Arbitration of Disputes Involving Incentive Problems: A Labor View,* CRITICAL ISSUES IN LABOR ARBITRATION (Washington: The Bureau of National Affairs, 1957).

Gomberg, W., *The Work Rule Problem and Property Rights in the Job,* 84 MONTHLY LAB. REV. 595 (1961).

Gottlieb, B., *Time Study and Union Safeguards,* 72 THE AM. FEDERATIONIST No. 11, at 15 (1965).

Gross, J. A., *Value Judgments in the Decisions of Labor Arbitrators,* 21 IND. & LAB. REL. REV. 55 (1967).

Halperin, J., *What is a Fair Day's Work?,* 39 PERSONNEL J. 91 (1960).

Handsaker, M., *Classification Problems,* MANAGEMENT RIGHTS AND THE ARBITRATION PROCESS (Washington: The Bureau of National Affairs, 1956).

Handsaker, M., *Grievance Arbitration and Mediated Settlements,* 17 LAB. L. J. 579 (1966).

Harris, P., *Supervisory Performance of Bargaining Unit Work,* 20 ARB. J. 129 (1965).

Haughton, R. W., *Arbitration of Disputes Involving Incentive Problems,* CRITICAL ISSUES IN LABOR ARBITRATION (Washington: The Bureau of National Affairs, 1957).

Hays, P. R., LABOR ARBITRATION: A DISSENTING VIEW (New Haven, Conn.: Yale U. Press, 1966).

Horvitz, A., *The Arbitrator Looks at Labor and Management,* 7 ARB. J. 66 (1952).

Hutchinson, J. G., MANAGING A FAIR DAY'S WORK (Ann Arbor, Mich.: Bur. of Indus. Rel., U. of Mich., 1963).

Hutchinson, J. G., *Stiffer Battles Ahead over Work Standards?,* 40 PERSONNEL 47 (1963).

Jones, E. A., *Evidentiary Concepts in Labor Arbitration,* 13 UCLA L. REV. 1241 (1966).

Justin, J. J., *Arbitrability and the Arbitrator's Jurisdiction,* MANAGEMENT RIGHTS AND THE ARBITRATION PROCESS (Washington: The Bureau of National Affairs, 1956).

Justin, J. J., *Arbitration under the Labor Contract—Its Nature, Function, and Use,* 24 PERSONNEL 286 (1951).

Kennedy, T., EFFECTIVE LABOR ARBITRATION (Philadelphia: U. of Pa. Press, 1948).

Kilbridge, M. D., *Effort Bargaining in Industrial Society,* XXXIII J. OF BUS. 10 (1960).

Krick, E. V., METHODS ENGINEERING (New York: John Wiley & Sons, 1962).

Lasser, D., *Labor Looks at Industrial Engineering,* XXI ADVANCED MGMT. 14 (1956).

Lehoczky, P. N., *Industrial Engineering and Collective Bargaining,* 17 LAB. L. J. 393 (1966).

Levitt, R. A., *When to Take a Grievance to Arbitration,* LABOR RELATIONS YEARBOOK—1967 (Washington: The Bureau of National Affairs, 1968).

Livingston, F. R., *Arbitration: Evaluation of its Role in Labor Relations,* NEW YORK UNIVERSITY TWELFTH ANNUAL CONFERENCE ON LABOR (New York: Matthew Bender, 1959).

Lytle, C. W., JOB EVALUATION METHODS, 2nd ed. (New York: The Ronald Press Co., 1954).

McCrensky, H., *Settling Work-Standards Disputes: A New Approach,* 38 PERSONNEL 68 (1961).

McCulloch, F. W., *The Arbitration Issues in NLRB Decisions,* 19 ARB. J. 65 (1964).

McCullough, J. V., *Basic Patterns that Emerge from the Arbitration of Grievances Associated with Incentive Wage and Piece Rate Plans,* 28 DISSERTATION ABSTRS. 4764-A (1968).

McLaughlin, R. P., *Custom and Past Practice in Labor Arbitration,* 18 ARB. J. 205 (1963).

McManus, G. J., *Right-to-Manage is Caught up in Arbitration Crosswind,* 192 IRON AGE No. 21, at 41.

Meyers, F., *The Task of the Labor Arbitrator,* 22 PERSONNEL ADMIN. 24 (1959).

Mittenthal, R., *Past Practice and the Administration of Collective Bargaining Agreements,* ARBITRATION AND PUBLIC POLICY (Washington: The Bureau of National Affairs, 1961).

Murphy, F. J., *Job Classification Arbitrations under Bethlehem Steel Agreements,* 16 ARB. J. 8 (1961).

Murphy, J. S., *Arbitration: Evaluation of its Role in Labor Relations,* NEW YORK UNIVERSITY TWELFTH ANNUAL CONFERENCE ON LABOR (New York: Matthew Bender, 1959).

Myers, A. H., *Arbitrating Industrial Efficiency,* XXXI HARV. BUS. REV. 60 (1953).

Myers, M. L., *Challenges to Labor Arbitration,* LABOR RELATIONS YEARBOOK—1967 (Washington: The Bureau of National Affairs, 1968).

Northrup, H. R., *Plain Facts about Featherbedding,* 35 PERSONNEL 54 (1958).

O'Connor, T. F., *Wage Incentives,* XIV J. OF INDUS. ENG'R 41 (1963).

Ostrin, H. H., *Reserved Rights in Labor Arbitration,* NEW YORK UNIVERSITY TWELFTH ANNUAL CONFERENCE ON LABOR (New York: Matthew Bender, 1959).

Phelps, J. C., *Management's Reserved Rights: An Industry View,* MANAGEMENT RIGHTS AND THE ARBITRATION PROCESS (Washington: The Bureau of National Affairs, 1956).

Platt, E., *The Duty to Bargain as Applied to Management Decisions,* LABOR RELATIONS YEARBOOK—1968 (Washington: The Bureau of National Affairs, 1969).

Platt, H. H., *The Silent Contract vs. Express Provisions: The Arbitration of Local Working Conditions,* COLLECTIVE BARGAINING AND THE ARBITRATOR'S ROLE (Washington: The Bureau of National Affairs, 1962).

Prasow, P., & Peters, E., *The Development of Judicial Arbitration in Labor-Management Disputes,* IX CALIF. MGMT. REV. No. 3, at 7 (1967).

Prasow, P., & Peters, E., *New Perspectives on Management's Reserved Rights,* 18 LAB. L.J. 3 (1967).

Presgrave, R., *Grievance Arbitration and the Industrial Engineer,* XVIII J. OF INDUS. ENG'R 605 (1967).

Rubin, M., *The Right of Management to Split Jobs and Assign Work to Other Jobs,* 16 INDUS. & LAB. REL. REV. 205 (1963).

Scheiber, I. B., *An Experiment in Cutting Labor Arbitration Costs and Delays,* 19 ARB. J. 148 (1964).

Seitz, P., *Grievance Arbitration and the National Labor Policy,* NEW

York University Eighteenth Annual Conference on Labor (New York: Matthew Bender, 1966).

Seitz, P., *Reply to Gross article—"Value Judgments in the Decisions of Labor Arbitrators"*, 21 Ind. & Lab. Rel. Rev. 427 (1968).

Sembower, J. F., *Halting the Trend Toward Technicalities in Arbitration*, Critical Issues in Labor Arbitration (Washington: The Bureau of National Affairs, 1957).

Seward, R. T., *Arbitration and the Functions of Management*, 16 Ind. & Lab. Rel. Rev. 235 (1963).

Seward, R. T., *Man in the Middle Talks Shop*, 15 Modern Indus. 67 (1948).

Seward, R. T., *Reexamining Traditional Concepts*, Work Assignments and Industrial Change (Washington: The Bureau of National Affairs, 1964).

Sherman, H. L., Jr., Arbitration of the Steel Wage Structure (Pittsburgh: U. of Pittsburgh Press, 1961).

Sherman, H. L., Jr., *Arbitrator's Analysis of Job Evaluation Disputes*, 43 Personnel J. 365 (1964).

Shulman, H., *Reason, Contract, and Law in Labor Relations*, Management Rights and the Arbitration Process (Washington: The Bureau of National Affairs, 1956).

Simkin, W. E., *The Arbitration of Technical Disputes*, New York University Sixth Annual Conference on Labor (New York: Matthew Bender, 1953).

Slichter, S. H., Healy, J. J., & Livernash, E. R., The Impact of Collective Bargaining on Management (Washington: The Brookings Institution, 1960).

Smith, R. A., *Arbitrability—The Arbitrator, the Courts and the Parties*, 17 Arb. J. 3 (1962).

Steelworkers of America, United, The Steelworkers Handbook on Arbitration Decisions (Pittsburgh: United Steelworkers of America, 1960).

Steiber, J., *Work Rules Issue in the Basic Steel Industry*, 85 Monthly Lab. Rev. 267 (1962).

Stessin, L., The Practice of Personnel and Industrial Relations (New York: Pitman Publishing Corp., 1964).

Stone, M., Managerial Freedom and Job Security (New York: Harper & Row, 1964).

Taylor, G. W., *Arbitrating Wages and Working Conditions*, Current Problems in Labor Relations and Arbitration (Ithaca, N.Y.: N.Y.S. School of Indus. & Lab. Rel., Cornell U., 1954).

Taylor, G. W., *Effectuating the Labor Contract Through Arbitration*, 26 Personnel 232 (1949).

Teple, E. R., *Contract Provisions Affecting Job Elimination*, 17 W. Res. L. Rev. 1253 (1966).

Tibbetts, N., & Gottlieb, B., *Protecting the Worker on Job "Standards,"* 73 The Am. Federationist No. 5, at 9 (1966).

Torbert, F., *Making Incentives Work*, XXXVII Harv. Bus. Rev. 81 (1959).

Unterberger, S. H., *Arbitration of Job Evaluation Cases,* 17 ARB. J. 219 (1962).

Unterberger, S. H. *The Arbitration of Wage Incentive Cases,* 23 ARB. J. 236 (1968).

Unterberger, S. H. *Technicians as Arbitrators of Wage Disputes,* 4 LAB. L.J. 433 (1953).

Updegraff, C. M., ARBITRATION AND LABOR RELATIONS, 3rd ed. (Washington: The Bureau of National Affairs, 1970).

Vaughn, R. C., INTRODUCTION TO INDUSTRIAL ENGINEERING (Ames, Iowa: Iowa State U. Press, 1967).

Waite, W. W., *Problems in the Arbitration of Wage Incentives,* ARBITRATION TODAY (Washington: The Bureau of National Affairs, 1955).

Wallen, S., *The Arbitration of Work Assignment Disputes,* 16 IND. & LAB. REL. REV. 193 (1963).

Wallen, S., *Arbitrators and Judges—Dispelling the Hays Haze,* IX CALIF. MGMT. REV. 17 (1967).

Wallen, S., *How Issues of Subcontracting and Plant Removal are Handled by Arbitrators,* 19 IND. & LAB. REL. REV. 265 (1966).

Wallen, S., *The Silent Contract vs. Express Provisions: The Arbitration of Local Working Conditions,* COLLECTIVE BARGAINING AND THE ARBITRATOR'S ROLE (Washington: The Bureau of National Affairs, 1962).

Warren, E. L., & Bernstein, I., *A Profile of Labor Arbitration,* 4 IND. & LAB. REL. REV. 200 (1951).

Werner, C. A., *Industrial Engineers, Incentive Systems, and the Contract,* XI J. OF INDUS. ENG'R. 231 (1960).

Wiggins, R. L., *Arbitration of Industrial Engineering Cases,* 26 DISSERTATION ABSTRS. 5105 (1966).

Wolff, S. A., *Management's Reserved Rights,* MANAGEMENT RIGHTS AND THE ARBITRATION PROCESS (Washington: The Bureau of National Affairs, 1956).

Young, S., *The Question of Managerial Prerogatives,* 16 IND. & LAB. REL. REV. 240 (1963).

Allowances, 49 BUTCHER WORKMAN No. 7, at 24, 40 (1963).

Candid Camera Helps Solve Labor-Management Disputes, 112 FACTORY (MODERN MFG.), Oct. 1954, at 106.

Challengeable Trends in Labor Arbitration, 7 ARB. J. 12 (1952).

Code of Ethics and Procedural Standards for Labor Management Arbitration, THE PROFESSION OF LABOR ARBITRATION (Washington: The Bureau of National Affairs, 1957).

Editorial, 16 ARB. J. 1 (1961).

Experts Give You Practical Answers on Arbitration Grievances, 27 FOOD ENG'R. No. 12, at 63 (1955).

How to Get Better Results from Labor-Management Arbitration: Benjamin C. Roberts and G. Allan Dash, Jr. Exchange Views with Representatives of Parties, 22 ARB. J. 1 (1963).

INDUSTRIAL ENGINEERING HANDBOOK (2nd ed. H. B. Maynard) (New York: McGraw-Hill, 1963).

New Tool for Arbitration, BUS. WEEK, Dec. 26, 1953, at 78.

Prescription for Curing "Troubled" Grievance Procedures, Labor Relations Yearbook—1966 (Washington: The Bureau of National Affairs, 1967).

Rating Factor, or Leveling the Study, 49 Butcher Workman No. 6, at 24 (1963).

Six Cues to Better Arbitration, 114 Factory, (Modern Mfg.), No. 9, at 108 (1956).

The Steel Arbitration Digest, 2 vols. (Washington: Pike & Fischer, 1962, 1970).

Steel: 2B or not 2B, 60 Fortune, Aug. 1959, at 174.

What Work Rules?, 60 Fortune, Dec. 1959, at 215.

TABLE OF CASES

2 LA 214: Fairchild Camera & Instrument Corp. (David L. Cole).
2 LA 217: Goodyear Tire & Rubber Co. (Whitley P. McCoy).
2 LA 223: Linde Air Products Co. (John E. Dwyer).
2 LA 225: Fulton Sylphon Co. (John E. Dwyer).
2 LA 469: John Deere Tractor Co. (Clarence M. Updegraff).
2 LA 478: Forstmann Woolen Co. (David L. Cole).
2 LA 572: Colgate-Palmolive-Peet Co. (Jacob J. Blair).

3 LA 309: Henry Disston & Sons (Joseph Brandschain)
3 LA 353: Borg-Warner Corp. (Charles O. Gregory).
3 LA 454: Standard Oil Co. (John E. Dwyer).
3 LA 677: Reliance Mfg. Co. (Dudley E. Whiting).
3 LA 855: Reynolds Alloys Co. (William M. Hepburn).

4 LA 136: California Shoes, Ltd. (Paul Prasow).
4 LA 189: National Malleable & Steel Castings Co. (Harold M. Gilden).
4 LA 399: Fruehauf Trailer Co. (Dudley E. Whiting).
4 LA 415: SKF Indus. (Hayward H. Coburn).
4 LA 482: La Follette Shirt Co. (John E. Dwyer).
4 LA 716: E. F. Houghton & Co. (Sidney L. Cahn).

5 LA 30: Goodyear Tire & Rubber Co. (Whitley P. McCoy).
5 LA 115: Cranston Print Works Co. (Maxwell Copelof).
5 LA 231: Monarch Mach. Tool Co. (Paul N. Lehoczky).
5 LA 241: Electric Boat Co. (Maurice S. Trotta).
5 LA 247: Continental Can Co. (Clarence M. Updegraff).
5 LA 278: Ohmer Corp. (Paul N. Lehoczky).
5 LA 290: Jones & Lamson Mach. Co. (Maxwell Copelof).
5 LA 304: Gardner-Richardson Co. (Dudley E. Whiting).
5 LA 540: North Am. Aviation Inc. (Benjamin Aaron).
5 LA 712: Carnegie-Illinois Steel Corp. (Herbert Blumer).

6 LA 119: North Am. Aviation Inc. (Benjamin Aaron).
6 LA 156: Copco Steel & Eng'r Co. (Harry H. Platt).
6 LA 200: U. S. Pipe & Foundry Co. (William M. Hepburn).
6 LA 218: Container Co. (Dudley E. Whiting).
6 LA 236: Yale & Towne Mfg. Co. (Martin Raphael).

6 LA 304: Hood Rubber Co. (Saul Wallen).
6 LA 366: Chrysler Corp. (David A. Wolff).
6 LA 575: Pittsburgh Steel Co. (Robert J. Wagner).
6 LA 579: Wilson Steel & Wire Co. (Charles G. Hampton).
6 LA 681: Goodyear Tire & Rubber Co. (Whitley P. McCoy).
6 LA 695: St. Joseph Lead Co. (Verner E. Wardlaw).
6 LA 774: Ashland Oil & Ref. Co. (Jacob J. Blair).
6 LA 924: Goodyear Tire & Rubber Co. (Whitley P. McCoy).
6 LA 979: Timken Roller Bearing Co. (Paul N. Lehoczky).

7 LA 21: Master Elec. Co. (Charles G. Hampton).
7 LA 27: Verney Corp. (A. Howard Myers).
7 LA 368: General Motors Corp. (John A. Griffin).
7 LA 467: Armstrong Cork Co. (Jacob J. Blair).
7 LA 575: National Tube Co. (Herbert Blumer).
7 LA 585: M.T. Stevens & Sons Co. (Maxwell Copelof).
7 LA 691: General Cable Corp. (J.M. Klamon).
7 LA 718: Minneapolis-Moline & Power Implement Co. (Nathan P. Feinsinger).
7 LA 943: Blackhawk Mfg. Co. (Clarence M. Updegraff).

8 LA 88: Slatersville Finishing Co. (James A. Healy).
8 LA 234: Aluminum Co. of America (Spencer D. Pollard).
8 LA 503: Central Screw Co. (Alex Elson).
8 LA 572: Pittsburgh Plate Glass Co. (Aaron Horvitz).
8 LA 846: American Steel & Wire Co. (Herbert Blumer).

9 LA 66: Hoover Co. (Paul N. Lehoczky).
9 LA 83: Spartan Mills (Paul N. Guthrie).
9 LA 239: Carlile & Doughty Inc. (Joseph Brandschain).
9 LA 659: Neon Prods., Inc. (Paul N. Lehoczky).
9 LA 735: Huron Portland Cement Co. (Harry H. Platt).

10 LA 20: Anaconda Wire & Cable Co. (Israel Ben Scheiber).
10 LA 94: Electric Boat Co. (Emanuel Stein).
10 LA 143: United Aircraft Prods., Inc. (Verner E. Wardlaw).
10 LA 480: Geuder, Paeschke & Frey Co. (Leonard E. Lindquist).
10 LA 535: Associated Shoe Indus. (A. Howard Myers).
10 LA 812: Distillers Co. (Maurice S. Trotta).

11 LA 108: Central Screw Co. (Samuel Edes).
11 LA 432: Jenkins Bros. (Joseph F. Donnelly).
11 LA 490: Lockheed Aircraft Corp. (Paul Prasow).
11 LA 544: Bethlehem Steel Co. (Mitchell M. Shipman).
11 LA 633: Sloane-Blabon Corp. (Thomas Kennedy).
11 LA 703: Champion Lamp Works (James J. Healy).
11 LA 822: McQuay-Norris Mfg. Co. (Harry Abrahams).

12 LA 273: Brickwede Bros. Co. (Paul N. Lehoczky).

12 LA 603: Michigan Tanning & Extract Co. (Russell A. Smith).
12 LA 631: National Tile & Mfg. Co. (Charles G. Hampton).
12 LA 676: Continental Carbon Co. (A. Langley Coffey).
12 LA 865: Youngstown Sheet & Tube Co. (Clarence M. Updegraff).
12 LA 949: Ford Motor Co. (Harry Shulman).
12 LA 1055: W. H. Fisher Co. (Harold M. Gilden).
12 LA 1084: Advanced Alum. Castings Corp. (Peter M. Kelliher).
12 LA 1126: Fabet Corp. (Saul Wallen).

13 LA 217: Rheem Mfg. Co. (Monroe Berkowitz).
13 LA 220: Central Screw Co. (Peter M. Kelliher).
13 LA 223: Consolidated Chem. Indus. (Carl White).
13 LA 227: Bemis Bros. Bag Co. (Benjamin Aaron).
13 LA 414: International Harvester Co. (Whitley P. McCoy).
13 LA 763: Dumont Elec. Corp. (Jules J. Justin).

14 LA 487: Baer Bros. (Joseph F. Donnelly).
14 LA 490: Ohio Steel Foundry Co. (Paul N. Lehoczky).
14 LA 638: Pennsylvania Transformer Co. (Jacob J. Blair).
14 LA 802: A.D. Julliard & Co. (Charles O. Gregory).
14 LA 815: International Harvester Co. (Ralph T. Seward).

15 LA 195: Wolverine Shoe & Tanning Corp. (Harry H. Platt).
15 LA 314: Pacific Mills (Saul Wallen).
15 LA 603: Emge Packing Co. (Charles G. Hampton).
15 LA 754: West Virginia Pulp & Paper Co. (Maxwell Copelof).
15 LA 945: National Lock Co. (Bert L. Luskin).

16 LA 76: Branch River Wool Combing Co. (Maxwell Copelof).
16 LA 115: American Seating Co. (Dudley E. Whiting).
16 LA 252: American Zinc. Co. (Harold M. Gilden).
16 LA 331: International Harvester Co. (Whitley P. McCoy).
16 LA 770: Thor Corp. (Otto J. Baab).

17 LA 268: Hershey Chocolate Corp. (R.P. Brecht).
17 LA 293: Huffman Mfg. Co. (Paul N. Lehoczky).
17 LA 361: Mengel Co. (Peter A. Carmichael).
17 LA 391: Kroehler Mfg. Co. (John A. Lapp).
17 LA 472: A.C.L. Haase Co. (Wayne L. Townsend).

18 LA 166: Huron Portland Cement Co. (Harry H. Platt).
18 LA 352: Sigfrid K. Lonegren, Inc. (Arthur Lesser, Jr.).
18 LA 459: National Lock Co. (Bert L. Luskin).
18 LA 462: Librascope Inc. (John D. Gaffey).
18 LA 513: Safeway Stores Inc. (Maurice S. Trotta).
18 LA 612: Bethlehem Pacific Coast Steel Corp. (Hubert Wyckoff).
18 LA 827: American Zinc Co. (Clarence M. Updegraff).

19 LA 358: Koppers Co. (B. Meredith Reid).
19 LA 856: Carborundum Co. (A.B. Cummins).

20 LA 289: Jack & Heintz Precision Indus. (Dallas M. Young).
20 LA 309: Continental Baking Co. (Clarence M. Updegraff).
20 LA 362: Tin Processing Corp. (Jack Johannes).
20 LA 370: Republic Steel Corp. (Harry H. Platt).
20 LA 455: Allegheny Ludlum Steel Corp. (Whitley P. McCoy).
20 LA 463: Central Soya Co. (D. Emmett Ferguson).
20 LA 586: Jenkins Bros. (Joseph F. Donnelly).
20 LA 639: Sangamo Elec. Co. (C.F. Penniman).
20 LA 890: St. Joseph Lead Co. (Clarence M. Updegraff).

21 LA 84: Jones & Laughlin Steel Corp (Sidney L. Cahn).
21 LA 124: International Harvester Co. (David L. Cole).
21 LA 244: John Deere Harvester Works (Harold W. Davey).
21 LA 387: Veeder-Root Inc. (Mitchell M. Shipman).
21 LA 424: McDonnell Aircraft Corp. (Joseph M. Klamon).
21 LA 449: John Deere Waterloo Tractor Works (Harold W. Davey).
21 LA 461: Brown & Sharp Mfg. Co. (William W. Waite).
21 LA 550: International Shoe Co. (Le Roy A. Rader).
21 LA 586: Bethlehem Steel Co. (Ralph T. Seward).
21 LA 609: U.S. Steel Corp. (Frederick Harbison).
21 LA 755: Jones & Laughlin Steel Corp. (Sidney L. Cahn).
21 LA 784: John Deere Waterloo Tractor Works (Harold W. Davey).
21 LA 814: International Harvester Co. (David L. Cole).

22 LA 336: Dow Chem. Co. (Joseph M. Klamon).
22 LA 450: Dayton Steel Foundry Co. (Paul N. Lehoczky).
22 LA 785: Nebraska Consol. Mills Co. (James A. Doyle).

23 LA 188: San Francisco Bakery Employers' Assn. (Sam Kagel).
23 LA 206: John Deere Des Moines Works (Harold W. Davey).
23 LA 228: Virginia-Carolina Chem. Corp. (Alpheus R. Marshall).
23 LA 340: Bethlehem Steel Co. (Ralph T. Seward).
23 LA 490: Union Malleable Iron Works (Harold W. Davey).
23 LA 522: Modine Mfg. Co. (Bert L. Luskin).
23 LA 782: Wheeler Insulated Wire Co. (Joseph F. Donnelly).
23 LA 804: Lockheed Aircraft Corp. (John D. Gaffey).
23 LA 829: Lear, Inc. (M.S. Ryder).

24 LA 665: Cameron Iron Works, Inc. (Clyde Emery).
24 LA 713: Faultless Caster Corp. (John F. Sembower).

25 LA 44: Reynolds Metal Co. (Paul Prasow).
25 LA 394: John Deere Des Moines Works (Harold W. Davey).

26 LA 3: Worthington Corp. (Thomas P. Whelan).
26 LA 114: Deere & Co. (Maurice H. Merrill).
26 LA 172: Babcock & Wilcox Co. (Samuel S. Kates).
26 LA 564: John Deere Dubuque Tractor Works (Harold W. Davey).
26 LA 812: U.S. Steel Corp. (Sylvester Garrett).

27 LA 81: Rockwell Spring & Axle Co. (Peter M. Kelliher).
27 LA 324: Simonds Saw & Steel Co. (Robert S. Thompson).
27 LA 389: American Air Filter Co. (Peter M. Kelliher).
27 LA 689: Clark Bros. Co. (Harry Pollock).
27 LA 758: Hunter Fan & Ventilating Co. (Carl A. Warns, Jr.).
27 LA 784: McDonnell Aircraft Corp. (Joseph M. Klamon).
27 LA 906: Bethlehem Steel Co. (Ralph T. Seward).

28 LA 126: Pittsburgh Steel Co. (Sidney L. Cahn).
28 LA 129: Allegheny Ludlum Steel Corp. (Whitley P. McCoy).
28 LA 132: Barboursville Clay Mfg. Co. (Paul N Lehoczky).
28 LA 144: Walworth Co. (Wayne L. Townsend).
28 LA 259: Timken Roller Bearing Co. (Vernon L. Stouffer).
28 LA 394: Ironrite, Inc. (Ronald W. Haughton).
28 LA 530: Bethlehem Steel Co. (Rolf Valtin).
28 LA 651: Bethlehem Steel Co. (Ralph T. Seward).

29 LA 123: White Motor Co. (Eli Rock).
29 LA 687: National Container Corp. (Alpheus R. Marshall).
29 LA 784: Allegheny Ludlum Steel Corp. (Ralph T. Seward).
29 LA 828: Singer Mfg. Co. (Sidney L. Cahn).

30 LA 31: Lockheed Aircraft Corp. (Carl A. Warns, Jr.).
30 LA 46: Ford Motor Co. (Harry H. Platt).
30 LA 115: Standard Oil Co. (Clarence M. Updegraff).
30 LA 194: Harsco Corp. (George F. Hayes).
30 LA 290: McCord Corp. (John F. Sembower).
30 LA 316; Bethlehem Steel Co. (Ralph T. Seward).
30 LA 423: Trane Co. (Leonard E. Lindquist).
30 LA 705: Celanese Corp. (B. Meredith Reid).
30 LA 1014: Allegheny Ludlum Steel Corp. (Rolf Valtin & Ralph T. Seward).

31 LA 20: Bethlehem Steel Co. (Ralph T. Seward).
31 LA 111: Butler Mfg. Co. (Maurice O. Graff).
31 LA 121: Koppers Co. (Myles S. Boothe).
31 LA 447: Kaiser Steel Corp. (Ralph T. Seward).
31 LA 659: Lockheed Aircraft Corp. (Charles A. Reynard).
31 LA 662: Libbey-Owens-Ford Glass Fibres Co. (Donald A. Crawford).

32 LA 115: Simoniz Co. (R.W. Fleming).

32 LA 216: Johnson Bronze Co. (Stanton W. B. Wood).
32 LA 383: Thor Power Tool Co. (Paul Prasow).
32 LA 640: Singer Mfg. Co. (Sidney L. Cahn).
32 LA 836: Continental Baking Co. (R.W. Fleming).
32 LA 888: Sherwin-Williams Co. (Peter M. Kelliher).

33 LA 1: Marsh Stencil Mach. Co. (Joseph M. Klamon).
33 LA 29: Johns-Manville Fiber Glass, Inc. (Robert P. Brecht).
33 LA 169: Quaker Oats Co. (Clarence M. Updegraff).
33 LA 188: Kroger Co. (Robert G. Howlett).
33 LA 296: Kroger Co. (Milton H. Schmidt).
33 LA 300: Fairmont Alum. Co. (John R. Coleman).
33 LA 357: Lockheed Aircraft Corp. (Carl A. Warns, Jr.).
33 LA 385: Reynolds Metals Co. (Paul L. Kleinsorge).
33 LA 421: Television Station KXTV (Arthur M. Ross).
33 LA 442: Penn-Dixie Cement Corp. (B. Meredith Reid).
33 LA 537: Dana Corp. (Richard Mittenthal).
33 LA 557: Desilu Prods., Inc. (J.A.C. Grant).
33 LA 725: Simmons Co. (Arthur M. Ross).
33 LA 758: Mallory-Sharon Metals Corp. (Edwin R. Teple).
33 LA 913: Mosler Lock Co. (Milton H. Schmidt).
33 LA 916: Philco Corp. (Alex Elson).

34 LA 209: Diamond Gardner Corp. (John D. Regester).
34 LA 226: H.J. Heinz Co. (Harry Pollock).
34 LA 278: Continental Emsco Co. (Byron R. Abernethy).
34 LA 365: Johnson Bronze Co. (Thomas J. McDermott).
34 LA 827: W-K-M (E.E. Hale).

35 LA 63: Fabricon Prods. (Paul Prasow).
35 LA 72: Bethlehem Steel Co. (I. Robert Feinberg).
35 LA 113: United States Ceramic Tile Co. (Walter G. Seinsheimer).
35 LA 367: Borg-Warner Corp. (Jerome A. Klein).
35 LA 434: Mansfield Tire & Rubber Co. (Frank R. Uible).
35 LA 575: Goodyear Tire & Rubber Co. (Charles C. Killings-
worth).
35 LA 662: Magnavox Co. (James J. Willingham).
35 LA 664: Linde Co. (Joseph Shister).
35 LA 856: Western Union Tel. Co. (Mitchell M. Shipman).
35 LA 859: Pur-O-Lator Prods. Co. (David L. Kabaker).

36 LA 86: Publishers' Assn. (Peter Seitz).
36 LA 162: Bethlehem Steel Co. (Ralph T. Seward).
36 LA 740: American Hard Rubber Co. (Milton Rubin).
36 LA 1097: Triangle Conduit & Cable Corp. (Jacob J. Blair).
36 LA 1442: Whitewater Electronics (Robert J. Mueller).

37 LA 155: U.S. Steel Corp. (Clare B. McDermott).
37 LA 192: General Motors Corp. (Nathan P. Feinsinger).

37 LA 279: Hydril Co. (Paul N. Lehoczky).
37 LA 711: Lukens Steel Co. (Donald A. Crawford).
37 LA 758: United States Ceramic Tile Co. (Robert G. McIntosh).
37 LA 915: Hillbro Newspaper Printing Co. (George E. Hildebrand).

38 LA 228: Pickands Mather & Co. (Paul N. Lehoczky).
38 LA 584: Line Material Indus. (Paul N. Lehoczky).
38 LA 799: National Biscuit Co. (Harold M. Gilden).
38 LA 1068: Monarch Mach. Tool Co. (Walter G. Seinsheimer).
38 LA 1208: Houdaille Indus. (Paul N. Lehoczky).

39 LA 4: U.S. Steel Corp. (Sylvester Garrett).
39 LA 9: U.S. Steel Corp. (Sylvester Garrett).
39 LA 11: Stuart-Christy, Inc. (Vernon H. Jensen).
39 LA 102: Wolverine Toy Co. (Paul N. Lehoczky).
39 LA 173: Bonney Forge & Tool Works (Paul N. Lehoczky).
39 LA 341: Reserve Mining Co. (John F. Sembower).
39 LA 432: American Chain & Cable Co. (Thomas J. McDermott).
39 LA 483: Transport Workers (Sidney A. Wolff).
39 LA 801: Harchem Div. (Harry J. Dworkin).
39 LA 1058: Continental Oil Co. (A. Langley Coffey).
39 LA 1065: Ohio & W. Pa. Dock Co. (Harry J. Dworkin).
39 LA 1265: Metal Specialty Co. (Marlin M. Volz).

40 LA 33: Rockwell Mfg. Co. (Paul N. Lehoczky).
40 LA 67: Pittsburgh Steel Co. (Thomas J. McDermott).
40 LA 70: Pittsburgh Steel Co. (Thomas J. McDermott).
40 LA 73: Republic Steel Corp. (Joseph G. Stashower).
40 LA 199: F & M Schaefer Brewing Co. (Burton B. Turkus).
40 LA 487: Pittsburgh Steel Co. (Thomas J. McDermott).
40 LA 565: National Cash Register Co. (Paul Prasow).
40 LA 700: Nebraska Consol. Mills Co. (Harold W. Davey).
40 LA 866: Rockwell Mfg. Co. (Edwin R. Teple).
40 LA 875: H.K. Porter Co. (Paul N. Lehoczky).
40 LA 879: Sandia Corp. (John E. Gorsuch).
40 LA 1106: A. O. Smith Corp. (Paul N. Lehoczky).

41 LA 24: Air Reduction Chem. & Carbide Co. (Carl A. Warns, Jr.).
41 LA 120: Flintkote Co. (Carl R. Schedler).
41 LA 268: Flintkote Co. (Maurice H. Merrill).
41 LA 285: Shenango, Inc. (Donald A. Crawford).
41 LA 300: U.S. Steel Corp. (Clair V. Duff).
41 LA 510: Diamond Crystal Salt Co. (Frank R. Uible).
41 LA 651: Kennecott Copper Corp. (John E. Gorsuch).
41 LA 721: Kuhns Bros. Foundry Co. (Carl A. Warns, Jr.)
41 LA 884: U.S. Steel Corp. (David C. Altrock).
41 LA 953: Rola Div. (Maurice E. Nichols).
41 LA 997: Carborundum Co. (Robert G. McIntosh).
41 LA 1038: Mead Corp. (George E. Strong).

41 LA 1053: Armstrong Cork Co. (Joseph Shister).
41 LA 1076: U.S. Slicing Mach. Co. (James J. Willingham).
41 LA 1140: FMC Corp. (LeRoy Autry).
41 LA 1147: Quaker Oats Co. (Sam Davis Tatum).
41 LA 1150: Anaconda Am. Brass Co. (Sidney A. Wolff).
41 LA 1161: Lone Star Cement Corp. (Harry J. Dworkin).
41 LA 1169: Groveton Papers Co. (Charles O. Gregory).

42 LA 125: Arketex Ceramic Corp. (Walter G. Seinsheimer).
42 LA 294: Gulf Oil Corp. (Charles M. Rehmus).
42 LA 298: Lloyd Mfg. Co. (John F. Sembower).
42 LA 638: Rockwell-Standard Seating Corp. (Howard S. Block).
42 LA 643: Mead Corp. (Langston T. Hawley).
42 LA 647: American Oil Co. (Byron R. Abernethy)
42 LA 661: Minnesota Mining & Mfg. Co. (Dale S. Beach)
42 LA 697: Bienville Furniture & Mfg. Co. (LeRoy Autry)
42 LA 944: Allegheny Ludlum Steel Corp. (Donald A. Crawford).
42 LA 945: Oswald Jaeger Baking Co. (Phillip G. Marshall).
42 LA 965: Ingersoll-Rand Co. (Israel Ben Scheiber)
42 LA 1025: Olin Mathieson Chem. Corp. (Joseph M. Klamon).
42 LA 1056: Automatic Elec. Co. (John F. Sembower).
42 LA 1123: Chrysler Corp. (Gabriel N. Alexander).
42 LA 1127: Mead Corp. (L. Drew Redden).
42 LA 1162: Kelly-Springfield Tire Co. (Whitley P. McCoy).
42 LA 1327: Acme-Newport Steel Co. (Milton H. Schmidt).

43 LA 33: Orr & Sembower, Inc. (Jacob Seidenberg).
43 LA 193: Detroit Edison Co. (Russell A. Smith).
43 LA 318: Curtis-Wright Aeronautical Corp. (Donald A. Crawford).
43 LA 353: Great Atlantic & Pacific Tea Co. (Marlin M. Volz).
43 LA 364: General Dynamics Corp. (A. Howard Myers).
43 LA 380: Lockheed Aircraft Corp. (Irving Berstein).
43 LA 427: Pickands-Mather & Co. (Paul N. Lehoczky).
43 LA 491: Gulf States Utils. Co. (Paul M. Hebert).
43 LA 583: Jones & Laughlin Steel Corp. (Clair V. Duff).
43 LA 651: New Jersey Bell Tel. Co. (James V. Altieri).
43 LA 722: Peoria Malleable Castings Co. (John F. Sembower).
43 LA 770: Pittsburgh Steel Co. (Thomas J. McDermott).
43 LA 1006: Overmyer Mould Co. (Peter M. Kelliher).
43 LA 1028: Firestone Tire & Tubber Co. (M.S. Ryder).
43 LA 1048: U.S. Steel Corp. (Peter Florey).
43 LA 1181: Reliance Elec. & Eng'r. Co. (Paul N. Lehoczky).
43 LA 1208: Patent Button Co. (George Savage King).

44 LA 33: Morton Salt Co. (Robert G. Howlett).
44 LA 353: Kaiser Steel Corp. (Irving Bernstein).
44 LA 359: General Am. Transp. Corp. (Harry Abrahams).
44 LA 469: Joy Mfg. Co. (Richard Mittenthal).

44 LA 563: Electronic Instrument Co. (Hubert T. Delany).
44 LA 774: U.S. Steel Corp. (Clare B. McDermott).
44 LA 840: Gidholt Mach. Co. (Thomas J. McDermott).
44 LA 992: Socony Mobil Oil Co. (Joseph Shister).
44 LA 1006: Hinson Mfg. Co. (Harold W. Davey).
44 LA 1219: Shell Oil Co. (Burton B. Turkus).
44 LA 1230: National Lead Co. (James J. Willingham).

45 LA 104: U.S. Steel Corp. (Peter Florey).
45 LA 201: Tennessee River Pulp & Paper Co. (Louis C. Kesselman).
45 LA 557: Pure Oil Co. (Clarence M. Updegraff).
45 LA 778: Bethlehem Steel Co. (Gerald A. Barrett & Ralph T. Seward).
45 LA 812: American Welding & Mfg. Co. (Harry J. Dworkin).
45 LA 860: Los Angeles Herald Examiner (Sanford H. Kadish).
45 LA 923: Yale & Towne, Inc. (Jacob Seidenberg).
45 LA 955: Chris-Craft Indus. (Adolph M. Koven).
45 LA 964: Jessups Farms (Thomas T. Roberts).
45 LA 996: Sperry Rand Corp. (Paul N. Lehoczky).
45 LA 1015: Wooster Sportswear Co. (Harry J. Dworkin).

46 LA 4: Yale & Towne, Inc. (Clair V. Duff).
46 LA 36: International Paper Co. (Eugene H. Hughes).
46 LA 39: Square D Co. (John Day Larkin).
46 LA 62: Fruehauf Corp. (Peter Di Leone).
46 LA 70: Mead Corp. (George Savage King).
46 LA 140: Mobil Oil Co. (Paul M. Hebert).
46 LA 193: Golden Foundry Co. (Ben F. Small).
46 LA 295: Diamond Power Specialty Corp. (Clair V. Duff).
46 LA 335: FMC Corp. (Richard Mittenthal).
46 LA 396: American Sugar Co. (Harry J. Dworkin).
46 LA 499: Franklin Assn. (John Day Larkin).
46 LA 503: Barton Salt Co. (Maurice H. Merrill).
46 LA 517: Union Carbide Corp. (Sidney L. Cahn).
46 LA 532: American Sugar Co. (Harry J. Dworkin).
46 LA 557: Stubnitz Spring Div. (Vernon L. Stouffer).
46 LA 572: Metro Glass (Harry J. Dworkin).
46 LA 660: U.S. Steel Corp. (Clare B. McDermott).
46 LA 707: Weyerhaeuser Co. (Peter M. Kelliher).
46 LA 730: Bethlehem Steel Corp. (Ralph T. Seward).
46 LA 733: Pittsburgh Steel Co. (Thomas J. McDermott).
46 LA 746: Burgmaster Corp. (Melvin Lennard).
46 LA 750: Burgmaster Corp. (Melvin Lennard).
46 LA 865: Lockheed-California Co. (Howard S. Block).
46 LA 870: Lockheed-California Co. (Howard S. Block).
46 LA 890: Allegheny Ludlum Steel Corp. (Saul Wallen).
46 LA 920: American St. Gobain Corp. (Clair V. Duff).
46 LA 978: Reactive Metals, Inc. (Rankin M. Gibson).

46 LA 1018: Western Elec. Co. (Frank J. Dugan).
46 LA 1027: Rheem Mfg. Co. (Howard S. Block).
46 LA 1065: Worthington Corp. (Harry J. Dworkin).
46 LA 1189: Addressograph-Multigraph Corp. (Edwin R. Teple).
46 LA 1196: Pacific Outdoor Advertising Co. (Thomas T. Roberts).
46 LA 1203: New Haven Board & Carton Co. (Daniel Kornblum).
46 LA 1208: C. Schmidt Co. (Marlin M. Volz).

47 LA 170: Faultless Rubber Co. (Freeman F. Suagee).
47 LA 282: Sewanee Silica Co. (Lee S. Greene).
47 LA 382: Square D Co. (John Day Larkin).
47 LA 396: Marble Cliff Quarries Co. (Harry J. Dworkin).
47 LA 414: John Deere Plow Works (John F. Sembower).
47 LA 425: Brooklyn Union Gas Co. (Benjamin H. Wolf).
47 LA 541: American Cyanamid Co. (Sidney L. Cahn).
47 LA 547: Darling & Co. (Martin A. Cohen).
47 LA 577: Warren Wire Co. (Milton Rubin).
47 LA 601: Penn-Dixie Cement Corp. (Joseph Shister).
47 LA 609: Courtaulds N. Am. Inc. (Whitley P. McCoy).
47 LA 716: Vickers Inc. (M. David Keefe).
47 LA 748: Teeters Packing Co. (Wayne T. Geissinger).
47 LA 756: Dierks Paper Co. (Lawrence S. Morgan).
47 LA 761: Dierks Paper Co. (Paul M. Hebert).
47 LA 836: Pipe Fitters Local 205 (Maurice H. Merrill).
47 LA 929: F.M.C. Corp. (Paul N. Lehoczky).
47 LA 930: F.M.C. Corp. (Paul N. Lehoczky).
47 LA 986: Daniel W. Mikesell Inc. (Freeman F. Suagee).
47 LA 1045: Eaton Mfg. Co. (Samuel S. Kates).
47 LA 1089: Dayton Tire & Rubber Co. (Harry J. Dworkin).
47 LA 1150: McLouth Steel Corp. (M.S. Ryder).
47 LA 1157: Carrollton Mfg. Co. (Clair V. Duff).

48 LA 24: Omaha Cold Storage Terminals, Inc. (James A. Doyle).
48 LA 52: Penn-Dixie Cement Corp. (Clair V. Duff).
48 LA 55: U.S. Steel Corp. (Peter Florey).
48 LA 72: American Cement Corp. (Howard S. Block).
48 LA 124: Interchemical Corp. (Louis Yagoda).
48 LA 305: Virginia Elec. & Power Co. (Alexander B. Porter).
48 LA 339: VR/Wesson Co. (Harold W. Davey).
48 LA 518: Lockheed-Georgia Co. (George Savage King).
48 LA 524: Hupp Corp. (J.K. Hayes).
48 LA 563: Joy Mfg. Co. (David C. Altrock).
48 LA 691: O'Keefe & Merritt Co. (Adolph M. Koven).
48 LA 746: Great Lakes Carbon Corp. (Howard S. Block).
48 LA 751: Alabama Asphaltic Limestone Co. (Ralph Roger Williams).
48 LA 819: General Fireproofing Co. (Edwin R. Teple).

48 LA 893: Diebold, Inc. (George S. Bradley).
48 LA 901: Penn-Dixie Cement Corp. (Calvin L. McCoy).
48 LA 941: National Rejectors Inc. (J.V. McKenna).
48 LA 957: Victor Mfg. & Gasket Co. (Paul N. Lehoczky).
48 LA 974: Ranco Inc. (Rankin M. Gibson).
48 LA 1000: General Cable Corp. (Peter M. Kelliher).
48 LA 1138: Kaiser Foundation Hosps. (Edgar A. Jones, Jr.)
48 LA 1192: Wisconsin-Michigan Power Co. (Neil Gundermann).
48 LA 1239: Newport News Shipbuilding & Drydock Co. (Donald A. Crawford).

49 LA 202: Peerless Wire Goods Co. (Daniel E. Lewis).
49 LA 271: Montgomery Ward & Co. (Clarence M. Updegraff).
49 LA 294: Hercules Inc. (Daniel J. Dykstra).
49 LA 320: Borg-Warner Corp. (David C. Altrock).
49 LA 355: Chamberlain Corp. (Clair V. Duff).
49 LA 445: Humble Oil & Refining Co. (Paul M. Hebert).
49 LA 471: U.S. Stoneware, Inc. (Vernon L. Stouffer).
49 LA 487: McDonnell-Douglas Aircraft Corp. (Stanford C. Madden).
49 LA 515: Great Atlantic & Pacific Tea Co. (Donald A. Crawford).
49 LA 521: Dallas Publishers (Sylvester Garrett).
49 LA 544: Gibson Refrigerator (M. David Keefe).
49 LA 581: Buddy L. Corp. (Robert G. McIntosh).
49 LA 669: Kimco Auto Prods.. Inc. (John P. Owen).
49 LA 744: Douglas Aircraft Co. (Leo Kotin).
49 LA 841: Johnson & Johnson and Ethicon, Inc. (Edward F. Murphy).
49 LA 874: Phoenix Closures, Inc. (John F. Sembower).
49 LA 912: Shuron Continental (Donald A. Crawford).
49 LA 922: Tappan Co. (Harry J. Dworkin).
49 LA 981: Lockheed-California Co. (Francis E. Jones).
49 LA 1014: Bethlehem Steel Corp. (Alexander B. Porter).
49 LA 1018: Birmingham News Co. (Harry H. Platt).
49 LA 1036: United Eng'r. & Foundry Co. (Robert J. Wagner).

50 LA 1: Zoological Soc. (Edgar A. Jones, Jr.).
50 LA 107: International Nickel Co. (Richard Calhoon).
50 LA 136: Industrial Wire Prods., Inc. (Calvin L. McCoy).
50 LA 157: Thompson Grinders Co. (Samuel S. Kates).
50 LA 186: Memphis Publishing Co. (Clair V. Duff).
50 LA 194: O & A Elec. Cooperative (Herbert V. Rollins).
50 LA 287: Wallace-Murray Corp. (Myron L. Joseph).
50 LA 293: Bethlehem Steel Corp. (Seymour Strongin).
50 LA 322: Ethyl Corp. (Harry J. Dworkin).
50 LA 344: International Paper Co. (William I. Prewett).
50 LA 357: Farmlea Dairy, Inc. (Banjamin H. Wolf).
50 LA 361: Kaiser Steel Corp. (Howard S. Block).
50 LA 458: Lone Star Brewing Co. (Paul M. Hebert).

50 LA 624: Vertol Div. (W. Roy Buckwater).
50 LA 677: Essex Chem. Corp. (William B. Gould).
50 LA 752: Mobil Oil Corp. (John W. Leonard).
50 LA 804: Coyne Indus. Laundry, Inc. (John E. Waldron).
50 LA 823: E.W. Bliss Co. (Monroe Berkowitz).
50 LA 871: Owens-Illinois, Inc. (Joseph M. Klamon).
50 LA 882: Herff-Jones Co. (Samuel S. Kates).
50 LA 888: Whirlwind, Inc. (Lewis E. Solomon).
50 LA 927: Moloney Elec. Co. (Paul N. Lehoczky).
50 LA 930: Allegheny Ludlum Steel Corp. (Herbert L. Sherman, Jr.).
50 LA 997: Hercules Engines, Inc. (Bruce B. Laybourne).
50 LA 1001: Ingalls Shipbuilding Corp. (George V. Eyraud, Jr.).
50 LA 1048: Strippit (Sylvester Garrett).
50 LA 1086: Blaw-Knox Co. (Bernard D. Meltzer).
50 LA 1165: Minnesota Mining & Mfg. Co. (Thomas P. Lewis).
50 LA 1186: Stardust Hotel (Edgar A. Jones, Jr.).

51 LA 35: Wilson Jones Co. (Carroll R. Daugherty).
51 LA 37: National Carbide Co. (Marlin M. Volz).
51 LA 101: Timken Roller Bearing Co. (Harry J. Dworkin).
51 LA 189: Great Atlantic & Pacific Tea Co. (Carroll R. Daugherty).
51 LA 293: Duraloy Co. (Clair V. Duff).
51 LA 296: Ingalls Shipbuilding Div. (Ralph Roger Williams).
51 LA 303: Great Atlantic & Pacific Tea Co. (Jacob Seidenberg).
51 LA 411: Portland Co. (Harold G. Wren).
51 LA 494: Western Elec. Co. (Nathan Cayton).
51 LA 549: Ruralist Press, Inc. (J. Fred Holly).
51 LA 600: Videotape Prods. (Burton B. Turkus).
51 LA 660: Air Reduction Co. (Paul M. Hebert).
51 LA 682: Flexsteel Indus. (Clark A.J. Hazlewood).
51 LA 842: West Virginia Pulp & Paper Co. (Walter G. Seinsheimer).
51 LA 902: General Dynamics Convair Tech. Div. (Irving Helbling).
51 LA 970: Eagle Mfg. Co. (Marlyn E. Lugar).
51 LA 1031: A.M. Byers Co. (Harry J. Dworkin).
51 LA 1051: Virginia Folding Box Co. (A.R. Marshall).
51 LA 1159: Meadow Gold Dairies, Inc. (Myron L. Joseph).
51 LA 1174: Cleveland Newspaper Publishers Assn. (Harry J. Dworkin).
51 LA 1194: Cyclops Corp. (Edwin R. Teple).
51 LA 1221: KIRO-TV, Inc. (Cornelius J. Peck).
51 LA 1269: Southern Union Gas Co. (Paul M. Hebert).
51 LA 1280: Magnetics, Inc. (Samuel Krimsly).

TOPICAL INDEX

A

Allowances (see Standards problems)
Arbitration
—*ad hoc* arbitrations, judicial viewpoint
  as applicable to 13
—arbitral judgment 10
—arbitral process, nature of 13
—changes, arbitral review of 142
—consensus arbitration 11
——harmony-promotion viewpoint,
    applicability to 12
—existing standards and the basis
  thereof, company's right to change,
  arbitrability of issue 135
—principal feature of arbitration 5
Arbitrators
—capabilities of 6
—industrial engineering disputes,
  critique 301-304
—practice 159-186
—qualifications of 301-313
——technical knowledge
    requirement 313
——technical qualifications, need
    for 306-312
—role of 7
—test of arbitrator's art 11
Automation, elimination of job,
  general manufacturing 209

B

Balancing of interests 19
Bargaining unit (see Unit for
  bargaining)
Bedeaux System 134
Bonuses
—present rate effective prior to
  updated incentive plan 135
Break periods
—(see also Standards problems)
—changes in, past practice 179

C

Classification and evaluation
  issues 91-121
—by commodity 105
—by location 105
—by size 107
—by union 108
—classification matters, rule of
  reason 115

—CWS plan 103
—evaluation plans and concepts 103
—high skill, use of 112
—job evaluation 120
—NMTA plan 103
—overlapping capabilities and incidental work, major borderline cases 113
—plans and their utilization 134-140
—precepts and principles 108
—procedures and practices 115
——job evaluation 120
——procedure, changes in 117
——time, element of 116

Classification of jobs
  (see Job classifications)
Collective bargaining
—changes in jobs and wages by
  negotiations only 95
—effects of 18
Collective bargaining agreements
—allowances for personal time, wash-up
  time, etc. 292-293
—average piecework earnings, provision
  for payment 130
—classification system, purpose of 96
—downtime, payment for 297
—effort bargain 265
—fatigue allowance contract clause,
  grievance issue turns on
  interpretation of 295
—inherent- or reserved-rights view 14
—job changes (see Job changes)
—management rights clause permitting
  the altering, adding to, or subtracting from employees' duties 41
—pace as sometimes defined in
  contractual provisions 284
—past practice, functional use of 161
—practice (see Practice)
—production standards 60
—rights and limitations 14
—"standard relationships" between
  parties to agreement 100
—standards and incentive issues
  (see Standards and incentive issues)
—technological changes or improvements, advance notice required 101
—10-percent personal allowance in
  standards 295
—wage-rate bargain (per time or per
  output) 265

345

Collective bargaining agreements—
Contd.
—work-output standards, fixing of, and
imposition of demotion for just cause,
company's right to   63
—zipper clauses, use of   133, 159
Crew size (see Workload and crew size)
CWS plan, evaluation plans and concepts, steel industry   103

D

Discharge
—inefficiency, time allowance   62
—production standards, company's
"carte blanche authority" to discharge
employees for failure to meet   63
—rules infractions, required
performance   289
Downtime, payment for, provision in
contracts   297

E

Earnings guarantees (see Wages,
subhead: earnings guarantees)
Equal pay for equal work   82, 94, 124
Evaluation issues (see Classification and
evaluation issues)

F

Fair day's work   75-90, 265
—definition   75
—employee reactions   87
—meaning and measurement   77
——comparisons   81
——measurement, methods of   78
—quantification, (see Quantification)
—understanding   90
—workload   78

G

Grievances
— (see also specific subject heads)
—company's right to change existing
standards and the basis thereof,
arbitrability   135
—incentive rates, alleged violation of
contract permitting company
to set   66
—problems presented through grievances, interpretations of provisions as
they apply to   91
—stewards' time spent in grievance meetings, payment for, zipper clause in
contract   133

H

Hours
—standard, changes in   142
—"wait time," hourly earnings for   132

I

Incentives (see Methods and incentives;
Standards and incentive issues)

Industrial engineering
—basic problem
——change, adjusting to   16
——change, aspects of   15
—definition of   2, 5
Interests, balancing of   19

J

Job changes
—abolishment of job   224
——insufficient work in
classification   225
——primary function continues   226
—by negotiations only   95
—combining or splitting jobs   227
——splitting   230
——wage issue   228
—duties, adding or removing
——added duties   232
——duties, removal of   234
——money issue in removal-of-duties
cases   234
——money issue in added-duties
situations   233
—elimination of jobs, management's
right   223
—impact of change on job   217-240
—management's right to make
changes   98
—new jobs or classifications, establishing
of   101, 218
——company initiative   219
———limitations on   220
———union requests supported by
arbitrator   222
—right of management to make, restrictions on   99
—"standard relationship" between
parties to agreements   100
—views about   95
Job classifications
—efficiency, classification changes
for   48
——new or combined jobs   49
—errors in classifications, claims of   236
——higher rates, claims for   239
——setup, pay for   238
—establishing of   218
—higher classification, requests for   237
—job or duties eliminated   51
—new jobs or classifications (see Job
changes, subhead: new jobs or classifications, establishing of)
—new or combined jobs   49
—purpose of classification system   96
—setup, pay for   238
—skilled journeymen to semiskilled production workers, changes from   41
—unilateral elimination of classification
and assignment of functions to another classification   41, 53

Job descriptions
—changes by negotiations only 95
—importance of 40, 110
Job evaluation
—arbitral handling of problems 120
—parties' approach to, importance of, cases cited 108
—understanding the issue 92
Job Structuring
—changes in, company-initiated action 101
—definition 2
Jurisdictional disputes
—removal of equipment 190
—skilled trades (see Skilled trades)

L

Layoffs
—job descriptions, importance of 40

M

Machine speeds and feeds
—standards problems (see Standards problems, subhead: machine speeds and feeds)
Management and union rights 21-74
Management rights
—added duties 53
—company operations, right of management to make studies for efficiency purposes 65
—discretion and ability to make choices to fulfill its function 70
—efficiency, classification changes for 48
—job or duties eliminated due to recession in the industry 51
—job changes, right to make 98 (see also Job changes)
——restriction on 99
—skilled journeymen to semiskilled workers, changes from 41
—unilateral elimination of classification and assignment of functions to another classification 41
Manufacturing, general
—bulk handling problems 206
—inspection 207
—job requirements 209
—substantiality of changes in methods 208
Master Standard Data (MSD) 134, 295
Metal forming, methods and processes
—changes, impact of 199
—crew and job changes 198
—pot ramming 197
Metal working, methods and processes
—changes, employee-initiated 204
—job requirements, changes in 203
—machining operations, changes in 201

Methods and incentives 64
—(see also Standards and incentive issues)
—economic changes 66
—employee problems 68
—incentive changes 67
—incentive case, comments 89
—management initative with respect to incentives supported by arbitrators, general rule emerging from cited cases 70
—methods, changes in 65
——past practice 178
Methods and processes 187-215
—assembly operations, changes in 194
—equipment 190
——changes in, major and minor 192
——machines, combination of 191
—general manufacturing (see Manufacturing, general)
—metal forming (see Metal forming)
—metal working (see Metal working)
—methods changes, significance of 189
—processes 210
——job duties or requirements 211
——other process changes 212
—product design change 202
—standards problems 265
Methods-time-motion measurement (MTM) 134, 273
Motion-time analysis (MTA) 134

N

New jobs
—company's right to establish recognized in contract 101
—creation of, union initiative 221
—removal of duties from existing job to create, union protest 101
NMTA plan, evaluation plans and concepts 103

O

Operations
—changes in, pay adjustments 19
—history of 170

P

Past practice (see Practice)
Performance standards
—measurements 139
—plans and their utilization 134
—workload yardsticks 138
Practice 159-186
—classification and assignment practices 164
——classification practice, meaning of 165
——interunit practices (see subhead: interunit practices)

Practice—Contd.
—definition, function,
   interpretation   160
—diverse assignment situations   172
—employee improvements   179
—functional use of   161
—inertunit practices
——interdepartmental practice   176
—interunit practices
——practice, unusual claims of   176
—job assignments, company change of,
   grievance   177
—operations, history of   170
—skilled trades assignments   171
—technical cases, practice in   163
—time considerations   167
—work breaks   179
—workload and methods practices   177
——changes in workloads or
     methods   178
—work standards and incentive
   practices   181-186
——formula requirements   183
——output requirements   182
——rate applications   184
—zipper clause, use of in contracts to
   eliminate past practice   133
Production standards
— (see also Standards and incentive issues; Standards problems)
—constraints   61
—discharge for inefficiency, application
   of test requirement   62
—discipline and standards   62
—output bargain   281-282
—rights issue   60
—standards and discipline   62
Promotions
—sex, problems of, practical
   considerations   47

Q

Quantification of fair day's work
—quantification, bases of   85
—reasonable effort   83

R

Red circle rates
—personal or job   111
Responsiveness to parties' wishes   12
Rights
—implied obligations   73
—role of reason   72
—union function is protection, "establishing limits on, or guideposts for,
   the exercise of management's
   discretion"   70
Role of reason   72

S

Seniority
—"Job Family," seniority established
   by   113

—single system, establishment of   46
Sex discrimination
—problems of   44
——practical considerations   47
——seniority considerations   45
——single seniority system,
     establishment of   46
Skilled trades   43
—assignments, past practices   171
—jurisdictional problems of   43
—new skilled classifications, job
   requirements   209
—overlapping capabilities, past practice,
   significance of   171, 172
Standards and incentive issues
— (see also Methods and incentives;
   Standards problems)
—bonuses, present rate effective prior to
   updated incentive plan   125
—changeovers   144
——day work to work standards   141
——incentive to day work   145
—changes
——arbitral review of   142
——requiring justification   135
—check studies, use of to resolve
   disputes over   152
—classified and quantified contract
   clauses on procedures for establishing
   incentive rates   123
——earnings guarantees   129
——maintenance of earnings   131
——nonstandard operating
     conditions   129
——off-standard conditions   130
——earnings opportunity   125
——opportunity, meaning of   126
——workload and crew size   128
—error correction   154
—errors found in standards   153
—incentives
——creepage   123
——earnings opportunity   125
——problems and principles   149
——steel contracts, some applications
     in   140
———effect on other operations   213
—measurement of standards application,
   sufficiency of   143
—money "piecerate plan" replacement
   with new incentive based on time   134
—nonstandard operating conditions,
   earnings guarantees   129
—off-standard conditions, welding operation performed under, earnings
   guarantees   130
—opportunity, meaning of   126
—plans and their utilization,
   measurement systems   134
—principles and procedures   148
—performance standards
   (see Performance standards)

—standard data 150
—standards, setting of, union right
  to data 151
—steel industry
——incentives, applications in steel
  contracts 140
——two-step, trial process for introducing new incentives 141
—wage incentives for productive classifications, contract provision 134
—workload relationship to application
  of earnings-opportunity clauses,
  cases cited 128
Standards problems
—allowances
——claims 298
——delays and interferences 296
——determinations and
  interpretation 294
——fatigue 295, 299
——interpretation and
  interferences 297
——personal allowance usage 294
——types of 292
—assembly line problems 274
—details, knowledge and administration
  of plan or plans used in setting
  standards 266
—effort-earnings relationship 286
—levelling arguments 287
—loose rates 274
—machine feeds and speeds 276
——feed, right to specify 278
——increased machine speed,
  effects of 279
——speed, right to specify 277
——methods, changes in 266
—pace
——concept of 281
——definition 281, 285
——normalizing process 282
——performance 288
——practice, effect on pace 284
——required pace, interpretation
  of 287
—policy 265-266
—production
——deliberate control by employee 289
——established level of 288
——"480 standard minutes" of
  work 287
—ranges of 265
—temporary standards 265, 267
——error, correction of 270
——grievances, company-initiated 269
——time limits 268
—10-percent personal allowance
  specified in agreement 295
—work-cycle problems 271
——idle time in work cycle 273
——work cycle, changes in 272

Steelworkers trilogy
—effects of 8
—philosophical impact 9
Strikes, no-strike pledge, violation of 17
Summary and conclusions 315-324
Supervisors
—bargaining-unit work, performance 32

T

Technological changes, effect on rate
  change and incentive quota 128
Technological changes or improvements,
  advance notice requirement in
  contract 101
Time study program, initiation of,
  discussion of 77

U

Unions
—management and union rights 21-74
—standards, setting of, union right
  to data 151
Unit for bargaining
—bargaining-unit work affected by
  change 22
—changes within 39
—duties
——addition of 26
——concurrent duties 36
——elimination of 25
——transfers of 23
—job descriptions, effects of 40
—legally imposed changes 27
—nonunit personnel, bargaining-unit
  work performed by 28
——nature of work 29
——practice and practicality 34
——technological changes 30
——work locale 31
—operational requirements 41
—supervisors, performance of
  bargaining-unit work by 32
—transfer of duties under management-
  rights clause from bargaining-unit
  workers 31
—two unions involved 37

W

Wages
—changes by negotiations only 95
—crew size, reduction in, maintenance
  of earnings 131
—earnings guarantees 129
——average piecework earnings, contract
  provision for payment for 130
——maintenance of earnings 131
——personal, fatigue, and miscellaneous
  allowances, sufficiency of 133
—earnings opportunity 125
——meaning of 126
—incentive rates (see Methods and incentives; Standards and incentive
  issues)

Wages—Contd.
—job classification
  (see Job classifications)
—jobs, combining or splitting,
  wage issue 228
—mongrel type rate not subject to
  earnings-opportunity provision
  requirement 127
—operations, changes in, pay
  adjustments 19
—stewards' time spent in grievance meetings, payment for, zipper clause in
  contract 133
—wage-rate bargain
  (per time or per output) 265
—"wait time," hourly earnings for 132
Warrior & Gulf Navigation Co.
  case 9, 10
Work Factor 134, 273
Workload and crew size
—crew size 57
——crew reductions, impediments
    to 256
——cumulative changes, effects of 258
——expanding or changing
    operations 254
——newspaper operations 252
——reduction in, maintenance of
    earnings 131
—crew, what constitutes 255
—multiple assignments 55
—practice (see also Practice)
——changes in workloads 178

——workload and methods
    practices 177
—problems of workloads 246
——indirect effects 250
——manufacturing issues 249
——multiple-machine assignments 248
——processing issues 246
—working conditions 259
——beneficial conditions, maintenance
    of 263
——protected work conditions, bases
    for 261
——steel industry; other
    industries 259, 260
—workload
——increases to production workers,
    hourly pay raise, indirect effects
    250
——yardsticks 138
—workloads 54, 128
—workloads, nature of 241
——effort component (quality) 243
——evaluation aspect of workload 244
——performance component
    (quantity) 242
——fair day's work (see Fair day's work)
Work Performance (Measurement)
—definition 2

Z

Zipper clause, use of in
  contracts 133, 159